Contesting French West Africa

France Overseas: Studies in Empire and Decolonization

SERIES EDITORS: A. J. B. Johnston, James D. Le Sueur, and Tyler Stovall

CONTESTING FRENCH WEST AFRICA

Battles over Schools and the
Colonial Order, 1900–1950

HARRY GAMBLE

University of Nebraska Press   LINCOLN AND LONDON

Portions of this book have previously appeared, in
different form, in "La crise de l'enseignement en
Afrique occidentale française (1944–1950)," *Histoire de
l'Éducation* 128 (2010): 129–62, http://histoire-education
.revues.org/2278; doi:10.4000/histoire-education.2278.
© ENS Éditions. Used with permission.

Library of Congress Cataloging-in-Publication Data
Names: Gamble, Harry, author.
Title: Contesting French West Africa:
battles over schools and the colonial
order, 1900–1950 / Harry Gamble.
Other titles: France overseas.
Description: Lincoln: University of Nebraska
Press, 2017. | Series: France overseas | Includes
bibliographical references and index.
Identifiers: LCCN 2017008064
ISBN 9780803295490 (cloth: alk. paper)
ISBN 9781496202321 (epub)
ISBN 9781496202338 (mobi)
ISBN 9781496202345 (pdf)
Subjects: LCSH: Education—Political aspects—
Africa, French-speaking West. | Education—Africa,
French-speaking West—French influences. |
Educational change—Africa, French-speaking
West. | Africa, French-speaking West—History. |
France—Colonies—Africa—Administration.
Classification: LCC LA1661 .G36
2017 | DDC 370.966—dc23
LC record available at https://lccn.loc.gov/2017008064

Set in Sabon Next by Rachel Gould.
Designed by N. Putens.

For April

CONTENTS

ILLUSTRATIONS

ACKNOWLEDGMENTS

In ways that I cannot fully explain, my trajectory as a scholar and educator connects back to my years as a Peace Corps volunteer in southern Mali. Although my time in Diou and surrounding villages was filled to the brim with present-oriented activities, many of my developing questions already had to do with the past. My first thanks go out to the many Malians who generously welcomed me into their homes and lives. I am particularly indebted to Mariam and Ndoh Kone and their children, who served as my host family; even though many years have passed, their warmth and easygoing friendship are still fresh in my mind.

Important foundations for this book were put down during my years as a doctoral student at New York University. Although much has happened during the intervening years, I remain deeply grateful to Herrick Chapman for his generous, hands-on mentoring, which was second to none. Herrick skillfully guided me through the dissertation process and more deeply into the historian's craft.

A series of study and research trips to France and Senegal helped me ground this project in promising ways. I would like to thank Christian Baudelot for the unforgettable welcome he extended during my stint as a *pensionnaire étranger* at the École normale supérieure in Paris. Christian's teaching did much to fuel my interest in the history of education in France and my thinking about educational inequalities. At l'ENS I also benefited from stimulating conversations with Benoît de L'Estoile and other members of the Département de Sciences Sociales. A subsequent year in France, generously supported by a Chateaubriand grant from the French government, allowed me to conduct foundational archival research—in Aix, Fontainebleau, Nantes, and Paris as well as in Dakar. As I combed through boxes and bundles of colonial-era documents, I received help from a succession of generous and skilled archivists too numerous to name here.

Since coming to the College of Wooster, my work on this long-running project has benefited from sustained support in the form of two research leaves and additional course releases granted through the Henry Luce III Fund for Distinguished Scholarship. This invaluable "time away" allowed me to return to archives in France and Senegal and to find the sustained quiet time I needed to nurture my writing process through its various twists and turns. As I moved into the publication process, the college's Faculty Development Fund assisted with the acquisition of illustration rights and the production of the book's index.

At the College of Wooster, I am lucky to work alongside dynamic and dedicated colleagues, many of whom are close friends. I would especially like to thank Greg Shaya for sharing his passion for French and European history, his friendship, and his enthusiasm for things as diverse as Ultimate Frisbee, folk guitar, and ping pong. I am lucky to be surrounded on a day-to-day basis by colleagues doing exciting work on Africa. Upon first arriving at the College of Wooster I was immediately welcomed by Boubacar N'Diaye, who has remained an exceptionally generous friend ever since. I have also had the good fortune to work alongside Ibra Sene, a dynamic historian of Africa whose research program intersects in exciting ways with my own. With their broad interests and deeply collaborative spirits, David McConnell and Amyaz Moledina have both helped me to make connections with other disciplines and geographic areas. Laura Burch and Marion

Duval have been exemplary and inspirational colleagues, on more levels than I can mention here. My work on this book has been greatly facilitated by the library resources of the College of Wooster and by Ohio's world-class library consortia. I would like to thank the many talented and devoted librarians who have kept me supplied with an amazing range of hard-to-find sources. I am particularly grateful to our digital curation librarian, Catie Newton, who helped prepare some of the illustrations for this book.

My heartfelt thanks go out to colleagues elsewhere, who have shared their intellectual excitement and camaraderie across three continents and a range of academic conferences. I have learned much from exchanges with other scholars working on the history of education in France and in various colonial and postcolonial settings. I would like to extend special thanks to Pascale Barthélémy, Kelly Duke Bryant, Jean-Hervé Jézéquel, Laurent Manière, Rebecca Rogers, and Marie Salaün.

During the gestation of this book Alice Conklin offered much-appreciated encouragement at several key junctures. Herrick Chapman provided timely insights and astute advice as I began to think more seriously about the publication process. I would like to thank Elizabeth Foster for closely reading and perceptively commenting on a particular chapter of this study. My thanks also go to Eric Jennings, who generously agreed to read the entire manuscript just prior to publication. As I carried out final manuscript revisions, I was able to draw on the detailed and insightful reports of two anonymous readers selected by University of Nebraska Press. I would like to thank both of these readers for their careful engagement with my project and their collegial support.

Along the way many other scholars and colleagues have enriched my journey, in ways big and small. I would particularly like to extend my thanks to Brian Arganbright, Jennifer Boittin, Kristen Stromberg Childers, Judith DeGroat, Michael Gomez, Scott Gunther, Janet Horne, the late Tony Judt, Elizabeth Campbell Karlsgodt, Alexander Keese, Alison Murray Levine, Mary Lewis, Ken Orosz, Louisa Rice, Rachel Riedner, Nicole Rudolph, Emmanuelle Saada, Benoît Trépied, David Wilkin, and Sarah Zimmerman.

Since first taking an interest in this project, Bridget Barry, the history editor at the University of Nebraska Press, has been a committed supporter, going out of her way to make the entire publication process as smooth and transparent as possible. The final shape of this book has benefited in numerous ways from the careful work of Sara Springsteen, the project editor. I was also fortunate to be able to count on the carefully honed skills and keen eye of Sally Antrobus, my copyeditor.

Researching and writing this book would have been far less enjoyable without the steadfast companionship of my family. My mother has inspired and sustained me through the years with her wisdom and generosity of spirit. An academic himself, my father has been a devoted supporter and vital mentor for as long as I can remember. I am lucky to be able to rely on the sparkling and nourishing friendship of my sister Allison, whose life's journey—in the United States, France, and francophone Africa—has been remarkably intertwined with my own. Throughout the researching and writing of this book, my wife April has been a generous and loving companion who has helped to keep me attuned to the fullness of life. Through long walks, countless conversations, and a succession of everyday joys, April has helped to shape this book and so much more. Finally, I would like to thank Henry and Sophie, our children, for the stream of happiness they have brought into our lives. Having, in their own ways, grown up with this book, both Henry and Sophie have frequently asked, half-pleadingly, half-jokingly: "Papa, est-ce que tu as fini ton livre aujourd'hui?" I am happy to be able to reply at last: "Mais oui!"

Contesting French West Africa

Introduction

First founded in 1895, the sprawling Federation of French West Africa stretched from the tip of the Cap-Vert peninsula, on Senegal's Atlantic coast, across the bulge of West Africa, all the way to the present-day country of Niger. The northern reaches of French West Africa (Afrique occidentale française, AOF) extended deep into the Sahara desert, while the federation's densely forested southern fringes eventually ran into the Gulf of Guinea. Across the first half of the twentieth century French officials struggled to give solidity and purpose to this vast collection of conquered territories covering an area eight and a half times the size of metropolitan France. But despite these ongoing efforts, AOF remained in many respects a deeply contested entity.

By the turn of the twentieth century the period of military conquest was winding down, and most, but not all, of the territory of French West Africa had come under civilian control. On the ground, however, there were still very few civilian institutions capable of making French rule a more concrete reality. Although a federal administration, or Government General, had been established in 1895, this inchoate entity initially remained fused with the more established administration of the Colony of Senegal. It was not until the first years of the new

FIG. 1. Postcard showing the Palace of the Government General in Dakar as it was nearing completion, circa 1907. From the author's personal collection.

century that the Government General acquired clearer structures and broadened powers. Its headquarters moved from the older Senegalese town of Saint-Louis to the up-and-coming Dakar, after the latter was designated in 1902 as the federation's new administrative capital. Amid these and other events, colonial authorities soon began to think more seriously about the development of AOF and the forms that it might take.

Given how provisional French West Africa remained at the opening of the twentieth century, it is hardly surprising that French authorities felt the need to project bold confidence. In 1903 construction crews in Dakar began work on the Palace of the Government General, a towering structure located near the westernmost point of the African continent. Boasting neoclassical lines, this Palace recalled grand buildings in metropolitan France (see fig. 1). As a result of major building projects like this one, Dakar soon acquired some of the trappings of a young imperial capital, beckoning toward the future. But it was one thing to erect imposing buildings in Dakar and quite another to give shape and purpose to a sprawling colonial federation inhabited by populations that had only recently, and reluctantly, come under French control. Moreover, in a number of regions, colonial authorities were still engaged in an ongoing process of conquest, which they euphemistically dubbed "pacification."

In many cases the boundaries of the various West African colonies had still not been delineated with precision. Authorities understood that space had to be mapped and depicted before it could be appropriated, not only by the colonial administration but also by the metropolitan French, who were beginning to take note of their nation's vast new holdings south of the Sahara. Comparing maps from 1888 and 1912, one can observe these efforts to symbolically recast and domesticate space (see maps 1 and 2). The seemingly unbounded tracts represented on the earlier map have been enclosed by borders and colors on the 1912 map, even as some spaces within the northern and eastern reaches of the federation remained rather undefined. Although the mapping of AOF had progressed considerably by 1912, colonial boundaries were not consolidated until after World War I. By that time the federation had come to include the colonies of Senegal, Mauritania, French Soudan, Guinea, Ivory Coast, Dahomey, Upper Volta, and Niger. Across the first half of the twentieth century, colonial maps proliferated—in schoolbooks, travel literature, the popular press, and the promotional materials of geographical societies and the colonial administration. These maps tended to represent AOF as a solid and often brightly colored space that had been resolutely attached to France, despite its remote location. Maps thus functioned to obscure the very real struggles and hesitations that continued on the ground.[1]

Officials in Dakar were keenly aware that turning French West Africa into a more concrete reality would require more than just administrative headquarters, boundaries, and maps. During the first decade of the twentieth century the Government General planned and launched a number of large infrastructure projects, designed to frame and catalyze the development of the young federation. Through the construction of ports and railroads, colonial authorities sought to create new corridors that would stimulate the production and flow of exports.[2] As of the 1880s, colonial authorities had already constructed

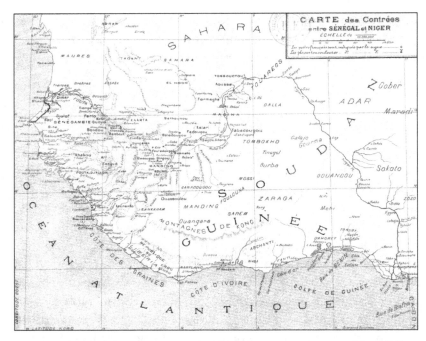

MAP 1. "The lands between Senegal and Niger," 1888. Courtesy of the Bibliothèque nationale de France.

a rail line along the Senegalese coast, between Saint-Louis and burgeoning Dakar, which lay closer to the colony's peanut-growing basin. Around the same time, work began on a second rail line that would eventually extend deep inland, from Dakar all the way to the Niger River. After the turn of the century several other railway projects pressed forward into interior regions of French West Africa. The 1912 map (map 2) depicts both completed railways and planned extensions, which were to form the beginnings of a federation-wide network.[3] From the outset, railway construction involved large numbers of forced laborers, who toiled in appalling conditions and often died on worksites.[4]

During the opening years of the twentieth century colonial officials also realized the limitations of large infrastructure projects, which might help to lay foundations for colonial economies but could do

MAP 2. "French North and West Africa." From Gouvernement général, *L'Afrique occidentale française: janvier 1912*. Courtesy of the Bibliothèque nationale de France.

rather little to orient human beings to the new order. Schools quickly came to be seen as a powerful means to promote and direct the human development of French West Africa. During the expansion of France's West African empire in the second half of the nineteenth century, authorities had mounted only sporadic initiatives in the area of education and had often been content to leave the founding and running of schools to Catholic congregations.[5] The Government General announced a major new departure in 1903, when it published plans for a comprehensive educational system in the newly founded federation. Although it would take years to turn the 1903 blueprints into a concrete reality, colonial officials did not hesitate to express their confidence in the transformative power of schooling. After taking over as governor general in 1908 William Ponty resolutely declared to his administration: "I repeat that education is, to my mind, the most effective means to which we can resort to assure the rapid development, from all standpoints, of this land and of the influence that we wish to exercise here."[6] Ponty was hardly the only official to view schools as a central driver of the entire colonial project. More than their European counterparts, French colonizers seemed intent on placing schools at the heart of their activities overseas.

In many ways, such faith in the power of education was rooted in the recent experiences of metropolitan France. When the Third Republic was first founded, in 1870, sizeable portions of the French countryside still functioned as semi-autarkic *pays*, defined more by local dialects and customs than by their participation in the life of the French nation.[7] After securing their hold over the new regime in 1879, republican officials quickly turned their attention to educational matters. Under the leadership of Jules Ferry—who twice served as prime minister (*président du Conseil des ministres*) during the early to mid-1880s—a devoted group of politicians and pedagogues worked to found a new primary school system, offering universal education that was free, secular, and "republican." Officials hoped that schools would not only promote cultural and linguistic integration but also begin to pull children away from Catholic congregations, which had long served as important purveyors of primary education. Given that most of these congregations continued to profess monarchist sympathies, officials were all too aware that the new regime would not be firmly established until it was equipped with its own schools, capable of cultivating republican sensibilities and virtues in French children.[8] Within a few decades, the sturdy architecture of the republican primary school system had proven its effectiveness by helping to consolidate the Third Republic and the nation's cultural and linguistic unity.[9]

Although they were designed to promote national integration and shared frames of reference, republican schools accommodated themselves to a society that remained heavily marked by class distinctions. While encouraging a limited kind of social mobility and meritocracy, the new primary school system remained quite separate from France's fee-charging secondary schools, which continued to cater to the offspring of bourgeois families. Many children of privilege began their schooling in the lower grades of collèges and lycées and thus never attended republican primary schools, which were generally understood as *écoles du peuple*. Although not absolute, educational segregation along class lines remained an everyday feature of the republican body politic. This bifurcation would help to inform French thinking about education in the colonies: there was already a metropolitan precedent for parallel and unequal educational regimes. However, overseas colonial administrations soon went much further, as they began to organize educational segregation—not around social class but around legal status and racial distinctions. The schools of AOF were deliberately designed to educate "colonial subjects" and not French citizens.

Officials trying to imagine the education of subject populations never considered making secondary education broadly available. Secondary education did make its way to the towns Saint-Louis and Dakar, where growing European populations lived alongside sizeable numbers of rights-bearing Senegalese, known as the *originaires des Quatre Communes*.[10] However, until the end of World War II these exceptional institutions remained outside AOF's educational system. For colonial officials, it quickly became axiomatic that the education of indigenous populations should take place in primary schools.[11] Officials also generally agreed that metropolitan primary education was itself ill suited for African populations: however modest they were, French primary schools had nonetheless been designed for citizens. From the beginning of the twentieth century, officials in AOF worked to develop schools that would be adapted to the "different" needs and aptitudes of subject populations and to the specific requirements of the expanding colonial state.

However, it was one thing to make general policy statements and something else to build and operate a colonial school system. As they went about this work, French authorities struggled to reconcile competing goals. On the one hand, authorities expected schools to facilitate new contacts and collaborations and otherwise bring Africans into the colonial order. On the other hand, schools were supposed to ensure that students understood and internalized their distinct and subordinate positions. From the turn of the twentieth century to World War II these two roles—one incorporative and the other distancing—remained in almost constant tension. More often than not French officials worried that the incorporation of African students and school graduates was proceeding too far, and that boundaries were being blurred or overstepped. Fears of this sort helped to spawn a succession of reforms, designed to firm up distinctions between colonizers and the colonized, and the education that each group received. Carried out during the interwar period, these reforms quieted but did not fully allay French concerns about the content and consequences of colonial schooling. Although it was meant to help clarify and reinforce the colonial order, the school system frequently exposed the anxieties and tensions that hovered over French West Africa.

Studies of colonial education have traditionally focused heavily on the pronouncements and plans of prominent French officials while devoting far less attention to the responses of local populations. Adopting a different approach, *Contesting French West Africa* deliberately tacks back and forth between French and African actors and perspectives. Rarely if ever mere recipients of colonial education, Africans who attended colonial schools often worked to bend their education to their own purposes, through complex processes of appropriation and contestation. Even after completing their studies, many school graduates continued to treat educational policy as a vital arena that could not be left entirely to the colonial administration. After all, schools conditioned the advancement of new African elites and the kinds of positions they could go on to hold in the various spheres of the colonial state. Several chapters of this book investigate the public engagement of African elites in broad contests over education and the colonial order. If many elites attached considerable importance to these battles, it was also because schools, by their very nature, gestured beyond the existing order, toward a shifting horizon of future possibilities. Time and again, controversies over schooling came to serve as proxies for broader contests over the future of French West Africa.

NARRATIVE AND ARGUMENTS

The eight chapters of this book examine specific moments, when struggles over education, the colonial order, and the shape of the future burst into an expanding public sphere. Chapters 1 and 2 focus on contests that took place in the Four Communes of Senegal between the turn of the twentieth century and the early 1920s. Throughout this period these coastal towns contained an unrivaled concentration of schools. And yet these schools quickly became key sites of broadening conflicts between the colonial administration and the rights-bearing originaires. While many originaires saw access to metropolitan education as one of their rights, colonial officials increasingly sought to direct the children of the originaires toward schools designed for subject populations. Whereas the originaires have been confined to the margins of most studies of French West Africa, chapters 1 and 2 underscore the need to write these populations—and their struggles— more fully into the history of AOF. Throughout the first decades of the twentieth century the originaires used their unique position to mount fundamental challenges to the expanding colonial state. This became especially evident after the originaires collectively acquired French citizenship in 1916. Whereas authorities in AOF remained committed to developing a colonial order predicated on African subjecthood, the originaires worked to imagine and build other futures.

Chapters 3 and 4 move beyond the Four Communes and fully into the interwar period. After World War I, the administration in French West Africa sought to frame a colonial order that would look away from the restive populations of the Four Communes and other coastal towns. After being drawn into escalating conflicts with the originaires, French officials increasingly imagined that the vast interior of French West Africa offered more reassuring prospects. Colonial schools were used to map out these shifting priorities. Whereas schools had often been clustered in coastal towns and settlements, the administration now sought to develop a ramifying network of schools in interior regions. These efforts were pursued most vigorously during the Great Depression, when the Government General promoted a new generation of rural schools. As they worked to reorient the colonial order toward interior regions, colonial officials also developed new approaches to the training of African elites, particularly schoolteachers. By reforming more advanced schools, and especially the highly symbolic École William Ponty, authorities hoped to produce more "grounded" elites, who would remain closer to rural societies and less attuned to the struggles of urban Africans. Whereas many studies of French West Africa have tried to identify an interwar colonial project, chapters 3 and 4 highlight important shifts within the interwar period. The depression years ushered in new thinking and bundled reforms, as key officials in Dakar and other administrative capitals worked to revise the colonial project in significant ways. Changes proved especially striking in the field of education.

As the administration strove to frame a less threatening colonial order that would be anchored in the federation's vast rural interior, urban populations found ways to reassert themselves. This was especially the case after the Popular Front came to power. Chapter 5 explores the activism that spread across Senegal's coastal towns during the period 1936–38. Although urban populations expressed many grievances and made any number of demands, they remained especially focused on schooling. Many of the inhabitants of Senegal's towns viewed the administration's new focus on rural education as a concerted assault on educational standards and opportunities. As was so often the case, disputes over education quickly fed into larger debates about the very future of French West Africa. Although the Popular Front period ended rather abruptly in late 1938, spirited debates soon resumed during the first years of the war. As chapter 6 shows, even during the repressive wartime context, African elites found ways to publicly contest the future of AOF.

The final two chapters examine competing attempts to recast French West Africa in the wake of World War II. As of the Brazzaville

Conference, in early 1944, Gaullist officials insisted on the need to assemble and advertise a bold new program of development that could help secure the future of the African colonies. Gaullists rather quickly concluded that interwar approaches to "native education" would not suffice in a changed postwar environment. However, even as they asserted the need to fundamentally rethink and greatly expand the educational system in AOF, Gaullist officials struggled to break out of established frameworks and habits of mind. Contests over education erupted more fully during the first years of the Fourth Republic, as the practice of mass politics began to spread across French West Africa and as all the federation's inhabitants obtained de jure citizenship. The dramatically expanded class of African politicians elected at the end of the war was keenly aware that the citizenship won in Paris would have to be enacted on the ground, in the face of strong resistance from the colonial administration. The experiences of Senegal's originaires served as a cautionary tale. After winning citizenship in 1916, the originaires struggled throughout the interwar period to practice many of their citizens' rights. During the early Fourth Republic, contests over schooling burst more fully into the expanding public sphere. As they struggled to win equal education, and qualifications that would allow them to compete for the same positions as the metropolitan French, Africans tested the new possibilities of citizenship, while also confronting the legacies and rigidities of the colonial state.

1

Conflicting Visions

FRAMING FRENCH WEST AFRICA

As officials began to contemplate and plan the development of French West Africa, they had to contend immediately with the complex legacies of nineteenth-century colonialism. These legacies proved particularly strong along Senegal's Atlantic coast, where French influence stretched back several centuries. By the 1830s political rights had already begun to take root in the old settlements of Saint-Louis and Gorée. These rights eventually became more established during the second half of the nineteenth century, as urban centers along Senegal's coast became staging grounds for new French conquests in West Africa. Soon after the founding of the Third Republic, Saint-Louis, Gorée, Dakar, and Rufisque were reorganized as *communes de plein exercise* (full communes) and equipped with some of the institutions that defined the communes of metropolitan France. However, while the Four Communes harbored small but growing numbers of rights-bearing Africans, the rest of France's expanding West African empire was increasingly predicated on hardening notions of African subjecthood.

The first two chapters of this book investigate the conflicts that erupted as the rights-bearing originaires sought to negotiate their place within a colonial order grounded in stark contrasts between citizens and subjects. Given how central the originaires were to struggles over the developing colonial order, one can reasonably wonder why these populations have been relegated to the margins of many historical accounts of French West Africa. For years, G. Wesley Johnson's pioneering work *The Emergence of Black Politics in Senegal* remained a rather isolated study.[1] Although his book begins by situating the originaires broadly within the nineteenth century, Johnson's main focus is on the transformations that reshaped these communities during the first two decades of the twentieth century. In several articles and book chapters Johnson has partially extended his analysis to the interwar period.[2]

In recent years scholarly interest in the originaires has finally begun to pick up. However, newer work has tended to examine the originaires largely within the context of the second half of the nineteenth century.[3] This sort of framing can reinforce the widely held view that the originaires were rather quickly pushed to the sidelines in the early twentieth century, as colonial authorities consolidated their hold over French West Africa. Studies of AOF often bring the originaires back into view when assessing World War I and its impacts. But even when it comes to the war, there is a tendency to recycle a rather tidy group of facts relating to political activism of Senegal's first black deputy, Blaise Diagne. With the end of the war, historical accounts tend to shift sharply away from Diagne and the originaires. Such treatment is rather surprising, given that the number of originaires grew steadily across the first two decades of the twentieth century, reaching eighteen thousand by 1921.[4] Concentrated in some of the most central nodes of the colonial state, these populations represented a standing challenge to French projects.

SITUATING THE ORIGINAIRES

At the opening of the twentieth century the newness of the Federation of French West Africa contrasted with the long history of Senegal, France's oldest sub-Saharan colony. French involvement along the Senegalese coastline reached back all the way to the seventeenth century, when chartered companies first established *comptoirs*, or fortified trading posts, in Saint-Louis and on the island of Gorée.[5] These coastal comptoirs quickly became important nodes in the transatlantic slave trade, which flourished through the eighteenth century and continued into the early nineteenth century.[6] As long as French involvement in West Africa was primarily oriented toward slaving, settlements remained largely confined to a handful of coastal enclaves. But with the progressive decline of slave trading during the first half of the nineteenth century, and France's official abolition of slavery in 1848, authorities soon began to experiment with new forms of colonization.[7]

During the Second Empire (1852–70) Senegal's older towns became important staging areas for new territorial conquests stretching along the Senegalese coast and into interior regions. Spearheading many of these conquests was the ambitious Louis Faidherbe, who served as governor of Senegal from 1854 to 1861 and then again from 1863 to 1865. Although some of the newly conquered territories were placed under direct rule, most of the expanding colony of Senegal came to be organized differently, through protectorate agreements with African communities and states and a developing system of colonial administration. During Faidherbe's two stints as governor Senegal was transformed: from the old coastal enclaves, the colony's boundaries were extended far inland, following the Senegal River and other routes. As a sign of their growing strategic importance as established bridgeheads to a rapidly expanding colony, Senegal's most important coastal towns soon acquired new infrastructures and institutions, including schools.[8]

In many ways the founding of the Third Republic in 1870 signaled even greater transformations in Senegal's towns. While republican authorities did not immediately push forward with further inland conquests, they quickly moved to reorganize Senegal's main urban centers. In 1872 Saint-Louis and Gorée-Dakar were administratively and politically recast as communes de plein exercise.[9] The town of Rufisque acquired the same status in 1880, and in 1887 Dakar was split off from Gorée and established as a separate commune. These four towns were soon equipped with many of the institutions that helped to define metropolitan communes.[10] Along with local French populations, the African inhabitants of these towns elected municipal councils, whose members went on to choose town mayors.[11] Together, voters in these communes also elected a Conseil général du Sénégal (General Council), modeled after the bodies by the same name that existed in each department of metropolitan France.[12] Beginning in 1871 voters in the Four Communes also began to elect a representative to the French Chamber of Deputies. Throughout the rather long life of the Third Republic, this would remain the only deputyship in French West Africa.[13]

The creation of these metropolitan political institutions has led most scholars to view the Four Communes as a case study in the ideology and practice of assimilation. In reality, however, the situation in these towns remained considerably more ambiguous. Local colonial authorities expressed reservations early on about the creation of communes in Senegal.[14] Moreover, after failing to prevent these reforms, colonial officials in Senegal actively sought to limit the influence of the Four Communes. By the 1890s officials were already pressing forward with plans to shrink the size of the territories placed under direct administration, through a process known as "disannexation." As a result of these measures the boundaries of the communes of Saint-Louis and Dakar were significantly trimmed.[15] Colonial authorities increasingly found that they could rule more flexibly and expediently in the protectorate regions of Senegal (*les pays de protectorat*), where French legal norms and metropolitan-style political institutions did not hold sway. By contrast, rule in the Four Communes was coming to seem more complicated and contentious.

There are other factors that should prevent us from viewing the Four Communes as a straightforward case study in assimilation. Most important, these towns were equipped with some but not all of the institutions that defined communes in metropolitan France. In what was an important derogation from metropolitan norms, republican schools were never introduced in these communes. From the founding of the Third Republic to the first years of the twentieth century, schools in Senegal's coastal towns continued to be operated by Catholic missionaries and their congregations, which received direct subsidies from the colonial state. Given how fundamental republican schools became to the new regime in France, the decision not to extend metropolitan school legislation to the Four Communes raises important historical questions about the limits of assimilationist ideology and practice.

During the last decades of the nineteenth century the inhabitants of Senegal's communes were perhaps most defined by their in-betweenness: even as they developed urban modes of sociability and a certain familiarity with local French populations, many originaires maintained strong connections to interior regions of Senegal. These dual anchorings allowed the originaires to serve as important middlemen, who facilitated trade along the Senegal River and in the increasingly important peanut-growing regions closer to Dakar and Rufisque. Recent studies by Hilary Jones and David Robinson have underscored just how involved many originaires were in broad trading networks that stretched across Senegal and beyond. By the end of the century, however, the position of these middlemen had weakened, as French conquests of inland regions and improved transportation systems lessened the need for intermediaries who knew how to work on the fringes of empire.[16]

As their roles in trading networks ebbed, the originaires turned increasingly to careers in colonial administration and local politics. During the 1880s and 1890s French officials had to contend with prominent mixed-race (*métis*) elites, who made steady inroads into local political institutions, particularly in Saint-Louis.[17] For a time French officials maintained the upper hand, even as they shared political positions with the métis. However, by the turn of the century métis politicians were clearly becoming a more formidable political force. With the election of François Carpot to the French Chamber of Deputies in 1902, Senegal's mixed-race populations seized the colony's preeminent political position for the first time. Although French politicians still remained in charge of Dakar, Gorée, and Rufisque, local métis soon took control of both the municipal government in Saint-Louis and Senegal's General Council.[18] As they observed the rising political fortunes of the métis, colonial authorities began to express growing misgivings about the originaires and their place within the expanding colonial order.

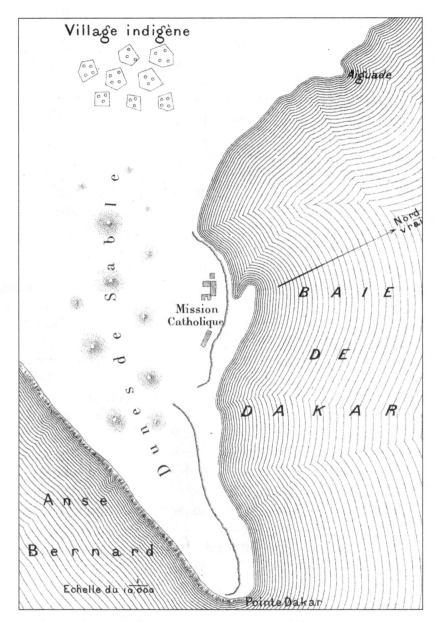

Village indigène

Aiguade

Nord Vrai

B A I E

D E

D A K A R

Dunes de Sable

Mission
Catholique

Anse

Bernard

Echelle du 1/10,000

Pointe Dakar

MAP 3. The outpost of Dakar in 1850. From Louis Faidherbe, *Le Sénégal: La France dans l'Afrique occidentale*. Courtesy of the Bibliothèque nationale de France.

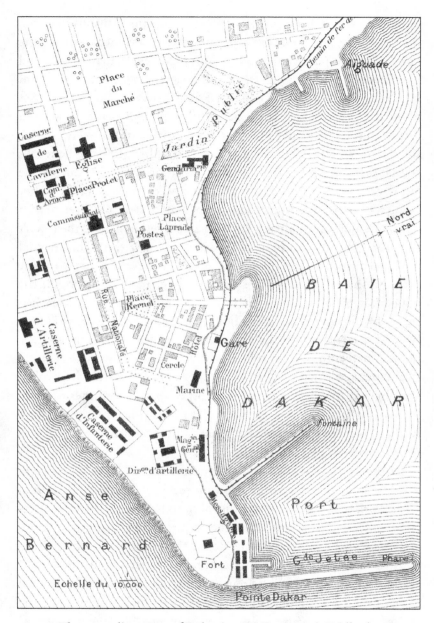

MAP 4. The expanding town of Dakar in 1888. From Louis Faidherbe, *Le Sénégal: La France dans l'Afrique occidentale*. Courtesy of the Bibliothèque nationale de France.

Demographic trends only added to mounting tensions between the originaires and the colonial administration. Prior to the founding of the Third Republic, the populations of Senegal's main towns had remained small. With some 15,000 inhabitants in 1865, Saint-Louis was by far the biggest urban center in Senegal. That same year Gorée's population stood at around 3,000. With tiny populations of around three hundred residents, Dakar and Rufisque could scarcely be classified as towns at all. However, the demographic profile of Senegal's coastal towns soon began to change. Dakar grew steadily during the last decades of the nineteenth century and even more rapidly after being named as the administrative capital of AOF in 1902 (see maps 3 and 4). By 1910 Dakar already boasted 24,914 residents, and the town's expansion showed no signs of slowing down. With its commercial port and central role in the peanut trade, Rufisque also took on new proportions, its population reaching 12,457 in 1910. Although the population of Saint-Louis grew more gradually, it nonetheless reached 22,093 by the same year.[19] Histories of the young Federation of French West Africa tend to portray the Four Communes as awkward artifacts of the nineteenth century, whose influence was increasingly eclipsed as the new colonial order took shape. But rather than becoming marginal to the new colonial order, the Four Communes actually served as dynamic urban nodes, radiating out into interior regions. As they observed these trends, colonial authorities found new reasons to want to hem in the originaires.

By the first years of the twentieth century the Government General had become increasingly committed to developing a colonial framework that rested on stark distinctions between African subjects and French citizens.[20] Although the corpus of administrative decrees and *arrêtés* that would eventually define the category of "subjects" was hardly complete, it was already clear that the latter would enjoy few if any of the rights of French citizens. As they worked to bring additional clarity to colonial frameworks, many French officials came to see the rights-bearing originaires as a standing challenge. But whereas colonial authorities moved to curtail the rights and influence of the originaires, these populations frequently found ways to reassert their positions and claims. Although these contests played out in any number of spheres, they became particularly pronounced in the field of education.

INVENTING COLONIAL EDUCATION

With the rapid expansion of empire during the last decades of the nineteenth century, French officials came to think more about the education of conquered populations. Claiming a broad educational mission became one of the ways in which French authorities sought to justify colonial conquests, both to metropolitan populations and to international observers. Notwithstanding the high-flown rhetoric touting France's "civilizing mission," the fact remained that embryonic colonial administrations were often ill prepared to open and operate their own schools. During the late nineteenth century many of the schools that came to dot the empire were founded not by colonial administrations but by far-flung French missionary societies. In his insightful book *An Empire Divided: Religion, Republicanism, and the Making of French Colonialism, 1880–1914,* J. P. Daughton has shown just how active French missionaries remained in imperial settings. However, as Daughton makes clear, overseas missions and their schools routinely pursued their own agendas, often with little regard for the ideology of the early Third Republic or the practical needs of colonial rule.[21] Elizabeth Foster has exposed a similar divide in her detailed study of tense and tenuous relations between missionaries and colonial officials in the Colony of Senegal.[22] Relationships between missionary societies and colonial administrations grew more strained around the turn of the twentieth century, as church-state conflicts in metropolitan France intensified. When the Dreyfus Affair precipitated a new round of confrontations between anti-clericalists and clericalists, Left and Right, republicans and anti-republicans, the very foundations of the Third Republic trembled.

In the face of renewed challenges from the anti-republican right, government officials took a dimmer view of the various Catholic congregations that operated schools in metropolitan France. The position of these schools was called into question in 1901, when the government of Pierre Waldeck-Rousseau sponsored an important new law on associations. In many respects this law was liberal in spirit, since it established the right to form associations freely. However, the 1901 law also included a restrictive provision requiring all religious congregations to be officially authorized by the state. Unauthorized congregations, of which there were many, were given three months to request state approval. In the end government officials turned down almost all the requests that they received, prompting many teaching congregations to close down or to send their members abroad. A separate law, passed in 1904, went even further by banning—at least on paper—even recognized congregations from operating schools in France.[23] The campaign to rein in *écoles congréganistes* deepened church-state antagonisms in France and helped to spur republican officials to seek broader solutions. It was in this tense context that the Chamber of Deputies eventually passed a far-reaching 1905 law providing for the separation of church and state.[24]

In practice these church-state controversies were only partially exported to the empire, and even then, they tended to be more informed by local concerns and power dynamics than by metropolitan scripts.[25] Moreover, by World War I there were clear signs of a rapprochement between missionaries and overseas colonial administrations.[26] But in many cases the clampdown on écoles congréganistes that occurred in turn-of-the-century France did precipitate changes overseas. In various parts of the empire, colonial administrations sought to reduce their reliance on mission-run schools by founding, or consolidating, their own school systems. As we will see, officials in Dakar soon began to take important steps in this direction.

At the turn of the century almost all the schools in Senegal's Four Communes were still operated by Catholic teaching congregations. Boys' schools had been turned over to the Brothers of Christian Instruction of Ploërmel, who received direct subsidies from the colonial administration. At the same time the Sisters of Saint-Joseph de Cluny and the Sisters of Our Lady of the Immaculate Conception of Castres ran all the girls' schools in the Four Communes. Over the years the originaires had developed a long familiarity with these congregations: the Brothers of Ploërmel had operated schools in Senegal ever since the middle of the nineteenth century, and the Sisters of Saint-Joseph de Cluny had opened their first schools in the colony even earlier.[27] During the second half of the nineteenth century missionary-run schools evolved considerably. Although religious instruction remained an established part of the school day, the curricula came to contain more and more standard school subjects. This was partly a response to local populations and their elected leaders, who repeatedly pushed the teaching congregations to introduce higher educational standards.[28] Whereas schooling within the Four Communes had been entrusted almost entirely to French missionaries, the colonial administration operated a scattering of its own schools in the rest of Senegal, which had been constituted as a French protectorate in 1882. However, compared to the more established schools of the Four Communes, these administration-run schools remained small and poorly attended.[29] Elsewhere in French West Africa colonial authorities had also made some rather haphazard attempts to found schools. But at the turn of the century administration-run schools tended to be precarious local enterprises that received little outside support or guidance.[30]

The educational order that had developed in Senegal's Four Communes during the second half of the nineteenth century was abruptly called into question in 1903, as metropolitan officials pressured colonial authorities to reduce their reliance on Catholic teaching congregations. Faced with this changing context the governor general of AOF, Ernest Roume, sought advice from key collaborators on how to proceed. Roume asked Camille Guy, the lieutenant governor of Senegal, to prepare a report that would make recommendations regarding the *laïcisation* of existing schools and the creation of a new administration-run school system. Guy's twenty-nine-page report titled "The State of Education in Senegal in 1903" included an unsparing assessment of missionary-run schools. The lieutenant governor noted that the teachers in these schools had themselves received little formal education and even less pedagogical training. Unprepared for the task that had been handed to them, these *congréganistes* fell back on formalistic, bookish approaches to education that encouraged students to parrot phrases in French without fully grasping their meaning. As far as Guy was concerned, the problem went beyond poorly trained teachers and inappropriate pedagogies. The lieutenant governor also deplored the fact that schools in the Four Communes continued to use books produced by missionary societies, "which do not take any account of recent discoveries or the advances made in all the branches of science."[31] For all these reasons Guy supported a process of laïcisation that would lead the colonial administration to assume direct control over the schools of the Four Communes.

The lieutenant governor stressed, however, that such a transition should occur gradually, so as not to arouse needless opposition among the originaires, many of whom had grown attached to existing schools.[32] Moreover, Guy contended that new administration-run schools would need to remain sensitive to the educational precedents that had been established in the Four Communes. Guy was especially concerned about a recommendation that the minister of colonies had recently forwarded to Governor General Roume. The minister had suggested that AOF take inspiration from Madagascar, where, under the leadership of Joseph Galliéni, local officials had begun to develop a brand new school system for *indigènes*. In his 1903 report to Roume, Guy highlighted the problems that such an approach would produce in Senegal's towns: "The system of General Galliéni could perhaps be introduced in new colonies such as Dahomey or Ivory Coast where nothing or almost nothing exists [in the way of French-run schools]. To try this in Senegal would be to deeply disturb local opinion and to rile up a population which has, for sixty years, been satisfied with its current schools and which considers them sufficient. One cannot proceed in a colony that is two centuries old as one can in a recently conquered land, where newcomers can attempt all manner of experiments and try out all kinds of systems."[33] Guy understood that many originaires would oppose an abrupt turn toward new forms of education, expressly designed for subject populations. Seeking to avoid controversy, the lieutenant governor contended that new administration-run schools in the Four Communes should be modeled after the primary schools of France.

It would be wrong to view Guy as being in the thrall of assimilationist ideology; more than anything, he sought to stake out a pragmatic position. The lieutenant governor's main concern was with métis populations, whose leaders had acquired increasing influence in the Four Communes. After consulting with various elected officials in Saint-Louis, Dakar, Gorée, and Rufisque, Guy concluded that "the white and mulatto populations of the established communes would not accept anything other than metropolitan education."[34] What Guy chose to elide was the fact that most originaires were black and that these populations were beginning to enroll more of their children in local schools. As we will see in a later section of this chapter, racial considerations would increasingly inform the colonial administration's approach to educational policy in the Four Communes.

While seeking to respect certain precedents within the Four Communes, Guy advocated a different approach to schooling in the rest of the Colony of Senegal. In his 1903 report on the state of education the lieutenant governor estimated that approximately three hundred students attended, "more or less regularly," the eleven schools that the colony's administration had established in inland areas. Describing the failures of these administration-run schools, Guy noted: "The mistake was to believe that we could reach our goals by simply transporting metropolitan education to the colony. Curricula, pedagogies, schoolbooks, personnel, and examinations—everything must be thoroughly redesigned." Guy then sketched out some steps that could be taken in the colony's interior to bring schools closer to African realities and the needs of the developing colonial state. He explained that "at inland schools [les écoles des escales] we must resolutely decide to only teach reading, writing, and basic math, a few very elementary aspects of Senegalese and French geography, while leaving aside the teaching of history, which is difficult to provide and which can only have unfortunate consequences. The more practical and rudimentary education is, the more useful schools will be; it's a matter of turning young natives into workers who speak and write French."[35] In short, what Guy recommended was a bifurcated approach to schooling in Senegal: whereas metropolitan-style primary education would be the norm in the Four Communes, schools in the rest of Senegal would provide truncated forms of education designed with subject populations in mind. Evidently impressed by these recommendations, Governor General Roume soon asked Guy to begin outlining a school system for the entire Federation of French West Africa.

In October 1903 Guy sent Roume drafts of three arrêtés, along with an introductory report explaining the new educational mission that the colonial administration was about to undertake. The first of these arrêtés established the structures and goals of the new colonial school system, while the second and third arrêtés created the *cadres*, or administrative categories, in which French and African teachers would serve.[36] Promptly approved by Roume, the new directives called for a school system that would resemble a pyramid. The system's base was to be made up of an expanding network of village schools. Guy and other colonial officials imagined that most African students would be educated exclusively in village schools providing only a few years of basic primary education. Smaller numbers of more promising students would be sent on to regional schools, which were to be opened in larger villages and smaller towns with a certain French presence. Whereas village schools might have either an African or a French director, depending on their size, regional schools would be systematically placed under the authority of a French director. And unlike village schools, regional schools would offer a full course of colonial primary education.[37]

While providing a fuller program of primary education, regional schools were not supposed to imitate the primary schools of metropolitan France. The 1903 school blueprints made it clear that both village schools and regional schools should provide education that was "adapted" to the needs of French West Africa. In general this meant that colonial school curricula should be rudimentary and clearly oriented toward local subjects and practical applications. According to the 1903 arrêté, regional schools were to teach the following subjects: "the French language; the Arabic language (in Muslim lands); reading; writing; basic math and the metric system; elements of geometry; drawing; basic elements of modern and contemporary history, studied in its relationship to the diverse regions [*pays*] of French West Africa;

elements of physical and natural sciences applied to hygiene, agriculture and local industries." In addition to these subjects, regional schools were required to provide practical training in agriculture; when local resources permitted, these schools were encouraged to add manual sections devoted to woodworking, metalworking, and other *travaux pratiques*.[38] French officials considered that such training would orient African students toward useful subaltern roles. Regional schools were also charged with selecting small numbers of students who would go on to complete more advanced studies at professional schools located in the Four Communes.[39]

The 1903 arrêté proposed different guidelines for urban schools, which were to be established only in the federation's largest towns. Charged with educating European children and select African students whose families were sufficiently assimilated, these schools were expected to have a French director and an entirely European teaching staff. And whereas village schools and regional schools now ran on colonial curricula, urban schools conformed to the primary school curricula of metropolitan France. Although the 1903 regulations did stipulate that "modifications [to the curricula of urban schools] can be introduced in order to meet local needs," it was understood that such adjustments would remain minimal. Whereas children attending regional schools could only work toward a colonial primary school certificate, students at urban schools studied for "a primary school certificate analogous to that instituted in the metropole by the law of 28 March 1882."[40]

As it happened, newly defined urban schools came to be clustered in Senegal's Four Communes. By converting the congregation-run schools of the Four Communes into urban schools, Guy hoped to avoid a public showdown with the originaires. In a report to Governor General Roume, he noted: "It is this desire to not destroy everything that explains the preservation, under the name of urban schools, of educational institutions that have been functioning for a long time in these urban centers."[41] While classifying all eleven of the primary schools of the Four Communes as urban schools, Guy's administration proceeded very differently in the rest of the Colony of Senegal. No additional towns were equipped with an urban school. Moreover, in

1904–5, the Colony of Senegal possessed only two regional schools, one in Thiès and the other in the town of Ziguinchor. That same year the colony operated twenty village schools. However, because they were larger and more solidly established, the urban schools of the Four Communes still accounted for two thirds of all students in the colony's "official" schools.[42] Clearly, by maintaining eleven urban schools in the Four Communes, Guy's administration was hardly complying with the Government General's 1903 directives, which established that the overwhelming majority of African students should attend village and regional schools following "adapted" curricula. The network of urban schools found in Senegal's towns contrasted sharply with the situation elsewhere in AOF: at the time, most of the other colonies did not even boast one urban school.[43]

But even as he helped to establish the urban school model within the Four Communes, Guy worked to rein in opportunities for more advanced forms of education. In his 1903 report on the state of education in Senegal, Guy pointedly criticized the secondary school in Saint-Louis, which the Brothers of Ploërmel had operated ever since the mid-1880s. Over the years this school had produced small but influential cohorts of Senegalese elites, which had included Blaise Diagne.[44] As far as the lieutenant governor of Senegal was concerned, this school turned out graduates who were maladapted to colonial society. Guy declared that "the students who have come out of it [the secondary school], misled, like their parents by the school's pompous name, have always considered themselves the products of a superior education that predestines them for high positions. Those who, forced to make a living, have entered the postal service, the customs service or the offices of the administration are not far from considering that they have been stripped of their rights; many have become *déclassés*, too educated to accept petty positions, not educated enough to render useful services."[45] Guy was hardly the only official to denounce the untoward effects of secondary education and to recommend that the school be closed. In the end the secondary school was converted into the École Faidherbe, an *école primaire supérieure et commerciale*, designed to train a more modest kind of African elite.[46] As we will see, these reforms aroused considerable consternation among the originaires, who clearly understood that their educational rights and opportunities had suffered a serious blow.

TOWARD SEGREGATION IN THE FOUR COMMUNES

After arriving in Dakar in 1908, Amédée William Merlaud-Ponty soon became a highly influential governor general, who would play an outsize role in the framing of French West Africa. In the introduction to this book, we heard Ponty profess his faith in the power of colonial schools, when he declared to his administration: "I repeat that education is, to my mind, the most effective means to which we can resort to assure the rapid development, from all standpoints, of this land and of the influence that we wish to exercise here."[47] But while underscoring the centrality of schools to the colonial project, Ponty made it clear that he was not proposing metropolitan solutions. In his inaugural address to his administration, Ponty went on to describe the kinds of schooling that he planned to promote:

> But rest assured, I intend only to increase the number of schools providing a very simple primary education. We must effectively take our populations where they are in their development. To teach natives to speak our language, to read it, to write it, to instill in them a few basic math skills, along with a few notions of morality, this is sufficient for the moment. They can learn these things in schools run by native schoolteachers. Once these lessons have been learned, the education of our young natives must—with the exception of an elite of a higher culture which we have a duty to promote—become and remain practical.[48]

But while Ponty initially saw schools as a rather straightforward means to consolidate the new colonial order in French West Africa, he would soon realize that schools could also become complex battlegrounds. Nowhere was this more evident than in Senegal's Four Communes. Ponty would spend most of his long tenure in Dakar enmeshed in protracted battles with the originaires over schools, political rights, and the future of French West Africa.

Soon after he arrived in Dakar, Ponty began looking for ways to curb the exceptionalism of the Four Communes. The new governor general took exception to Guy's decision to generalize the urban school model in Senegal's old towns. Anxious to revisit this question, Ponty sent a series of notes on educational policy to the headquarters of Senegal's administration, in Saint-Louis. In a September 1909 letter Ponty explained to the acting lieutenant governor of Senegal, Edmond Gaudart, that "it is important to multiply rural or regional schools as much as possible, for they are the very foundation of our educational program for natives." The governor general went on to stress that "urban schools must be reduced to a minimum. This is the logical consequence of, on the one hand, the increase in the number of regional schools and rural schools designed for natives in towns and their outlying areas as well as in the *cercles*, and on the other hand, the fact that, according to the terms of the arrêté of 24 November 1903, these urban schools are meant to meet the particular educational needs of students of European origin."[49]

In seeking to link rural and regional schools clearly with "natives," and urban schools with Europeans, Ponty sought to downplay questions of legal status, while placing new emphasis on the deepening racial divide. While noting that the primary vocation of urban schools was to educate European children, the governor general nonetheless conceded that these schools did not need to be "officially closed to natives recognized to be capable of receiving a superior education."[50] Although the governor general did not specify how these more "capable" African students should be chosen, racial criteria were clearly coming more fully into play. As we will see, Ponty remained open to the continued inclusion of a certain number of métis in Senegal's urban schools. What Ponty and other officials now questioned was whether black originaires should be able to send their children to urban schools, offering metropolitan education.

The colonial administration's relationships with métis families had become increasingly tense, as prominent métis began to assert themselves more fully in local government. In other respects, however, French authorities continued to view the métis of the Four Communes somewhat favorably. After all, most were Catholics, who spoke French and had adopted French-inflected lifestyles. But although the métis had come to wield considerable influence in local politics, they made up dwindling minorities; most originaires were black Muslims.[51] And while colonial administrators harbored growing misgivings about the métis, attitudes toward black originaires usually proved considerably more hostile. Many officials resented the fact that French rights had been conceded to black populations maintaining different religious affiliations and lifestyles.

In the face of increasing pressure from Ponty and the Government General, officials in Saint-Louis sought to show that they were tightening access to urban schools. In April 1909 Lieutenant Governor Gaudart wrote Ponty to explain his plans to reduce the number of urban schools in the Four Communes.[52] In October of that year Gaudart went on to publish an arrêté officially reclassifying many of the schools in Saint-Louis, Dakar, Gorée and Rufisque. Up until this point the Four Communes had been home to eleven urban schools, seven for boys and four for girls. With the 1909 reclassification, the number of urban schools for girls remained unchanged, whereas the number of urban schools for boys dropped precipitously, to just two. As part of this reform process, five urban schools for boys were downgraded to the status of regional schools.[53] With these changes, new forms of colonial education made inroads into the Four Communes and opportunities for metropolitan schooling shrank considerably.

Officials in Senegal would soon go even further in their efforts to curb originaire access to French primary education. The October 1909 reform had not clearly defined the populations that were to be served by the remaining urban schools; Gaudart's arrêté had merely stated that "urban schools are reserved for children capable of following the metropolitan school curricula that correspond to their age."[54] In practice, however, school officials and French teachers used the new regulations to winnow out many students who were not of European origin. Black children, most of whom were Muslims, turned out to be the primary targets. At the time black students tended to be older than their European classmates, largely because they often completed several years of Koranic education prior to enrolling in a French-run school. The 1909 reforms led to the dismissal of a number of these students, who were now considered too old for their respective grades.

Colonial officials also began to demand greater fluency in French from Senegalese children wishing to attend the remaining urban schools. With the introduction of the October 1909 arrêté, non-French children were required to pass an exam—administered by the school director and the appropriate teacher—to determine whether they were capable of following the metropolitan curricula. The stakes were quite high indeed, since only students at urban schools could work toward the *certificat d'études primaires élémentaires*, a school-leaving certificate equivalent to that which was awarded in metropolitan France. Students at regional schools could study only for the *certificat d'études primaires professionnelles*, a certificate with no equivalent in France that served to limit students' educational and professional prospects. Village schools did not award any certificate at all.[55]

Although Senegal's urban schools had brought together children of very diverse backgrounds, there was clearly growing pressure from the colonial administration and European populations to reduce racial intermixing. Colonial officials hesitated to introduce overt color bars, such as those found in the British colonies.[56] Although republicanism had never been fully implanted in Senegal's Four Communes, the strains of republicanism that had taken root were enough to make official color bars problematic. Nonetheless, there were clear signs of a new willingness to invoke racial distinctions.[57] After taking over as lieutenant governor of Senegal, Jean Peuvergne continued Gaudart's efforts to "whiten" the colony's urban schools.[58]

Peuvergne's own views on racial intermixing had been partially shaped by the work of Léon d'Anfreville de la Salle, an employee in Senegal's hygiene department who had already begun to publish a range of texts on the African colonies. D'Anfreville de la Salle was especially prolix when it came to the subjects of racial differences and public hygiene.[59] In his 1909 book on the past, present, and future of the Colony of Senegal, this official sought to ridicule the old ideology of assimilation for ignoring fundamental and enduring racial distinctions.

Although he could approvingly note the broad movement away from assimilationist thinking, d'Anfreville de la Salle clearly thought that more needed to be done, particularly in Senegal's towns. This official opined that "we have still not been able to completely separate, in the schools of the large towns, the black and the white races." In explaining the need for school segregation, d'Anfreville de la Salle reached for any argument he could find, emphasizing not only differences in physical appearance but also dissimilarities in hygiene, upbringing, morality, religion, and civilization. Summing up, this official contended that "we should not bring together, in the same classes, children who are separated from each other by diametrically opposed atavisms, by natural or acquired mentalities that are totally contradictory."[60]

While openly calling for school segregation, d'Anfreville de la Salle was ready to make some minor concessions, so as not to completely ignore the links that bound certain local elites to the French. He thus proposed "to bring together, in special classes, European students, the *assimilés*, and the few blacks brought up according to our principles."[61] D'Anfreville de la Salle's rather tortured explanations shed light on some of the ways in which race and racial separations were constructed in Senegal and AOF in the early twentieth century. As the historian and sociologist Emmanuelle Saada has shown, categorizations according to phenotype represent only part of the story. As they struggled to draw and enforce lines between colonizers and the colonized, and to resolve the vexed "question" of the métis, French officials frequently factored in more personal considerations relating to such things as home environments and lifestyle.[62] If the métis—referred to rather allusively by d'Anfreville de la Salle as the assimilés—could still sometimes find spaces in urban schools, it was not only because of their physical features but also because they were often viewed as possessing other kinds of affinities with the French. By contrast, d'Anfreville de la Salle and other officials worked to underscore the fundamental alterity of black populations, regardless of whether they possessed originaire status.

In a report produced in early 1910, d'Anfreville de la Salle reiterated his warnings about the promiscuous and unhealthy intermixing taking place in Senegal's urban schools. After receiving this report, Lieutenant Governor Peuvergne promptly wrote Ponty to express his growing anxieties. In his letter Peuvergne directly referenced d'Anfreville de la Salle's admonitions, which drew attention "to the dangers, from a sanitary point of view, of too large a grouping of Europeans, métis, and natives, intermixed in the same locale." Peuvergne went on to note that the opinions of d'Anfreville de la Salle were in keeping with recent approaches to urban planning in Senegal. The lieutenant governor mentioned "the sustained efforts and the considerable expenditures" that had already been made to protect public health by separating "the French element from the native element" in the colony's main towns.[63] Peuvergne remarked that some European families had refused to send their children to racially mixed urban schools. These families were apparently concerned not only about the allegedly poor hygiene of African students but also about the moral influence that the latter might have on their sons and daughters, particularly when it came to sexuality. After observing that African students were often considerably older than their European classmates, Peuvergne warned of the "moral contamination" that might occur in urban schools. Citing these and other fears, European families had at various times requested that special schools, or at least special classes, be established for their children.[64]

Attempting to develop a pedagogical argument in favor of segregation, Peuvergne noted that the African students who attended urban schools often lacked a firm command of the French language. The lieutenant governor contended that French children frequently ended up wasting their time as their African classmates labored through school lessons at a slower pace. Peuvergne flatly rejected this sort of "democratic equality," which was achieved "by bringing down" European students. In making his case to Ponty, Peuvergne made one final argument. He predicted that the racial intermixing taking place at Senegal's urban schools would sooner or later become the subject of unflattering reports that would find their way to metropolitan France. He predicted that certain metropolitan newspapers might seek to turn this situation into a scandal that could embarrass authorities in AOF. For all these reasons Peuvergne, like Ponty himself, supported additional restrictions on access to Senegal's remaining urban schools.[65] As they pursued this goal, both men could count on the support of other influential French officials.

Émile Masson, the French mayor of Dakar, did not hesitate to criticize the schools of the federal capital. In a report filed in early 1909 Masson lamented that too much money was being spent providing metropolitan education to undeserving indigènes. Masson emphasized that "it would be more than sufficient to teach children to speak French, to read and to write, to do basic math: our ambitions should be limited to that and our efforts should stop there. Why should we want to adhere to complicated and learned curricula that natives do not understand in the least? While trying to understand them, they waste time that could be much more usefully spent on basic primary and professional education." Ponty indicated his full agreement with all of these points by scrawling "yes!!" in the margins of Masson's report and by noting that he had himself developed similar arguments in his recent address to the Council of the Government General. In his report Masson went on to explain that the commune of Dakar planned to reduce expenses on education, partly by pushing the town's African inhabitants toward regional and even rural schools. Attempting to justify such measures, the mayor declared: "It is not by creating déclassés, proud of the knowledge that they think they possess that France's civilizing work will be consolidated." By way of conclusion, Masson added that the primary effect of education reforms would be "to eliminate the bulk of these déclassés [since] most children who have attended school would remain in the situation of their fathers, [namely] workers or farmers."[66]

THE ORIGINAIRES FIGHT BACK

Seeing their educational rights and opportunities called into question, the originaires soon began to mobilize themselves in new ways. Discussions of educational policy became quite heated in Senegal's General Council over which métis politicians held controlling influence. The actual prerogatives of this body were rather limited: its most important official charge was to vote on non-obligatory administrative expenditures in the parts of Senegal that had been placed under direct administration (principally, the Four Communes). The colony's lieutenant governor controlled the budget for the protectorate regions of Senegal as well as the obligatory expenditures within the Four Communes. However, since non-obligatory budget items in the Four Communes were not negligible, the General Council maintained a certain leverage over colonial policy. Moreover, the members of this body often chose to debate a broad range of issues that did not fall within their official purview. After holding such debates, councilors sometimes formulated and approved recommendations, which could influence public opinion and, at times, colonial policy.[67]

No councilor spoke out more forcefully against educational segregation in the Four Communes than Justin Devès.[68] After his political grouping won control over the municipal council in Saint-Louis in 1909, Devès emerged as a dominant figure in local politics. In addition to being named as the new mayor of Saint-Louis, Devès also won a seat on Senegal's General Council.[69] Part of Devès's success stemmed from his efforts to reach out to black originaires, who had formerly played rather minor roles in local politics. If the métis and French communities had long constituted the two main political forces in Senegal's towns, black originaires were beginning to develop new forms of political consciousness and activism.

During a December 1909 session of the General Council, Devès denounced the recent reclassification of schools within the Four Communes. Devès observed that schools with a high percentage of European and métis children were still designated as urban schools, while schools with large numbers of blacks were being reclassified as regional schools. All this led the new mayor of Saint-Louis to declare that "the administration has established an unacceptable distinction since it is based not on abilities, but on the color of students. There is now one primary school curriculum and one primary school certificate for whites and another for blacks. These curricula and certificates no longer provide the same opportunities." Devès went on to note that "this distinction is not only hurtful, but also persecutory for natives whose interests are undermined the moment you bar them from entering liberal careers and seek to turn them into workers." Making a final point, Devès added that the 1909 reclassification of schools was not only unjust but also illegal, insofar as the Government General's 1903 education guidelines had not called for regional schools to be set up in the federation's largest towns.[70]

Following Devès's opening salvos, other members of the General Council added their voices to this heated discussion. Whereas Justin Devès was something of a political newcomer, his brother Hyacinthe had been a longstanding presence within the General Council.[71] Turning toward the representative of the colonial administration, who sat listening, Hyacinthe Devès declared that "schools are public, free and secular, thus you must open them to everyone. Students' origins don't concern the administration."[72] This councilor took issue with newly announced plans to sort students according to their French language skills—a measure clearly destined to favor the metropolitan French over all others. Hyacinthe Devès explained that most students learned French at school rather than at home. Reflecting candidly on his own experiences, he noted that despite being brought up "à la française," he had been slow to express himself in French and had only become truly comfortable in his adopted language after traveling to France for university studies. Directly addressing the representative of Senegal's administration, Hyacinthe Devès declared that if measures of proficiency in French were used to shunt the originaires into regional schools, providing manual training, "you will no longer see anyone in your schools, I warn you!"[73]

At this point Galandou Diouf spoke up to denounce recent attempts to segregate schools in the Four Communes. Having just been elected to the General Council, Diouf symbolized the rising political influence of black originaires. Although a few black politicians had already sat in the General Council, none had acquired the prominence that Diouf would soon enjoy.[74] Pointing up the consequences of the turn toward the regional school model, Diouf observed that "natives are prevented from going to school unless they [agree to] learn a trade." Diouf then advised: "Leave natives free to learn as they wish and give them simply the means to educate themselves like others."[75] Intervening repeatedly in this discussion, the representative of Senegal's administration tried to contain the rising tide of criticism. But unswayed by the administrator's remarks, a majority of councilors came together to pass a resolution calling for all primary schools in the Four Communes to follow the same curricula and award a common school-leaving certificate, equivalent to that of metropolitan France.[76]

Scholars have sometimes been dismissive of the originaires' demands in the area of education. The French historian Denise Bouche, for example, presents these demands as little more than fanciful thinking, which revealed the originaires' disregard for the true needs of Africans.[77] In reality the originaires were usually motivated by pragmatic considerations that reflected a careful understanding of their predicament, as rights-bearing populations in a colonial federation that was increasingly predicated on African subjecthood. The colonial school system set up after 1903 was clearly meant to educate subjects and not citizens. Village schools provided only a few years of basic education that did not lead to any sort of school-leaving certificate. Although students at regional schools received a somewhat fuller primary education, they could only work toward a "colonial" school certificate that led to a narrow band of lower-level positions within the colonial state (the *cadres indigènes*). By contrast, metropolitan education—and metropolitan school certificates and diplomas— could open up a much broader array of opportunities.

During the late nineteenth century and into the first decade of the twentieth century, a number of originaires had been able to obtain metropolitan educational credentials and subsequently enter professions usually reserved for the French (the *cadres européens*). Within the various branches of the colonial state, administrative cadres determined everything from pay scales and benefits to levels of responsibility and opportunities for promotion. Whereas the cadres européens codified French privilege, the cadres indigènes were designed to structure African subordination. By the first decade of the twentieth century colonial authorities were clearly moving to restrict originaire access to the cadres européens. This process could be observed across many categories of employees, ranging from postal and telegraph workers to teachers.[78]

In Saint-Louis, originaire politicians were ready to use every tool at their disposal to impede the consolidation of a racially defined colonial order. Financial control over educational expenditures remained one of their most effective tools. A decree signed in 1896 had established that each of Senegal's Four Communes was required to bear the full cost of its schools and teachers.[79] These costs became more onerous with laïcisation since the salaries and other expenses associated with lay schoolteachers were invariably higher than the modest sums that had been paid to missionary teachers. The situation was very different in metropolitan France, where the French state covered the salaries of public schoolteachers, among other expenses.[80] Originaire politicians had often insisted that Saint-Louis, Dakar, Gorée, and Rufisque should enjoy similar access to state funding, since they had been officially designated as full communes.[81] French authorities ultimately chose to ignore these appeals. However, because Senegal's communes continued to finance local schools, mayors, municipal councils, and the General Council could often exert a certain amount of influence over educational policy.

As part of the 1909 reclassification of schools in the Four Communes, colonial authorities attempted to force newly created regional schools to open *sections de travail manuel*. These sections were essentially school workshops providing introductory training in trades such as woodworking and metalworking. Convinced that the addition of manual training could only undermine the academic programs of these schools, the municipal government in Saint-Louis refused to approve financing for school workshops. Subsequently the General Council also voted against these expenditures. Tactics like these succeeded in slowing down the development of manual activities in the regional schools of the Four Communes. In the face of such obstruction, Lieutenant Governor Peuvergne finally decided that his only recourse was to finance school workshops through another budget, over which the originaires did not have any discretionary authority. But even then the lieutenant governor wondered whether these efforts would overcome the originaires' staunch opposition to manual training in schools.[82]

Obstruction took other forms as well. As a result of the 1909 reforms, two urban schools in Saint-Louis were downgraded to the status of regional schools. The town's sole remaining urban school for boys—the École Blanchot—drew disproportionately large numbers of European and métis children.[83] Rather than allowing the École Blanchot to become a school for whites and select métis, the mayor of Saint-Louis—Justin Devès—used his authority to close down this school. In this way European and métis children were forced to attend the two remaining boys schools (the École Duval and the École Brière-de-L'Isle), both of which were regional schools drawing large numbers of black students. In making this move, Devès and his allies sought not only to block the growing trend toward school segregation but also to force a general return to the urban school model. Devès and his political allies knew all too well that Europeans would be unwilling to send their children to schools adhering to colonial curricula and providing manual training.[84]

Maneuvers like these could tie colonial officials up in knots. Peuvergne found himself caught between Ponty, who continued to demand resolute changes, and originaire politicians, particularly in Saint-Louis, who had dug in their heels. In the face of these competing layers of authority and these divergent demands, Peuvergne eventually became quite flustered. In a March 1910 letter to Ponty, the lieutenant governor flailed around, proposing at one point to reintroduce the metropolitan curricula and eliminate manual education in all the schools of the Four Communes. He added that "using this approach we might have some chance of reestablishing, when it comes to schooling, a good understanding with the General Council and the municipality of Saint-Louis. However we must not fool ourselves too much in this regard; it is very possible that such a concession would only produce additional demands." Anticipating that Ponty would never countenance these concessions to the originaires, Peuvergne went on in the remainder of his letter to defend the education reforms that had been introduced in 1909.[85]

Although originaire leaders actively worked to influence education reform, they ultimately failed to block creeping school segregation.

In 1911 Galandou Diouf informed Senegal's General Council that the director of the urban school for boys in Dakar had recently established a "whites-only" class. Not one black or métis student had been admitted. After explaining that the creation of this class was "solely motivated by considerations of origins and color," Diouf demanded that the matter be investigated. As was so often the case, the French officials who were present countered by noting that segregation was not the goal, and that school officials made decisions on pedagogical grounds. However, the line between pedagogical and racial reasoning could be fine indeed, as was the case when a French member of the General Council remarked that "European children come to school with a knowledge of the French language, learned while at the breast [à la mamelle], which native children do not have."[86] In the end the creation of this whites-only class in Dakar was just one of many examples of the growing trend toward segregation in the Four Communes.[87]

In its struggle to find workable solutions, Senegal's administration eventually cast aside the classification of urban, regional, and rural schools that had been introduced in 1909. A 1912 arrêté stipulated that schools in the Four Communes would henceforth be internally compartmentalized, so that individual schools could include classes following the urban school curricula alongside others following the curricula of regional or rural schools. Combinations of classes were to vary from school to school.[88] This reform soon provoked considerable disgruntlement among school officials and teachers, who were left to figure out how a single school could keep two—and sometimes three—different tracks straight.[89] Originaire politicians also denounced the new measure, imagining all too easily that classes following the urban school curricula would serve as refuges for European children, while non-Europeans would be relegated to the two remaining tracks.

More than anything else, the convolutions of education reform in the Four Communes underscore just how difficult it was to force the originaires—with their unique history, institutions, and rights—into newer colonial structures. As late as 1912 the schools of the Four Communes had still not been brought firmly into the federal school system that had first been announced in 1903. Authority over schooling in Senegal's largest towns remained awkwardly divided between the Government General in Dakar, Senegal's administration in Saint-Louis, the General Council, municipal councils, and local mayors. The complexities and skirmishes surrounding urban schools suggest that the Four Communes need to be viewed not as a case study in assimilation but rather, as contested, liminal spaces with large implications for the rest of French West Africa.

CONSOLIDATING THE FEDERAL SCHOOL SYSTEM

The dynamics of education reform would soon shift in the Four Communes and in the rest of French West Africa. As of 1912, authorities in Dakar began to implement a series of measures designed to strengthen the Government General's control over educational policy. Many of these reforms were the work of Georges Hardy, the newly appointed inspector of education, who first arrived in Dakar in October 1912.

Historians have rightly viewed Hardy as an influential figure, who left an important imprint on the educational system in AOF. Whereas most other education officials possessed rather modest academic credentials, Hardy boasted an elite education that had taken him all the way to the École normale supérieure in Paris. Along the way he had obtained the prestigious *agrégation* in history and geography.[90] Although new to the colonies, Hardy would soon become a figurehead in France's colonial establishment, serving for seven years in Dakar before going on to become the director of education in French Morocco between 1919 and 1926. Thereafter he was named as the new director of the École coloniale in Paris, a position he would hold until 1933.[91] While most scholars present Hardy as an energetic reformer, assessments of his years in Dakar vary greatly. Denise Bouche has painted an admiring picture of Hardy as a clear-sighted man of action, who knew what was required in the area of colonial education.[92] Others have offered more critical accounts, which underscore Hardy's racializing and essentializing approaches to colonized peoples and colonial rule.[93]

Adopting Ponty's priorities, Hardy sought to strengthen the

Government General's control over schools throughout the federation and to drastically reduce the exceptionalism of the Four Communes. In many ways Ponty had been pursuing these twin goals ever since he had arrived in Dakar. In 1908 he had created a federal corps of primary school inspectors, who were subsequently assigned to the various colonies to oversee local schools and to advise the lieutenant governors on educational matters. However, prior to Hardy's arrival, only a few men had been integrated into this corps. Moreover, these officials seem to have been rather poorly prepared for their new duties.[94] Determined to foster increased professionalism, Hardy helped to prepare a 1913 reform, which established that education inspectors would henceforth be recruited through a *concours*, or competitive examination.[95] Hardy looked for other ways to professionalize the education administration in AOF. In 1913 he also oversaw the creation of a Conseil supérieur de l'enseignement primaire, or High Council on Primary Education. Composed mainly of senior officials at the Government General, this advisory body was to meet twice a year for discussions of personnel issues and educational policy.[96]

Like Ponty, Hardy was well aware that the Government General would not have effective control over education as long as the Colony of Senegal retained the ability to define its own policies. At a time when local colonial administrations remained rather inchoate, Senegal was the only colony to possess its own education department. As the Government General became more institutionalized, its education department began to claim roles that had formerly been ceded to Senegal's administration.[97] An important turning point came in 1912, when the Government General assumed direct control of three professional schools that had previously been run by authorities in Saint-Louis.[98] These institutions included the federation's normal school, which was charged with training African schoolteachers for service throughout AOF. As part of these reforms, the normal school was soon moved from Saint-Louis to a new site on Gorée Island, just off the coast of Dakar. In the years that followed, Hardy worked to fundamentally recast this important teacher-training center, which was soon renamed the École William Ponty.[99]

The consolidation of educational policymaking in Dakar accelerated in 1914, when the Government General published detailed instructions on schooling and comprehensive new curricula. Like the 1903 curricula, those of 1914 continued to distinguish among village, regional, and urban schools and the types of education that each was to provide. However, the curricula drafted by Hardy and his associates did much more to flesh out the content of colonial education.[100] And whereas the 1903 curricula had never been fully implemented in Senegal, the 1914 curricula were adopted by all the colonies without exception. Writing a few years later, Hardy reflected back on the reform process that had finally brought Senegal's schools fully into the federal school system: "Senegal long occupied a privileged position in the organization of our African education: it is the oldest colony in the Federation of French West Africa, it possessed the most schools, it benefited from having its own specific director of education, it was responsible for administering the Normal School and the two most important professional schools. But the rapid development of the other colonies, and the determination of their governors to multiply the number of schools, have put an end to Senegal's exceptionalism, and the organization of education [in Senegal] is now modeled exactly after that of the Government General."[101] The integration process that Hardy described was exactly what many originaires had struggled to avoid.

Hardy worked not only to consolidate the federal school system but also to pioneer new forms of colonial education. At the time many officials continued to argue that schools—not just in Senegal but throughout AOF—remained too heavily indebted to their metropolitan counterparts. As inspector of education, Hardy encouraged experimentations and innovations, in the hope that these would eventually lead toward pedagogies and practices more fully grounded in "colonial realities." It was partly with this goal in mind that Hardy founded the *Bulletin de l'Enseignement de l'A.O.F.* in 1913. The mission of this monthly publication was to publicize federal education policies, while also fostering a sense of common purpose among AOF's schoolteachers.[102] If this bulletin dispensed regular doses of pedagogical guidance to teachers, it also published reports from the field, in which teachers described their initiatives and reflected on their results. Explaining his objectives in the bulletin's very first issue, Hardy noted that "we are developing, little by little, a native pedagogy, which is very different, and surely none of you would dare claim that we see clearly the methods or even the goal of our teaching. We are going to strive to carry out this project collectively. . . . Bringing together collaborators, coordinating ideas and experiences, such will be purpose of this bulletin."[103] While candidly acknowledging that this "native pedagogy" was still in its infancy, Hardy made it clear that colonial education was a distinct field of activity, which would become even more distinct as new expertise and practices were developed.

During his years in Dakar Hardy also sought to put an end to the confusion and controversy that had swirled around urban schools, particularly in Senegal's Four Communes. For the first time, authorities in Dakar designed local curricula for the federation's urban schools. Published in 1914, these curricula pulled urban schools more fully into the colonial school system. With this turn away from metropolitan norms, colonial authorities felt less compelled to restrict access to these schools. Hardy went so far as to propose that "urban schools . . . admit all the children or adolescents that come forward." Sounding a note of realism, the 1914 instructions asserted that urban populations had already been deeply marked by their contact with the French, and that "like it or not, most of the students of our urban schools will go on to look for jobs in the administration or with local firms. Even those whose parents still practice humbler trades will most often escape from the pull of the paternal profession, which elsewhere remains a powerful force, but which cannot govern the population of a city."[104]

However, while broadening access to urban schools, Hardy and his associates also worked to preserve and indeed reinforce European privilege. In what was a new departure, the 1914 instructions explicitly called for urban schools to create special "European classes." These instructions explained that "children whose maternal language is French, who will likely continue their studies in the metropole will be brought together, to the extent possible, in separate classes, called 'European classes,' in which the metropolitan curricula will be scrupulously followed."[105] Among other things, the 1914 directives showed just how explicit authorities in Dakar were now willing to be when it came to referencing the link between race and access to metropolitan education. I have not found statistics on the composition of the new *classes européennes*; it is quite possible that small numbers of métis children continued to slip in. What is clear, however, is that colonial authorities increasingly viewed racial segregation in urban schools as a normal and necessary practice. Attitudes within the administration had hardened considerably since the opening years of the century, when the urban schools of the Four Communes had brought together students of very different backgrounds.

From the turn of the century to the outbreak of World War I, colonial officials came to expect that schools would help to reify boundaries between colonial subjects and French citizens. However, as I have sought to make clear in this chapter, drawing and enforcing such boundaries often proved to be a tortuous exercise that aroused considerable opposition, especially in the Four Communes. Nonetheless, by the time war broke out in Europe, colonial officials had made some important strides in their quest to cut the originaires off from metropolitan education and the cadres européens. Although colonial authorities in Dakar and Saint-Louis hoped to go even further in their efforts to contain the originaires, the outbreak of war soon introduced mounting uncertainties. In a rapidly changing context originaire communities soon found new ways to reassert their claims to French rights.

2

The Lessons of War

RETHINKING THE ORIGINAIRES

The consolidation of the colonial order in French West Africa was hardly complete when World War I broke out. In many ways local officials were ill prepared for a war that would soon reach deep into the West African colonies. As tens of thousands of African soldiers began to be recruited for service on European battlefields, it became clear that the war had the potential to destabilize the very foundations of French rule. Ultimately the war years produced not only new anxieties within structures of command but also broad reflections on colonial practices and the ways in which they might be reformed. It was not immediately clear what the lessons of the war would be. However, by the time peace returned, many colonial officials had already begun to advocate a more conservative order, which would be better equipped to contain urban Africans and their escalating demands.

African populations would also draw lessons from the war. As military recruiting drives siphoned off more and more able-bodied men, the hardships of war became obvious to many. Programs of forced crop cultivation only added to these strains. However, for some, the war brought not only adversity but also new horizons. This was certainly true for freshly conscripted soldiers, whose journeys led to new parts of French West Africa, and often, all the way to Europe. For many of these men the war years gave rise to vastly new experiences and expectations. Even for those who never left their home colony, the war frequently proved quite formative. Aware of the large debt that France was contracting through the mass conscription of African soldiers, many urban elites began to position themselves so as to make new demands on the colonial state. This was certainly true in Senegal's Four Communes, where local populations were especially well equipped to press their claims. Having been drawn into broadening confrontations with the colonial administration since the beginning of the century, many originaires now hoped to use the wartime context to consolidate and extend their rights.

OF CITIZENS AND SUBJECTS

Before turning our attention to the wartime period, we need to pause a moment longer over the conflicts that roiled the Four Communes during the years leading up to the war. Throughout his tenure as governor general (1908–15), Ponty waged a long-running battle to contain the originaires.[1] If this battle played out partly around urban schools, it also came to focus on the legal status and rights of the originaires. Along with many other colonial officials, Ponty remained convinced that the originaires had been allowed to accrue a range of rights without the necessary scrutiny. However, as officials began to revisit the status of these urban populations, they were forced to grapple with the historical complexities of the originaire category. During the nineteenth century a veritable tangle of laws, decrees, and *arrêtés* had coalesced to define the unique position and rights of the originaires. What was relatively clear was that, over the decades, the group of Africans known as the *originaires des Quatre Communes* had been collectively recognized to possess an array of political and civic rights. What remained considerably less clear were the boundaries of the originaire category and the extent of originaire rights.

Until the end of the nineteenth century the colonial administration in Senegal had generally been willing to live with these ambiguities. But with the founding of French West Africa in 1895, and subsequent efforts to consolidate this federation after the turn of the century, many officials felt the need to clarify and restrict the position of the originaires. As the new order came to be grounded increasingly in core distinctions between citizens and subjects, the existence of sizeable populations of liminal, rights-bearing Africans posed direct challenges. As has already been stressed, the originaires did not inhabit tidy enclaves that could be cleaved off from the expansive Federation of French West Africa. On the contrary, these populations remained heavily concentrated in some of the most central nodes of the colonial state. As Ponty and his associates looked for new ways to contain these urban populations, they ran into a range of impediments. Most fundamentally, perhaps, officials often found it difficult to determine who was—and who was not—an originaire.

Scholars have often conflated the rights-bearing populations known as the originaires with the geographical spaces known as the Four Communes. In reality the demographics of these communes had grown quite complex by the early twentieth century, as migration patterns continued to bring in newcomers. Figures compiled in 1921 can be used to highlight trends that were already well established before the war. When authorities in Senegal conducted a rather detailed census in 1921, they learned that French "subjects" (*sujets français*) accounted for almost 60 percent of the total population of the Four Communes (41,262 out of a total population of 69,808). Numbering 18,458, the originaires (*citoyens français originaires*) made up the second largest group. But the 1921 census also revealed that the Four Communes were home to 6,645 foreign subjects (*sujets étrangers*), 3,334 European French (*Européens français*), and 109 European foreigners (*Européens étrangers*).[2] With so many different groups and statuses present, it is not surprising that French authorities had come to see the Four Communes as a standing challenge to their efforts to distinguish more clearly between colonizers and the colonized.

As growing numbers of migrants flowed into the Four Communes, determining who could rightfully claim originaire status often proved a contentious matter. To be officially classified as an originaire it was necessary to demonstrate that one had been born within one of the

Four Communes. In certain cases originaire status was also conferred on children born to originaire parents residing outside the Four Communes, although this remained a less certain pathway into the originaire category.[3] As colonial authorities attempted to police these boundaries more effectively, they had to contend with the fact that official records of names, marriages, births, and deaths were often poorly kept in the Four Communes.[4] Uniform recordkeeping in the form of an *état civil* developed only slowly, and in the meantime French officials often had to rely on oral testimonies to ascertain whether an individual qualified for originaire status. Between 1913 and 1921 courts in Saint-Louis and Dakar recognized—through decisions known as *jugements supplétifs*—a total of 8,496 people, without birth certificates, as having a rightful claim to this status.[5] Although concrete proof was hard to come by, authorities imagined that a considerable number of these decisions were based on fraudulent testimonies.

As they took stock of changing demographics and political dynamics within the Four Communes, officials developed a number of new strategies for curbing the rights of the originaires. Ponty's administration focused increasingly on the question of courts and tribunals. At the time, the originaires lived under a hybrid judicial regime that was the product of a complex history. The originaires were not subject to the provisions of the 1903 judicial code that had been developed for other Africans, classified as colonial subjects. This code of "native justice" provided for a network of tribunals of several different levels, charged with hearing and deciding legal cases involving Africans. These tribunals were supposed to apply customary law, except when the latter was deemed "contrary to the principles of French civilization." In practice, however, new native courts left wide discretion to judges appointed by the colonial administration. These judges frequently handed down harsh and arbitrary sentences that did not refer to established legal precedents. Moreover, defendants enjoyed few protections, since native courts did not guarantee the right to legal counsel and offered only a very limited right of appeal.[6] This system of native tribunals coexisted with the harsh code of administrative justice known as the *indigénat*, which was also used to discipline

African populations.[7] The indigénat sidestepped tribunals and trials altogether by placing a broad range of disciplinary powers in the hands of local colonial officials.[8]

Like European populations in AOF, the originaires enjoyed access to a parallel system of French courts that settled cases according to French law and provided a range of protections not found in native tribunals. However, when it came to certain civil matters such as marriage, divorce, and inheritances, the originaires could also choose to have their cases settled by Muslim tribunals. The first of these tribunals had been established in Saint-Louis in 1857; in subsequent years additional Muslim tribunals were founded in Dakar, Rufisque, and Kayes. If many originaires took advantage of these tribunals when it came to civil matters, it was because they had chosen to retain their *statut personnel musulman*, or Muslim personal status.[9] The historian Mamadou Diouf has shown just how hard many originaires fought to defend their personal status, even as they pressed for full French political rights during the nineteenth century. Much of Diouf's basic argument could be extended to the first half of the twentieth century.[10]

The compromises that defined the originaires' access to different kinds of courts were upset by an August 1912 decree, "reorganizing native justice" in AOF.[11] This decree upheld the originaires' established right to use French courts as long as they remained within the boundaries of the Four Communes. However, in what was an important new departure, originaires residing or traveling outside the Four Communes would now be required to have their criminal cases heard by native tribunals.[12] Originaire politicians and notables found many reasons to oppose this new restriction. It was not difficult to see that the colonial administration was seeking to link their rights to a narrow geographic perimeter—a move that would further distinguish the originaires from French citizens, whose rights suffered no such limitation. The problem was not just that, by residing or traveling outside the Four Communes, originaires would now expose themselves to native courts. Many originaires also feared that, upon venturing outside the Four Communes, they might even be subject to the indigénat. It soon became clear that these fears were not unfounded.[13] For all these reasons the publication of the August 1912 decree touched off a wave of protests in the Four Communes.

To fully appreciate the stakes of this controversy we need to further complicate our understanding of the originaires. Historical studies still tend to situate the originaires rather squarely within the Four Communes. But although they did remain concentrated in Senegal's old towns, significant numbers of originaires had dispersed across Senegal and beyond. The 1921 census, mentioned earlier, revealed that eight other Senegalese towns had originaire populations in excess of one hundred. Specifically, there were 485 originaires in Tivaouane, 366 in Louga, 283 in Thiès, 201 in Meckhe, 148 in Diourbel, 127 in Fatick, 121 in Foundiougne, and 108 in Ziguinchor.[14] In reality the originaires were spread even more widely than the preceding figures suggest, since significant numbers of originaires had ventured beyond Senegal's borders to other colonies in French West Africa. In 1921 French Soudan was home to well over a thousand originaires, followed by Guinea with almost five hundred. Some three hundred originaires lived in Ivory Coast, while slightly more than one hundred resided in both Dahomey and Mauritania.[15] As they moved around, the originaires carried with them self-understandings and outlooks that challenged the colonial order. In short, the originaires represented a larger, more diffuse challenge to French authority than most historians have heretofore recognized.

As they mobilized to challenge the August 1912 decree, the originaires took their case to Senegal's General Council as well as to the Chamber of Deputies in Paris. Since 1902 François Carpot had represented Senegal in the French legislature. A prominent member of Saint-Louis's *métis* community and a lawyer by training, Carpot had not been involved in the drafting of the 1912 decree "reorganizing native justice." It was also true, however, that Carpot had failed to block the decree's controversial provision limiting originaire access to French courts. Facing mounting criticism from his constituents in the Four Communes, Carpot eventually began to mount a more vigorous defense of the rights of the originaires on the floor of the Chamber of Deputies.[16] On 19 December 1912, the Senegalese deputy delivered a lengthy speech in which he retraced the body of jurisprudence—stretching all the way back to 1794—that had awarded many French rights to these urban populations. Carpot's basic point was that there was a complex but demonstrable legal foundation for the rights of the originaires. He noted that "until recently, these natives had always been treated like French citizens; they found themselves in the same situation as the blacks of Guiana and the Antilles and, like them, they could enlist in the metropolitan army; they could aspire to all public positions and take part in all elections, as long as they satisfied the age and residence restrictions established by law."[17] After making these observations, Carpot went on to criticize the colonial administration's recent challenges to established precedent.

Several of these challenges had made it all the way to the Cour de cassation, France's highest court. In a series of cases, decided between 1907 and 1909, the Cour de cassation handed down some rather complicated decisions. While confirming the electoral rights of the originaires, and while invalidating the administration's efforts to summarily strike sizeable numbers of originaires from voting rolls, the court found that the originaires did not have a legitimate claim to full French citizenship. In the end these decisions satisfied neither the originaires nor the colonial administration.[18] Questioning the decisions of the Cour de cassation, and the assaults that continued to emanate from the Government General in Dakar, Carpot insisted that the time had come to offer all originaires a pathway to full citizenship, provided that they renounced their Muslim personal status and agreed to follow the provisions of the French Civil Code.[19] Although Carpot pushed for more than colonial authorities were willing to accept, his proposal fell well short of what Blaise Diagne would obtain four years later: French citizenship without any requirement that originaires give up their Muslim personal status.

As Carpot intervened in the Chamber of Deputies, officials at the Government General worked to make sure that their views would also receive a full hearing in Paris. In an August 1913 letter to the minister of colonies, Ponty sought to directly rebut the arguments that Carpot had developed at the end of the previous year. Ponty did his best to underscore juridical anomalies, particularly the fact that most originaires had acquired rights without renouncing their Muslim personal status or accepting the provisions of the Civil Code. Ponty clearly saw these aberrations as a wedge that could be used to discredit most originaire claims to French citizenship. In his letter to the minister of colonies, the governor general insisted that "the quality of French citizen can only be acquired individually, by decree, and on the condition that the beneficiary submits to the rules of French civil law."[20]

While categorically ruling out the possibility of a collective naturalization, Ponty was willing to support the individual naturalization of a limited number of deserving originaires, by which he meant the most acculturated elements, who could prove that their ancestors had acquired French rights as of 1833.[21] Ponty clearly realized that such a rigorous naturalization process would discourage most potential candidates.[22] Given the state of official records, and given the migrations that had reshaped the Four Communes over the years, formally tracing one's ancestry back to 1833 would present formidable challenges for many. Ponty probably also knew that most originaires would not be willing to trade away their Muslim personal status in exchange for naturalization.

As he worked to develop a new procedure by which select originaires might be individually naturalized, Ponty remained especially focused on a group sometimes referred to as the *assimilés*—originaires and originaire families who had chosen to identify with French cultural practices. Although the métis tended to make up the core of the assimilés, this group also included small numbers of black originaires who had visibly embraced French ways. In explaining why the assimilés could and should be offered a pathway toward naturalization, Ponty noted that "this part of the population [is] so French in its heart—and for a portion of them—the métis—so French in their blood." As he worked to identify the small numbers of originaires who could be made into citizens, Ponty thus referred to both cultural identities and racial affinities.[23] Although the governor general made only glancing references to religion, the fact that many mixed-race families were

Catholic clearly made it easier for him to imagine their inclusion as citizens. By the same token, Ponty viewed the Muslim identities of most originaires as a nearly insurmountable obstacle to citizenship.[24]

Mounting questions about the status of the originaires can be usefully compared to situations elsewhere in the French empire. Scholars have shown just how much attention colonial administrations devoted to métis populations, whose liminality was often viewed as a direct challenge to the divide between subjects and citizens. The "métis problem" took on growing proportions, particularly in Indochina.[25] Although authorities in AOF continued to view the métis as an awkward population deserving special attention, other groups were clearly coming to seem more threatening.[26] Over the years births within the Four Communes and the arrival of new migrants had reduced the influence of established métis families. Population growth was strongest in Dakar and Rufisque, where mixed-race communities had never been as prominent as they had once been in Saint-Louis. But even in Saint-Louis the métis increasingly had to make room for black Muslims, who had started to venture more deeply into civic life and local politics.[27]

Although new kinds of political activism had been developing for some time in the Four Communes, the first half of 1914 nonetheless stands out as a watershed moment. In February 1914 Blaise Diagne returned home to Senegal to announce that he would be running for the colony's seat in the French Chamber of Deputies.[28] Born on Gorée Island in 1872, Diagne had been raised in large part by an adoptive métis family, which had sponsored his education. After completing primary school on Gorée Island, Diagne had gone on to study in France before returning to Senegal to attend the newly founded secondary school in Saint-Louis.[29] After graduating at the top of his class in 1890, Diagne began a career in the customs service, which took him around the empire—to Dahomey, French Congo, Réunion, Madagascar, and French Guiana. During these postings and peregrinations, Diagne became known as an outspoken defender of racial equality.[30]

Even though Diagne had been away from Senegal for more than two decades, his upstart political campaign immediately caused great waves, largely because he was a black man who showed that he knew how to galvanize urban communities in new ways.[31] Many colonial officials and métis reacted with surprise and consternation when Diagne went on to win the legislative election in a run-off. A number of the losing candidates sought to have Diagne's election invalidated on various technicalities. Behind these and other challenges lurked the scarcely camouflaged belief that a black man should not be allowed to represent Senegal in the Chamber of Deputies. Despite objections of this sort, the local electoral commission in Senegal ended up recommending that the French Chamber of Deputies confirm Diagne's victory.[32]

The outbreak of the war soon gave Diagne new opportunities to defend and consolidate the rights of the originaires. Military recruitment had become an increasingly sensitive subject ever since February 1912, when French authorities published a decree introducing a partial draft in French West Africa.[33] This decree paved the way for growing numbers of West Africans to be recruited into colonial units known as the *tirailleurs sénégalais*. At the time, the originaires held the dubious distinction of not being subject to any military conscription at all. Although many were in fact ready to enlist, they insisted on their right to join the regular army, alongside French citizens.[34] It had initially appeared that the originaires might get their wish. After the 1905 law governing military recruitment in metropolitan France was finally extended to French West Africa, toward the end of 1909, small handfuls of originaires were conscripted along with select Frenchmen residing in the federation. Within a few months, however, almost all these originaires were summarily discharged.[35]

The tensions and uncertainties surrounding military recruitment in the Four Communes resonated with the situation in France's old colonies, where populations had long seen military service as a means to consolidate their French rights. Although citizens since 1848, the populations of Réunion, Martinique, Guadeloupe, and French Guiana were not subject to military conscription during the second half of the nineteenth century. As was the case in Senegal's Four Communes, the 1905 law calling for all French men to complete two years of military service was not initially implemented in the old colonies. After finally launching conscription campaigns in the French Antilles in 1912, authorities soon pulled back, amid racially inflected concerns about the robustness and usefulness of Antillean soldiers. Following many hesitations, the 1905 law was fully introduced in the French Antilles in 1915, when the wartime need for soldiers eventually trumped the lingering reservations of French authorities.[36] As was the case in the old colonies, the controversy over military recruitment in Senegal's Four Communes was filled with symbolism. All parties understood that service in the regular French army would bolster originaire claims to French citizenship, whereas conscription into tirailleur units would push the originaires back toward the status of "colonial subjects." Beyond this powerful symbolism, controversies over conscription also had far-reaching practical implications, given the enormous differences that separated the treatment of tirailleurs, serving in colonial units, from the treatment of ordinary French soldiers. Tirailleurs enlisted under a highly inferior regime, when it came to things such as pay, food rations, sleeping quarters, possibilities for promotion, and pensions.[37]

After his victory in the run-off election in May 1914, Diagne immediately turned his attention to the impasse that was keeping the originaires from enlisting for military service. The outbreak of war soon provided Diagne with the leverage he needed: determined to expand recruitment efforts in French West Africa, French authorities now found it less politic to bar the originaires from serving in the regular army. On 19 October 1915 the Chamber of Deputies voted in favor of a bill, prepared by Diagne, authorizing the originaires to join regular military units, in which they would be subject to the "same obligations and advantages" as metropolitan soldiers. Traveling home to Senegal at the end of 1915, Diagne explained the importance of the law he had just helped to enact, while also stressing the need for additional reforms. In the recently founded paper *La Démocratie du Sénégal*, Diagne declared that "the war, despite its horrors . . . has become for the people of Senegal an important instrument of social reform."[38]

After returning to Paris, Diagne continued his efforts to clarify and expand the rights of the originaires. Within a matter of months he introduced another bill that would have vast implications for the originaires and the colonial order in French West Africa. Approved by the Chamber of Deputies on 29 September 1916, the second "Diagne law" stated that "the natives [*natifs*] of the full communes of Senegal and their descendants are and remain French citizens subject to the military obligations set forth by the law of 19 October 1915."[39] Although couched as a rather mundane law on military recruitment, Diagne's legislation immediately made waves because of its direct reference to the citizenship of the originaires. With the passage of this law the swirling controversies over the status of the originaires seemed to have been resolved at last. In what would remain a unique arrangement, the originaires were collectively recognized as citizens, even as the vast majority retained their local Muslim personal status, rather than accepting the provisions of the French Civil Code.[40]

But if an important step had been taken in Paris, it remained to be seen how authorities in French West Africa would react to these events. The implementation of French laws could never be taken for granted in the colonies, which were usually defined as exceptional spaces, placed under administrative rule. To be sure, the situation was more complicated in the Four Communes, where at various times French laws had been promulgated. But in many ways these towns continued to sit problematically in between metropolitan law and the localized rule of the colonial administration. As we will see in the next section, these ambiguities immediately complicated the "practice" of originaire citizenship.

WARTIME REFORM AND COLONIAL REACTION

By paving the way for originaires to enlist in the regular French army, Diagne acquired new influence in Paris. He could now claim to be an instrumental supporter of the broadening war effort. Diagne's standing increased even more in January 1918, when he was tapped by Prime Minister Georges Clemenceau for a cabinet-level position, as commissioner of the republic, charged with leading recruiting efforts in West Africa.[41] This was an unprecedented move, since it gave Diagne an official rank that rivaled that of the governor general of French West Africa. By the summer of 1918 Diagne's highly publicized recruiting campaign had brought in record numbers of new African soldiers—a stunning sixty-three thousand men.[42] And whereas earlier campaigns had relied heavily on coercion, Diagne and his associates worked to convince Africans to enlist voluntarily.[43]

Before agreeing to lead recruiting efforts in AOF, Diagne had extracted a series of promises from the Clemenceau government. Presidential decrees signed on 14 January 1918 established that African veterans would be exempted from taxation and the indigénat. Veterans were also promised preferential access to certain types of jobs, and, for a few, a new pathway to French citizenship. In addition, Diagne obtained formal assurances that two new professional schools would be opened in AOF, an agricultural school and a colonial medical school.[44] In certain quarters these bundled decrees were hailed as the beginning of a new native policy in French West Africa.[45]

With the success of Diagne's recruiting mission, Gabriel Angoulvant, the interim governor general of AOF, clearly felt pressure to announce additional reforms. In a November 1918 circular to the lieutenant governors of the various colonies, Angoulvant underscored the federation's heavy contributions to the war effort, before going on to ask:

> How could France not take full account of such a sum of sacrifices and how could she not admit that she has contracted, with the natives of AOF ... particular obligations of gratitude? But for this gratitude to be real, we must not imagine that France's debt can be paid exclusively in cash, through recruitment bonuses and retirement pensions; this is a long-term debt that we must accept without reservation and pay fully, so that future generations will benefit from the sacrifices of their elders. By this I mean that we must resolutely commit ourselves to vast enterprises of social progress.

This circular went on to explain that such social progress would not be possible without the collaboration of expanded cohorts of African technical agents. Angoulvant reminded the lieutenant governors of promises that had recently been made in Paris, regarding the founding of an agricultural school and a colonial medical school, and explained that these institutions would help consolidate a new layer of colonial education, which he referred to as "higher technical education."[46]

If building and equipping new professional schools would have to wait until the end of the war, Angoulvant insisted that it was already possible to increase enrollments and educational levels at existing elite schools, such as the École William Ponty. The governor general noted, however, that broadened cohorts of new elites would never materialize unless the various colonies did their part by increasing enrollments at feeder schools, such as regional schools and higher primary schools.[47] Sensing that local administrations might prove less than cooperative, Angoulvant cautioned: "As long as the colonies of AOF are not committed to this necessary effort, we will stomp around in place; recent events do not allow for inaction."[48] But while some officials—especially in Paris—acknowledged the need to recognize the sacrifices and solidarity of overseas populations through new gestures and a strengthened commitment to colonial development, many officials in AOF demurred. As we will see, prominent local officials were already calling for the reassertion of colonial authority after the disruptions and contestation of the wartime period.

As lieutenant governor of Senegal between 1914 and 1916, Raphaël Antonetti had directly witnessed the rising tide of originaire politics and the surging influence of Diagne—events that Antonetti had described in ominous tones. After being named as the new lieutenant governor of Ivory Coast in 1918, Antonetti continued to criticize the emboldened attitudes that he observed in many Senegalese "expatriates" and local school graduates, or évolués. Although they overlapped at times, the originaire and évolué categories were actually constructed quite differently. To be recognized as an originaire, one had to have been born in the Four Communes or to have been born to originaire parents residing outside the Four Communes. Although originaire communities did produce a good number of French-educated elites, originaire status was never contingent on educational level or even the ability to speak French. In point of fact, many originaires never attended French-run schools. The évolué category, on the other hand, was closely tied to colonial schooling, knowledge of French, and

French-influenced lifestyles. During the war colonial officials worried increasingly about the impact that emboldened, politicized originaires were having on évolué populations around the federation.

As they worked to limit contacts between these two groups, officials ran up against the internal logic of the colonial school system, which funneled a narrow but influential stream of young elites from around the federation to professional schools in the Four Communes. The number of students heading to these schools increased during the war: whereas entering classes at the École William Ponty had hovered at around thirty students between 1913 and 1916, the class of 1917 jumped to one hundred, a figure that was reached again the following year.[49] Lieutenant Governor Antonetti openly resisted Angoulvant's calls for the colonies to send more students to the Government General's professional schools in and around Dakar. In a sharply worded letter written in mid-1918 Antonetti criticized the École William Ponty for turning out rebellious schoolteachers who did not hesitate to challenge colonial authority. Antonetti declared to Angoulvant that "the experiment being carried out" at the École William Ponty was "extremely dangerous" and that many newly trained African school-teachers were "completely unhinged and consumed with pride." The lieutenant governor went so far as to blame Georges Hardy personally, for centralizing elite education and for introducing curricula that were excessively ambitious.[50]

In the years that followed, Antonetti continued to draw direct links between the Government General's professional schools and African contestation.[51] In a December 1921 letter to Dakar, the lieutenant governor of Ivory Coast again questioned the wisdom of sending African students all the way to the Four Communes. Repeating arguments he had already developed on several other occasions, Antonetti declared that "it is dangerous to search all the regions of French West Africa, among the most diverse tribes, for the brightest young men, whose intelligence appears to invite a more complete education, and then uproot them, give them an exaggerated notion of their own merit, allow their young minds to conceive of dreams they will never be able to fulfill, and bring them to Dakar."[52] Antonetti's pessimistic view of AOF's professional schools tapped into broad colonial anxieties about the deracination and mobility of young African elites and the spread of new outlooks and modes of contestation. However, what Antonetti denounced most vigorously was the way in which the colonial school system routinely brought elite students into contact with the originaires.

Antonetti did not seek to paint all originaires with the same broad brush. In his December 1921 letter to the governor general, he conceded that "when I write about the Citizens of the Four Communes, I discuss, in fact, only a minority. I have lived in Senegal too long to ignore the good qualities and basic loyalty of most." But after these anodyne remarks, Antonetti went on, as was his custom, to sound a series of alarmist notes. Describing the influence that the originaires could have over other Africans, the lieutenant governor wrote: "That is what's most dangerous about the action of the Senegalese citizens, even if they are not ill intentioned. They have, one could say, a rebellious way of flaunting their privilege; they boast about it, they glory in it, they take advantage of it to speak contemptuously to our subjects and, by a natural reaction, drive the latter to make their ambitions clear: 'Them yesterday, why not us tomorrow?' our young intellectuals ask each other. They become intoxicated with these idle dreams." Convinced that the contagion had already begun, Antonetti denounced the contentious environment that had supposedly developed at the École William Ponty, declaring that the school had become the site of "collective acts of insubordination, almost revolts." To drive home his point, Antonetti included a chart, which revealed that a total of 74 students had been dismissed from the École William Ponty between 1918 and 1921.[53] As we will see, officials in Dakar had already begun to take the warnings of Antonetti and other likeminded officials quite seriously.

Although he had been named as the new governor general of AOF in early 1918, Martial Merlin did not take up his new post in Dakar until the fall of 1919. As it happened, Merlin arrived in Dakar just as Diagne and his political allies were poised to score a string of political victories that would put them in charge of all the elected bodies of the Four Communes. In an election held on 30 November 1919,

FIG. 2. Blaise Diagne in 1921. Photograph by l'Agence Meurisse. Courtesy of the Bibliothèque nationale de France.

Diagne easily won a second term as Senegal's deputy. In elections the following month, Diagne's party went on to take complete control of all four municipal councils. Although French and métis politicians were not entirely eliminated, most of those who survived had rallied to Diagne's party. The landslide continued in January 1920, when "Diagnist" candidates won a majority of seats in Senegal's Conseil général.[54] The surging Diagne continued to enjoy support from key allies in Paris, such as the minister of colonies, Henry Simon. After hearing about Diagne's reelection, Simon telegrammed: "Very hearty congratulations on your magnificent success. Faithfully yours."[55] But while Simon was supportive, many officials in AOF had begun to express growing consternation.

Upon taking up his new post, Merlin made no secret of his intention to challenge Diagne and his broadening base of supporters. Like Antonetti, Merlin was no stranger to the politics of the Four Communes. As a young colonial administrator during the 1890s, Merlin had served as director of native affairs in Senegal's administration. After the turn of the century, Merlin had gone on to become second in command (secretary-general) in the administration of Governor General Roume.[56] At the end of World War I many colonial officials welcomed Merlin's return to Dakar in the hope that the newly appointed governor general would know how to rein in the emboldened originaires. As long as the war lasted, local officials found it difficult to challenge Diagne bluntly. However, with the end of the war, many officials quickly set aside their former restraint.[57]

At the beginning of the 1920s a flurry of tendentious reports cast the Senegalese deputy as a dangerous demagogue, bent on spreading anti-French sentiment. The political affairs department in Dakar folded many of these warnings into an alarmist thirty-one-page document titled "Politics of M. Diagne in Senegal—Diagnism." According to this document Diagne's objectives included the "affirmation of the equality of all blacks with whites and even of the superiority of many of them, [a] call for racial fraternity so that blacks who make up the majority will supplant Europeans who are the minority, [and] finally the prospect, for natives, of 'self-government.'" This compendium of complaints and warnings went even further by trying to connect Diagne with international political movements such as pan-Africanism and Bolshevism.[58] Designed to discredit Diagne, these claims bore little relation to reality. Even during the early 1920s, when hostilities between the Senegalese deputy and the colonial administration reached their climax, Diagne continued to profess his allegiance to France. His main objective was to secure fair and equal treatment for his constituents in the Four Communes and to gradually improve the condition of populations elsewhere in Senegal and French West Africa.[59] Diagne did project a powerful reformist vision, but the latter was almost completely inscribed within the parameters of French republicanism and the "French Imperial Nation-State."[60]

Nonetheless, during the early 1920s rumors and reports about "Diagnism" continued to command the attention of many colonial officials. After completing a tour of Senegal in 1922, a police inspector by the name of Vallet filed a lengthy report on the "state of mind" of the Senegalese. Rather than distinguishing between the originaires and other urban populations, this inspector attributed contentious attitudes to most urban Senegalese. Vallet worried not only about the climate in Senegal's major towns but also about the spread of Senegalese attitudes to other parts of French West Africa. As this police inspector himself noted, containing such attitudes was no easy matter, since "the Senegalese spread themselves everywhere through their presence in the state-run administrations: postal and telegraph services, teaching, the army, etc." Even as he urged colonial authorities to do much more to contain Senegal's urban populations, Vallet doubted that these efforts would suffice as long as contingents of West African students continued to be brought into the Four Communes for professional training. In the words of this police inspector: "They go there to get an education and return contaminated."[61]

As he added up incoming reports on the attitudes of elites who had been trained on Gorée Island, Merlin eventually felt pressured to respond.[62] In August 1921 Merlin wrote to the interim director of education to express concern about the dispositions and conduct of these new elites. The governor general observed: "The education they have received has seemingly engendered, in the overwhelming majority of them, an excessive vanity, which is without any proportion to their knowledge, and which is not mitigated by feelings of duty or respect for discipline."[63] In response to similar concerns, officials in certain colonies had gone so far as to recommend the closing of the federal schools, so that new African elites could be trained in their home colonies, far from the effervescence of the Four Communes. Merlin was not ready to accept these proposals, which would have trimmed the prerogatives of the Government General significantly. However, by 1921 he had clearly decided that the time had come to rethink the education of African elites. More than anything else, Merlin concluded that the professional schools had failed to provide young elites with adequate moral education.[64]

Recognizing that a full reconsideration of elite education would take time, Merlin began by reducing the number of students attending the Government General's schools. In 1920–21 the École William Ponty still enrolled 279 students, while turning out 112 new graduates. By the following school year, however, Merlin's administration had already slashed the school's enrollment to 102 students. That year the school produced only 61 graduates. Although the total number of students rose slightly in 1922–23—to 111—the number of graduates fell to a mere 26. By the early 1920s wartime plans to expand the École William Ponty had been completely rolled back, and the very future of the school seemed increasingly uncertain.[65]

NEW CONFLICTS OVER EDUCATION IN THE FOUR COMMUNES

During and immediately after the war, colonial officials were not the only ones to demand new educational policies. After being officially recognized as French citizens in 1916, many originaires expected that they would at last be able to send their children to schools providing metropolitan education. However, throughout the war, authorities at the Government General resisted these demands. The refusal of Hardy and other officials to rethink educational policies in the Four Communes soon provoked loud denunciations in certain Senegalese newspapers. As the political campaigns of 1919 heated up, condemnations of educational policies became a recurrent theme in the Diagnist paper *La Démocratie du Sénégal*. Criticisms continued unabated after this paper changed its name to *L'Ouest Africain Français* in April 1919.[66] Articles on educational policy frequently included unflattering comparisons between the current educational regime and the schools that the Brothers of Ploërmel had operated up until 1903. After noting sharp declines in the quality of education and in the value of diplomas, contributors to these papers did not hesitate to speak of a deliberate program of "sabotage."[67]

The most outspoken critic of official educational policies wrote under the pen name of Amadou l'Artilleur, so as to call up the sacrifices that many Africans had recently made on European battlefields. In one of his many articles in *La Démocratie du Sénégal*, Amadou l'Artilleur noted: "We can observe that none of our colonial administrators has been capable of drawing from the war the lesson that lies in the progress of our natives, voters or not, who lived in the trenches where our brave French soldiers (the true Frenchmen) completed their education."[68] By the end of the war at least 7,200 originaires had enlisted for military service; and unlike other African troops, these men had served in regular military units where they had prolonged contact with French soldiers.[69] Originaire soldiers fought as citizens alongside other French citizens. However, upon returning home, these soldiers found that most colonial officials were anxious to limit the fallout from the war.[70]

The man who wrote under the name of Amadou l'Artilleur was none other than Amadou Duguay Clédor Ndiaye, a schoolteacher turned politician, who had become one of Diagne's closest collaborators. "Duguay-Clédor" had accompanied the Senegalese deputy on his highly publicized recruiting mission in 1918.[71] In another article, Duguay-Clédor explained that wartime experiences had led to new expectations regarding republicanism and its application in the colonies. But after declaring his support for "republican principles that are indispensable to the successful education of our youths," this Senegalese politician went on to highlight the lived reality of race prejudice. In a rhetorical appeal to his compatriots, Duguay-Clédor declared: "Oh proud people of Senegal, they hope that tomorrow people whose only merit (if it is one!) is to have 'white skin' will forever be superior to your children, sons and nephews of the Great War, whose competition could become troublesome." Adopting the voice of an imagined colonial official or *colon*, Duguay-Clédor then added: "Negro! you are inferior to the European [and] that is how you will remain whatever your capacities might be!" This article concluded with some pointed advice for Hardy and other senior education officials in AOF: "Gentlemen, start making your arrangements to leave and pack your bags. Get ready to go to other lands more suitable to your work, because we want, and we will have true Frenchmen, good, sincere republicans to whom we will entrust without fear the future of our children. Leave; but leave quickly. Otherwise the voice of the people will purely and simply expel you from French West Africa."[72] In the event, this ultimatum proved rather premonitory: Hardy left AOF in April 1919 for what was billed as a three-month convalescence leave. In reality, Hardy's departure was precipitated by mounting pressure from the originaires and by Diagne's continued lobbying in Paris.

With Hardy out of the picture, many originaires hoped that some of their longstanding demands would finally be met. By 1921 it seemed as if the originaires might at last be granted access to French primary schooling. After a flurry of correspondence, Governor General Merlin signed an arrêté stipulating that "the official curricula of primary schools in metropolitan France will be implemented in the primary schools of the communes of Saint-Louis, Dakar, Rufisque, [and] Gorée."[73] However, Merlin made it clear that this was just an experiment and that within a year or two the results of this reform would have to be evaluated. It soon became apparent that this experiment did not have the backing of colonial officials. Less than two years later— after what must have been a very partial implementation—officials were already preparing to reverse course. At their June 1923 meeting in Dakar, education officials collectively decided that "after a two-year trial period, the use of metropolitan curricula in certain native classes does not seem to have produced promising results." After reaching this peremptory conclusion, these officials promptly recommended that "the metropolitan curricula be eliminated in all of the schools in which they are in effect." Only special classes for Europeans would continue to follow metropolitan curricular guidelines.[74]

These reforms were reaffirmed the following year, when the Government General issued a new corpus of instructions regarding the schools of AOF.[75] Among other things, these instructions stipulated that urban schools should clearly distinguish between *classes européennes* and *classes indigènes*. Whereas the former would follow the primary school curricula of metropolitan France, the latter were now required to use the same curricula as AOF's regional schools.[76] The 1924 guidelines went on to specify that European classes would be reserved for "the European and assimilated element," students "whose maternal language is French."[77] Written in this way, the new regulations probably allowed small numbers of métis students to study alongside European children. However, it was quite clear that vast majority of children attending school in the Four Communes would continue to study colonial curricula designed for subject populations.

One might have expected different outcomes, given that the originaires had been recognized as French citizens. For many originaires, the passage of the 1916 law confirming their citizenship remained a defining event that would color outlooks and claims throughout the interwar period. However, in determining who should have access to metropolitan education and the privileges that it conferred, local authorities continued to look beyond formal questions of citizenship. As the originaires discovered, much to their consternation, authorities remained committed to using to racial criteria to segregate students in the Four Communes.

Histories of France's overseas empire have often highlighted the crucial divide that separated citizens from subjects. But while the category of "subjects" has been examined from many angles, far less attention has been paid to the various ways in which the category of "citizens" was constructed and deployed in the colonies. As scholars such as Silyane Larcher have shown in telling detail, the extension of citizenship to formerly enslaved populations in Martinique and Guadeloupe in

1848 did not usher in a period of equal treatment within the French body politic. For darker-skinned populations, what followed emancipation tended to be a form of junior—or probationary—citizenship, which often served to prolong distinctions and stratifications that were rooted in local plantation-based societies. Larcher writes that "as a result of their servile past, ex-slaves or their descendants thus found themselves closed into the identity of an always suspect and potentially incompetent citizen, [who is] condemned to be a flawed citizen, in short, a second-class citizen."[78]

In similar ways the history of the originaires also underscores the need to complicate traditional understandings of an abstract and undifferentiated French citizenship. For the originaires, incorporation into the juridical category of "citizens" rarely led to straightforward inclusion in the republican body politic. Throughout the interwar period, officials made a habit of introducing and enforcing invidious, race-based distinctions between "European" and originaire citizens. Moreover, when it came to a range of practical matters, such as education, colonial officials did not hesitate to downplay—or even ignore—the legal status of the originaires. Through these maneuvers, local authorities openly questioned whether laws passed in Paris could really turn black Africans into bona fide French citizens.

3

Toward the Interior

RURAL SCHOOLS AND COLONIAL REFORM

Held under the auspices of the 1931 Colonial Exposition, the Intercolonial Conference on Education in the Colonies and Overseas Territories brought together education officials from around the French empire for broad discussions of recent reforms and remaining challenges in the burgeoning field of "native education." The task of organizing this conference had fallen largely to Paul Crouzet, the Ministry of Colonies' point man on educational matters. As he called the conference's first session to order, Crouzet felt obliged to note that old stereotypes about the schools of the French empire continued to circulate. "The myth persists," Crouzet conceded, "that all the colored students continue to read in their schoolbook and repeat: 'the Gauls, our ancestors . . .'"[1] Crouzet then explained that one of the conference's central objectives was to dispel this myth permanently by highlighting the multiform reality of education in the empire: "It is important that we show once and for all that next to the metropolitan school systems, there are, overseas, numerous other school systems, which, in each of the colonies, were specially constructed for the needs of the populations that have been entrusted to us."[2]

Most of the French officials attending this conference were eager to declare assimilation an outdated ideology that had little remaining purchase on colonial thinking or policy. Even officials at the French Ministry of Public Instruction seemed to have accepted that the education of colonial subjects meant something very different than the education of French citizens. This was certainly the view of Henri Gautier, the official who had been selected to represent the Ministry of Public Instruction at this conference. As he welcomed participants and tried to set the stage for the various sessions to follow, Gautier proposed that "there is one principle, in any case, on which I think we can all already agree: it's that France does not ask for us to produce a series of fake Europeans [*contrefaçons d'Européens*]. She needs, to serve her and love her, human beings who have not been stripped of their own nature, and who come to her language, to her thought, and to her genius, less by negating themselves than by clarifying their own identity [*en se dégageant*]."[3] As we were able to closely observe in chapters 1 and 2, colonial authorities in French West Africa had long been deeply reticent about the prospect of assimilation. This was true even when it came to Senegal's Four Communes, where officials regularly tried to back away from assimilationist precedents, however partial these remained. But as the statements of Gautier and Crouzet suggest, by the early 1930s, French authorities were seeking to do even more to disprove myths about assimilation by showcasing the directions that colonial policy had taken, especially since World War I.

SURVEYING THE SCHOOLS OF THE EMPIRE

In many ways the 1931 Colonial Exhibition served as an elaborate tribute to Louis Hubert Gonzalve Lyautey, the first resident-general of the Moroccan Protectorate, who had worked to discredit assimilationist approaches to colonial rule and to pioneer new forms of "association."[4] During his years in Morocco (1912–25) Lyautey regularly inveighed against centralized, bureaucratic thinking and standardized solutions, while simultaneously arguing that enlightened colonial administration needed to be a supple, local creation that could respond to realities on the ground. Lyautey worked to turn French Morocco into a laboratory for associationist policies that aimed to preserve traditional elites, institutions, and décors, as foundations for a more conservative colonial order.[5] Lyautey's visions were structured by the notion of separate spheres: while European sectors of Moroccan towns came to project a daring modernism, most of the protectorate was to develop in more restrained ways, within traditional frameworks that protectorate authorities set out to preserve and renovate.[6] After leaving Morocco in 1925 Lyautey remained a towering figure in France's colonial establishment.

Named as general commissioner of the Colonial Exposition as of 1927, Lyautey brought his visions to developing plans for the Vincennes fairgrounds. After the exposition opened, Lyautey continued to serve as a tutelary figure, who made highly noted appearances at various events.[7] During his brief appearance at the Intercolonial Conference on Education, Lyautey described the progress that colonial ideology and practice had made, especially since the war. He explained that "there was a time when we dreamed only of applying French methods. This was true not only of education but also of administrators, judges, soldiers. ... Everyone, in the beginning, was fixated on uniformity; it was the *théorie départementale*; we had to do the same thing in Diego Suarez, in Haiphong, in Marrakesh." Lyautey added that "then the colonial spirit began to develop," and French officials began to adopt more flexible approaches that took account of local realities.[8]

Many of the reports delivered at the Intercolonial Conference on Education sought to demonstrate that overseas school systems had been fashioned not by central authorities in Paris but by specialists in the various colonial administrations, who possessed first-hand knowledge of local populations and their specific "needs." Although they had once been threadbare operations, the education departments in Hanoi, Tananarive, Rabat, Dakar, and the other administrative capitals of the empire had eventually gained more staffing and solidity, especially since the war. In most cases local school systems had come to possess their own administrative architectures, their own corps of inspectors and teachers, and their own curricula and diplomas. With these developments, the school systems of the empire had come to function more autonomously, looking less and less toward France's powerful Ministry of Public Instruction.

In his report on the schools of Indochina, Georges Taboulet (the head of education in the Cochin China region) began by noting that "the seductive and fallacious theory concerning the assimilation of colonized peoples has few remaining partisans today."[9] After rhetorically pushing the theory of assimilation into the past, Taboulet went on to describe the future-oriented initiatives that had reshaped the schools of Indochina. He explained that "the thoughtful and gradual efforts of two generations of technicians and administrators have led to the creation of a living and coherent system [of education], which, although certainly not opposed to the French system, is clearly differentiated as a result of its adaptation to local realities."[10]

During his second term as governor general of Indochina, Albert Sarraut had presided over the drafting of a new Code of Public Instruction (introduced in 1917–18), which helped to consolidate colonial forms of schooling, known as *l'enseignement franco-indigène*. The overhaul of the educational system in Indochina continued during the 1920s. Particularly important was the bundle of reforms introduced in 1924, which split primary education into two distinct cycles. Intended for the masses, the "elementary cycle" lasted three years and culminated in the *certificat d'études élémentaires indigènes*. During this cycle, education took place almost entirely in local languages.[11] Most students never progressed beyond these first three years of primary education. Sharply reduced cohorts of students continued on to the "primary cycle," which included three additional years of instruction, provided in French. Only a tiny fraction of those who completed both cycles were allowed to enroll in more advanced schools. Like other reports presented at the Intercolonial Conference on Education, Taboulet's paper pointed to heavy restrictions on elite education and a new focus on rudimentary schooling for rural populations.[12]

The report on schooling in Madagascar highlighted a clear trend toward educational segregation—something that could be observed across the empire. The rapporteur for Madagascar (Louis Devaux) began by noting that Europeans and Malagasies now attended completely separate school systems. Devaux explained very matter-of-factly that "this separation is justified by the different intellectual aptitudes of the two categories of students." After indicating that "academic levels in European schools are the same as in the Metropole," he added that "as to the native schools, their curricula have been adapted as precisely as possible to the aptitudes and current needs of their clientele."[13] As was the case in Indochina, the vast majority of indigenous students were confined to the first cycle of primary instruction, which lasted only three years. The curricula used in this cycle were "simple and utilitarian," devoted largely to local subjects and to agricultural and manual activities adapted to particular regions. Although students were taught French, lessons on other school subjects often took place in local languages.[14] Devaux concluded by noting that Madagascar's education department "has attempted to choose methods that tend to maintain and encourage the rural mentality, [and] to remove only a small number of carefully selected natives from their natural milieu, to give them a fuller education."[15]

In France's Moroccan Protectorate, the school system for "natives" had taken on a somewhat different configuration, emphasizing social class above all else. The protectorate's delegate to the Intercolonial Conference on Education was Louis Brunot, who served as head of Muslim education throughout the interwar period. During the first half of the 1920s Brunot had collaborated with Resident-General Lyautey and with Georges Hardy, the director of education in Morocco between 1919 and 1926. In his report Brunot explained that it had taken time to wean schoolteachers and protectorate officials off metropolitan educational models. He noted that "natives, far from opposing it, often demand education that is identical to that of the French, convinced that by this means they will manage to equal us and to be, like us, powerful and rich. For them, 'to instruct' has its Latin sense of 'to arm.'"[16] After mentioning these early impediments, Brunot went on to describe the more promising educational approaches that had eventually taken shape. He listed "the dogmas of native education," which included: "respect for what is most commendable in the native mentality, respect for customs and for religion, care to not denature [dénaturaliser] our charges through education, to not turn them into déracinés, misfits caught between two civilizations, but accepted by none."[17] Unlike the more complicated language policies that had been worked out in both Indochina and Madagascar, primary education in the Moroccan Protectorate continued to take place predominantly in French.[18]

While reforms in Indochina, Madagascar, and Morocco suggested a broad-based move away from metropolitan-style education, there were some notable exceptions to this trend. Throughout the interwar period, schools in the "old colonies" of Martinique, Guadeloupe, French Guiana, and Réunion remained broadly aligned with those of metropolitan France. In practice this alignment did not prevent some glaring disparities.[19] At the Intercolonial Conference on Education delegates from these colonies tried to suggest some minor ways in which schools had been adjusted to local populations and their needs, but in the end these rather awkward efforts highlighted just how foreign the notion of adapted education remained in these particular settings. The delegate from Martinique—a secondary school teacher named Marie Magdeleine—noted more candidly that "Martinique is an old colony that aspires to be assimilated to the French provinces.... We do not think it advisable to make the slightest modification to the French curricula in use in Martinique."[20] As a result of their outlier positions within the French empire, the old colonies and their schools received little attention at the Intercolonial Conference on Education.

What did this conference reveal about French West Africa and its relationship to the burgeoning field of native education? Whereas delegates from Indochina, Madagascar, and Morocco could boast of major education reforms, the official representative from AOF (André Davesne) struck a more pessimistic note. Davesne quoted extensively from the most recent school guidelines, which the Government General had published in 1924.[21] However, after noting that "all these recommendations are excellent," he explained that "the goal they define is very far from being reached."[22] As far as this official was concerned, French West Africa had yet to develop a school system that was truly adapted to the needs of Africans and the colonial state. Davesne noted that practical training in gardening and manual trades was still underdeveloped and that schools still maintained an "excessive" focus on academics. In Davesne's words: "teaching, despite the official recommendations, is theoretical, bookish, [and] fairly poorly adapted to the needs of the present time."[23] After issuing this indictment of the schools of AOF, Davesne proceeded to make a series of recommendations, which, he contended, would put schools on a more promising path. If Davesne felt free to offer a disparaging assessment of the schools of AOF, it was partly because major education reforms were already being announced in Dakar.

DEVELOPING RURAL SCHOOLS

After taking over as governor general of French West Africa in late 1930, Jules Brévié promptly announced his intention to boldly reform colonial schools. In his first formal address to his administration Brévié emphasized the need to develop a more ramified school system that would be capable of reaching deep into the federation's interior: "We must think more and more about collective education, about the mass education of the peoples of French West Africa."[24] It was not difficult to point up the thinness of existing schools. Brévié noted that after several decades of French occupation, the colonial administration still operated a mere 335 schools in AOF. Moreover, the schools that did exist tended to be concentrated in nodal points of the colonial state, whereas in many interior regions, schools remained few—and often very far—between. But as he announced a new focus on mass education, Brévié made it clear that he was not proposing to add more schools of the existing varieties. What was urgently needed, the governor general argued, was a new type of rural school.[25]

During his tenure in Dakar, Brévié did not tire of promoting these new schools, which quickly become one of the hallmarks of his administration. By the end of 1930 Brévié had already offered a revealing description of rural schools and the educational philosophy that lay behind them. The governor general explained that "this native school, which we must see one day in each group of villages, is the rural school, liberated from ambitious academic curricula, it is a farm and a workshop, a dispensary and an experimental field ... we need to concern ourselves with practical realities, with improving native

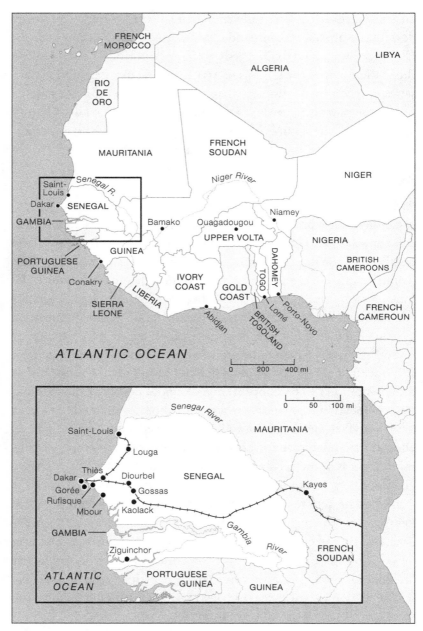

MAP 5. French West Africa and Togo, circa 1931. The Senegal inset shows towns with populations of at least five thousand (in 1934). Cartography by Erin Greb.

life right on the spot. In order for natives to go to school, schools must first go to the natives."[26] For Brévié, taking education "to the natives" implied several different things. While seeking to disperse schools broadly across the African interior, Brévié also emphasized the need to develop smaller, more informal schools, which would be able to commingle with village settings and lifeways. Finally, the governor general made it clear that taking schools "to the natives" meant leaving behind academic pretensions so that teachers and students alike would be free to focus on more practical things, such as "improving native life" in situ.

Given the way that language policies had developed in French West Africa, Brévié did not seek to link rural schools with a clear move away from instruction in French. Many others, particularly in Britain's colonial establishment, continued to insist that "adapted education" necessitated—almost by its very definition—the use of local languages. As has been noted, such thinking had already made some notable inroads into the French empire, especially in Indochina and Madagascar. By contrast, language policies in French West Africa had remained more constant. The Government General's 1924 education instructions clearly stipulated that "only French is to be used in schools. Schoolteachers are forbidden to use local idioms with students."[27] Nonetheless, support for education in local languages was clearly growing within colonial circles.[28] After being named as governor general, Brévié went so far as to encourage the use of local "idioms," when these seemed a more efficient means of reaching rural populations. Addressing his administration at the end of 1931, Brévié explained: "So that this education can immediately have its full useful effect you must not hesitate to have recourse to local idioms when it comes to indispensable knowledge for natives.... The urgency of this practical education is beyond any doubt. The local idiom must be called upon if French cannot be of service."[29] Although French remained the dominant language of instruction during the 1930s, the interdiction against using local "idioms" seemed to have broken down.[30]

If Brévié took a direct role in defining and promoting rural schools, so too did Albert Charton, who served as inspector general of education in AOF throughout Brévié's tenure in Dakar. In a set of recommendations that he forwarded to Brévié in late 1930, Charton emphasized the need to develop truncated forms of education, oriented almost entirely toward local life and its improvement. Underscoring just how narrow the scope of education should be, Charton insisted: "No curricula that are too academic, no pompous lessons, no civic education, we are staying in the bush, in our village, the horizon stops there. It's about practical, concrete, and collective education."[31] After completing several years of summary schooling, students were to return to the land, where they would become agents of progress, spreading techniques and habits of mind that would improve local life, stimulate agricultural production, and bring rural villages more fully into the colonial economy.

After 1930 the Government General pressured the various colonies to convert their village schools, of an older conception, into new rural schools. No colony embraced Dakar's directives with more alacrity than did French Soudan.[32] Having already experimented with various kinds of rural education during the 1920s, Soudan's seasoned director of education, Frédéric Assomption, now pushed his efforts further.[33] In a circular to all of Soudan's teachers, Assomption stressed the need to limit the scope of academic subjects, by concentrating on the local, the familiar, and the observable. Assomption recommended that lessons on morality touch on the following points: "Family, the village, France. Life in a society. The nourishing earth, the charm of rural life, its advantages. The farmer: the satisfaction of being useful, of producing. The good farmer: thrifty, provident, assiduous, tenacious, etc." Regarding history lessons, the head of education in French Soudan urged: "Teach the history of the village and the canton, exclusively through anecdotes. Three essential points. a) the village before the French arrived b) the village at the beginning of and during the French conquest c) the village under French rule." All of the subject matter for geography lessons was also to be found within a small radius, encompassing the village and its immediate environs. "Do not take up general subjects," Assomption admonished, "keep to things that are visible and verifiable. The village, its location, its different quarters. The surrounding land and its features." Lessons on science and hygiene were to follow similar patterns.[34]

Agricultural education quickly emerged as a key feature of rural schools. Since the beginning of the century French officials had often emphasized the importance of providing African children with practical education, particularly in agriculture. Such a concern had been clearly articulated by the 1903 *arrêté*, which had first sketched out the contours of the federation's school system. In the years that followed, colonial authorities had gone to even greater lengths to stress the importance of practical lessons in agriculture. While some agricultural education could take place in classrooms, colonial officials concluded early on that students also needed to spend time practicing agriculture in school gardens. As part of the comprehensive education directives that it published in 1914, the Government General stipulated that all village and regional schools should maintain a garden, and that all students should receive agricultural education under the supervision of a teacher.[35]

But it was one thing to issue directives in Dakar and something else to monitor and enforce these instructions at schools across French West Africa. In 1916 interim Governor General Angoulvant concluded that the 1914 guidelines regarding school gardens and agricultural education still remained, in many cases, "a dead letter." Determined to change this situation, Angoulvant tried to implement more stringent requirements.[36] These initiatives came just as AOF was being summoned to supply the metropole with increased quantities of agricultural exports as part of the war effort. School gardens now commanded more attention, not only as sites for lessons on agriculture but also as potential sources of exportable goods.[37] However, with the end of the war, this emphasis waned and school gardens often became neglected plots that generated little interest among teachers or students. The federation-wide school curricula that were published in 1924 still claimed that "school gardens exist at almost all schools during part of the year at least."[38] But while these curricula encouraged the teaching of some basic agricultural skills, agricultural education did not even figure in the official schedule specifying how the thirty-hour school week was to be divided up.[39]

With the onset of the Great Depression, the colonial administration quickly developed a much fuller commitment to agricultural education. This trend began to take shape even before Brévié was appointed as governor general in late 1930. In the spring of that year Brévié's predecessor, Jules Carde, had already stressed the need to align schools more fully with the needs of the colonial economy. In a circular to the various lieutenant governors Carde explained that "the fundamental principal is that the general education provided in schools will be, as far as possible, oriented toward agricultural life and working life. Every branch of education must consequently adopt, as its focal point, manual work and economic activity in all of its forms."[40] Although Carde was replaced before these instructions could be carried out, agricultural and manual education quickly took on new proportions under Brévié's administration. It was no coincidence that this focus intensified just as the Great Depression was beginning to unfurl across French West Africa.

The economic crisis came somewhat later to France and its West African colonies than it did to more industrialized countries such as Great Britain, Germany, and the United States. But although it was slower to settle in, the Depression eventually proved more protracted, hanging over France and its empire for the better part of the 1930s.[41] To weather the Depression, French authorities worked to bring the metropole and the empire into a more heavily protected trading bloc—a strategy sometimes referred to as *le repli impérial*. Although the empire had already become France's leading trading partner just prior to the onset of the Depression, this interdependence increased during the 1930s. As part of this arrangement, the colonies were expected to provide the metropole with increased quantities of raw materials and agricultural goods.[42]

Brévié would spend his entire tenure in Dakar responding to the economic crisis and its fallout. Soon after he arrived in Dakar, the new governor general asked all Europeans in positions of authority to devote themselves to the goal of boosting production: "I want to tell you of my intention . . . to make production in general the linchpin of the policy of West Africa . . . I call on the participation of all those who, in whatever capacity, as colons, traders, military officers, or civil servants of any kind, are able to exercise influence over the native population, and I ask them to focus all of their will and energies on this one goal: production."[43] When Brévié issued this call, the Depression was only beginning to be felt in AOF. During the months that followed, steep declines in the market prices of export crops soon compromised the financial position of the colonies, producing a wave of cutbacks in local administrations and trading firms. It was in this inauspicious context of budget austerity that colonial officials set out to stimulate and better harness agricultural production in French West Africa. As we will see, schools were quickly hitched to these broader efforts.

Rural schools often came to include not only gardens but also barnyards, livestock, fields, and small plantations. School farms were meant to demonstrate to schoolchildren and villagers the immediate advantages of new crops and improved farming techniques. However, from the beginning, the boundary between agricultural education and agricultural production proved tenuous. This was especially the case in French Soudan. Assomption, the colony's long-serving head of education, had issued a circular on "practical agricultural education" as early as 1923. In his circular Assomption had instructed schoolteachers: "You must strive to cultivate a fondness for agricultural work, to raise the prestige of farmers, and to develop the natural qualities of your students, almost all of whom must return to farming." Assomption went on to urge teachers to expand school gardens so as to include not only vegetables but also export crops.[44] But if agricultural education was already becoming a clearer priority during the 1920s, school gardens and fields took on far more importance during the Great Depression. By 1933 the schools of French Soudan were farming a combined total of 102 hectares, a figure that would grow to 404 hectares by 1936. By the latter date the colony's schools had also come to possess a total of 159 oxen, 1,000 sheep, 600 goats, 1,500 chickens, 138 hogs, 250 rabbits, and 530 pairs of pigeons.[45] Throughout Brévié's tenure the Government General held French Soudan up as a model that other colonies would do well to follow. To spur local authorities on, officials in Dakar published colony-by-colony figures showing the extent of agricultural initiatives in school gardens and on school farms.[46] As these reports suggest, success in rural education was increasingly measured in agricultural—as opposed to academic—terms.

The proceeds of school farms also became a gauge of success. Money earned from the sale of school produce, crops, and livestock was funneled into school-run savings associations, known as *mutuelles scolaires*. These savings associations were not a new invention; a scattering of mutuelles scolaires had sprung up as of the first decade of the twentieth century. In 1913 Governor General Ponty had invited the colonies to promote and formally organize these entities.[47] Mutuelles scolaires came to be more fully endorsed during World War I, as schools were drawn into broader efforts aimed at boosting agricultural production.[48] But while many school-run savings associations were created during the war, their organization usually remained rather haphazard. Moreover, by the early 1920s the administration's enthusiasm for mutuelles scolaires had already begun to wane. The 1924 school curricula gave them only a passing endorsement, noting that "without being compulsory, mutuelles scolaires are worthy of encouragement."[49]

After 1930 the Government General worked to make mutuelles scolaires an integral part of rural education. According to the Government General's news bulletin, these associations were to serve as "a school of work, solidarity, and providence," which would contribute to the moral and material progress of rural Africa.[50] A well-worn colonial stereotype held that Africans looked down on agricultural work, considering it the lot of the lowest social categories. Another colonial stereotype suggested that Africans farmed only enough to meet their basic needs, spurning innovations and surpluses. Still another trope related to the profligacy of Africans, who supposedly lived large immediately after harvests, failing to set aside adequate reserves for the rest of the year.[51] Colonial officials imagined that mutuelles scolaires could help to correct or at least mitigate these "moral deficiencies," while also bringing rural communities more fully into the colonial economy.

School-run savings associations returned some of their profits to students in the form of meals, clothing, and occasionally toolkits and plows. However, in the end much of the money taken in was funneled back into school budgets, where it was often used to expand and better equip school farms. After amassing 25,000 francs in 1933, mutuelles scolaires in French Soudan increased their annual proceeds to 65,000 francs in 1936.[52] Education officials hoped that these tidy sums would allow schools to become partially self-supporting. The Government General, and the individual colonies, had never been inclined to devote large sums of money to educating Africans, and despite Brévié's calls for mass education the 1930s would be no different. Expenditures on education stagnated during the Depression years.[53] As it promoted the development of rural schools, the Government General made sure to explain just how inexpensive these schools were to build and operate. Moreover, far from seeing these rustic schools as a Depression-era expedient, officials in Dakar increasingly presented rural schools as the way of the future.

Established rather quickly in French Soudan, rural schools met strong resistance in coastal regions of Senegal, Ivory Coast, and Dahomey, where populations had grown accustomed to an earlier generation of colonial schools. Given the extent of local resistance, authorities in these colonies were slower to implement directives coming out of Dakar. However, Brévié and Charton kept pressuring local administrations, and by the mid-1930s these three colonies were beginning to fall into line. In its report on the 1934–35 school year, Charton's office could tout the progress of rural education in almost all the West African colonies. The section on Senegal noted that "all the schools in the interior have become rural schools, equipped with gardens, fields, nurseries, draft animals, and some livestock. At many schools, students are learning to yoke oxen, horses and donkeys, and to use plows, seeders and harrows." Describing the situation in Dahomey, this report explained that "after overcoming some initial reticence, education in Dahomey has been clearly oriented toward agricultural activities; the results of this past year are most encouraging."[54]

Officials in Dakar continued to criticize authorities in Ivory Coast for not doing enough to reform their schools. In response to these mounting pressures, that colony's administration eventually introduced a series of new measures in 1935–36. These measures stipulated that rural schools would henceforth provide only three and a half hours of classroom instruction per day, so that the rest of the school day (two to three hours) could be devoted to manual tasks in school workshops and, more often, on school farms. Whereas children had previously started school as early as age six, a new policy now established that students needed to be at least nine years old. Rural schools involved difficult agricultural work—clearing land, digging, plowing, planting, and watering—which could not be readily done by children younger than nine. With these reforms, the Government General could finally write that "practical, artisanal, and agricultural education is vigorously expanding in Ivory Coast."[55]

In their efforts to recast colonial education, Brévié and Charton initially focused on converting village schools into newly designed rural schools. Rather quickly, however, both officials also began to rethink the purpose of the federation's regional schools. Since the beginning of the century village schools had offered only the first few years of primary schooling (the *cours préparatoire* and the *cours élémentaire*), whereas regional schools usually included the full course of primary education, through the *cours moyen*.[56] Regional schools played a central role in the training of new African elites. Students at these schools could often work toward the local primary school certificate—a modest diploma that could nonetheless lead to broadened career prospects, whether in private firms or in the various branches of the colonial administration.[57] The primary school certificate also opened up the possibility of further studies at higher primary schools, even though there was only once such school per colony.[58]

With the onset of the Depression the Government General began to clamp down on the federation's seventy-two regional schools, which were now accused of turning out too many potential elites. In a 1932 circular to the lieutenant governors, Brévié warned: "If we are not careful, it is at regional schools that we run the risk of producing 'déracinés,' unable to find their place among Africa's new elites, but resistant to traditional native life, in which they appear as foreign bodies." Brévié worried most about students who were weeded out of regional schools after a few years, before earning a primary school certificate. As far as the governor general was concerned, these byproducts of regional schools could play no useful role in colonial society: "Most of these young people who fail to make the cut at school become part of the floating masses of potential, importunate candidates for petty jobs. Proud of their useless knowledge, embittered by their early disappointments, they are incapable of readapting to their native milieu."[59] While recognizing that regional schools needed to retain small competitive sections to train the required numbers of young elites, Brévié now called for these schools to add other sections oriented toward rural life, farming, and manual trades.

In response to these directives, regional schools soon began to assemble working farms, so that students could devote a portion of each day to hands-on agricultural activities. And whereas farms at understaffed and underfinanced rural schools usually remained somewhat modest in size, those associated with regional schools often became larger operations. Even students who secured spots in the academic sections of regional schools were now required to spend a portion of their time in school-run barnyards, gardens, and fields. Education officials contended that their goal was to ensure that all students developed a healthy fondness for the land and physical work, which might counterbalance the more "academic" dimensions of regional schools.

The invention of rural schools and the reform of regional schools need to be seen as part of broader efforts to reconfigure the colonial project during the Depression years. As we will see in the final section of this chapter, French understandings of progress and what it should mean for the inhabitants of AOF were increasingly colored by peasantist tropes. Many colonial officials were coming to view Africans as natural-born peasants, or at least as peasants-in-the-making.

PROMOTING *PAYSANS NOIRS*

While prompting renewed interest in the agricultural potential of French West Africa, the Great Depression also brought attention to plight of rural African societies. Sharp declines in the prices of export crops had added significantly to the hardships of rural communities already beaten down by heavy taxation and various forms of forced labor. Mounting hardships now pushed unprecedented numbers of villagers to migrate toward urban centers.[60] As they observed these trends, many colonial officials expressed growing anxiety.

The impact of migration patterns proved particularly spectacular in and around Dakar. During the first three decades of the twentieth century steady population growth had already become a defining feature of the federal capital. As part of broader efforts to manage the town's growth, colonial authorities had moved, in 1924, to create a new administrative entity known as the Circonscription de Dakar et dépendances, which included Dakar and its suburbs as well as the island of Gorée.[61] The population of this metropolitan area had already surged during the years leading up to the Depression from forty thousand in 1926 to fifty-four thousand in 1931. However, it was during the Depression itself that the population of greater Dakar exploded, reaching ninety-three thousand by 1936.[62] Officials worried out loud about Dakar's ability to absorb all these newcomers, at a time when opportunities for formal employment were in sharp decline. As colonial businesses and administrations retrenched in response to rapidly deteriorating earnings on export commodities and customs receipts, urban unemployment became a growing—although still relatively new—problem. Concerns about migrants, and the precarious existences they often led on the fringes of towns, became a steady refrain of colonial officials during the Great Depression. Many officials spoke ominously of "floating populations" and "déracinés," and of the looming threat they posed to the colonial order.

Senegal had always been home to the largest concentration of urban centers in French West Africa. By 1934 this colony included ten towns of more than five thousand inhabitants, including AOF's two most populous towns, Dakar and Saint-Louis. At the time French Soudan had seven towns of more than five thousand residents, while Guinea and Ivory Coast each had five. The corresponding figures for Niger, Dahomey, and Mauritania were respectively four, three, and zero. Although migration toward urban centers had clearly accelerated,

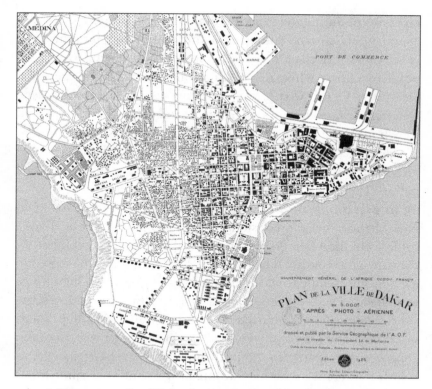

MAP 6. The metropolis of Dakar in 1925. Produced by the Service géographique de l'A.O.F. Courtesy of the Bibliothèque nationale de France.

there were still only four towns in AOF with populations in excess of twenty thousand: Dakar, Saint-Louis, Porto-Novo, and Bamako. Dakar stood out as the only town with a population over thirty thousand.[63] Colonial officials still found it possible to imagine that towns were exceptional spaces, and that the true vocation of French West Africa was to remain overwhelmingly rural and agricultural.

No colonial official did more than Robert Delavignette to popularize and normalize pastoral visions of French West Africa. After graduating from the École coloniale in 1922 Delavignette had gone on to serve as a field administrator in Niger and Upper Volta, before returning to Paris to work at the Ministry of Colonies. Although he had proven to be a relatively able commandant, Delavignette's rapid ascent during the 1930s owed more to his success in Paris as a colonial publicist and author, who knew how to tap into the spirit of the times.[64] At the Ministry of Colonies, Delavignette worked on publicity efforts, while also finding time to write rather personal accounts of French West Africa. In evoking AOF and its development, Delavignette drew heavily on regionalist and peasantist tropes, which were flourishing in the climate of the Great Depression.

Delavignette joined a long list of interwar French authors who turned their attention to peasants and their place within the French nation. The experience of World War I had prompted new interest in peasants. France's agricultural population had contributed more than any other professional category to the war effort: all told, some 3.7 million farmers were mobilized to fight in the conflict. By the time peace returned between 500,000 and 700,000 of these soldiers had been killed, while another 360,000 to 500,000 went home wounded.[65] These staggering losses were seen by many to accelerate the longer decline of France's rural populations.[66] While peasants were some of the most obvious victims of the Great War, they also contributed mightily to the ultimate victory over Germany. As a disoriented French nation confronted the extent of wartime losses and the uncertainties of peace, peasants were increasingly venerated for their sacrifices and sheer tenacity.

Views of peasants had not always been this positive: during the nineteenth century, French elites had often portrayed peasantries as uncivilized populations, who resided in secluded and insalubrious worlds.[67] With the growth of interest in folklore and regionalism during the last decades of the nineteenth century, representations of peasants grew more complex. But although the refiguring of French peasants was well under way by the time World War I broke out, the war greatly accelerated this trend. By the time the conflict finally ended, many French elites were coming to describe peasants as archetypal Frenchmen, whose lives evoked steadfastness, harmony, and authenticity.[68] Discourses of this sort served to assuage interwar anxieties about accelerating societal changes and what they portended for the future. Although some had begun to speak of an *exode rural*, or rural exodus, during the century's first two decades, it was during the interwar period that this expression became something of a mantra, capturing a range of apprehensions, not only about rural decline but also about the associated processes of urbanization, industrialization, and intensifying class conflict.[69]

When the Great Depression struck, many French elites found even more reasons to publicize French peasants and the stabilizing role that they could play. Compared to neighboring countries such as Great Britain and Germany, France still retained large rural populations throughout the interwar period.[70] Only partially integrated into broader economies, these populations had helped to delay the arrival of the Depression in France and then to limit its impact. In writing *Les paysans noirs*, Delavignette hoped to transfer a portion of the positive publicity surrounding French peasants to the populations of French West Africa. Although few in France had thought of Africans as "peasants" prior to the publication of Delavignette's book in 1931, peasantist rhetoric would soon make deep inroads into colonial discourse.[71]

Delavignette sought to show how rural Africans could become effective producers of cash crops without abandoning their villages and traditional modes of work. *Les paysans noirs* chronicles the efforts of a commandant (a thinly disguised Delavignette) who is determined to win the confidence of local farming communities in Upper Volta. This particular commandant succeeds where others had failed, largely because he actively builds a ground-level understanding of local populations, by bypassing intermediaries and consulting directly with farming families and village leaders. The commandant in *Les paysans noirs* has been charged with overseeing the installation of a mechanized oil press that will soon begin to process peanuts. Knowing that he will have to "feed the machine," the commandant works to convince local populations of the advantages of peanut cultivation, rather than turning to the more familiar solution of coercion. After following the agricultural calendar, and the progression of the peanut crops, *Les paysans noirs* concludes with a coming together, as colonial authorities and farming communities celebrate record harvests and the beginnings of a new rural prosperity. We are led to understand that this commandant succeeded largely as a result of his willingness to seek out new compromises, such as the grafting of peanut production onto family and community-based modes of farming.

The timing of *Les paysans noirs* was highly significant. As the Great Depression settled in, Delavignette worried that the drive to spur colonial production would lead to increased exploitation of African labor, without consideration for the fabric of rural communities. In their efforts to promote cash-crop production in French West Africa, colonial authorities had turned, early on, to a variety of coercive schemes. During World War I authorities had summoned African populations to supply the metropole with record quantities of agricultural products. To meet production targets, administrators and their African agents often forced local populations to work in fields tellingly known as *les champs du commandant*. Another arrangement required individual African farmers to produce specified quantities of cash crops in their own fields. Failure to comply with any of these demands could result in punishment through the indigénat.[72] Programs of forced cultivation were maintained during the 1920s, as the imperative of wartime *ravitaillement* gave way to a postwar focus on agricultural *mise en valeur*.

During the interwar period, forced labor took many other forms. Colonial authorities regularly helped to round up contingents of laborers for shipment to European-owned plantations and forestry concessions, especially in the Ivory Coast. As a result of the exploitative working conditions and wages that they proposed, these European ventures had rarely been able to attract sufficient amounts of free labor. But rather than improving working conditions and raising wages, European planters and loggers preferred to turn to the colonial administration for help.[73] More densely populated than other parts of AOF, the colony of Upper Volta came to serve as a vast labor reservoir. Between 1920 and 1930 this colony exported some eighty-four thousand laborers to neighboring colonies, particularly the Ivory Coast. This figure does not include the laborers who were requisitioned to work on agricultural or public works projects in Upper Volta.[74]

Colonial authorities also directed large amounts of forced labor toward expanding irrigation projects. After World War I authorities began to push forward with plans to irrigate extensive swaths of land along the Niger River, in the hope of creating cotton and rice-growing basins that could serve as economic engines for the entire federation. By the mid-1920s the first irrigation projects had already begun to siphon large sums of money from colonial budgets. With the official creation of the semi-autonomous Office du Niger in 1932, these irrigation schemes came to be pursued even more vigorously. Large labor gangs were assembled to build the dams, canals, and other structures that would eventually make irrigated farming possible. Once lands were finally irrigated, farming families were recruited to live and work on tracts directly administered by the Office du Niger. To recruit the necessary families, the staff of the Office du Niger and local colonial authorities turned to the familiar expedient of coercion.[75] The Office du Niger, and the visions that sustained it, had had never been above criticism; but it was not until the Popular Front period (1936–38) that French authorities began to probe more deeply into the labor abuses and illusory promises of these large-scale irrigation schemes.[76]

In 1930 the International Labor Organization drafted a convention which proposed to end "forced or compulsory labor in all its forms within the shortest possible period." This convention immediately banned forced labor "for the benefit of private individuals, companies or associations," while temporarily authorizing the continued use of forced labor for public works, provided that certain conditions were met.[77] In the end the French government joined the governments of Belgium and Portugal in refusing to sign this agreement. But even as they rebuffed these international efforts to phase out forced labor, French officials clearly felt new pressure to confront this issue.[78] If Delavignette's visions of African peasants gained support across the 1930s, it was partly because French authorities were challenged to imagine forms of agricultural production and development that would begin to move beyond forced labor.

Delavignette contended that peasant communities could become powerful motors of production once they were properly understood and guided by colonial authorities. It was the role of commandants living in contact with local communities to introduce judicious changes that could be blended with more traditional practices. Delavignette counseled: "Leave the family free to choose its land and its work traditions. Endorse the religious rites of the farm. Control the use of the seed and make sure that the experiment that is going to be carried out does not undermine traditional crops. Exercise this control through tours [*tournées*]."[79] Concerned with balancing preservation and modernization, Delavignette promoted what he termed "l'Afrique du juste-milieu." Drawing yet another connection between France and French West Africa, Delavignette added: "And we French, who like the cultivated earth, who value a sense of balance and of divine moderation, we can only feel at home in such an Africa."[80]

Having worked to reveal and normalize the peasantist vocation of French West Africa, Delavignette found it rather easy to support the development of rural schools. He expressed little concern about the paring back of academic lessons or about the development of agricultural activities on school farms. In a 1935 article Delavignette could approvingly note that the rural school "does not award diplomas; it does not open up doors to professions. It is turned toward the land. It will be truthful to a particular region [*pays*]; here a school of riverside communities; there a school of the savannah; elsewhere a school of the forest. It will express all of the rural and artisanal truth of this land. It will bring the entire village to school."[81] Through descriptions such as this one, Delavignette suggested that colonial schools were finally reaching down to what was most authentic and essential in French West Africa.

During the 1930s a new focus on indigenous peasantries and their improvement developed in many colonial settings. Georges Hardy, who served as director of the École coloniale between 1926 and 1933, underscored this this trend in 1932, when he declared that "the word peasant has lately made its official entry into the colonial vocabulary. It is given a place of honor in governmental speeches. Some original and profound works such as *Les paysans noirs* have taken this as their title; in all of our possessions, policies are being shaped which aim to reinforce or restore peasant farmers [*le paysannat*]."[82] This empire-wide priority had already been revealed at the International and Intercolonial Conference on Native Society—a major conference convened under the auspices of the 1931 Colonial Exposition. After presiding over this six-day gathering, Hardy summed up the conclusions that had emerged, noting that "all the reports have concurred in their calls for, depending on the case, the establishment or the restoration of true peasant farmers [*un véritable paysannat*], capable of providing native societies with the material well-being, the moral security, and the stability that seem to be indispensable conditions for any progress."[83]

But if peasant farmers and peasantries were now seen as essential foundations for safe and enduring progress, they were found to be everywhere deficient. Hardy explained that in some parts of the empire "true peasant farmers" did not yet exist, while in other areas native peasantries were archaic and disintegrating. In either case, peasants were unable to progress on their own and thus required the guidance of a colonial power such as France. Both Delavignette and Hardy contended that France, with its deep peasant traditions, was particularly well qualified to carry out such a mission. But even as they stressed newfound affinities between metropolitan and overseas populations, Hardy and Delavignette were careful to avoid anything that might signal a return toward discredited notions of assimilation. Native peasants, they insisted, should be understood within colonial contexts that were quite distinct. At the close of the International and Intercolonial Conference on Native Society, Hardy stressed that "the reports have also stated their opposition to any general formula that would simply equate native peasant farmers with our European types of peasant farmers. Here more than elsewhere, we must take into account local customs and respect, as far as possible, traditional frameworks.... Solutions can only be local, and must vary according to region and ethnic group."[84] In coining the expression "les paysans noirs," Delavignette sought to evoke both the familiar and the "other." On the one hand, he hoped that metropolitan populations and colonial authorities would develop new respect for rural Africans, once the latter had been incorporated into the intuitively familiar category of "peasants." But on the other hand, Delavignette used the adjective "noirs" to reference essential differences. In his various writings from the 1930s Delavignette was careful to make clear that black peasants belonged to a colonial sphere that remained far removed from the French countryside.

If they had little in common with the ideology of assimilation, the peasantist discourses that developed during the 1930s should not be viewed as a simple variation on the ideology of association. Members of France's colonial establishment were drawn to new discourses about African peasants and their gradual progress partly because these discourses seemed to move beyond abstract ideologies, so as to suggest earthy compromises that many could find intuitive. Delavignette himself insisted that it was pointless to look for ideological consistency in something as hybrid as French colonialism. Writing at the end of the 1930s, he observed: "One is tempted to bring ideas about native policy back to the classic debate: Assimilation or Association. But the experience in Black Africa is filled with contradictions and transactions between these two theories. . . . Assimilation *and* Association, both formulas are often combined; and their proportions vary according to the dexterity of the operator and the temperature of events. . . . Reality escapes the categories in which we claim to enclose it. And these very categories, which appear to us to be clear and practical, are not or are no longer methods for understanding. They immobilize the mind."[85]

During the depression years, the colonial administration found many reasons to embrace peasantist visions. African peasants had come to be viewed as a stabilizing force around which gradual and non-threatening programs of modernization and production could be constructed. The new focus on peasants drew attention to the agricultural potential of the African interior while deflecting attention away from expanding urban populations and the challenges that these populations now seemed to represent. Normative visions of hardworking, "rooted" peasants were seen as a way to discredit urban Africans, as "déracinés," who did not have a clear place in the colonial order. Finally, harmonious depictions of a placid *Afrique paysanne*, which was finally coming into its own, were used to mask the oppression and dislocation that were the lot of many rural populations, especially in the 1930s. During the Great Depression, the combined pressures of steeply declining prices for agricultural crops, heavy taxation, forced labor, and an increasingly intrusive colonial state made many parts of the African interior quite inhospitable. It was no mere coincidence that discourses touting the rustic virtues of African peasants gained widespread currency just as growing numbers of migrants were leaving the countryside in the hope of finding sanctuary in or around the federation's expanding urban centers.

Having observed some of the ways in which colonial authorities worked to recast the African interior during the Great Depression, we now move back to the coast of Senegal and to the École William Ponty. During the first half of the 1930s colonial authorities set out to fundamentally remake this elite school. This process of reinvention reveals much about the administration's changing understanding of African elites and their place within the colonial order.

4

Reorienting African Schoolteachers

AGENTS OF THE FUTURE

Throughout the early twentieth century the teaching profession constituted one of the major avenues of social promotion open to French-educated Africans. Colonial officials hoped that schoolteachers would serve as loyal foot soldiers, as they spread out to staff increasingly far-flung schools. And yet, early on, many officials began to fault schoolteachers for moving beyond their assigned roles and for providing education that overstepped official guidelines. Although tensions between African schoolteachers and the colonial state can be traced back to the founding of the federal school system in 1903, these tensions tended to increase with time, as schoolteachers became more numerous, and as colonial authorities grew more anxious about the place of newly trained elites within the colonial order.

Because of the important role it played in the production of African elites, the École William Ponty has continued to draw considerable attention from historians.[1] But while much is known about the history of "Ponty," existing studies have still not accounted adequately for the battery of reforms that reshaped the school during the 1930s. Reforms soon became so extensive that colonial authorities felt compelled to design and build an entirely new school campus to reflect changing priorities. After residing for more than two decades on Gorée Island, just off the coast of Dakar, the school eventually moved to a sprawling rural campus on the African mainland. Through the construction of this new campus and other reforms, colonial authorities worked to plot out revised sociocultural coordinates for future African elites. Before assessing the remaking of the École William Ponty during 1930s, this chapter begins by situating AOF's preeminent colonial school in the context of the 1920s. During this decade Ponty became the site of a number of controversial experiments, which highlighted lingering French hesitations about young African elites.

POSTWAR HESITATIONS

We have already had occasion to note the blunt criticism of African schoolteachers that was voiced during and immediately after World War I. In chapter 2 we saw Lieutenant Governor Antonetti describe many schoolteachers as "completely unhinged and consumed with pride." Not known for his restraint, Antonetti also declared that the École William Ponty had itself become the scene of "collective acts of insubordination, almost revolts." The criticisms of officials such as Antonetti helped to prompt a dramatic scaling back of the École William Ponty during the early 1920s, as the Government General reconsidered its approaches to teacher training and other forms of elite education. In the end, however, the 1920s brought more than just retrenchment. The École William Ponty experienced a protracted period of instability as school officials proceeded with several different experiments.

Although originally founded as a normal school, devoted solely to teacher training, the École William Ponty broadened its mission after the war when it opened two new sections. In 1920 the school added an administrative section, charged with training African agents for service in the lower echelons of the colonial state.[2] By 1924, however, the Government General had already decided to close this new section, in response to pressure from various colonies.[3] As they observed the politicized climate in the Four Communes at the end of the war, Antonetti and a range of other officials concluded that petty agents of the colonial administration could be trained more safely and expediently in their home colonies. Whereas the administrative section was promptly closed down, Ponty retained its medical section, which had also been opened in 1920. This section prepared students for eventual entry into Dakar's École de médecine, a newly established professional school that had begun to train auxiliary medical personnel for service across AOF.[4] However, even as the École William Ponty experimented with new roles, the teaching section continued to occupy a dominant position, producing almost 60 percent of the school's graduates during the 1920s.[5]

Two other experiments also added considerably to the uncertainties surrounding the École William Ponty and its mission. In a new departure the Government General established three scholarships in 1920, so that a small but steady stream of Ponty graduates could continue their studies at the normal school in Aix-en-Provence, in the south of France. At the same time the Colony of Senegal began to offer similar scholarships to Senegalese graduates of the École William Ponty.[6] Setting off for Aix in 1920, the first contingent of *boursiers* included three students who had received scholarships from the Government General (two students from Guinea and one from French Soudan), and nine additional students sponsored by the Colony of Senegal.[7] This scholarship program was part of the broader package of measures introduced at the end of the war, as colonial authorities were pressured to expand opportunities for elite education. In the end this program was inaugurated just before the Government General began cutting enrollments at the École William Ponty in response to mounting criticism of African schoolteachers.

Viewed from certain angles, these new scholarships seemed to renew patterns that had been established during the late nineteenth century, when the Four Communes regularly sent small cohorts of students to France for secondary or post-secondary studies.[8] There was even a precedent for sending students to Aix-en-Provence. During the 1880s Blaise Diagne had been one of a number of Senegalese students to study at a privately run pre-professional school in Aix, before this arrangement eventually broke down. In 1889 Diagne and several other originaires were expelled from this institution, after a falling out with the school's director. Returning to Senegal, Diagne was able to use his government scholarship to study at the secondary school in Saint-Louis, which had opened only a few years earlier.[9] While building on certain precedents, the scholarship program that was founded in 1920 also broke new ground. Unlike the trips of the late nineteenth century, which were generally reserved for the children of well-connected originaires, the new scholarships were earmarked for Ponty graduates, most of whom did not hail from the Four Communes. And whereas the scholarships of the late nineteenth century were granted by local authorities in the Four Communes, the program inaugurated in 1920 bore the imprimatur of the Government General.

The twelve boursiers who arrived in Aix in December 1920 had all earned the terminal diploma of the École William Ponty. However, since this diploma had no validity in France, the West African students first had to catch up with their French classmates, who had all completed the *brevet élémentaire* before enrolling at the normal school in Aix.[10] Students at French normal schools spent much of their time working toward a more advanced diploma known as the *brevet supérieur*.[11] After successfully passing the qualifying exam for the brevet élémentaire, the West African students were able to turn their attention to the normal school curriculum and the brevet supérieur. During their stay in Aix these students also worked toward the *certificat d'aptitude pédagogique*, the teaching certificate required of all full schoolteachers (*instituteurs titulaires*) in metropolitan France. Officials both in Dakar and at the normal school in Aix assumed that the twelve West African boursiers would return to AOF in late 1923 with all the credentials of metropolitan schoolteachers. This promised to be a highly symbolic event, since these schoolteachers would presumably qualify for admission to the European teaching cadre, which had generally remained closed to Africans.

By September 1923 most of the African boursiers were already beginning to make their way home. The director of the normal school in Aix (A. Gleyze) wrote to Dakar to express his satisfaction with some of the boursiers and his desire to receive more such students in the future. But while trying to remain broadly complimentary, the school director also made a point of criticizing the Senegalese students. Gleyze noted that "in general, the Senegalese can be distinguished from the students of the other colonies by their propensity to vanity and pride, by their less spontaneous and less complete acceptance of rules, and by their weaker desire to make themselves useful and to work hard."[12] As we will see, the director's disparaging views of the Senegalese boursiers only hardened during the months that followed.

Whereas most of this first cohort of boursiers returned to AOF in September 1923, four students remained behind to retake the qualifying examination for the brevet supérieur, which they had not passed the first time around.[13] Soon thereafter, two of these students—Guibril N'Diaye and Massire Coulibaly, both of whom were Senegalese—became embroiled in a growing dispute with school officials. The two boursiers were accused of repeatedly leaving the school's premises without permission and of refusing to do their chores willingly. When Gleyze confronted N'Diaye and Coulibaly, he found them unrepentant and arrogant. This conflict quickly led to the permanent expulsion of the two Senegalese students. While both had managed to earn the brevet supérieur, they were ultimately sent back to Dakar without having obtained the certificat d'aptitude pédagogique.[14]

In an explanatory letter to the Government General, Gleyze tried to make it clear that the recent problems only concerned the Senegalese students and that the behavior of the other students had been beyond reproach: "I must add (and I would like to emphasize this point in particular) that we were and still are completely satisfied with the other scholarship students from AOF, and that one cannot praise them enough; they earned the affection of everyone here and are perfectly deserving of the scholarships they received from the Governor General of AOF."[15] However, insofar as nine of the first twelve boursiers were from Senegal, the school director's remarks seem more than a little disingenuous. Moreover, while Gleyze clearly harbored particular animosity toward the Senegalese students, his correspondence also reveals broader racial prejudices regarding the physical and intellectual abilities of black Africans. For example, when describing students' abilities to lead gymnastics sessions, the school director felt comfortable observing that "in this area, blacks are very inferior to whites; their physical indolence and their slowness contrast with the vivacity and energy of the latter."[16]

Although archival sources tend to present these altercations from the vantage point of the school director, one suspects that the two expelled Senegalese students would have provided a very different account of their time at the normal school in Aix. How did they experience the school's paternalistic constraints? How heavily did the prejudices of school officials, teachers, and fellow students weigh on the West African boursiers? Some suggestive clues can be found in a 1925 letter that another Senegalese scholarship recipient addressed to Governor General Carde. In his letter this student remembered the expulsion of N'Diaye and Coulibaly in the following terms:

> Three days after my arrival at the École Normale d'Aix, I witnessed an unexpected spectacle. The school director chases two of my fellow countrymen from the school, in a way that made me want to request to be repatriated immediately. That is not all. After the departure of the expelled students, my remaining classmates from AOF and I had to endure remarks that were quite unfitting for a head of school charged with training educators. In short, disoriented since my arrival in France, I have never been able to find any support around me ... I have never complained, since at the École Normale, grievances are frowned upon.[17]

Clearly distraught and unsure of whom to turn to, this student had eventually decided to express his grievances directly to the governor general of AOF, despite the potential risks that this step entailed.

As they sorted through the correspondence coming back from Aix, authorities in Dakar seem to have found little reason to question the accounts of school director Gleyze. As the first contingent of boursiers headed home, colonial officials were already expressing doubts about the fledgling scholarship program. The Government General moved almost immediately to revise the process by which boursiers were selected. An *arrêté* published in September 1923 stipulated that the three federal scholarships would no longer be awarded to students who had just graduated from Ponty. Rather, the scholarships would go to recent Ponty graduates who had already begun their teaching careers in AOF. Moreover, the new guidelines stipulated that candidates should have demonstrated not only their "aptitudes for the profession" but also their "exemplary conduct."[18] In the event, these modifications did relatively little to quell the colonial administration's growing hesitations about sending future schoolteachers to France.

Officials in France and French West Africa soon observed the itinerary of Tiémoko Garan Kouyaté, a student from French Soudan who had graduated from Ponty in 1921. Kouyaté went on to work for two years as a schoolteacher in Ivory Coast before receiving a scholarship to study at the normal school in Aix. Kouyaté's time in Aix has not been well accounted for: he never finished his studies there and seems to have been expelled in late 1924, as a result of his "hidden hostility toward the French administration."[19] What is clear is that Kouyaté stayed on in France throughout the interwar period, becoming a notorious activist in the small but growing communities of colonial migrants that could be found in France's larger cities. Kouyaté partially affiliated himself with the French Communist Party, before moving in other directions after 1933.[20] Itineraries like that of Kouyaté helped to solidify concerns among colonial officials that educational pilgrimages to France might lead to various kinds of activism and radicalization. By 1926 the inspector of education in AOF, Aristide Prat, could write that "the unfortunate case of the École normale d'Aix seems to prove that stints in France have a regrettable influence on our students."[21] Before colonial authorities in Dakar finally phased out the scholarship program during the mid to late 1920s, some twenty-three Ponty graduates had completed journeys to Aix.[22]

Officials in AOF had other reasons for opposing study trips to Aix. This scholarship program ran counter to the administration's traditional policy of cutting Africans off from metropolitan diplomas and the opportunities that these diplomas opened up. During the late nineteenth century and into the first years of the new century, certain Senegalese students had been able to obtain the brevet élémentaire, since the Colony of Senegal had established a diploma by that name in 1884.[23] This situation changed in 1907, when Senegal's administration abolished the brevet élémentaire. The following year Governor General Ponty signed an arrêté creating new diplomas for African teachers—diplomas that no longer bore metropolitan names.[24] A number of Senegalese schoolteachers who had managed to obtain the brevet élémentaire sought to join the European teaching cadre and thereby to secure the same salaries and benefits as French teachers. While most of these schoolteachers failed in their quest, and were soon integrated into the native teaching cadre, a few succeeded in joining these European ranks, where they clouded distinctions between colonizers and the colonized. However, as a result of successive rounds of reform, routes into the European cadre, which had always been tenuous, became increasingly improbable.[25]

For a short time it seemed as if the Aix scholarship program might reverse this trend. Most of the Senegalese boursiers who left for Aix in 1920 were in fact integrated into the European teaching cadre upon their return home. However, like other postwar openings, this one proved ephemeral. When subsequent cohorts of Senegalese boursiers returned from Aix, they were summarily incorporated into the native cadre, despite their metropolitan credentials.[26] One can reasonably assume that non-Senegalese boursiers received similar treatment upon returning to AOF. With the phasing out of the scholarship program during the mid to late 1920s, the chances of breaking into the European cadre seemed to become even more remote.

However, just as they were winding down the scholarship program, colonial authorities began to move forward with another experimental program, which promised to open up new routes toward metropolitan diplomas. As of 1928 authorities created a special section at the École William Ponty, so that select students could begin working toward the brevet élémentaire and eventually the brevet supérieur. This program owed much to Ponty's new director, Désiré Dupont, who came to the school determined to raise academic standards, which he found troublingly low. After seeing Ponty students successfully adapt to a more ambitious curriculum during the 1927–28 school year, Dupont proposed to go further, by formally establishing a *section du brevet*.[27] In his correspondence with the Government General, Dupont requested better trained metropolitan teachers, who would be more capable of preparing select Ponty students for the abovementioned metropolitan diplomas. Although Dupont's immediate priority was to assemble a cohort of students who would begin working toward the brevet élémentaire, the school director expected that many of these students would subsequently move on to the brevet supérieur. In his annual report, written at the end of his first year at Ponty, Dupont declared: "When students are able to prepare for the brevet supérieur, the École William Ponty will be a true normal school."[28] Apparently supportive of these plans, Governor General Carde proceeded to sign an arrêté calling for the creation of a section du brevet.[29] But while many French-educated Africans applauded these reforms, influential members of the colonial establishment looked on disapprovingly.[30]

In his efforts to introduce metropolitan diplomas at the École William Ponty, Dupont enjoyed the backing of Aristide Prat, who headed up the Government General's education department throughout most of the 1920s.[31] However, with Prat's death in 1929, views at the Government General quickly began to shift. Prat was succeeded by Albert Charton, whom we encountered in chapter 3. After being named as inspector general of education, Charton almost immediately expressed his opposition to Dupont's reforms.[32] In the end the recent reforms remained in place through the end of Carde's term as governor general. However, with the arrival of Brévié in Dakar in late 1930, the Government General quickly suspended the section du brevet, even though a number of students had been preparing for the brevet élémentaire for two years and were about to take the qualifying examination.[33]

During the early 1930s both Charton and Brévié would seek to put a definitive end to the reforms that Dupont had pursued. In a policy note that he prepared for the new governor general, Charton recapitulated his opposition to the recent reforms, explaining that "the institution and the preparation of metropolitan brevets in AOF, especially if accompanied—and it could scarcely be otherwise—by the transformation of the École William Ponty into an exact replica of a metropolitan normal school, calls into question the very spirit of our teaching. It is true reversal, a renunciation of the realistic and fruitful principle of adaptation, which inspired the successive curricula of 1904, 1914, and 1924. . . . Moreover, I myself firmly believe that the education provided at Ponty is not yet sufficiently adapted."[34] As we will see in the remainder of this chapter, the new leadership in Dakar did not just bury plans to bring metropolitan diplomas to the École William Ponty. During the early to mid-1930s Brévié, Charton, and other officials worked to take the federation's premier colonial school in a very different direction.

NEW ORIENTATIONS AT THE ÉCOLE WILLIAM PONTY

In colonial circles, criticism of the École William Ponty took a variety of forms and was hardly limited to the Aix-en-Provence scholarship program or the recent plans to introduce metropolitan diplomas. Many detractors continued to take issue with the school's location on Gorée Island.[35] As we observed in chapter 2, doubts about the suitability of this location had already been expressed during World War I, as political activism in the Four Communes crested to new levels. After taking over as governor general of AOF in 1923, Jules Carde ultimately sought to defend the school's location. During his first year in Dakar, Carde informed the various lieutenant governors: "As to schoolteachers, it is preferable, in spite of certain disadvantages, that their intellectual training take place in a large center such as Dakar where they are in contact with European civilization and where the economic activities of a large port provide them with a continual *leçon de choses*."[36] However, with Carde's departure in 1930, officials began to question the setting of the École William Ponty more freely.

In his 1931 report to the Intercolonial Conference on Education in the Colonies and Overseas Territories, André Davesne criticized many aspects of the École William Ponty, including the school's location. Addressing education officials from around the empire and a selection of foreign observers, Davesne bluntly declared that "it is not an exaggeration to say that *the minds of future schoolteachers are completely unsettled by the years that that they spend on Gorée. . . . If* they are sent *to a bush school, they feel like exiles*, having 'lost touch' with their homelands [*pays d'origine*]."[37] Davesne went on to lament that Ponty students did their practice teaching at Gorée's primary school, which catered to the island's relatively assimilated population and thus did not reflect the realities that schoolteachers would later encounter elsewhere in the federation. If Davesne and other officials worried about the influence of Gorée Island on the development of future schoolteachers, they fretted even more about the impact of neighboring Dakar. Over the years Gorée had become more tightly tethered to the booming federal capital, to the point that the commune of Dakar officially absorbed that of Gorée in 1929.[38]

While criticizing the setting of the École William Ponty, Davesne made it clear that the school also suffered from a range of other problems. Echoing well-worn complaints that extended at least as far back as far as World War I, Davesne claimed that the school plied its students with vast quantities of information, much of which was of little use in African villages, where most Ponty-trained schoolteachers went on to serve. Davesne contended that "excessive" book learning destabilized the minds of Ponty students: "They study too much and too quickly. They don't have the time to understand, to engage in a personal project, or even to learn their profession. They fill their memories right up to the breaking point."[39] What French West Africa needed, Davesne maintained, were schoolteachers devoid of intellectual pretensions, who would feel at home in rural communities. The inspector of primary education explained that "in African villages the schoolteacher must not be a professor who teaches up on a rostrum. Responsible for educating workers and peasants, he must, on occasion, know how to become a worker or peasant again. Practical subjects of all kinds—manual work, agriculture, hygiene—must make up a large part of his professional training." Stressing just how unassuming the African schoolteacher should be, Davesne added: "We will be very content if he has some common sense, a well organized mind that is not overloaded, and especially if he does not feel insulted when he is called upon to handle a pickax with his students."[40] As he imagined the future of the École William Ponty, Davesne looked sharply away from the reforms that Dupont had introduced during the late 1920s. As we will see, a range of other officials were also working to push the school in a very new direction.

During the early to mid-1930s the staff of the École William Ponty invented a series of pedagogical activities designed to mitigate the influences of Dakar by pulling students back toward the African interior. Alfred Dirand, the school's director for most of the 1930s, placed particular emphasis on research projects, which required students to focus in new ways on their home regions. It had always been standard practice for Ponty students to return home at the end of the school year, during the European summer months. Beginning in 1933 Ponty students who had just completed their second year were required to conduct research on a particular topic during their trips home. Upon returning to Gorée for their final year of training, students drew on the information they had gathered as they prepared written reports under the guidance of school officials.[41]

While students had a degree of choice when it came to the subjects of their research projects, officials also sought to impose clear parameters. At the end of 1933 Charton reported on the process that Ponty teachers had followed when they introduced research projects for the first time. The inspector general of education explained that "specific subjects relating to native life were proposed to students who could then choose. Here are the main native subjects: the agricultural year, the native diet, native fêtes, hunting, fishing, dwellings, [and] the rearing of farm animals."[42] Charton's comments reveal not only the orientation but also the clear limits of these projects, which were to focus on "native life" in particular regions. School officials insisted that students scrupulously avoid studies of life in towns, since one of the pedagogical goals of these projects was to redirect students' attention toward more traditional settings. School officials also prevented Ponty students from investigating larger geographical entities, such as entire colonies, or the Federation of French West Africa. Charton made it clear that "the subject had to be strictly limited in geographical terms."[43] The Government General had imposed similar constraints in 1931, when it established yearly prizes totaling three thousand francs to be awarded to the Africans who produced the best reports on specific regions of AOF. For this competition, topics could include local history, ethnology, folklore, local languages, local geography, and natural history.[44]

School officials hoped that research projects would require Ponty students to have sustained interactions with rural communities and local traditions. It was partly for this reason that officials discouraged the use of published sources. But while summoning Ponty students to explore and reaffirm their connections to their home regions, officials also hoped that students would learn to see local cultures through new eyes. Thanks to their French training, students were supposed to recognize not only the value but also the limits and imperfections of their native cultures. Charton contended that research projects would help "turn the gaze of our future schoolteachers toward the rational understanding of their native environment." He added that "in this sympathetic return to the realities of native life our schoolteachers will find respect for living traditions and an awareness of necessary transformations."[45] As these comments suggest, Charton and other colonial officials imagined a "re-rooting" of a very particular kind, designed to encourage both a "sympathetic return" and the internalization of a new critical distance.

Colonial officials hoped that these real and symbolic pilgrimages back home would counterbalance the other journeys that Ponty students had already undertaken. Students who made it as far as the École William Ponty had already piled up years of travels. The internal logic of the colonial school system funneled a trickle of students from regional schools, scattered across the federation, to higher primary schools, located in the administrative capitals of the various colonies. From there an even smaller trickle of students went on to study at the professional schools in Dakar and Gorée. As late as the 1930s, students' journeys to the federal capital could still require a week or two of travel, across vast distances, made even vaster by the state of the federation's roads. As Benedict Anderson has observed, the disparate itineraries of Ponty students all shared a defining feature: they eventually converged on Dakar. Anderson concludes that these analogous journeys led Ponty students to understand themselves within a broader "imagined community" that increasingly corresponded to the Federation of French West Africa.[46] But if Anderson is right to underscore the new "federal" outlook that took root at Ponty, he overlooks the other more localized identities that the school actively worked to foster, especially during the 1930s and World War II.

Throughout this period school officials consistently promoted a layering of identities. While encouraging Ponty students to imagine themselves within the broader community of French West Africa, school officials also pressed students to reaffirm their attachment to their home region and home colony. Normative notions of layered identities were never confined to the colonial sphere. François Chanet and Anne-Marie Thiesse have both underscored similar norms in their work on primary schools in France, particularly during the interwar period. Through circulars, official curricula, schoolbooks, and more informal advice, officials encouraged teachers and students alike to take an active interest in their *petites patries*, even as they deepened their attachment to their *grande patrie*.[47]

The layering and articulation of local and federal identities that was promoted at the École William Ponty can be seen rather clearly in the school's theatrical productions, which became a celebrated tradition during the 1930s. First launched during the 1932–33 school year, "Franco-African theater" soon generated considerable interest among education officials and students. During the first two years, productions took place at the school and only featured one theatrical troupe, made up of students from Dahomey.[48] In subsequent years Ponty students were divided up according to their colony of origin so as to form multiple theater troupes. Under the guidance of teachers, students developed artistic programs composed not only of plays but also of skits, songs, and dances. Although they were creations of the École William Ponty, programs were supposed to take inspiration from local history, legends, and folklore. More than anything else, education authorities hoped that Franco-African theater could be used to inflect the cultural position and outlook of young African elites.[49]

Much of the original inspiration for these productions came from

Charles Béart, who helped guide the reinvention of the École William Ponty during the second half of the 1930s and World War II. Béart had first experimented with school theater and locally inspired plays during his stint as director of the higher primary school in Bingerville (Ivory Coast) during the early 1930s. He brought these experiences with him when he came to teach at Ponty in 1935–36. Béart subsequently served for one year as the principal of the higher primary school in Saint-Louis before heading up Senegal's education department between 1937 and 1939. Thereafter he became director of the École William Ponty—a position he held throughout the war years.[50] Although he viewed theatrical productions as healthy entertainment, Béart expressed particular interest in the pedagogical uses of Franco-African theater. Like personal research projects, theatrical activities were seen as a way to rekindle students' connections to local cultural traditions. Béart contended that "nothing will do more to preserve in them the poetry of their homelands than native theater, with its music, its dances, its choruses." He added: "Tomorrow, as functionaries, they will gladly associate with their brothers back in the villages. They will study and work to restore the prestige of art forms that have been neglected for too long."[51] If the plays, skits, songs, and dances that students presented often contained distinct messages, the process by which these productions were developed was also intended to be deeply pedagogical.

During their trips home at the end of the school year, students were asked to transcribe traditional tales and songs in local African languages. Upon returning to Ponty, students worked to translate this material into French, the primary linguistic medium of Ponty's theatrical productions. Béart explained that "our students who ordinarily think in French, and only in French, were forced to go back to their maternal languages, to study them as they never had before, to penetrate the meaning of their words and proverbs, to find the French equivalents, the French images that come closest to capturing images in Mandinka, Agni, or Nago. It makes for an excellent lesson in French, but moreover, it is one of the rare times when French thought has been able to commingle closely with native thought."[52]

Although accuracy was sometimes valued, Béart and other officials also made it clear that productions were meant to breathe new life and expressive potential into local cultural traditions.[53]

On a thematic level, productions tended to navigate between a legendary African past, the colonial conquest, and the new Franco-African world that was taking shape. Plots often revolved around characters struggling to negotiate these transitions. Characters who remained in the sway of traditions that were particularly outdated were frequently held up for ridicule or scorn. A telling example can be found in the "Dahomean" play *Sokamé*, which came to occupy a prominent place in Ponty's theatrical repertoire. Tapping into European tropes about African primitivism, the play centered around a Dahomian village suffering from intense drought and impending famine. The play opens as this village is preparing to make an annual human sacrifice to the rain fetish, which takes the form of a snake. The girl who is about to be sacrificed (Sokamé) desperately turns to her young suitor, Egblamakou, for help. The two plan to run away, but while Egblamakou runs home to fetch his protective charm belt, Sokamé is apprehended and brought back to the village for the sacrificial ceremony. After visiting a local fortuneteller, Egblamakou decides that he must act. Returning to the village center, he rushes into the unfolding ceremony with a dagger and proceeds to sever the head of the fetish serpent. The chief fetishist and the crowd of villagers promptly call for Egblamakou to be put to death for the sacrilege he has just committed. But before any action can be taken, the sky opens up and rain begins to fall. As the villagers rejoice, the king pardons Egblamakou.[54]

Although plays and skits often underscored the need to update tradition, they also mocked Africans who spurned tradition altogether. This function was clearly on display in February 1935, when Ponty students performed for the first time at the Chamber of Commerce in downtown Dakar. The program consisted of two plays (one "from" Dahomey and one "from" Soudan) and four choirs (representing Senegal, Guinea, Dahomey, and Ivory Coast). The Government General's official news bulletin proceeded to publish a telling description of the skit put on by the choir from Ivory Coast. The bulletin noted that "in front of a chorus of young men and young women nicely draped in their pagnes [large sections of dyed cloth] appears a detribalized native [*un indigène affranchi*], decked out in European style. The ludicrous native [*le grotesque*] is intensely amused by his fellow creatures, who have remained themselves. They [the chorus] contemplate the déraciné with knowing looks and continue their beautiful song from Ivory Coast: 'Sawa-Sawa.' Little by little the ludicrous native becomes less sure of himself, and finally he gives in to the incantation and sings 'Sawa-Sawa' with the others." As the verbal violence of this description suggests, even choral performances often carried blunt messages. Making no attempt to mute his own views of African elites and the position they should occupy, the author of this summary—probably Béart himself—went on to praise Ponty teachers for making sure that students maintained "an interest in their race and their roots."[55] Colonial officials hoped that Franco-African theater could be used to plot out and reinforce cultural coordinates that would help keep young African elites at the juncture of European and African worlds. The messages embedded in plays and skits were directed not only toward Ponty students but also toward other French-speaking Africans, who might attend or hear about these end-of-the-year performances.[56]

Officials at the École William Ponty and at the Government General also hoped that Franco-African theater could be used to shape metropolitan perceptions. In July 1937 thirty Ponty students boarded a steamer bound for France and the Paris World's Fair. The following month the Ponty delegation gave two performances at the Théâtre des Champs-Élysées, where Josephine Baker had made her Paris début in 1925.[57] Noting the departure of these students, and the spectacles that this group would bring to the French capital, the Government General's official bulletin observed: "Thirty young blacks have left Dakar for Paris. Thirty young blacks who are among the most Europeanized, wearing school uniforms. Visitors to the fair will see them dressed in showy rags, pounding tom-toms, singing, jumping, and, like natural-born actors, bringing back to life legendary heroes and the life of the village but mocking half-civilized Africans [i.e., Africans who acted 'too European']. The performances they are going to present, which they have put together themselves, are intense, colorful, dizzying. It's the Africa of yesterday and today, by turns frenzied and sensible [*tour à tour endiablée et sage*]."[58] The author of this article went on praise the enlightened pedagogical work being carried out at Ponty, where the dissemination of French culture was now coupled with a new concern for preserving students' attachment to their own cultural and racial heritage. However, this author wondered whether audiences in Paris would fully grasp the school's balanced approach to the uplift of African elites: "Will they appreciate the merit of the educators who, while opening these young minds, not only kept them from spurning and rejecting their race but also succeeded in making them value and like it more?"[59]

Scholars have made conflicting claims about Ponty's theatrical productions and the context in which they were produced. Some have argued that the school maintained a liberal climate that allowed students to take charge of the creative process.[60] Others have described a more complex climate that offered a modicum of freedom, while also imposing, whether explicitly or implicitly, certain norms that school officials deemed important.[61] Still others have argued that school officials were the true creators of "Franco-African theater."[62] None of these accounts is entirely satisfactory. By virtue of its position at the apex of the colonial school system, the École William Ponty was heavily bound up in the structures and normative visions of the colonial state. Productions put on by Ponty students were written, rehearsed, and performed under the watchful supervision of school officials, who sought to frame Franco-African theater in specific ways.[63] In practice, however, the meanings of songs, skits, and plays proved more unstable than colonial officials imagined: performances created complex semiotic arenas where a profusion of signs circulated and where divergent meanings could be constructed. Ponty students frequently did find theatrical productions powerful, as did other African spectators. However, this power often derived from meanings that were unintended by colonial authorities.[64]

Colonial officials contended that personal research projects and theatrical activities were helping to lead the way toward a new

Franco-African culture, of which the École William Ponty would be something of a standard bearer. Convinced that new elites needed to maintain closer connections with local African societies, and greater distance from European lifestyles, officials worked to carefully map out an intermediate position. The administration presented Franco-African culture not as neatly defined object, but rather, as an ongoing project that Ponty officials, students, and graduates would continue to pursue. Governor General Brévié had begun to call for the development of a new Franco-African culture as early as 1932. That year, in his annual address to the Council of the Government General, Brévié asked: "Has the time not come to promote and institute here, among the colonials as well as among the educated and cultivated natives, a type of Franco-African culture?" Brévié went on to explain that "a true culture cannot be entirely imported; it must draw its force from the earth itself. To link native elites more and more tightly to French life and to make them aware of their African position, to interest them in their country [*pays*] and their region are not contradictory aims."[65] Convinced that the development of a Franco-African culture could help to resolve the cultural predicament of new African elites, Brévié presented cultural "in-betweenness" less as a passing stage than as a permanent condition, which needed to be more carefully mapped out.

As the inspector general of education in French West Africa, Charton sought to help define the relationship between French and African cultures. While urging students to devote new attention to their native cultures, Charton tried to make it clear that these cultures remained primitive and deficient and in need of French guidance. In 1932 he explained that "if one can speak in the sociological sense of African cultures, that is to say of complete social systems, in a state of static equilibrium, Black Africa does not have a veritable native civilization."[66] Two years later Charton further developed his ideas, when he declared that "the Black African peoples have not achieved a coherent and complete civilization; they cannot find within themselves the power to develop a true educational system." As a result of these supposed deficiencies, education and progress could only come from an outside civilizing force. The inspector general of education added that "the great contribution of colonization is precisely the joining of rudimentary civilizations to our universal civilization, which in taking on such a responsibility must justify its superiority and its authority."[67] Charton's remarks point up some of the deep ambiguities that resided in the educational and cultural policies of the 1930s. We can observe a growing willingness to recognize African cultures and even "civilizations," but only on the condition that the latter would continue to be defined in debilitating terms that justified French intervention and domination.[68]

Alfred Dirand, the director of the École William Ponty between 1931 and 1937, also saw the future in terms of an unequal coupling of French and African cultures. Describing the new priorities of his school in 1937, Dirand noted that "the general culture is French-inspired, but we want our students to remain Africans; we want their preoccupations to be oriented toward the native environment, which they need to study." The school director added that summer research projects, theatrical productions, and other innovations "attest that they [Ponty students] observe, study, analyze native life, that they remain in contact with their milieu, which they know well and appreciate; their efforts also prove their desire to link themselves to our civilization without turning their backs on their homeland [*pays*] and race."[69] It was ironic indeed that efforts to "re-root" elites in African societies were launched on Gorée Island, where the École William Ponty had been located ever since 1913. After all, Gorée stood out as one of the most urbanized and Europeanized corners of French West Africa. These incongruities were not lost on Dirand, Charton, and Brévié. By the mid-1930s these officials were beginning to make plans to relocate the École William Ponty to a rural site on the African mainland. As we will see in the next section, plans for the new school campus reveal much about the administration's shifting understandings of African schoolteachers and other young elites.

FROM GORÉE TO SÉBIKOTANE

By the mid-1930s officials at the Government General were moving forward with plans to relocate the École William Ponty to the village of Sébikotane, some forty kilometers outside Dakar. Planning and construction continued for several years, and the new site was not officially opened until January 1938. More than anything else, the Sébikotane campus was meant to signify a turning away from the Four Communes and a corresponding move toward the interior regions of French West Africa. Although not especially far from the federal capital, Sébikotane offered a distinctly rural setting. Whereas the premises of the École William Ponty had long been scaled to tiny Gorée, the new campus would soon sprawl over a full 250 hectares. Once completed, the school's grounds would include a large vegetable garden, a woodlot, an orchard, fields, a barnyard, herds of livestock, and artisanal workshops.

Addressing a group of educational policymakers at the Government General in late 1935, Charton sought to explain the rationale behind these new spaces: "Future schoolteachers cannot remain indifferent to manual work; they must be capable of organizing agricultural education at their school. To this end, Sébikotane will have its own agricultural station, complete with livestock, where education will be both practical and experimental. Our students will no longer be pure intellectuals, incapable of even the slightest amount of manual labor; they will have their own workshop and will know how to handle tools."[70] On a rather practical level, the school's agricultural station was seen as a way to prepare future schoolteachers for the roles that they would be expected to play at rural and regional schools, where agricultural activities and other *travaux pratiques* had taken on considerable importance. However, school officials also hoped that agricultural training would influence the habits and attitudes of Ponty students. Although they were especially concerned about the outlooks of future schoolteachers, officials also imagined that the agricultural station would have salutary effects on students in the school's administrative and medical sections.[71]

During Ponty's years on Gorée Island, agricultural activities had rarely if ever been entirely absent. But while school officials had tried to maintain a garden, endeavors of this sort had remained quite limited, partly because the school's mission had continued to be defined largely in academic terms, and partly because the diminutive, long-settled island of Gorée was particularly ill suited to agriculture. In his 1931 report on the school system in AOF, inspector of primary education André Davesne found it rather easy to ridicule the agricultural training provided at Ponty. Davesne observed that "practical agricultural training is provided in a minuscule garden where European vegetables are grown using water brought in from Dakar by tankers."[72] With its extensive agricultural station, the Sébikotane campus marked a shift toward more developed forms of agricultural training. This is not to say that Ponty students came to spend long hours doing routine farm work. As a school that trained African elites, Ponty differed from lower-level colonial schools, where agricultural chores often became quite onerous. In the end, outside laborers were brought in to perform many of the more physically arduous tasks on the Sébikotane campus.[73] More than anything else, the school's agricultural station was meant to shape the character and sensibilities of students, who were expected to evince a comfortable closeness to rural societies and pastoral preoccupations.

The remaking of the École William Ponty needs to be situated within the broader context of interwar educational reform, not only in the colonies but also in metropolitan France. As they set about reforming Ponty, colonial authorities drew inspiration from newer conceptions of *éducation*, sometimes referred to as *éducation nouvelle*. For many of those associated with this reform movement, the goal was to temper the traditional French emphasis on *instruction*, which implied the rather formal study of academic subjects. The term "éducation" was used to denote more holistic approaches to the development of children, which included not only academic learning but also such things as personal exploration and discovery, character formation, practical training, and physical education.[74] In a clear sign of the growing influence of these reformist currents, the Ministère de l'Instruction publique et des Beaux-Arts changed its name in 1932 to the Ministère de l'Éducation nationale. Notions of éducation were inherently open-ended, which meant that they could appeal to men and women across the political spectrum; in the end reformers associated with both the Popular Front and the Vichy Regime would take inspiration from these broadened conceptions of learning.[75]

From beginning of the twentieth century, colonial authorities had sought to avoid a narrow focus on academic instruction that would exclude such things as character formation and practical training. However, by the 1930s the Government General was clearly ready to move more fully toward broadened forms of éducation. Shifting perspectives could be seen in the Government General's publications: first founded in 1913, the *Bulletin de l'Enseignement de l'A.O.F.* was rebranded as *L'Éducation Africaine* in 1934. These general shifts in thinking shaped the course of reform at the École William Ponty. Through the introduction of research projects and Franco-African theater, colonial authorities sought to counterbalance academic lessons with personal activities that took students outside classrooms. Although these changes were already in evidence during Ponty's final years on Gorée Island, the move to Sébikotane soon allowed school officials to move much further in this direction.

Well before the new site opened, authorities at the Government General began to announce the long list of activities that would be organized at the new campus. Charton explained that in addition to providing training in agriculture and certain artisanal trades, the relocated school would also allow for "the intelligent organization of leisure activities," which would include such things as "troupes of musicians and artists organized according to regions, physical education and sports groups, a mutuelle agricole, [and] an arts and culture society." Charton went on to note that the creation of these new groups and structures would demonstrate that "the Sébikotane center is focused on the total training of its students, from an intellectual point of view, as well as from a physical, material, social, and moral point of view."[76] Although metropolitan normal schools also came to propose a broadened list of educational activities between the wars, the move away from academic instruction proceeded much further at the École William Ponty.[77] Normal schools in France remained part of a unified school system, governed by a powerful education ministry, which continued to ensure the integrity of national curricula and standards. In the more decentralized, illiberal context of the empire, local authorities could proceed with a much freer hand.

To more fully grasp the distance that now lay between metropolitan and colonial forms of teacher training, one also needs to look beyond the École William Ponty. Even after it had been remade, Ponty continued to be understood as an elite institution. During the Depression, officials at the Government General increasingly stressed the need to establish other teacher-training centers, which could produce a more modest kind of African schoolteacher. In 1935 Brévié issued a major circular in which he proposed new functional divisions among three distinct categories of schoolteachers. The governor general announced his intention to pull European schoolteachers out of classrooms, so that they could devote themselves almost entirely to supervisory tasks, as directors of regional and urban schools and as supervisors of surrounding rural schools. Only at more advanced schools, such as higher primary schools and the École William Ponty, would schoolteachers from France continue to be in charge of classrooms. The second category of teachers would be made up of Ponty graduates, who would serve as directors of rural schools, and as teachers at regional and urban schools. The third and final category was to be composed of peasant schoolteachers, who would be assigned to teach in rural schools.[78] Given that the federation's school system was expanding primarily at its base, Brévié saw the training of this last category of teachers as a particular priority. In 1934 Brévié declared to his administration that "the rural schoolteacher, of common extraction, trained right on the ground, kept and incorporated within the structures of native society, will play a leading role in the renewal of rural Africa."[79]

With this goal in mind, Brévié and Charton began to draw up plans for two écoles rurales normales (rural normal schools).[80] The first and most important of these training centers opened its doors in 1935, in Katibougou, a village in French Soudan, some sixty kilometers outside Bamako. Two years later officials inaugurated a second rural normal school in the village of Dabou, in southern Ivory Coast, about forty kilometers to the west of Abidjan. The Government General intended for there to be a functional division between the two schools: whereas

"Katibougou" was charged with training peasant schoolteachers for service in Sahelian and Sudanic regions of French West Africa, "Dabou" was expected to produce schoolteachers for heavily forested areas.

The Government General presented the founding of the École normale rurale de Katibougou as a crowning moment in the development of rural education. At the school's inauguration, Charton enthused: "With Katibougou, the new schools, rural schools are definitively established and consecrated."[81] Having embraced the rural school movement more energetically than other colonies, French Soudan was now rewarded with a teacher-training facility that recruited students from across the federation. Like the new Ponty campus being developed at Sébikotane, the Katibougou site encompassed an extensive tract of land, covering more than three hundred hectares and including vegetable gardens, tree nurseries, orchards, a school farm, and fallow parcels. By 1938 the farm at Katibougou already stretched out over thirty hectares, while the school's herd of cattle had grown to seventy head. And whereas hands-on agricultural training remained somewhat limited at Sébikotane, no such restraint was shown at Katibougou. Students devoted a full four hours a day to agricultural tasks, which left four or five hours a day for classroom lessons, and one hour for physical education and sports. However, at Katibougou even classroom lessons were meant to be concrete and practical—a continuation of what students learned on the school farm.

Explaining the educational philosophy that underpinned this new rural normal school, Assomption, the director of education in French Soudan, noted that "the sciences are studied in relationship to agriculture, livestock and hygiene. Mathematics are limited to knowledge necessary for an understanding of the principal operations of surveying, leveling and measuring land." During their fourth and final year students received nothing but agricultural training.[82] The entire curriculum was oriented toward the acquisition of skills that could be put to immediate use in peasant communities. Assomption emphasized that "rural teachers need to possess practical knowledge that is urgently important and immediately useful at schools and in school fields. . . . We will thus remove from the curriculum less essential subjects [*les matières 'de luxe'*] that are of no use in village schools; student teachers will not learn to learn, their studies will not be an end in and of themselves."[83] At the school's inauguration in 1935 Charton echoed these points, noting that "here more than elsewhere we must not fill up minds, but train and shape them. Moreover, we must not separate minds from arms, from the whole body."[84]

If colonial officials spent an inordinate amount of time and energy trying to reorient schoolteachers, it was largely because the latter were considered important agents of the future. As they fanned out, taking up their positions at schools around the federation, newly minted teachers brought with them habits, ideas, and visions of the future. Although they often had little evidence to go on, colonial officials worried almost constantly that Ponty-trained teachers were contesting French authority and privilege and imagining futures of their own. Through the reforms examined in this chapter, colonial officials sought to produce more modest schoolteachers who would remain grounded in African societies and cultures even as they learned to work in proximity to the French. Officials hoped that the reinvention and relocation of Ponty, along with the founding of rural normal schools, would help to push new cohorts of schoolteachers back toward the interior and away from the federation's expanding towns.

These efforts soon ran into considerable opposition. With the election of the Popular Front in April–May 1936, towns across French West Africa experienced a new effervescence. As we will see in chapter 5, Senegal's larger towns quickly became major focal points, as local populations worked to understand and exploit the possibilities of the Popular Front moment.

5

Léopold Sédar Senghor and the Popular Front

NEW POSSIBILITIES FOR REFORM

On the evening of 4 September 1937 Léopold Sédar Senghor strode before a crowd of some one thousand people who had come to hear him speak at the Chamber of Commerce in downtown Dakar. After studying in France for almost a decade, and earning several advanced degrees, Senghor had recently returned home to Senegal to assess the impacts and new possibilities of the Popular Front. Although this left-leaning coalition had been in power for over a year, relatively few colonial reforms had been passed. By the middle of 1937 Senegal's main towns were filled with broadening forms of activism, as local populations mobilized to demand bolder action. At this pivotal moment, when the future seemed as if it might be opening up in new ways, Senghor seized a rare opportunity to address his compatriots.

Many of those in attendance probably expected Senghor to wade into the protracted conflicts that had long opposed Senegal's originaires and the colonial administration. With the victory of the Popular Front, many originaires hoped that they would finally be able to consolidate their citizenship. Although they had been legally classified as French citizens ever since the passage of the second Blaise Diagne law in 1916, the originaires often found it difficult to practice their French rights. This was certainly the case when it came to education. With few exceptions, colonial authorities continued to direct the children of the originaires toward colonial schools, offering truncated courses of instruction, local diplomas, and sharply limited career prospects. When the Popular Front came to power, originaire politicians and notables renewed their longstanding demands for access to metropolitan schooling and an end to educational segregation in the Four Communes.

As it happened those who came to hear Senghor speak at the Chamber of Commerce did not hear a defense of the rights of the originaires or a critique of educational discrimination. Rather, Senghor used his speech to unveil the incipient Negritude movement that he and a group of diasporic black intellectuals had been developing in Paris. More than anything else, the founders of this movement sought to discredit the goal of cultural assimilation, so that young elites in the colonies would turn their attention to native cultures and their hidden potentials. Negritude had significant, but still largely unformulated, implications for schooling. Directing his remarks primarily to the African elites who had come to hear him speak, Senghor now sought to translate the Negritude movement to the field of education by calling for an autonomous educational system that would give new priority to African subjects, cultures, and languages. Senghor concluded his talk with a provocative charge. Quoting the black expatriate protagonist of a novel by the Jamaican writer Claude McKay, he declared: "Getting down to our native roots and building up from our own people ... is not savagery. It is culture."[1]

This chapter investigates the ways in which Senegalese elites— and especially Senghor—responded to real and perceived openings during the Popular Front period (1936–38). While the Popular Front's engagement with imperial reform has been the subject of a growing number of studies, less is known about indigenous responses to this heady moment.[2] No African elite engaged more directly and deeply with the Popular Front than did Senghor, who fully emerged as a public intellectual at precisely this time. And yet, scholars have not adequately examined Senghor's early activism within the context of this high-stakes moment.

Studies of Senghor's activism during the 1930s tend to foreground the imperial capital of Paris. Such a focus is understandable, given that the young Senegalese intellectual spent almost all of this decade in metropolitan France. However, once the Popular Front came to power, in the late spring of 1936, Senghor sought to bring the priorities of Negritude back to his home colony of Senegal. As we will see throughout this chapter, adapting the Negritude movement to the context of colonial Senegal was no straightforward endeavor. The literary critic Brent Edwards has illustrated some of the complex and uncertain ways in which black internationalism was "translated" as it migrated across the Atlantic world. As Edwards makes clear, this translation process created not only far-reaching exchanges but also significant gaps, or *décalages*. Edwards has urged scholars to examine the complex ways in which the translation process unfolded, rather than assuming connectedness and transmission.[3] As he tried to take his ideas from the metropole to the colonies, and from the level of theory to that of practice, Senghor was forced to grapple with the realities of the colonial situation and the limits of the Popular Front moment.

NEW OPENINGS: THE POPULAR FRONT AND COLONIAL REFORM

In France the legislative elections of April–May 1936 resulted in a sweeping victory for the left-leaning coalition of Socialists, Radical Socialists, and Communists that had come to be known as the Popular Front. Never, since the founding of the Third Republic, had the Left achieved such a commanding position in the Chamber of Deputies. Having won the most seats in the legislative elections, the Socialist Party (officially known as the Section française de l'internationale ouvrière, or SFIO) was charged with forming the new government. For the first time in its history the Socialist Party not only entered but also led a French government: Léon Blum became the new prime minister (*président du Conseil des ministres*), while Marius Moutet took over as minister of colonies.[4] As a well-known critic of colonial abuses and a longstanding member of the Ligue des droits de l'Homme, Moutet brought a reformist spirit to the Ministry of Colonies.[5] But upon taking office, neither Blum nor Moutet had drawn up anything resembling a roadmap for colonial reform. Although it had once included some of the harshest critics of French colonialism, the Socialist Party had moderated its positions by the interwar years, accepting the idea of empire even as it continued to inveigh against abuses overseas. By the time the Popular Front took power most Socialists had come to understand colonial reform as a process of gradual integration into the institutions of the Third Republic.[6]

Within the Popular Front coalition, Socialist leaders had to contend with both Communists and Radicals, who were poles apart when it came to colonial matters. Although the French Communist Party (PCF) had tempered its views upon joining the Popular Front, the anticolonial positions that the party had staked out in the 1920s and early 1930s had not been forgotten. Having distinguished itself during those years as the sole anticolonial party in France, the PCF was poorly positioned to shape colonial reform under the Popular Front. If the PCF now belonged to a governing coalition, Communists were still treated as dangerous outcasts in most colonial circles.[7] Unlike the Communists, the Radicals enjoyed broad representation in colonial milieus—indeed, no party was more closely connected to France's colonial establishment. This fact made it unlikely that the Radicals would throw their weight behind bold reforms overseas.[8] As a result of these internal tensions, the Popular Front government struggled to frame a coherent vision of colonial reform. And since the new government was immediately faced with a series of other crises— ranging from massive strike movements in France to the Spanish Civil War—reforming the empire often became a rather secondary concern. Scholars have generally concluded that the Popular Front raised high hopes among indigenous populations, while failing to implement meaningful and lasting reforms.

The parliamentary commission that was appointed to investigate conditions overseas and to recommend reforms has often been cited as a telling example of the Popular Front's dysfunction and inaction. Created in January 1937, this high-profile commission was composed of forty-two members, including five senators, eleven deputies, and an assortment of colonial officials, professors, writers, and journalists.[9] The commission was supposed to conduct its work in a systematic fashion over a period of eighteen months before submitting its recommendations. However, as the result of various delays, the group did not hold its first meeting until 8 July 1937.[10] By the time many of the investigating teams were finally ready to head overseas, the conservative French Senate had already cut off funding for such trips.[11] Protesting the Senate's obstructionism, the parliamentary commission collectively resigned in July 1938.[12] After garnering a great deal of publicity and generating huge amounts of documentation, the commission disbanded without making any official recommendations. Given this result it is rather easy to conclude, as most scholars have, that the parliamentary commission was a colossal failure.[13]

However, when viewed from another angle, this commission can appear more consequential. For a time it helped to sustain far-reaching conversations about the future of the empire. The commission's official mandate was to determine the "the needs and legitimate aspirations of the populations living in the colonies, protectorates and mandates."[14] As they took up their charge, members of the parliamentary commission consulted with the overseas colonial administrations, which eventually submitted reams of documentation. Taking a more unusual step, the commission also sought to obtain information through other channels. Although trips overseas were ultimately blocked, the commission did manage to reach out to various local constituencies. Among other things, the commission sent a form letter to registered political parties, trade unions, professional associations, and cultural groups, inviting them to express their "wishes, observations, suggestions, and general considerations."[15] No fewer than sixty-four groups were contacted in and around Dakar.[16] Realizing just how unprecedented this gesture was, many local groups responded by drafting what amounted to *cahiers de doléances*—catalogues of grievances. In many cases African constituencies had not waited for this official invitation to make their views known. After taking over as minister of colonies, Moutet almost immediately began to receive letters of support along with appeals for specific reforms. The same was true of Marcel de Coppet, after he was named as governor general of AOF during the summer of 1936.[17]

The sense of possibilities that accompanied the Popular Front could be seen in the new forms of associational life that sprang up in French West Africa. In the spring of 1937 the Popular Front government passed decrees authorizing the formation of trade unions and professional associations across the federation. Membership in trade unions remained rather restrictive, since only those who could read and write in French and produce a primary school certificate could join. Those who did not meet these requirements could become members of professional associations, whose legal status was less formalized.[18] Despite restrictions, de Coppet could report that as of November 1937, forty-two trade unions and sixteen professional associations had been founded in AOF.[19] Most of these groupings were located in Senegal's larger towns, where Western-style associational life already had deep roots. No fewer than thirty of the new trade unions were based in the city of Dakar. The numerous strikes that came to mark the Popular Front period followed similar patterns: of the fifty-five strikes that were recorded, forty-one took place in Dakar or elsewhere in Senegal.[20] Several historians have examined this surge in labor organization and strikes, along with the colonial administration's efforts to manage these events.[21]

Less attention has been given to the other types of associations that developed during the Popular Front period. Particularly important in the context of the present chapter are the thirty-one cultural, artistic, and sports associations that were founded between May 1936 and November 1937. The same period also saw the creation of nineteen mutual aid societies and eleven "assorted societies," which included a number of veterans groups.[22] As was the case with trade unions, many of these groups were based in Senegal. But if Senegalese towns acquired an exceptional dynamism, urban populations in other parts of French West Africa also experimented with new forms of associational life as they worked to collectively formulate their demands. Many of these demands had to do with schooling.

Although Senegal's urban elites had long criticized the educational

policies of the colonial administration, criticisms had become particularly pronounced during the first half of the 1930s, as colonial
authorities promoted more truncated forms of education and especially
rural schools. First developed in interior regions, rural schools soon
began to creep into more urban settings. By 1935 colonial authorities
were even announcing the opening of a rural school in the Médina
neighborhood of Dakar. Although this school included an academic
section, where select students could work toward the local primary
school certificate, the emphasis was clearly shifting toward agricultural
and vocational training. This new school included a large vegetable
garden of one and a half hectares, a modern chicken coop, and a
barn for dairy cows. Equipped with three workshops, the school also
provided training in carpentry, metalwork, and weaving.[23] By establishing a rural school in a quarter of Dakar, colonial officials hoped
to drive home the point that, even in the administrative capital of
AOF, African students needed to remain connected to manual work
and pastoral lifestyles, rather than imagining that they could live as
Europeans. As one might expect, many of Dakar's African residents
saw the opening of this rural school as a direct assault on their rights.[24]

With the victory of the Popular Front, the originaires mobilized in
new ways to beat back recent education reforms and to assert their
right to metropolitan schooling. The Association of Notables from
Saint-Louis summed up the views of many when it declared, in a
letter to Moutet, that "schooling, for which the Senegalese people
thirsts, has preoccupied all fathers for the last several years. Under the
pretext of adaptation, the curricula of our schools are deprived each
year of the very subjects that should be kept in order to maintain the
good French spirit that you can see in all of our elders. In spite of our
three centuries of loyalty ... we notice with regret that certain officials
still fear that widespread education would have harmful effects on
native society."[25] This petition went on to demand the introduction
of French curricula and metropolitan school certificates in the Four
Communes, along with the creation of scholarships so that certain
students could pursue more advanced studies in France.

Since the end of World War I, originaires elected to serve on

Senegal's Colonial Council—the successor to the General Council—had regularly invoked republican principles and the rights of citizens as they demanded metropolitan schooling for the populations of the Four Communes.[26] A motion approved by the Colonial Council in June 1935 declared that "the originaires of Senegal's assimilated communes are French citizens in every sense of the word," before going on to state that "the metropolitan curricula must be implemented in the schools of our assimilated communes as in those of the old French colonies." This motion drew attention to the fact that Senegal's schools remained under the authority of a colonial education inspector. After criticizing this state of affairs, the signatories demanded that the colony's schools be placed under the responsibility of a primary school inspector certified by the French Ministry of National Education.[27] Once the Popular Front had come to power, members of the Colonial Council continued to denounce reigning educational policies in Senegal, while demanding integrationist reforms.[28]

Similar demands were formulated by Lamine Guèye, the prominent originaire politician who presided over the founding the Senegalese Socialist Party in 1934. Campaigning in the spring of 1936, in his unsuccessful bid to replace Galandou Diouf as Senegal's representative in the French Chamber of Deputies, Guèye called for nothing less than the "the application of metropolitan school laws and curricula in the Four Communes."[29] Demands of this sort appeared frequently in the columns of originaire-run newspapers, such as Guèye's *L'AOF*, and the equally prominent *Le Périscope Africain*. Louis Martin, the *métis* editor in chief of the latter paper, wrote a string of articles denouncing the administration's handling of educational policy. In one of these columns, published soon after the victory of the Popular Front, Martin reiterated: "We have said and written many times that if we support the extension of primary education among the masses and the full development of professional training, we also consider it unacceptable to deprive the colony's elites of the means to pursue advanced studies that will open doors to prestigious careers in industry and administration as well as in the liberal professions." Martin noted that local elites were routinely cut off from more advanced studies by virtue of the fact that schools in the Four Communes continued to be organized differently from those in the metropole.[30]

Many originaires hoped that Popular Front officials would look more favorably on their demands. After all, integrationist reforms had long been associated with the republican Left. In an article titled "The Detractors of Education in the Colonies," one contributor to *Le Périscope Africain* blasted the educational reforms of the first half of the 1930s before noting, more optimistically, that "fortunately a new era is beginning and the torch of the Popular Front is coming to shed some light on our future."[31] In other urbanized corners of French West Africa, local elites also expressed similar hopes. This was particularly the case in coastal Dahomey, where the African-run paper *La Voix du Dahomey* published blunt critiques of the recent turn toward rural education, along with renewed calls for broadened educational opportunities.[32] Having briefly assessed the climate of Senegal's towns, I now shift to Paris and the beginnings of the Negritude movement.

NEGRITUDE: TOWARD A NEW CULTURAL ACTIVISM

Like urban elites in French West Africa, Léopold Sédar Senghor also sought to take advantage of the Popular Front moment. Since the fall of 1935 Senghor had been teaching French, Latin, and Greek at the Lycée Descartes in the French town of Tours. In his free time Senghor continued to pursue his own studies of Africa, through the disciplines of linguistics and ethnology. He also wrote poetry, in which he often recalled the lands, people, and traditions he had known as a child.[33] Senghor was active in a number of political and intellectual circles, both in Tours and in Paris. Nonetheless, it was not until the Popular Front period that he decided to fully assume the role of a public intellectual. Sensing that new possibilities were opening up, Senghor hoped that he might be able to help frame discussions of reform in French West Africa.

Senghor's thinking had been deeply informed by his unique educational trajectory. He had managed to bypass the "official" school system in French West Africa completely, by working his way up through several mission schools. When he finished his studies at the Collège-Séminaire Libermann in Dakar, in the spring of 1926, the school's director, Father Albert Lalouse, steered him toward a secular secondary school: the Cours secondaire de Dakar.[34] During the interwar period there were only two public secondary schools in AOF. Founded at the end of World War I and intended primarily for the European community in Senegal, the Cours secondaire de Dakar admitted a sprinkling of Senegalese students, most of whom hailed from the Four Communes.[35] Born outside the Four Communes to parents who were not originaires, Senghor was one of the rare "colonial subjects" to gain entry to this school. Although his route into this secondary school had been quite tenuous, Senghor quickly showed himself to be an exceptionally able student. In 1928 he earned his *baccalauréat* while also winning all the academic prizes awarded by the school that year. On the strength of these successes, Senghor received a half scholarship that allowed him to continue his studies in France.[36] By the late 1920s, scholarships of this sort had become rarities; despite his academic achievements, Senghor might not have been able to continue his education were it not for the determined interventions of Aristide Prat, who served both as director of the secondary school in Dakar and as inspector of education for French West Africa. Impressed by Senghor's academic talents, Prat apparently threatened to resign if this young prodigy did not receive a scholarship from the Government General.[37]

After making his way to Paris, Senghor entered the *classes préparatoires* of the prestigious Lycée Louis-le-Grand, where students prepared for the entrance exams of various *grandes écoles*. Senghor had his sights set on the École normale supérieure. But despite his sedulous work ethic, he failed in his two attempts to pass the entrance exam of this grande école. After these setbacks Senghor chose to study letters at the Sorbonne. At the same time he moved from the rather closed environment of the Lycée Louis-le-Grand to the newly opened Cité internationale universitaire on the southern side of Paris.[38] Within a few years he had completed a *license* and a *diplôme d'études supérieures* and was beginning to work toward a doctoral degree.[39] Along the way Senghor had also become the first black African to pass the prestigious *agrégation*, a competitive examination that served, among other things, to select elite secondary school teachers. As an *agrégé* Senghor was able to secure a teaching position at the Lycée Descartes in Tours. In the event the agrégation also had other important consequences for Senghor. Upon discovering that this competitive examination was only open to French citizens, he decided to apply for French citizenship, which he obtained in 1933, thanks in part to the timely interventions of Blaise Diagne.[40] Almost alone in his generation of African students, Senghor had managed to pursue a liberal, "classical" education at some of France's finest schools. At the time the few other African students who received public funding for studies in France were usually required, by the terms of their scholarships, to pursue technical degrees in fields such as veterinary medicine.[41]

In many ways Senghor's exceptional educational trajectory mirrored those of Aimé Césaire and Léon-Gontran Damas, whose studies took them from the Lycée Schoelcher, in Fort-de-France, Martinique, to Paris's institutions of higher learning.[42] As black students in the French capital, Senghor, Césaire, and Damas discovered a shared a sense of cultural displacement and alienation, along with a common longing for a cultural home. They also shared the experience of color prejudice, which helped to give rise to a heightened feeling of racial solidarity. In developing what would become known as the Negritude movement, Senghor, Césaire, and Damas drew attention to their cultural predicament and the ways in which it might be overcome.[43]

Scholars have convincingly shown how these three fathers of Negritude built on cultural themes and sensibilities that stretched back well into the 1920s. Moreover, it has become increasingly clear that several influential women also helped to lay the groundwork for Negritude.[44] The prehistory of the Negritude movement has often been traced through a series of ephemeral publications, such as *Les Continents* (1924), *La Voix des Nègres* (1927), *La Dépêche Africaine* (1928–32), and especially *La Revue du Monde Noir* (1931–32). In the first issue of *La Revue du Monde Noir*, the journal's editors declared that their goal was "to create among the Negroes of the entire world, regardless of nationality, an intellectual, and moral tie, which will permit them to better know each other[,] to love one another, to defend more effectively their collective interests and to glorify their race."[45] Related themes were later taken up and renewed in the first—and probably the only—issue of *L'Étudiant Noir*, which came out in March 1935. Historians and literary critics have often viewed *L'Étudiant Noir* as a sort of founding document of the new Negritude movement. Although its impact was actually less decisive, this ephemeral journal did mark something of a coming out for Senghor and Césaire.[46]

In their contributions to the inaugural issue of *L'Étudiant Noir*, Césaire and Senghor both sought to chart a course away from cultural assimilation by gesturing to a more authentic future that would allow the black peoples of the French empire to rediscover and reassert their distinctive selves. Seeking to discredit an older generation of West Indian elites who did not believe in their cultural and racial difference, Césaire declared: "That's why the African youth is turning its back on the tribe of the elders. The tribe of the elders says: 'assimilation,' we answer 'resurrection!'"[47] In his contribution to *L'Étudiant Noir* Senghor called, more mildly, for the development of "a cultural movement that has as its goal the black man, with Western reason and the black soul as research tools, for both reason and intuition are necessary."[48] Although Césaire, Senghor, Damas, and others were working to frame a distinct type of cultural activism, the term "Negritude" came into use more slowly and had hardly taken root by the time the Popular Front came to power.[49] Nonetheless, when he set off for Senegal, in the summer of 1937, Senghor clearly saw himself as the emissary of a new cultural movement.

A MOMENTOUS TRIP HOME

In 1937 Senghor agreed to take part in a colonial conference that was being organized as part of the Paris World's Fair: the International Conference on the Cultural Development of Colonial Peoples. Given how closely the subject of this conference dovetailed with Senghor's own interests and concerns, it is hardly surprising that he agreed to participate. The conference organizers asked Senghor to travel to Senegal to investigate the public controversies over schooling, which had recently reached something of a paroxysm. After completing his fact-finding mission, Senghor was to return to Paris in time to present his findings at the announced conference.

Senghor began to wade into controversies over education before he even set off for Senegal. In January 1937 he sent a provocative article, titled "Reflections on African Education: On Assimilation," to Senegal's largest paper, *Paris-Dakar*. Senghor began his article by noting just how contested educational policy had become in Senegal. From Paris, he observed that "schools have rarely generated so much interest in AOF, or rather so much emotion. The cause lies in the creation of rural schools." Stressing the broad implications of this controversy, Senghor went on to declare: "What is at stake is the future of the country [*pays*], which depends on what will be done with today's youth. Assimilation or non-assimilation, this seems to be the dilemma for many."[50]

At this point in his article Senghor began to unveil his own thinking about educational and cultural dilemmas and how they should be framed. He contended that the real choice was not between assimilation and non-assimilation but rather, between two different kinds of assimilation, one that was passive and objective and another that was active and personal. Senghor expressed his clear preference for the latter and noted that such a process was analogous to the digestion of foods: "assimilating a food means transforming it until it becomes one's flesh and blood; it means growing by absorbing foreign substances." Developing this physiological analogy, Senghor explained that civilizations, like human bodies, needed to draw on foreign substances in order to grow and prosper. He cautioned, however, that these foreign substances should enrich civilizations without altering their fundamental orientations: "One must advance along one's own trajectory and grow while remaining oneself." Making what would become a famous remark, Senghor insisted that "only one kind of assimilation is worthwhile, active assimilation. It's a matter of assimilating not being assimilated."

Having offered these general thoughts about cultures and their development, Senghor then went on to hint at what "active assimilation" might mean when it came to educational policy. He explained that "practically speaking, any kind of education worthy of its name must preserve the essence of African civilization which resides less in certain customs than in the Negro temperament or soul. French contributions must, above all, help it to blossom. But these contributions must be carefully chosen and tested. They must be healthy and fertile—not those old sterile routines, which, even in the Metropole, are a hindrance." Senghor had only begun his efforts to map Negritude onto the complex, bitterly contested terrain of educational policy. For the time being, he merely stated that education in AOF should have a distinct mission and that borrowings from the metropolitan school system should be intentional and selective, so as not to alienate Africans from their own cultural heritage. But despite the generality of his remarks, Senghor had clearly begun to distance himself from the views of the originaires and other urban elites.

Senghor knew all too well that the populations of Senegal's towns were intensely focused on their long-running political battles with the colonial administration and that schooling was a key component of these struggles. He was willing to support the originaires in their quest for full political assimilation. In his article in *Paris-Dakar*, Senghor remarked that "the democratic regime corresponds to the most elementary and most essential needs of justice. It can function normally even among less developed populations. Besides, Africans are not without experience when it comes to a certain form of democracy." But while offering passing support for full political rights in the Four Communes, and for the extension of political rights to other West African towns, Senghor indicated that his priorities lay elsewhere. He was convinced that the future also needed to be defined in cultural terms and that, when it came to field of culture, different solutions were required. By foregrounding cultural concerns, Senghor managed to see the colonial administration's recent education reforms as a step in the right direction. From Paris, Senghor went so far as to praise rural schools, for their supposed connectedness to the earthy cultures of French West Africa.[51]

When the steamship carrying Senghor docked in Dakar on 26 July

1937, most local residents knew little about this young poet-professor and even less about the budding Negritude movement. After being apprised of Senghor's arrival, Governor General de Coppet sent a note to the lieutenant governor of Senegal, requesting that he "kindly provide every facility to M. Senghor in order that he might complete his fact-finding trip in the best possible conditions (free transportation, access to schools, etc.)."[52] During his six-week visit, Senghor did not neglect his official mission. Touring around the colony, he conducted visits to schools and interviewed local education officials, teachers, and students. He also met with various associations and reviewed opinions that had been expressed in local newspapers.[53] On a more personal level Senghor spent time reacquainting himself with a colony that he had not seen since his last visit in 1932.[54] However, without a doubt, the high point of Senghor's trip came on 4 September, when he delivered his widely publicized talk in downtown Dakar.

The opening paragraphs of this chapter have already alluded to the publicity that Senghor's talk generated. Two days before he was scheduled to speak, Senghor met with the editors of *Paris-Dakar* to discuss the subjects that he would be taking up. The next day this newspaper ran an article that sought to reintroduce Senghor to local populations. The paper's readers were reminded of Senghor's many academic accomplishments and of his recently published comments on educational controversies. When asked by the editors of *Paris-Dakar* about the message that he would be delivering in his speech, Senghor responded: "I feel that the Franco-African cultural movement must and will succeed in spite of the imperfections that have marked its implementation. All we have to do is to educate public opinion better."[55] On the day of the talk a front-page article in *Paris-Dakar* reported that "for several days, all the native milieus have been talking about nothing but the talk that M. Léopold Sédar Senghor will give tonight, at 9 o'clock, at Dakar's Chamber of Commerce."[56] Both *Paris-Dakar* and the originaire-run paper *Le Périscope Africain* went on to publish Senghor's talk in its entirety.[57]

Prior to the Popular Front, young African intellectuals had not been invited to speak publicly at central nodes of the colonial state.

By helping to organize and publicize Senghor's speaking engagement, de Coppet self-consciously worked to signal the new times.[58] The day before the talk the governor general invited Senghor to a dinner that he was hosting at a local restaurant.[59] On the evening of his talk Senghor was picked up by de Coppet's personal limousine and driven the governor general's palace, where a dinner had been organized in his honor. All this build-up made a distinct impression on the inhabitants of Dakar, who were hardly used to seeing a young African receive such ceremonious treatment from colonial officials. After dinner Senghor finally made his way to the Chamber of Commerce. As he prepared to speak Senghor looked out on an audience of more than a thousand people, composed of colonial officials, businessmen, local politicians, notables, and students.[60]

Senghor directed his remarks primarily toward the young Africans who had turned out and to the others who would soon read or hear about his talk. He began by announcing that "my intention is not to convince you to adopt my point of view, but only to help you properly frame the cultural problem in AOF, the most serious problem of the moment, which we urgently need to resolve."[61] Many of the Africans in attendance probably found this claim surprising. For if the Popular Front period had been marked by a variety of contests—especially over politics, labor issues, and schooling—cultural issues had not been foregrounded. After announcing his purpose, Senghor proceeded to define culture as an active, creative force that resides inside different peoples and races: "It is imagination, active spirit, since, in the word, there is essentially the idea of a creative dynamism."[62] Senghor added that culture was also "a racial reaction of man to his environment." So as to temper the essentialism that this definition suggested, he added that "since environments, like races, are never immutable, culture becomes a perpetual striving toward a perfect equilibrium, a divine equilibrium." This was not a conventional definition of the word "culture," particularly in Senegal's major towns.[63]

Senghor's understanding of cultures had been partly shaped by the writings of the German ethnologist and archeologist Leo Frobenius, who belonged to a long line of German idealist thinkers that included Georg Wilhelm Friedrich Hegel. Both Frobenius and Hegel contended that independent forces or spirits helped to drive the development of peoples and history. But whereas Hegel had dismissed Africans, as immersed in a natural world and as bereft of cultural striving or accomplishment, Frobenius insisted that Africa was made up of larger cultural units with rich, if often overlooked, histories. Frobenius had been one of the first Europeans to readily invoke African "civilizations."[64] Frobenius's views contrasted with the very constrained understandings of African cultures and civilizations that colonial authorities promoted (see chapter 4).

By showing culture to be an active, immanent force residing in peoples and races, Senghor hoped to open up new ways of thinking about education and the very future of French West Africa. He spoke of cultures as animated subjects that should drive educational policies, noting that "education is the workman or the instrument of culture" and that "in a word, culture uses education to realize its ideal of man."[65] Having made all these broad prefatory statements about culture, Senghor was finally ready to outline his vision for the school system in French West Africa. He insisted that the first goal of schooling should be to root children in African cultures, values, and languages. Only after this process was well under way, he explained, should students be introduced to French academic subjects and the French language. Outlining the progression that should govern the entire school system, Senghor stated that "the study of West Africa and of France must constitute the two poles of education in AOF and this bipolarity, so to speak, will be found at every level. As students advance, the African pole will lose some of its attractive force to the French pole. What is important is to start from the local environment and from the Negro-African civilizations in which children are immersed. They must learn about these things and begin talking about them, first in their maternal languages, then in French. Little by little, they will broaden their horizons."[66] While accepting that French academic subjects, and the French language, would take on growing importance as students advanced, Senghor made it clear that even older students should remain actively engaged in the study of Africa.

In the context of the 1930s Senghor's view of African languages and their place in schools stood out as particularly novel and ambitious. He contended that African languages should be studied not only in primary schools but also at Senegal's two lycées. Professing his confidence in some of the more widely spoken West African languages, Senghor declared: "There are mother languages, dynamic languages, languages of conquest: Bambara, Hausa, Yoruba, Peul, Wolof." While insisting that they should be studied in their own right, Senghor also described West African languages as conduits to other fields of inquiry. Explaining how these languages should be taught, he noted: "And I mean, not only the grammar, but also the history, the geography, the folklore, and the civilization in general."[67]

Senghor emphasized not only the importance of teaching and studying African languages but also the new ways in which these languages needed to be used. While accepting that certain endeavors, and particularly work in scientific fields, could be pursued more effectively in French, he insisted that the mission of African intellectuals was also "to restore the truth and excellence of black values," and that this mission needed to be carried out at least partially in local languages. After proposing that African languages should be used "for the literary genres that best express the genius of the race: poetry, theatre, tales," Senghor asked, rhetorically: "How can one conceive of a native literature that is not written in a native language?" He then went on to explain:

> A black literature in French seems possible to me, it is true. Haiti has proved this; and other black literatures have been born, which have borrowed a European language: Negro-American, Negro-Spanish, Negro-Portuguese. To be completely frank, I would consider this a little premature. On the whole, our people is not yet capable of tasting all the beauties of French; and our writers would first need to be able to distinguish and use all the resources of the French language. Lastly, such a literature would not be able to express our entire soul. There is a certain flavor, a certain smell, a certain accent, a certain black tone that cannot be expressed through European instruments.[68]

These statements about the relative advantages of different languages surprised many of those who had come to hear Senghor speak.[69] After all, he had completed advanced studies in French, Latin, and Greek and had become—more than any of his contemporaries—a master of European languages.

While challenging the views of many urban Senegalese, Senghor's defense of African languages also clashed with the positions of the colonial administration. By the 1930s the ban on education in local languages was clearly breaking down in AOF. In chapter 3 we observed Governor General Brévié's support for education in local "idioms," when these seemed a more efficient means of reaching peasant populations. After being named governor general in 1936, de Coppet also proved receptive to the idea of delivering some basic education in local languages.[70] This new openness to the instructional uses of African languages led to several experiments on the ground. In the end language policies had been unsettled enough for the Ministry of Colonies to consider that new directives were necessary. In October 1938 this ministry eventually published a decree authorizing the use of local languages for practical education, while reasserting the principle that general education was to be provided exclusively in French.[71] Although increasing numbers of colonial officials were coming to accept that African "idioms" could have a certain practical utility, no French official came near to suggesting, as Senghor did, that major African languages could be of academic value in schools of all levels, as *langues de civilisation*.

For Senghor, the "cultural problem," along with its twin, the "educational problem," might be summed up as follows: How could Africans sustain and develop the most essential components of their racial and cultural make-up even as they adapted to a competitive, modern world that was increasingly marked by France's heavy embrace? Senghor proposed a complex response that involved cultivating the cultural and racial heritages of West African peoples, while also acquiring necessary European skills and knowledge that would help Africans to compete on new terrain. Summing up these tensions and challenges, Senghor declared that "we are now joined together [*solidaires*] with all five continents by bonds stronger than the cables that link us to them, [and] especially ... [to] France. We now share a common destiny and they will be formidable competitors for us in economic battles and in peaceful competitions. If we want to live we cannot overlook the need to adapt and to assimilate. Our milieu is no longer West African, it is also French, it is international; in sum, it is Afro-French."[72] Here Senghor offers an ambivalent view of the encroaching world that new African elites had to navigate. On the one hand, the future seems severely constrained, as a result of "bonds stronger than cables" and the movement toward a "common destiny." But on the other hand, Senghor suggests ways in which African elites could strategically position themselves so as to participate more fully in the shaping of the future. In preparing his talk at the Chamber of Commerce, Senghor's overriding objective was to push his compatriots to think more seriously about their deep cultural aspirations and how these might be formulated and pursued now that the Popular Front was in power.

While prodding African elites to imagine and engage the future in new ways, Senghor also took his ideas to other audiences. Upon returning to France his first priority was to prepare his interventions at the International Conference on the Cultural Development of Colonial Peoples, the conference that had sponsored his investigative trip to Senegal. Convened on 26 September, this three-day conference took place amid the bustle of the 1937 World's Fair, which stretched out along the western side of Paris. The French empire had been given a relatively prominent place at this fair. Erected along a man-made island in the middle of the Seine, just beneath the Eiffel Tower, the colorful pavilions of the "Overseas France Center" invited fairgoers to contemplate France's vast and variegated empire.[73] In this overdetermined context, Senghor worked to give voice to the new priorities of Negritude.

UNSETTLING AN IMPERIAL CONFERENCE

The International Conference on the Cultural Development of Colonial Peoples drew together leading ethnologists, prominent colonial officials, and a collection of missionaries and educators. Presiding over this gathering was Paul Rivet, who had emerged as a dominant figure in French ethnology. After helping to found the Institut d'ethnologie in 1925, Rivet had gone on to hold the anthropology chair at the Muséum national d'histoire naturelle and to direct the Musée d'ethnographie du Trocadéro. More recently Rivet had been appointed as director of the soon-to-open Musée de l'Homme.[74] The conference's secretary-general was Marcel Griaule, a well-known ethnologist who had already completed four research missions to Africa.[75] Other notable ethnologists in attendance included Henri Labouret, Maurice Leenhardt, Michel Leiris, Marcel Mauss, and Jacques Soustelle. The official representative of the Ministry of Colonies was none other than Albert Charton, who had become the ministry's chief advisor on educational matters. While most participants were French, other colonial powers had also dispatched small delegations.[76] In short, this conference brought together a host of prominent figures, who, by virtue of their professional reputations and institutional positions, could claim to speak authoritatively about indigenous peoples and cultures and how they should "evolve" or progress.

Organizers had established several goals for this conference. First, by gathering together many leading researchers, they hoped to produce a synthesis of the latest findings in "colonial ethnology." Second, the conference was to make a strong case for "the rights of ethnology to be heard and used by colonial authorities." Finally, the organizers wanted this gathering to provide a space for broader reflections and deliberations on "the means and ends of colonialism."[77] Although participants were actively invited to contemplate the futures of colonized peoples, papers and discussions were to be confined primarily to the spheres of culture and education. The very title of the conference served to bracket off political considerations.

A few representatives of colonized populations had found their way to this very "European" conference. The official *liste des congressistes* includes the name of only one African—Paul Hazoumé, a Dahomian schoolteacher and amateur ethnographer.[78] Senghor's name does not figure in the list of participants, even though he clearly attended the conference, where he delivered a paper titled "The Resistance of the Senegalese Bourgeoisie to Rural Schools."[79] Although he was not present at the conference, Fily-Dabo Sissoko submitted a report titled "Blacks and Culture," which was later included in the conference's published proceedings. A schoolteacher and canton chief from French Soudan, Sissoko had begun to play an active role in debates over cultural and educational policy in AOF.[80] In the end, however, it was Senghor who did the most to unsettle the International Conference on the Cultural Development of Colonial Peoples.[81]

Whereas Senghor had directed his talk at Dakar's Chamber of Commerce primarily toward African elites, his conference paper was clearly prepared with French officials in mind. Senghor tried to help those in attendance understand why Senegal's urban elites remained so strenuously opposed to rural schools. Temporarily muting his own disagreements with the originaires, the Senegalese professor suggested that the latter had some solid reasons for resisting rural schools. He noted that professional and political considerations led the originaires to favor metropolitan education and metropolitan diplomas, which offered greater guarantees and opened up broader opportunities. Senghor indicated that the originaires were not entirely wrong to see rural schools as a danger. To underscore this point, he quoted from several recent articles in the colonialist press, which called for deeper and deeper cuts to the academic curricula used in colonial schools, along with an ever-greater emphasis on vocational training.

While accurately reporting on what he had learned during his trip, Senghor also began to suggest some of the ways in which his own thinking differed from that of Senegal's urban elites. Whereas the latter foregrounded the political and professional implications of education, Senghor emphasized the importance of cultural considerations. He explained: "It is not surprising that our bourgeoisie doesn't understand the Franco-African cultural movement of which rural schools are one of the expressions. This movement has sprung from an entirely modern conception of culture, which consists in 'cultivating differences.'"[82] Senghor let his audience know that a small but influential nucleus of African elites did approve of the cultural and educational reorientation that had been carried out in AOF. He observed that this was "a small minority, it is true, but of high quality. They are young schoolteachers and university students fresh out of metropolitan universities."[83]

Senghor further developed and defended his personal views during the conference's discussion sessions. In a room full of Europeans, who had gathered to weigh the destinies of colonized peoples and cultures, he injected provocative new ideas. Although Senghor's remarks were not directly transcribed, one can trace their broad outlines in the summary report produced by Denis Blanche, a secondary school teacher in Guadeloupe, who served as conference's rapporteur. Reviewing the discussions that had taken place during the conference, Blanche noted that "one question was debated more than anything else, to the point that it dominated the conference's work."[84] This question had to do with the end goal of colonialism: What should ultimately result from the culture contact taking place in the colonies? If this question concerned all colonized peoples, Senghor's interventions helped to focus discussions on the "cultural destiny of the black race." Describing the controversy that had ensued, Blanche noted that "two arguments confronted each other: one which advocates respecting the native's culture, and one which advocates, on the contrary, the progressive assimilation of blacks to Westerners."[85]

Blanche then fleshed out these two competing viewpoints. In his profile of the anti-assimilationist camp, he distinguished several different strands of thought, before describing Senghor's position, which sparked the most debate:

> The notion that indigenous civilizations should be respected has become fairly popular. It is especially in vogue among certain admirers of "art nègre" and it sleeps in the hearts of certain friends of colonized peoples and certain sociologists who, in the interests of science, are sorry not to be able to meticulously preserve—fossilized as it were—indigenous civilizations. Many travelers consider that the world would be monotonous and boring if the same type of civilization reigned over all the continents. Others simply argue

that all types of civilization are of equal value; still others go so far as to think that Western civilization is inferior to some other civilization. These anti-assimilationist ideas were taken up and renewed with authority by a young professor of Senegalese origin, M. Senghor.[86]

Turning to the arguments that Senghor had put forward, Blanche noted that the Senegalese professor "questioned whether civilizing nations had the right—under the pretext of spreading civilization—to standardize humankind." Senghor spoke of the "fundamental originality," the "congenital aptitudes" and the "deep aspirations" of black Africans and argued that "to apply to them the mold of a civilization, which is made neither by them nor for them, for which they are not made, would be to commit an error of orientation, a veritable injustice, which would end up producing cultural half-breeds, covered with an unassimilated and inassimilable varnish." In making his arguments, Senghor evoked a "Negro-African civilization," which had its own independent existence and calling.[87]

Senghor's views ultimately presented such a challenge that the conference's organizers felt compelled to deliver something of a formal rebuttal. Blanche crafted this rebuttal in his summary of the conference's proceedings. The secondary school teacher roundly declared that "'Negro civilization' is an empty word. . . . The 'Negro race,' understood as an anthropological reality and as a collective author of a given civilization, is a myth."[88] What Blanche and others rejected most categorically was the notion of an independent, coherent "Negro-African civilization" possessing some kind of agency. Arrayed against Senghor were most of the conference's participants, who believed that European civilizations would have to serve as the central matrices of progress in Africa.

But if progress required the hitching of indigenous peoples to European civilizations, most of those present considered that this should be a gradual and lengthy process. As has been noted, one of the conference's central objectives was to establish ethnology more firmly as a colonial science that could guide the advancement of indigenous peoples and cultures. In this spirit, Paul Rivet could assert that "good colonization is not possible without good ethnology."[89] Summing up what he presented as the majority view, Blanche noted that all the facts seemed

to justify entirely the approaches of the ethnologist, who desires to study before they die those countless moribund civilizations, and who sees them die with so much regret when they might still be "useful." The excessive confidence of certain civilizers, who have not had any training in ethnology, condemns a little too hastily a host of tried and tested institutions that have stood the test of time, and which are, in any event, temporarily useful. To colonize is to civilize. Certainly, but the policy of the tabula rasa runs the risk of being needlessly vexing without being any more efficient. Proceeding blindly, it produces repeated misunderstandings that are often hurtful to natives. . . . It is perhaps unnecessary to reject native customs and techniques in their entirety. On the contrary, many things should be respected, if only to avoid a superfluous uprooting. For example, tolerance, rightly understood, dictates that we investigate, above all else, the moral and religious beliefs of each population, each tribe, and each clan. Otherwise, the colonizing process, which to be successful must entail collaboration, will be impeded, slowed, perhaps nullified by clumsiness, errors and misunderstandings, humiliations and mutual incomprehension.[90]

Such a vision of cultural development (*l'évolution culturelle*) could scarcely have been more different from that which Senghor proposed.

Blanche described the colonized world as a repository of isolated and fraying ethnic cultures, which colonial officials should selectively "use," and even partially preserve, as they tried to smooth out the eventual transition toward European civilization. In Blanche's telling, colonial officials and ethnologists were masters of the future, charged with preparing the way forward for dependent peoples. Colonized peoples and cultures were denied any agency. Adopting a radically different optic, Senghor invoked the inner potential and dynamism of African cultures, along with the broad reach of Negro-African civilization. For Senghor, African cultures and civilization functioned not only as deep wellsprings connecting Africans to their past but also as powerful forces that could be used to engage and orient the future.

Senghor's challenge to this conference went further still. Whereas French authorities cast Africans as subjects of colonial rule and ethnological research, Senghor spoke of African actors, who were ready to begin forging their own destinies, albeit with the help of France. This had been a core part of the message that Senghor had delivered in downtown Dakar. At the International Conference on the Cultural Development of Colonial Peoples, Senghor presented himself as a new kind of spokesman, who could help articulate the profound cultural aspirations of his compatriots. In adopting this posture he directly challenged the authority of colonial administrators and ethnologists, who were all too ready to speak for Africans. In proposing to serve as a spokesperson, Senghor could lay claim to several kinds of legitimacy. As graduate of the Sorbonne, who possessed several university degrees and a deep classical culture, he was steeped in the *culture légitime* of Third Republic France.[91] In addition to his studies of classical cultures and languages, and French letters, Senghor had also audited a number of university courses in ethnology and African linguistics, which allowed him to speak from—and to contest—the points of view of these disciplines.[92] French authorities might have tried to dismiss Senghor, as they often did other *évolués*—as denatured souls who could no longer speak for Africans.[93] But in Senghor's case, this proved more difficult, since he so obviously cultivated and displayed a deep, passionate attachment to African peoples and cultures. As a result of his advanced French education and outspoken defense of Africa's cultural resources, Senghor presented a new kind of challenge.

After the International Conference on the Cultural Development of Colonial Peoples had ended, Senghor continued to press his case in France. He forwarded a written copy of his report on educational controversies in Senegal to Henri Labouret, the colonial administrator and ethnologist who was heading up the parliamentary commission's investigation of the African colonies.[94] Senghor chose to give his paper a new conclusion, written specifically for the parliamentary commission. In less guarded language, he now added: "The conclusion? That it is important to first understand the resistance of the 'évolués,' which is natural; that it will take time and patience to instill in them a more human conception of culture; finally, that the best means of persuasion is still a liberal set of policies that rejects the old imperialist dream."[95]

In his response to Senghor, Labouret did not hesitate to denounce the "total incomprehension" of the originaires when it came to rural schools and their objectives. Labouret went on to write: "As you know, I, like you … consider that there is an African culture and that this culture must be preserved against the onslaught of Western civilization. I will make sure to pass this summary along to the rapporteur who is in charge of native aspirations. I'm sure that he too will find it striking." So as to encourage future collaboration, Labouret ended by noting: "Don't forget that this Commission is made up of men of good will, and that you can enlighten them. We are waiting for your enlightening collaboration [*nous attendons les lumières de votre collaboration*]. I hope that you won't deprive us of it."[96] As we will see in the final section of this chapter, Senghor did seek to serve as an unofficial advisor to key Popular Front officials.

REFORMING SCHOOLS DURING THE POPULAR FRONT

While cultivating ties with influential figures in metropolitan France, Senghor also tried to stay well connected with officials in Senegal. During his trip home he had been able to communicate at some length with Governor General de Coppet, who had proven to be a receptive interlocutor. Senghor had clearly influenced de Coppet's thinking. Addressing his administration in November 1937, the governor general paraphrased a number of Senghor's core ideas. After calling for the rapid development of education, de Coppet added:

> But in a way that will lead to the free blossoming of the black race, not to a narrow and sterile assimilation. I have too much confidence in the black race to think that its leaders must limit their ambitions to the servile imitation of our civilization. Why would

Blacks content themselves with imitating us? Why would they blindly follow the paths that we have taken? Why wouldn't they place their trust in their wonderful youth, in the inner strength of their race, and attempt, with the help of our science and our experience, to conceive and found a new civilization? They should strive to be creators, not imitators.[97]

It was quite unprecedented for a governor general to draw so freely and publicly on the thinking of an African intellectual. In fact, during their conversations in Dakar, de Coppet had been so impressed by Senghor that he apparently asked the Senegalese professor to serve in his administration, as inspector general of education. Although Senghor turned down this offer, he did agree to advise the governor general more informally on educational matters.[98]

Before returning to France Senghor promised de Coppet that he would draft a report summing up what he had learned during his investigations of Senegal's schools. Although he was delayed in completing this report, Senghor made it a point to send de Coppet regular updates. The governor general remained encouraging. In response to one of Senghor's letters, de Coppet wrote: "I thank you for not losing sight of the report on education in AOF that you promised me. You are not unaware of my interest in this question and I would be very happy receive an opinion as authoritative as yours." Responding to another of Senghor's letters, de Coppet noted: "Take all the time you need to successfully complete this report, which will be a great help—of that I'm convinced—to those who are currently looking into the reform of primary education in West Africa."[99] Senghor's twenty-two-page report finally arrived in Dakar in early 1938.

As a result of his first-hand investigations in Senegal, Senghor had tempered his early enthusiasm for the school reforms of the period 1930–36. In his report he expressed his continued support for the new school curricula, in which he claimed to find "a spirit of Afro-French humanism." However, regarding these curricula, Senghor immediately added: "I'm afraid, however, that they have been cut back excessively."[100] During his visits to schools in Senegal, Senghor had observed the effects of policies that encouraged the continued trimming of school subjects to make room for ever greater quantities of practical training. He noted: "We could only applaud when manual and agricultural activities were introduced at primary schools. But this was a slippery slope, and it is perhaps in this area that abuses have been most noticeable and harmful." To correct these abuses, Senghor insisted that rural schools should provide a minimum of four hours of general education per day and no more than three hours of manual activities. He warned: "One must not forget the age of the students; they must be spared work that is excessively difficult and deforming during a period of rapid growth." Unlike most French-educated Africans, Senghor continued to support the rural school model, as long as these limits were observed.

Senghor was also troubled by what he had seen at urban schools.[101] During the tenure of Governor General Brévié, officials in Dakar had pressured the colonies to begin "ruralizing" these schools by scaling back academic subjects and by introducing increasing amounts of agricultural and artisanal training. While allowing that students in larger African towns might usefully learn to tend a garden, or to make small repairs using common tools, Senghor stressed that urban schools should provide a full six hours of general education each day, with manual activities not exceeding an hour and a half. If Senghor was concerned by the "simplification" of academic curricula at urban schools, he was even more troubled by the "campaign against books." He observed that "books have been much criticized in AOF in recent years. What frightens me is that the leaders of dictatorships are also waging a campaign against books." Senghor generally approved of the schoolbooks he did see—most notably the readers that were used to teach African students French. By the 1930s colonial schools used schoolbooks such as those in the new "Mamadou and Bineta" series, which focused almost entirely on village life. Although Senghor found these manuals to be well suited to rural schools, he did not understand why the same books were being used in regional and urban schools. He emphasized to de Coppet that these schools required manuals of their own, featuring not only village life but also "the Afro-European life of towns." While finding readers to be in relatively good supply in Senegal's schools, Senghor was struck by the near absence of other kinds of schoolbooks. He informed de Coppet that "it's perhaps especially in history, geography and in math that a campaign has been waged against schoolbooks. I asked to see the history text that is used in AOF; in vain."

But even as he took stock of the many ways in which academic subjects had been pruned at colonial schools, Senghor did not join Senegal's urban elites in calling for an alignment with metropolitan practices and standards. Rather, in his long report to de Coppet, he dismissed the "grousing" (*criailleries*) of Senegalese elites, noting that "most natives have a mistaken understanding of culture." Senghor insisted that with the right mix of policies, and the requisite amount of good faith on the part of the colonial administration, the schools of AOF could maintain their own orientation without compromising academic standards.

Like Senghor, Governor General de Coppet slowly pieced together a more accurate picture of colonial schools. After touring French Soudan in early 1938, and visiting a number of rural schools along his way, de Coppet returned to Dakar utterly disabused. In a note to the inspector general of education, he observed that this unappealing and physically arduous type of schooling had done nothing to improve village life or to make students want to become farmers. More than anything else, de Coppet had been struck by the oppressive atmosphere that hung over rural schools. He remarked that "this education has scarcely won the approval of local populations, upon which its success depends; the great majority of students endure it, against the will of their families, whose consent was obtained by coercion." After relating all these discoveries, de Coppet concluded: "I don't think I'm exaggerating when I write that rural schools . . . have failed and backfired. The matter needs to be completely rethought."[102] When it came to rural schools, de Coppet ultimately arrived at a position that was considerably more critical than that of Senghor.

However, de Coppet did not reach these conclusions until the spring of 1938, by which time the Popular Front was in rapid decline.

De Coppet's star was already falling when he left for France—in mid-July—for what was supposed to be a seven-month leave.[103] After scarcely more than a month in France, the governor general was instructed to return to Dakar, to resolve a railway strike that was gripping Senegal. However, as he returned to Dakar, de Coppet's standing continued to decline. For many colonial officials the railway strikes were further proof that de Coppet had allowed disorder to reign in French West Africa.[104] On 17 October the governor general set off again for France, ostensibly to resume the leave that he had had to cut short the previous summer. In reality officials in Paris were already moving to put a more definitive end to the Popular Front moment in French West Africa.[105]

The appointment of Pierre Boisson as interim governor general of AOF signaled a clear tightening of the colonial system. A similar rightward shift had already occurred in Paris, where Georges Mandel had succeeded Moutet as minister of colonies. Mandel quickly made it clear that there would be no rethinking of educational policies in AOF. Indeed, as the prospect of another European war grew more likely, Mandel sought to make colonial schooling even more "practical" in nature. In a November 1938 circular to the various governors general, Mandel emphasized: "In my instructions concerning economic development [*la mise en valeur*], I directed you, as to the education provided to the masses, to accentuate its professional, practical, agricultural, and artisanal character. Today, I want to further elaborate on these instructions and highlight the need to link education closely to the immediate and in-depth economic development of our overseas lands."[106] Mandel sought to put a quick end to criticisms of education policies in AOF. In a March 1939 letter to Boisson, the minister of colonies noted: "You have reported that opposition to rural schools has been voiced in certain regions. It is important to stress first that the academic institutions founded in French West Africa are firmly established; their principles and orientation cannot be put up for discussion." Seeking to reassure Mandel, Boisson promptly wrote back: "I will be careful to make sure that no doubts remain in this area."[107]

Scholars have offered different interpretations of Senghor's activism during the second half of the 1930s. Critics such as Guy Ossito Midiohouan and Christopher Miller have described Senghor's stance as essentializing, nostalgic, and accepting of the colonial order. Miller goes so far as to qualify Senghor's position as one of "comfortable accommodationism," which was "infinitely less hostile to French power" than the more politicized activities of his "proletarian precursors"—activists such as Lamine Senghor and Tiémoko Garan Kouyaté, who developed a radical critique of colonialism as of the 1920s.[108] But although Senghor sought to reform and not condemn the colonial order, his activism during the Popular Front period was hardly "comfortable." As the present chapter has shown, Senghor worked to spread a bold set of new ideas about education, culture, agency, and progress—ideas that challenged the positions of colonial officials and most French-educated Africans.

Other scholars have highlighted the ambiguities of Senghor's activism. The historian Gary Wilder concludes that Senghor and other figures associated with early Negritude remained enmeshed in colonial positions, even as they sought to rework them and reach beyond them.[109] Such a view captures important features of Senghor's engagement with cultural and educational reform during the mid to late 1930s. As we have seen in this chapter, the Senegalese professor found much that he could support in the new "Franco-African" orientation of colonial schools, even as he sought to help correct errors or abuses that he had observed during his tour of schools in Senegal, and even as he proposed more ambitious approaches to the teaching of African languages, cultures, and history. But whereas Wilder sees the activism of Senghor (and Césaire and Damas) largely as a response to interwar colonial reformism, broadly defined, I have sought to highlight the crucial importance of the Popular Front period. More than anything else, it was the real and perceived openings of this heady period that prompted Senghor to throw himself into new roles, as a public intellectual, determined to shape understandings of cultures, education, and the future.

In the end the openings of the Popular Front proved more limited and short-lived than Senghor and others had imagined. But although Senghor's activism ultimately had a very modest impact on cultural and educational policies in French West Africa, his calls continued to resonate, even after the Popular Front period had passed. As we will see in chapter 6, the ideas that Senghor brought to Senegal in 1937 helped to touch off broad debates, which played out in the very different context of World War II.

6

The National Revolution in AOF

DEBATING THE FUTURE DURING THE WAR YEARS

France's sudden military defeat to Nazi Germany and the signing of the armistice on 22 June 1940 opened up a deeply unsettled period in French West Africa. By July high officials in Dakar had rallied to the side of Marshal Philippe Pétain and the arch-conservative regime that was being assembled in the unoccupied portion of France. This alignment, which lasted for two and a half years, would have far-reaching consequences for AOF. It was long assumed that the Vichy regime's ideological program to purify and refound the French nation—the "National Revolution"—was intended for the metropolitan French, with little concern for the populations of the empire. Overturning this view, a series of more recent studies have highlighted the extent to which Vichy policies and propaganda were exported and adapted to imperial settings.[1] During the first years of the war many colonial administrators proved quite receptive to discourses and policies emanating from Vichy France. The same was true of many Europeans residing in the empire. But while historians have come to better understand the ways in which Europeans in the colonies appropriated Vichy's agenda, we still know far less about indigenous responses to the troubled, ideologically charged wartime period.

In many parts of the empire the Vichy period produced an expanded focus on indigenous youths, particularly those who had attended colonial schools. Although these populations had long produced anxieties in colonial circles, such sentiments intensified amid the uncertainties and rivalries of the war. Authorities in AOF often did not know how young African elites understood France's military defeat, the creation of Pétain's government, and the official alignment of AOF with Vichy France. Some fretted that the spectacle of a defeated, partially occupied France might embolden Africans and give rise to anti-French movements. After French Equatorial Africa (AEF) and French Cameroon aligned themselves with General Charles de Gaulle and the Free French at the end of August 1940, authorities in AOF also had to contend with the very real possibility that Africans might be receptive to Gaullist appeals. Questions of allegiance remained complex, as France's two African federations began a protracted face off and launched an escalating propaganda war.[2] The situation in AOF was further complicated by the proximity of Britain's West African colonies. Although French forces based in Dakar successfully repelled a British-led invasion in September 1940, local authorities remained concerned, not only about the possibility of future military incursions but also about Allied propaganda efforts. With so many allegiances and ideological options available, authorities in Dakar found compelling reasons to develop new programs of *encadrement* and indoctrination for African youths.

The present chapter explores the weekly publication *Dakar-Jeunes*, which was supposed to serve as a major conduit for National Revolution propaganda. Founded at the beginning of 1942, this new paper primarily targeted the *jeunesse évoluée*—graduates of AOF's more advanced schools who were proficient in French and often employed by the colonial state. Although *Dakar-Jeunes* was meant to function largely as a conveyor belt for Vichy's ideology, the paper became the center point of a broad debate after its editors asked African readers to express their opinions on cultural advancement and what it should mean in French West Africa. Each week the paper published an article presenting a particular point of view. At a time when public discussions of politics and the ongoing war remained heavily censored or banned altogether, the pages of *Dakar-Jeunes* became an unexpected forum for vigorous debate. Although ostensibly focused on cultural questions, this forum soon took on broader meanings, as African contributors and readers worked to collectively imagine and contest the postwar future.[3] Before turning to these contests, this chapter begins by providing a fuller backdrop to the war years in French West Africa.

THE ADMINISTRATION OF PIERRE BOISSON

During the critical weeks following France's military defeat, Pierre Boisson emerged as a pivotal figure. As part of its bid to gain control of the African colonies, the government taking shape around Marshal Pétain appointed Boisson as high commissioner of French Africa on 25 June 1940.[4] Although this newly created position was supposed to give Boisson authority over French West Africa, French Equatorial Africa, and the French mandates of Togo and Cameroon, events on the ground soon decided otherwise. As a result of the "defections" of AEF and Cameroon, Boisson's authority was soon limited to AOF and French Togo. If Boisson succeeded in consolidating his control over AOF, it was partly because he remained a well-known figure there. After being promoted in 1933 to the rank of *gouverneur des colonies*, Boisson was assigned to the Government General in Dakar, where he served as second in command in the administration of Jules Brévié. Boisson remained in this post until late 1936, when the first Popular Front government appointed him as the new commissioner of French Cameroon. Two years later Boisson returned to Dakar to serve as interim governor general of French West Africa, after de Coppet's departure. At that time Boisson's arrival in Dakar was interpreted as a clear end to the Popular Front period in AOF. Boisson then went on to hold the post of governor general of AEF briefly, before returning to Dakar in the summer of 1940 to serve as Vichy's most senior representative.[5]

Given the rather uncertain context that continued to reign in French West Africa, officials in Vichy and Dakar quickly began to mount new propaganda efforts. Writing in late August 1940, one official in

Vichy's Colonial Ministry noted not only the importance of official propaganda but also the new direction in which propaganda had begun to flow. This official explained that "the present situation, as paradoxical as it might seem, has forced the Ministry of Colonies to alter its propaganda and news services entirely. Whereas the latter were, until these last months, almost exclusively oriented from the colonies toward France, meaning that they targeted the metropolitan population, circumstances now require France to direct its propaganda and news efforts toward the colonies."[6] Whereas colonial propaganda had traditionally meant "selling" the empire to the metropolitan French, it now entailed defending Vichy France within a disoriented and fractious empire. Officials in Vichy hoped that by projecting the National Revolution abroad they would be able to firm up the loyalties of local populations. As we will see, however, transferring Vichy's ideology to French West Africa quickly proved to be an uncertain endeavor.

Certain aspects of the National Revolution could be rather easily adapted to the West African colonies. This was particularly true of Vichy's efforts to reassert forms of authority that were rooted in patriarchy, family, and tradition. In August 1940 Vichy's first colonial minister, Henry Lémery, issued directives concerning the "native policy" that was to be adopted in AOF. In a telegram to Boisson, Lémery warned that traditional authorities had "suffered a serious blow as a result [of the] rapid and disorganized evolution of youths, hungry for freedom and independence." Lémery went on to explain that "the fragile structures of native society have been weakened and [that the] grievances of notables all stress that traditions tend no longer to be respected, or to disappear altogether."[7] Vichy's colonial minister proceeded to outline a series of measures that could be used to counter these "erring ways" and to tighten French control over subject populations.

Boisson responded with a November 1940 circular, specifying the steps that local administrations should take to reinforce traditional authorities and tradition itself. In this detailed circular Boisson explicitly endorsed an entire corpus of interwar reforms that had been designed to shore up traditional frameworks. Insisting that such measures should now be pursued more vigorously, the high commissioner gave a very free hand to local colonial administrators and the African chiefs and notables with whom they collaborated.[8] By giving broadened prerogatives to these local agents, Boisson helped to accentuate authoritarian strains within the colonial state. In the end African populations often experienced the wartime "return toward tradition" as a move toward more despotic forms of colonial rule.[9]

The Vichy regime's enthusiasm for peasants, the soil, and "rootedness" could also be extended rather easily to French West Africa. As has been amply shown in previous chapters, the colonial administration had promoted these same priorities throughout the 1930s. Boisson was uttering familiar words when he declared, in 1941, that "Africa is a world of peasants [*l'Afrique est paysanne*]. She must, in her necessary development, remain a world of peasants. In the metropole we are attempting—with such good reason—to promote a return to the soil. Let's make sure not to promote the desertion of villages here."[10] In the new wartime context, colonial officials would seek to push peasantist visions and policies even further. In his November 1940 circular Boisson urged officials to "use disciplinary measures to combat desertions from villages," while underscoring "the crucial need to relieve the congestion of urban centers." The high commissioner recommended that officials make fuller use of existing powers, such as those granted by a 1923 decree designed to curb vagrancy, or those established by a 1928 decree restricting the travels of "natives." Boisson went on to spell out other methods that could be used to send unemployed migrants back to their villages and to ensure that they stayed there.[11]

While promoting peasantist visions of AOF, authorities in Dakar also devoted new attention to French-educated elites clustered in and around urban centers. Boisson was convinced that the administration had not done enough to structure the lives and secure the allegiances of these young Africans. In a circular drafted in August 1941 the high commissioner urged the various colonies to develop a more concerted approach to the jeunesse évoluée. Most of the recommendations contained in this circular were not new. During his stint as interim governor general of AOF on the eve of the war, Boisson had already drawn attention to the unsettled position of French-educated youths. Writing in April 1939 Boisson had warned the governors of the "dangerous isolation" of school graduates, who often lived outside the structures of traditional African societies but were rarely accepted by the European populations of AOF's towns. Boisson instructed local officials to build connections to French-educated African youths, "in order to keep them from coming under the hold of outside solicitations of all kinds, which might exploit their disappointments and resentments and deceptively orient their most legitimate aspirations toward hostile demands that would soon be transposed to a political or racial plane."[12]

While calling for a certain rapprochement between the jeunesse évoluée and European communities, Boisson's April 1939 circular made it clear that these efforts should not entail anything resembling assimilation. Struggling to define what rapprochement should mean in the race-conscious climate of the late 1930s, Boisson ended up suggesting that French-educated Africans needed to acquire some of the deeper moral traits of the French people: "What we seek is not for cultivated natives to join our own society definitively, but rather for them to have a favorable bias, which pushes them, while remaining faithful to their milieu, to draw near to the only sources from which they can acquire and assimilate that essential foundation of our civilization which resides less in formulas and ideas than in deep, slowly accumulated tendencies, in moral reflexes that are in a way atavistic, in a collection of moral traditions and intimately felt scruples [which are] difficult to define and even more difficult to inculcate."[13] Among other things, these tortuous recommendations show just how far key colonial officials had moved toward ethnic and racial understandings of Frenchness by the end of the interwar period.[14]

Boisson's April 1939 circular went on to present sports fields as ideal places for interracial contacts: "It is there that differences of intelligence and origin can subside, to make room for a reciprocal esteem and a voluntary spirit of order and discipline which grows out of competition and physical exercise." However, for Boisson, curbing the isolation of the jeunesse évoluée required more than broader contact with European communities. The high commissioner explained that young African elites also needed to organize themselves through the creation of a whole range of associations, which could be supported and monitored by colonial authorities. Boisson instructed the governors: "We must initiate a vast movement organized not only around sports associations, but also around cultural and artistic associations, clubs, libraries, foyers, etc."[15] All these directives were formulated in the spring of 1939, to ensure that French-educated Africans would remain disciplined and loyal as the nation and the empire prepared for another war in Europe. As it turned out local authorities hardly had time to implement these directives before war erupted. However, after the administration in AOF rallied to Vichy France, these same initiatives would be taken up more systematically.

In his August 1941 circular regarding the jeunesse évoluée, Boisson rehashed his directives from the spring of 1939. Far from seeking to mask these continuities, the high commissioner declared: "You must thus pursue the course that I suggested in 1939, namely, encouraging, as I requested you to do, occasions for contact between the two races." Boisson stressed once again the importance of sports, which had been receiving unprecedented attention ever since French West Africa had joined forces with Vichy France.[16] Boisson then instructed the colonies to "give substance to the plans, which I proposed to you in 1939, to create through and for the jeunesse évoluée a movement of cultural and artistic associations, libraries, clubs—a movement carefully supported and guided by the local administrations. You should inform me by the end of the year of actions you have taken in this area."[17]

As the wartime administration promoted new associations, it turned away from some older types of organization. Changes proved particularly striking in Senegal's Four Communes, where elective political bodies were dissolved and where local authority was henceforth concentrated in the hands of appointees. At the same time, political parties and trade unions ceased to function.[18] In Senegal's old towns and in larger population centers around the federation, the Légion française des combattants eventually became a particularly striking symbol of the new times. Led by veterans, the Legion cast itself as a vanguard for Pétain's regime, both in metropolitan France and in the empire. A federal Legion structure was founded in AOF in February 1941, and thereafter local sections were set up in the various colonies. The Legion took on considerable importance in Senegal's towns, which were home to sizeable European populations. By the spring of 1942 the Senegalese section could claim over ten thousand members, including a large percentage of the colony's European population and an untold number of Senegalese.[19] From its inception the Legion devoted significant energy to Vichy-themed pageantry. By 1942 certain colonial officials were proposing to give the Legion and its leaders a more prominent place in local power structures.

The Legion's more radical elements eventually came together to form the Service d'ordre légionnaire—squads of uniformed men who paraded around towns, heralding the new order and denouncing its enemies. In March 1942 Georges Rey, the very Pétainist governor of Senegal, sent a telegram to the colony's administrators, in which he went so far as to declare: "In a word, [you] must gradually turn over all [the] levers of power to legionnaires with a view to increasingly imbuing the masses with [the] ideas [of the] National Revolution."[20] In the end Rey's instructions were not carried out. Most colonial officials supported the Legion as long as it remained under the administration's wing. When the Legion showed signs of becoming an autonomous force, many officials became disabused. Clearly worried that Rey was sowing dangerous controversy, Boisson ended up writing the governor of Senegal to insist on a somewhat more limited vision of the National Revolution.[21]

As they worked to establish ideological orientations for French West Africa, authorities in Boisson's administration struggled with more than just competing understandings of the National Revolution. They also had trouble agreeing on what the new order should mean when it came to relations between Africans and Europeans. Just as Boisson himself was recommending new support structures for the jeunesse évoluée and a certain rapprochement between these elites and European communities, towns around AOF were experiencing a surge of antiblack racism. In Senegalese towns, populations now encountered racially segregated train cars and beaches and separate lines for rationed goods.[22] Verbal assaults on Africans eventually reached such levels that Boisson felt compelled to intervene. In a June 1941 circular the high commissioner stressed to the governors that racism was not the official policy of the Haut-Commissariat and that racist slurs would no longer be tolerated.[23] It is unclear whether Boisson's directives had a noticeable effect on the behavior of Europeans; many Africans would ultimately remember the war years as a time of open racism.[24]

YOUTH OF FRENCH BLACK AFRICA, THE DEBATE HAS BEGUN

It was in this general context that *Dakar-Jeunes* was founded, at the beginning of 1942, as a weekly supplement to the well-established daily *Paris-Dakar*. These papers were about all that was left of the press in Senegal, which had withered away under the strictures of wartime censorship.[25] *Paris-Dakar* was run by the enterprising Charles de Breteuil, who had recently founded a string of newspapers across French Africa. If de Breteuil managed to keep hold of his publishing interests during the first years of the war, it was largely because he agreed to collaborate closely with officials at the Government General. Officials in Boisson's administration initially imagined that both *Paris-Dakar* and *Dakar-Jeunes* were having positive effects on local populations. As late as April 1942 an internal report concluded that "the newspaper Paris-Dakar, which has been kept to a path of total orthodoxy thanks to daily censoring and excellent relations between its editors and the Haut-Commissariat, is leading a good fight for the Marshal's government. The same can be said of the recent weekly Dakar-Jeunes, which is having excellent effects on the federation's communities of colonial youths."[26]

Many of the regular columns that structured *Dakar-Jeunes* were closely tied to the priorities of the National Revolution. In keeping with the new regime's emphasis on physical education and sports, the paper provided extensive coverage of sporting events both in the metropole and in AOF. A series of articles, titled "Heroes and Builders of French Africa," lauded the exploits and dynamism of the men who had led France's African conquests—one legacy of the Third Republic that Vichy authorities clearly did not want to disown. A series called "Do You Know France?" consisted of articles on the French regions and their traditions. In launching this series the paper's editors explained: "When we think of France, we picture a village, even if we are city dwellers, for the land is our common heritage and we will never turn away from it. It this column we will evoke the most authentic France, through the words of those who have celebrated it."[27] Presenting the metropole through an essentializing regionalism, this series proposed articles with titles such as "Basque Country: A Land—Its Race—Its Traditions."[28] Building on interwar discourses about national identity, *Dakar-Jeunes* suggested that archetypal Frenchmen were those who cultivated their ties to their *petite patrie* while also professing allegiance to the *grande patrie*. The paper sought to encourage a similar dialectic in the West African colonies. As part of a series titled "Our Human Geography Contest," Africans were encouraged to submit articles describing lifeways and folklore in their native regions.

In the end, however, one section of *Dakar-Jeunes* garnered far more attention than any other. When the paper's editors decided to survey African opinion on the subject of cultural advancement (*l'évolution culturelle*), they did not realize that they were about to set off an explosive debate. Given the leading role that he had played in the cultural debates of the late 1930s, it was perhaps fitting that Ousmane Socé was selected to launch the *Dakar-Jeunes* survey. In late January 1942 the paper ran an article by Socé titled "One Testimony: The Cultural Advancement of AOF." Summing up arguments that he had been refining for several years, Socé announced that the future of French West Africa would be defined in large part by cultural *métissage*. He explained that "if one could, in an area as unmathematical as human progress, establish the equation for the march of civilization, one would surely have to write the following: It is a curve produced by successive métissages that are a function of the great military and commercial expansions of history; successive métissages of varying degrees."[29] Predicting that "a day will perhaps come when cultural métissage will be global," Socé announced that French West Africa would not escape the laws of human progress and that the federation's future civilization would be "Franco-African." After making these sweeping statements, Socé then encouraged other members of the jeunesse évoluée to submit their views on this controversial subject in the hope that some consensus might emerge. Socé concluded his article by declaring: "Youth of French Black Africa, the debate has begun."

Before examining how other French-educated elites responded to this call, something more needs to be said of Socé's exceptional trajectory, both as a student and as an author.[30] After graduating from the École William Ponty in 1928, Socé briefly taught at a primary school in Saint-Louis before returning to Ponty, where he served as head monitor (*surveillant général*) in 1930–31. During this period Socé found ways to continue his own studies. Along with a handful of other Senegalese schoolteachers, he prepared independently for the *baccalauréat*, without being enrolled in one of the colony's two secondary schools. Overcoming a range of obstacles, Socé succeeded in passing both parts of the baccalauréat by 1931. Soon thereafter he received a scholarship from the Government General that allowed him to continue his studies in France. In Paris Socé became a regular companion of Senghor. But whereas Senghor managed to study at some of France's most prestigious institutions of higher learning, Socé was required, by the terms of his scholarship, to study veterinary medicine at the École nationale vétérinaire, located in the town of Maisons-Alfort, outside Paris.[31]

Despite these constraints Socé soon became a prominent member of the community of black students who gathered in and around the French capital. Socé and Senghor both took part in the founding of the Association of West African Students during the early 1930s.[32] Whereas Senghor turned to writing poetry and articles about education and culture, Socé became one of the first Africans to produce novels in French. After publishing *Karim: Roman sénégalais* in 1935, Socé came out with a second novel, *Mirages de Paris*, two years later. He used both works to explore the cultural predicaments of young African elites, who oscillated dangerously between French and African worlds.[33] Although almost all Socé's young characters struggle to chart their way forward, they opt for different paths, somewhere between a full embrace and an outright rejection of French civilization. Highlighting deep differences of opinion, both novels include extended passages in which characters defend their competing ideas about cultural identity and the shape of the future. These passages were clearly informed by actual debates in which both Socé and Senghor actively participated. In both *Karim* and *Mirages de Paris*, Socé suggests that young African elites need to come together around a collective vision of the future. And yet, efforts to frame a common project continue to be complicated by large differences of opinion and formidable external forces. In the end neither novel proposes a cogent solution.

Shortly after he finished writing *Mirages de Paris* Socé completed his studies in veterinary medicine and returned home to Senegal. Arriving in the summer of 1937, he discovered the ebullient climate of Senegal's towns during the Popular Front period. Like Senghor, Socé was invited by Governor General de Coppet to give a public talk at Dakar's Chamber of Commerce.[34] By the time they gave their parallel talks, only a month apart, Socé and Senghor had come to represent rather different positions.[35] Both intellectuals imagined a future that would be marked by sustained cultural exchanges between France and French West Africa. But whereas Socé came out in favor a rather open-ended process of cultural métissage, Senghor avoided the latter term altogether and insisted that cultural borrowings should remain selective, so as not to compromise the originality and integrity of Negro-African cultures and civilization.[36]

Soon after he delivered his talk in Dakar, Senghor returned to France, where he remained until the end of the war. Socé, on the other hand, stayed in Senegal, where he became an influential public figure. During the late 1930s Socé contributed regularly to *Paris-Dakar*, publishing retellings of African legends as well as more present-focused articles on culture and education.[37] Given his established relationship with *Paris-Dakar*, and his ongoing engagement with cultural questions, it is hardly surprising that Socé assumed a leading role in the *Dakar-Jeunes* debates.

The novelty and importance of these debates was not lost on Fara Sow, a Ponty graduate who had begun a career as a schoolteacher.

After losing his teaching position in Rufisque as the result of an altercation with the local French community, Sow had taken a job in Dakar with Air France.[38] In his article in *Dakar-Jeunes* Sow noted: "'Dakar-Jeunes,' new paper, new spirit. The African youth finally has a say in the matter. It has been given center stage. It has already sent its paper several articles, which have caused a sensation." Sow went on to explain that the broadening debate over cultural orientation continued to be structured by the positions of Socé and Senghor. Whereas Socé presented cultural métissage as the surest way for Africans to advance, Senghor continued to be associated with African cultural authenticity. Although clearly torn between these competing positions, Sow eventually joined ranks with Socé, calling for a broad opening up toward the Western world. He argued: "We don't recommend departing from the universal method, namely, enriching ourselves through foreign and classical literatures as well as through the national literature. As to our industry, we can only gain by acquiring as much science as possible. Besides, it is well known that science belongs to all." Sow then concluded: "We advise African children, if we have to tell them something, to raise themselves up vigorously in order to follow the world in the march of Progress."[39]

But even as he clung to a certain universalism, Sow nonetheless expressed admiration for the bold positions that Senghor had staked out. Throughout the *Dakar-Jeunes* survey, even those who disagreed with Senghor usually paid tribute to the latter's powerful defense of African cultures and identities. Sow confided that "the point of view of Léopold is a pipe dream, the beautiful pipe dream of a young, very gifted man of letters, whose excessive love for his homeland [*pays natal*] led him to fanciful ideas about his race. Above all, this pipe dream is very dear to us and, for this reason, it is helpful. It has comforted and excited many young people, and made them realize their potential."[40]

Like other participants in these debates, Massata N'Diaye felt ambivalent toward those who encouraged Africans to stay culturally connected to their ethnicity and race. After all, such admonitions came not only from Senghor and his new followers but also from the colonial administration. As we saw in chapter 4, officials at the École William Ponty actively prodded students and school graduates to reaffirm and celebrate more localized cultural identities. Such prodding only increased during the first years of the war. In his article titled "Spiritual Loyalty," N'Diaye acknowledged that "those who have advised blacks to know themselves deserve praise; it is certainly necessary for them to be conscious of their original qualities." However, N'Diaye questioned whether French-educated Africans were really losing touch with their origins and true nature. He asked: "But this advice, which is given with such anxious concern, is it really necessary? Is it possible that an intelligent person, having grown up in his family, in his milieu, in frequent contact with his people, can still manage to be unaware of his specific condition?"[41]

Like others, N'Diaye saw inherent dangers in calls for a turn inward, toward localized forms of education and cultural advancement. In his contribution to *Dakar-Jeunes*, N'Diaye contended that

> the veneration of our individuality cannot make us forget its inadequacy. It is not reasonable to believe that a strictly Negro humanism will ever be able to bear fruit that is capable of satisfying our conception of progress. History shows that cooperation among individuals, nations, and cultures stems from an absolute necessity. Is civilization not the work of the world's elites, who are continuously being renewed? . . . Experience has disproved the absurd theory that held Africans to be incapable of assimilation. To urge them to give up modern education is to mistrust their intellect, to tacitly give them an inexorable badge of inferiority, to want to isolate them from the intellectual world. This cannot be our choice. . . . It is pointless to establish a static ideal for the African mind, for it is life, movement and progress.[42]

N'Diaye was hardly alone in concluding that Senghor's more particularist vision of culture, education, and progress would hem in the development of the African elite. Socé had voiced very similar concerns during the Popular Front period.

Soon after Senghor made his 1937 speech at Dakar's Chamber of

Commerce, Socé published what amounted to a direct rebuttal. In an article carried by *Paris-Dakar* and titled simply "The Danger," Socé suggested that Senghor was playing into the hands of reactionary elements within colonial administration who were all too eager to use notions of cultural and racial difference to constrain the advancement of African elites. Although not insensitive to the value of locally inspired schooling, Socé highlighted the risks of such an approach: "The danger is the men who are against our advancement and who would use the 'new spirit' to pursue 'reactionary plans' aimed at stifling our country's élite. In their hands, such a principle would result in this: our black brothers would know everything relating to Africa but they would lack general knowledge of mathematics, philosophy and history that every man in today's world must have. They would thus be only second-rate men, with limited intellectual horizons, and that is the danger."[43] As far as Socé was concerned, questions relating to cultural and educational orientation could not be considered in the abstract, without thinking about how policies would be implemented and exploited by colonial officials.

Joining the *Dakar-Jeunes* debates in April 1942, Daouda Diawara voiced concerns similar to those of Socé. Originally from French Soudan, Diawara had studied at the École William Ponty before going on to attend Dakar's School of Medicine. Thereafter Diawara began a career as a medical assistant, or "African doctor."[44] In his article titled "A Soudanese Opinion," Diawara focused on questions of language and particularly on several assertions that Senghor had made during his 1937 talk in Dakar. Like many African contributors to *Dakar-Jeunes*, Diawara shared neither Senghor's reservations about the French language nor his enthusiasm for education in local languages. At the time French enjoyed an exceptionally strong international position, not only as a language of diplomacy but also as a language that was frequently associated with *la civilisation*. In his article, Diawara asserted:

> We are lucky to have the French language, which is so beautiful and supple that civilized European peoples have adopted it as their language of diplomacy and have not resented seeing their maternal

languages relegated to a lower level. And what about us? We do not even have a written language and we do not want French anymore because it does not allow us to express ourselves in the same way that Bambara and Wolof do. Of course we have ways of expressing ourselves in our dialects that cannot be translated into French without losing their delightful flavor. Inventing our own form of writing, what a pipe dream, what an intentional delay, what lack of pragmatism. To express our feelings in a language that is not African does not belittle us or make us intellectual déracinés.[45]

While accepting that African languages had unique expressive capabilities, Diawara insisted that French was a powerful tool that Africans would do well to appropriate as quickly and as fully as possible.

Even as they recommended openness toward European cultures, knowledge, and languages, Socé, Sow, N'Diaye, and Diawara did not call for a turning away from African sources. These four contributors to *Dakar-Jeunes* considered that French influences would ultimately lead to the transformation and hybridization—but not the demise—of African cultures. What they feared most were not the effects of Westernization but rather the colonial administration's efforts to constrain the advancement of new African elites. As the wartime administration fully embraced essentializing and racializing discourses, Socé and his allies fought back, by defending open-ended notions of cultural métissage and universal understandings of progress.

RECASTING THE NATIONAL REVOLUTION

While some of the participants in the *Dakar-Jeunes* debates defended notions of cultural métissage, others came out in support of African cultural authenticity. Members of this latter group tended to identify broadly with the positions that Senghor had taken during the Popular Front period. At the same time, however, partisans of African cultural authenticity also sought to take advantage of opportunities that seemed to be opening up during the war. As French authorities worked to translate the National Revolution to the context of French West Africa, nativist cultural movements found new spaces in which to develop.

No one spoke out more powerfully in support of cultural authenticity than Mamadou Dia, a prominent Senegalese schoolteacher who was based in Saint-Louis.[46] Like Socé and a handful of other Senegalese schoolteachers, Dia had refused to let the École William Ponty be the end point of his formal education. After graduating from Ponty in 1930 Dia spent a good portion of the 1930s studying for and trying to pass the baccalauréat as an outside candidate. Although colonial officials generally frowned on his efforts, Dia eventually prevailed in 1937.[47] As a graduate of Ponty, and as a very rare African *bachelier*, Dia became a prominent member of the French-educated elite clustered in and around Saint-Louis. His outspoken cultural activism during the first years of the war soon brought him even more notoriety.

Dia injected a new intensity into the *Dakar-Jeunes* debates in March 1942, when he published a bold article titled "An African Culture." Taking inspiration from the positions that Senghor had defended during the Popular Front period, Dia declared that the most pressing task for new elites was to recover as much as possible from precolonial African civilizations, so that these materials could provide the foundation and inspiration for an African cultural renaissance:

> But since we have not yet been assimilated, since our development is only beginning, why would we not build with our own materials? Why strive to find in others, abroad, treasures that are buried in the ruins of old African civilizations? The debate has now been taken to a higher level: it is no longer a question of whether or not we are capable of taking courses at the Sorbonne; for us the most exciting question is to determine whether we should remain true to ourselves. Here we share all of the worries of Prof. Senghor, who is troubled at the thought of seeing African youths taken away from their true destinies. . . . It is truly audacious to dream of a cultural renaissance in AOF, which would be realized with specifically African components, free of any impurities. The important thing is for our culture to sink its roots down into our most ancient traditions and for us to learn to be proud of our naïvely wild Africa [*notre Afrique ingénument sauvage*].[48]

Although he readily invoked Senghor, Dia actually moved well beyond the latter's positions. While calling for a cultural movement that would tap deeply into the Negro-African experience, Senghor had also urged young African elites to strategically appropriate certain kinds of French culture and knowledge. Questioning the need for such appropriations, Dia now suggested that the time had come to purge these "impurities," so that West Africans could fashion a cultural identity that was entirely their own.

The fact that Dia was able to publish such views in *Dakar-Jeunes* shows just how much tolerance there was for cultural nativism during the first years of the war. We have already observed the ways in which Boisson's administration propagated essentialized views of cultural and racial differences, while providing encouragement and material support to a new crop of African associations. Rather quickly, however, Dia and a number of other elites in Saint-Louis moved beyond the cultural framework that colonial officials had imagined. In his published memoirs Dia reflects back on the wartime activism of his coterie, noting: "We preached authenticity; we said that we had no use for Western culture. We asserted our authenticity, the national identity, African identity." Dia insisted that the cultural movement he and some fellow teachers had founded was resolutely "anti-French."[49] By 1942 Dia and his cohorts had begun to promote something akin to cultural nationalism, even if the contours of their movement remained rather vague. In his memoires Dia explains that "our nationalism was, at the beginning, only cultural and not yet economic and political."[50] Throughout the first years of the war Dia professed a suspicion of politicians and politics, preferring, like Senghor, to stress the importance of cultural activism.[51]

While Socé chose to dismiss Dia and his companions as "revolutionaries," a number of other contributors to *Dakar-Jeunes* took up the cause of cultural authenticity, even if their calls remained somewhat more restrained than those of Dia.[52] Writing under the pen name "Sumus," one participant paid a lengthy tribute to Senghor, who had left "distant cultural summits" to come home and "make us feel the necessity of a truly African culture." This author went on to explain that "this moving warning cry is for us a precious token of loyalty and gratitude toward our origins of which we are proud, eloquent proof of our spiritual independence and dignity." After conjuring up the "still smoldering ruins of our old vanished cities," this contributor urged his peers to devote themselves to "a purely African civilization that we have the imperious duty to know deeply."[53] Like Dia, "Sumus" seemed to be calling for a new imagined community that would exist beyond the horizons of colonialism. By positing an independent African civilization that could spring forth again, these two authors suggested that France's impact on AOF was less deep than previously thought.

With opinions divided, some contributors to *Dakar-Jeunes* began to wonder how this vast debate would ever be resolved. Joseph M'Baye, a schoolteacher in Saint-Louis who collaborated closely with Dia, observed that "the cultural problem has given rise to two opposing schools of thought: 'métissage' versus purely African culture. Each school has its ardent supporters and its passionate advocates. The battle continues: each side has an abundance of arguments but the problem ... has yet to be solved; it awaits, unyielding, the synthesis of all the opinions. But who will produce this synthesis? This is a thorny question that will have to be answered at the end of the debates."[54]

M'Baye laid out the problem as he saw it: "On the one hand, métissage—if it is to be continuous and everlasting—seems to me like a renunciation of our own nature. On the other hand, a purely Negro culture is, for the current period of our history, a near impossibility." Trying to offer a way out of this conundrum, M'Baye went on to propose that "this being the case, we cannot escape a métissage where Western culture will predominate. Does this have to throw us into despair and cause us to abandon our most legitimate ambition, which is to create a purely Negro culture for Black Africa? Certainly not. If intellectual métissage resembles, at the dawn of our development, a rigorous law from which we cannot yet escape, it must not be viewed as an end but as a simple means, which will allow us to attain a fundamentally Negro culture." Whereas Socé imagined an Africa that was already culturally hybrid and would only become more so, M'Baye evoked the possibility that an *Afrique métissée* might one day regain its authenticity. M'Baye prophesied that "a time will inevitably come when a purely African culture will begin radiating across Black Africa. Only then will Black Africa begin to build on its own foundations."[55] In the interest of a certain realism, M'Baye pushed back the moment when Black Africa would begin returning to its cultural roots. However, the very fact that he could evoke a casting off of French cultural influences shows just how far debates progressed during the first half of 1942.

Although articles published in *Dakar-Jeunes* gained particular notoriety, debates over cultural identity and advancement extended far beyond the pages of this wartime newspaper. It is not hard to imagine the heated face-to-face discussions that must have taken place in many towns around French West Africa. Although these discussions have left relatively few traces in colonial archives, some of their contours can be seen in letters intercepted and reproduced by the colonial administration's censorship apparatus.

Joseph M'Baye, whom we have just encountered, further elaborated on his views in his private correspondence with Ibrahima M'Baye, a schoolteacher in the Senegalese town of Thiès. In a letter dated 5 May 1942, Joseph M'Baye declared to his correspondent:

> I'm very glad to see that you are taking an interest in the much-vaunted problem of cultural advancement to which the African youth is trying to find a solution. As you know, this problem is very complex and has thus elicited many opinions, most of which I find revolting and nauseating. . . . In reality, those who want a Franco-Negro culture to radiate eternally across Black Africa have not found or invented anything new; what they are presenting as a solution is just the reality of our current condition; no one is unaware of the fact that our present culture is Franco-Negro; the champions of that culture would have been more straightforward if they had called for "maintaining the status quo."

After roundly denouncing the supporters of cultural métissage, M'Baye went on to reiterate his own position: "Africa once had its own civilization that was the product of the Negro race.... You know that the intellectual influence of Timbuktu had reached the West—Why don't you want that civilization to live again? Why do you want Africa to lose its African character?"[56] For Joseph M'Baye, reining in French cultural influences and developing a culture that was rooted in "the genius of our race" did not seem to imply a general hostility toward France. Imagining that cultural autonomy could be pursued without breaking away from the colonial power, he continued: "Remaining Negroes does not undermine our attachment to beautiful France."

Ibrahima M'Baye remained unconvinced by these appeals. In his written response, which was also intercepted by postal monitors in Saint-Louis, this schoolteacher noted that "to improve our civilization—what you call civilization, for if it once existed, it is almost dead—we will have to go back four centuries and start from scratch, so to speak. Why put ourselves even further behind when, as it is, we will never be able to catch up?" Ibrahima M'Baye contended that it was through cultural exchanges with the European world that the inhabitants of AOF could more reliably—and more quickly—advance. Although he associated the future with increasing Europeanization, Ibrahima M'Baye did not think that full cultural assimilation was on the horizon. Rather, he concluded that "we can only be Europeanized Negroes" and added that "customs will never be dead."[57] Exchanges like this one point to the many different positions that African elites carved out, as cultural debates continued to spread beyond the columns of *Dakar-Jeunes*.

ENDING THE DEBATES

During the first half of 1942 *Dakar-Jeunes* was one component of the administration's broader plans to structure and guide the cultural and social life of French-educated elites, particularly those residing in and around towns. In response to Boisson's directives, colonial officials also facilitated the creation of a range of cultural associations. Officials were most supportive of associations devoted to the study and celebration of local traditions and folklore—themes that seemed to fit rather easily within the framework of the National Revolution.

As the *Dakar-Jeunes* survey was reaching its climax, a group of young elites came together to found the Foyer africain de Saint-Louis. The Vichyite paper *Sénégal* noted that the mission of this new association was "to group together the African youth under the auspices of the National Revolution" and "to contribute, through the research of its members, to a vast study of the civilization, names, and traditions of Black Africa."[58] While Saint-Louis proved to be an especially important hub for wartime cultural associations, similar associations also sprouted up in other towns. In September 1941 an official in Senegal's administration filed a report on the Dancing Club de Kaolack, an association "whose sole purpose seems to be to bring native folklore back to life, through theatrical performances."[59]

Like Boisson, the governor of Senegal, Georges Rey, imagined that such associations and their activities were concordant with National Revolution ideology. Writing to administrators across Senegal in March 1942, Rey emphasized that cultural associations and theatrical performances "must extol the inner qualities [*vertus foncières*] of the tribe [*race*] especially within a region corresponding to a *cercle*, so that elites will link themselves to their past and reintegrate themselves into [a] traditional framework of a worthy sort." Rey added: "You must also see to it that folklore fits, as usual, into the framework [of the] Fatherland and [the] Empire."[60] During the war years, efforts to encourage public celebrations of indigenous folklore were hardly confined to French West Africa. The historian Eric Jennings has documented the strong support that French officials in Indochina gave to local elites interested in celebrating identities of a neotraditionalist sort. The wartime administration of Admiral Jean Decoux went so far as to imagine that local patriotisms—complete with flags, hymns, emblems, and heraldry—would be compatible with a broader allegiance to French Indochina and Vichy France.[61]

However, in both Indochina and AOF, officials belatedly realized that such celebrations could take on other meanings that had little or nothing to do with Vichy's National Revolution. Indeed, in some cases indigenous elites seemed determined to use newly founded cultural groups to frame "national revolutions" of their own. As they observed the debates that had developed in and around *Dakar-Jeunes*, colonial officials eventually grew concerned. By late April 1942 Governor Rey had begun to blame the new paper for stirring up passions that were becoming difficult to control. In a "confidential" telegram to Boisson, Rey argued that by providing an open forum for "free opinions," *Dakar-Jeunes* was "swelling [the] innate vanity [of] second-rate intellectuals and encouraging them to seek honors [and] publicity." The governor of Senegal added that Africans, however well educated, were not qualified to resolve "complex cultural problems." If Rey found the *Dakar-Jeunes* survey an unwelcome distraction, he also noted, more ominously, that certain African elites seemed to be using this tribune to imagine a national revolution of their own. Rey warned that all the "intellectual agitation" was not unrelated to the emergence of "protest and separatist groups." Recommending that Boisson put an end to this situation, the governor argued that all of the commotion around *Dakar-Jeunes* ran counter to "national discipline, which requires: working silently, [the] renunciation of press campaigns, [and] patriotic doctrinal unity, [which is] incompatible with separatism, especially [when it is] of a cultural sort." Rey concluded: "This is no time for debates."[62]

Rey's concerns were shared by the director of political and administrative affairs in Dakar, who pointed out that the *Dakar-Jeunes* debates had caused the whole évolué community to get dangerously overheated.[63] Although the debates had been framed in cultural terms, it was not difficult to see how they might acquire political overtones. One African contributor to *Dakar-Jeunes* noted just this, when he wrote, in the paper's May 14 issue: "Who can't see that in the colonies every cultural question is a political question?"[64] This observation was particularly pertinent during the wartime period: with political expression essentially banned, cultural activism could serve as a potent proxy. In response to mounting criticism from colonial officials, the May 21 issue of *Dakar-Jeunes* peremptorily announced to readers that the survey was over. Having followed the cultural debates with growing unease, colonial authorities in Saint-Louis and Dakar now tried to reassert their own priorities.

Given that all, or almost all, of the African contributors to *Dakar-*

Jeunes were graduates of the École William Ponty, it is not surprising that the administration tasked Charles Béart with crafting something of a rebuttal. After helping to reshape Ponty during the second half of the 1930s (see chapter 4), Béart became the school's director in 1939 and remained in this position throughout the war. In a lengthy article published in the June 18 edition of *Dakar-Jeunes*, Béart tried to tamp down the recent debates. Adopting a paternalistic tone, the school director began by applauding the new interest that many African elites had taken in local traditions: "For a long time you thought your customs, tales, songs, [and] dances were the products of 'savages' and you avoided them, not long ago, with an air of disgust; now you have realized how detrimental that attitude was to your development, that it turned you into a detribalized caste [*une caste d'affranchis*] without a past or a future. All this is well and good." But after commending this turn back toward indigenous cultures, Béart went on to chide contributors to *Dakar-Jeunes* for getting "carried away" with their newfound enthusiasms.[65]

Béart insisted that the cultural advancement of French West Africa was still in its beginnings and that it would take years and years of tutelage before Africans would be capable of giving rise to a Franco-African civilization of their own. Béart urged new African elites to devote themselves, more modestly, to faithfully transcribing local African traditions, so that at some future time these stores of folklore might be turned into worthy works of art.[66] The school director's dismissive, infantilizing remarks provoked the ire of some of those who had participated in the *Dakar-Jeunes* debates.[67] More than anything else, however, Béart's article stood out as wooden coda bearing little to no relation to the spirited and wide-ranging debate that African elites had carried out during the first half of 1942.

In the existing scholarly literature, the contests that shaped wartime French West Africa are usually presented as Franco-French or European affairs. African actors often seem to retreat to the margins, waiting for the end of the war and the expansion of political life that would begin in 1945. Viewed from certain angles, these years were *des années de plomb* (literally, "leaden years"), when political and intellectual life were stunted by an authoritarian colonial administration and the many hardships brought on by the war. However, as I have tried to show in this chapter, this period also produced new openings, especially when it came to cultural debates and cultural associations.

The *Dakar-Jeunes* debates revealed complex African responses to the essentializing and racializing rhetoric of the Vichy regime and the local colonial administration. Although they defended competing visions of the future, African contributors to the *Dakar-Jeunes* nonetheless shared certain commonalities. Almost all the contributors distanced themselves from the cultural discourses that were proposed by Boisson's administration and the Vichy regime.[68] Colonial officials urged French-educated elites to turn their attention to quaint and colorful local traditions. In the words of one official, youths needed to work modestly, "to express, in a patiently developed French form, the richness of an often overlooked folklore."[69] Dismissing these narrow parameters, the elites we have encountered in this chapter all chose to think in terms of large cultural ensembles and a bold postwar future.

In the end these wartime efforts to imagine the future were cut short. Soon after the colonial administration terminated the *Dakar-Jeunes* survey, the Vichy period in French West Africa began to ebb. An important turning point came in November 1942, when the Allied landings in North Africa forced AOF to move beyond the orbit of the Vichy regime. Although uncertainty reigned for some time, the West African colonies joined the North African territories in an evolution that eventually brought them under the authority of the Algiers-based French Committee of National Liberation.[70] Boisson remained high commissioner of AOF until the summer of 1943, when mounting pressures from Algiers finally pushed him to resign.[71] This realignment, along with the return to war on the side of the Allies, would soon usher in new priorities and new contests. We now turn to the period 1944–45 and to the attempts of Gaullist officials to frame a revised colonial order. As we will see, Gaullist officials were hardly of one mind.

7

Gaullist Hesitations

FROM THE BRAZZAVILLE CONFERENCE
TO THE LIBERATION

Given the central place that Brazzaville came to occupy for Gaullist leaders and the Free French organization, it was perhaps inevitable that the Brazzaville Conference would become shrouded in myths. Before the conference had even broken up, in February 1944, Gaullist officials were already proclaiming that a major turning point had been reached and that the conference's recommendations would provide the foundations for a renovated African empire, confidently turned toward the future. In subsequent decades Gaullist spokespersons and a surprising number of historians sought to present the Brazzaville Conference as a different kind of turning point—as an opening event in the process of decolonization. More recent scholarship has tended to underscore the limits and ambiguities of "Brazzaville" as well as the rather indeterminate nature of the period that followed.[1] As we will see, when it came to education reform, the period 1944–45 was ultimately shaped both by new thinking and deep resistance to change.

As plans for the Brazzaville Conference began to take shape in late 1943, the French empire remained mired in uncertainty. Although the Allied landings of November 1942 had forced the administrations in Algeria, Tunisia, and French Morocco to sever their ties with the

Vichy regime, the administrations in North Africa remained filled with officials who had, until recently, professed some sort of allegiance to Vichy France. The same was true in French West Africa, where Boisson remained in charge until July 1943. New leadership structures developed rather slowly. Formed in Algiers as of June 1943, the French Committee of National Liberation (CFLN) was initially weighed down by internal struggles, as General Henri Giraud and General Charles de Gaulle competed with each other for authority. It was not until November 1943 that De Gaulle fully outmaneuvered his counterpart, becoming the sole head of the CFLN.[2] But even as the leadership in Algiers became clearer, Gaullist officials remained all too aware of the ideological battles and factionalism that had proliferated within the overseas administrations. By turning away from the recent past, and by initiating broad conversations about the postwar future, de Gaulle and his close associates hoped to generate new cohesion.

As they made plans for the Brazzaville Conference, Gaullist leaders focused not only on overcoming Franco-French divisions but also on defending the French empire in the court of international opinion.[3] During the war both the United States and the Soviet Union had expressed pointed skepticism about the future of European imperialism.[4] Anticipating new challenges, Britain had passed a Colonial Development and Welfare Act as of the summer of 1940. This package of reforms was part of a broader effort to recast British colonialism in terms of a comprehensive program of "development," to be methodically carried out after the war.[5] Gaullist authorities hoped to show that they too were making concerted, proactive plans for the postwar period. However, before plans could be announced, French officials first had to agree on what colonial development should mean in the wake of the war. Aware of how divided opinions remained on this question, Gaullist officials in Algiers hoped that the Brazzaville Conference would provide some needed clarification.

Convened on 30 January 1944, the Brazzaville Conference was scheduled to last ten days.[6] The conference's deliberations were limited to France's sub-Saharan possessions, which included French West Africa, French Equatorial Africa, Madagascar, the mandates of Togo and Cameroon, the French Somali Coast, and the island of Réunion. All told, the Brazzaville Conference brought together three governors general, fifteen sitting colonial governors, and twenty-two senior colonial administrators, all from the sub-Saharan colonies. Most of the remaining participants came from North Africa: the Provisional Consultative Assembly in Algiers sent a nine-member delegation, while the administrations of Algeria, Morocco, and Tunisia dispatched a total of six observers. The CFLN was represented by a few influential officials, such as Henri Laurentie, who served as chief organizer of the entire conference.[7] It was telling indeed that this major gathering did not include a single African.[8] From the beginning the Brazzaville Conference was predicated on the belief that veteran colonial administrators and key Gaullist officials should be charged with framing the postwar colonial order.

DEBATING COLONIAL SCHOOLING IN BRAZZAVILLE

Discussions of education reform began several weeks before the opening of the Brazzaville Conference, when officials in Algiers circulated a document that was meant to set the stage for the upcoming gathering. In its section on colonial schools, the "General Program of the Brazzaville Conference" asserted that "it is pointless to continue debating whether or not technical and manual training are preferable to academic education. Neither one has penetrated the masses or improved their quality of life. This type of mass education, which would provide the entire population with a recipe for a better, more productive, and healthier life, has yet to be invented." The authors of this document then asked: "How can we design schools that will teach native children nothing more than to stay in their villages and continue their family traditions, but with increased means and a concern for improving their standard of living?"[9] In many respects these remarks were hardly revolutionary. In describing the educational goals that should be pursued in French Africa, the general program echoed an entire corpus of policy statements from the 1930s. What was new in the general program was its blunt dismissal of existing schools and their results.

Caught off guard by this broad critique, education officials in AOF quickly called a meeting in Bamako to prepare their response prior to the opening of the Brazzaville Conference. More than anything else, this gathering revealed just how attached local officials remained to the rural school model. After posing some broad questions, which might have led to a reconsideration of educational policy, the director general of education in AOF (Yves Aubineau) quickly cut off debate, insisting that "competent people have studied this question. . . . I don't feel that I'm capable of developing a new type of school. We must take into account the experiences of our predecessors."[10] Like Aubineau, other education officials continued to view rural schools as a far-sighted solution to the problem of "native education." André You, the director of education in French Soudan, insisted:

> Before we search for a new type of school, before we declare null and void a type of education that has clearly proved its worth and its vitality, we must honestly and carefully . . . assess the results of rural schools. . . . What do we find in these schools and to what degree have they fulfilled their purpose? We find the education that village natives need: reading and writing a letter, making some simple calculations of purchases and sales. Hygiene, some lessons of morality based on native precepts, regional geography and history. Then there is hands-on agriculture in school fields, combined with animal husbandry, plowing, manuring, and crop rotation. Village life itself is the main focus of rural schools.[11]

Having been at the forefront of the movement to develop rural schools, officials in French Soudan were loath to see their efforts questioned and their credibility cast into doubt. Elsewhere in AOF other key officials also worked to head off any quest for new educational models.[12]

Begun prior to the opening of the Brazzaville Conference, this defense of rural schools continued at the conference itself.[13] Deliberations on educational policies and their reform were spearheaded by the Commission du plan d'enseignement, a working group composed of ten officials—five from AOF, one from AEF, one from Cameroon, one from Madagascar, and two from Algiers. This commission proceeded to develop a proposal that was subsequently submitted to the entire conference for discussion. Among other things, this proposal emphasized that "colonial education will ... avoid undermining traditional frameworks, for it is essential that peoples develop according to their own genius and that Black France [*la France Noire*], deeply rooted in the African soil, be an original creation, fertile and full of life. Education will, in general, adopt the methods and curricula of French education adapted to Africa, with a heavy emphasis on manual work, training in agriculture and home economics, and physical education. It will be as down to earth as possible [*le moins livresque possible*], well integrated into village life."[14] Hardly a rallying cry for new thinking, this proposal did little more than reaffirm principles that had inspired the rural school movement during the 1930s and into the wartime period.

When it came to girls' education, the Commission du plan d'enseignement also shied away from innovations. The commission underscored the importance of educating African girls, noting: "If we want our civilizing action to have a profound and lasting impact, if we want new standards of hygiene to be applied in each household, if we want farming methods to improve, if we want huts to be more sanitary and children to be brought up better, it is imperative that education also reach black women, who need to be made into sensible housewives and good mothers." The members of this working group went on to describe, in very restrictive terms, the kinds of education that African girls needed: "To know how to read, write, and count is more than enough for them. Moreover, their education should be mostly oral and direct. We must teach them to sew and to knit, to manage a budget, to make their gardens more varied, their huts cleaner and more attractive, and to care intelligently for their children."[15] In other words, girls' education was to be almost totally organized around the dissemination of practical skills that would supposedly allow students to become more enlightened mothers and homemakers in distinctly rural settings.[16]

However, even as they defended existing conceptions of colonial education, the members of the Commission du plan d'enseignement clearly felt pressured to propose something new. After all, the Brazza-ville Conference had been charged with laying the foundations for a renovated colonial order capable of demonstrating France's fitness as an imperial power. In this context, preserving the status quo was scarcely an option. In the end the solution that officials adopted was to define the problem of education, and new proposals for reform, in largely quantitative terms. After criticizing the limited reach of colonial schools, the commission called for a resolute turn toward mass education. This was not the first time colonial authorities had issued such calls; the turn toward rural schools after 1930 had been heralded as a bold move toward mass education. But while the col-onies did open some additional schools during the 1930s, the total number of students rose only incrementally. After four decades of efforts, the federation's "official" school system still reached only 61,792 children in 1943.[17] In a federation of some 16 million inhabitants, this amounted to a tiny sliver of the school-age population.

Although the number of boys enrolled in colonial schools remained quite modest, far less had been done to reach African girls. During the first two decades of the twentieth century, colonial authorities had often been content to leave girls' schooling in the hands of mis-sionary societies. As late as 1918 a mere 502 African girls attended administration-run schools. After World War I it seemed as if girls' education might finally become a higher priority; a series of official pronouncements stressed that French-directed progress would remain limited and uncertain without the sustained participation of African women. In the event, however, the new rhetoric led to rather meager results: the number of girls attending the administration's schools inched up slowly during the interwar period, to 2,500 in 1925, 4,343 in 1931, and then 5,507 in 1936.[18] These figures do not include girls studying at mission schools, who numbered 3,799 in 1937.[19]

Officials taking part in the Brazzaville Conference sought to break at last with the "Malthusian" logic that had long governed colonial schooling. The recommendations that were adopted at the conclu-sion of the conference, and published shortly thereafter, insisted that schooling should quickly "reach and penetrate the masses." The conference called for a school to be opened in every village where fifty students—boys and girls combined—could be assembled. The conference's recommendations also asserted that education for boys and girls should be developed in tandem and that continued neglect of girls' education would lead to "an imbalance fatal to native societies and families."[20] By making forceful declarations of this sort the Brazzaville Conference ultimately did help to prepare the ground for an important expansion of colonial schooling.

In 1944 Gaullist officials saw schooling as a vital glue that could help to bind the African colonies more tightly to France. There were many ways to understand the cohesiveness that colonial education might provide. Most obviously, perhaps, colonial schooling promised to create a growing community of French speakers. Spreading the French language had been a somewhat lesser priority during the interwar period, when the future of the colonies had seemed relatively assured. As we have seen, during the 1930s an array of high-ranking colonial officials evinced a new openness to the use of African languages for certain kinds of practical education. Striking a different posture, officials at the Brazzaville Conference sought to dispel any ambiguities surrounding language policies, by declaring that "EDUCATION MUST BE IN FRENCH, given that the use of local spoken dialects is absolutely prohibited, in private schools as well as in public schools."[21]

Although the published recommendations of the Brazzaville Conference signaled a new commitment to mass education and a fuller prohibition against the use of local languages in schools, it was not initially clear that these reforms would lead to a new educational model. Within a few weeks, however, colonial officials began to announce a rather decisive move away from rural schools. In a circular drafted in early March, Pierre Cournarie, the Gaullist governor general of AOF, informed the various governors that "the Brazzaville Conference decided that the native masses should be given a complete primary education, culminating in the primary school certificate." Cournarie went on to explain that all village (or rural) schools would have to align themselves with the regional school model, and that each colony would have to immediately launch "a vast school-building program."[22]

Addressing his administration at the end of 1944, Cournarie repeated the pledge, formulated at the Brazzaville Conference, to move rapidly toward mass education, but now added that "this education for the masses cannot be of inferior quality." Describing the changes that would be forthcoming, the governor general noted that "the plan that we propose to implement tends to establish in AOF a system of primary schools analogous to that of the metropole, taking students up to the primary school certificate, while still remaining fundamentally rural."[23] These reforms became clearer in August 1945, when the Government General published comprehensive instructions regarding the reorganization of primary education in AOF.[24]

The process of education reform that began in Brazzaville has usually been presented rather tidily: one historian has gone so far as to compare the move toward metropolitan-style primary schools to a *bourrasque*, or squall.[25] Upon closer inspection, however, this transition appears considerably more tentative. Although the reforms of the period 1944–45 did begin to break down the walls separating colonial schools from their metropolitan counterparts, the Gaullist leadership proceeded rather incrementally. In many cases, Gaullist officials were still struggling themselves to imagine what the postwar educational order should look like. When it came to imagining the future of secondary education, official thinking proved especially unsettled.

THE LONG ROAD TO SECONDARY EDUCATION

While devoting particular attention to the problem of mass education, officials attending the Brazzaville Conference also discussed the training of African elites and the ways in which such training should evolve after the war. The rather extensive plans for colonial development that were assembled in Brazzaville presupposed broadened cohorts of African elites, who would be able to take on expanded roles within the colonial state and colonial economy. However, rather than seizing this moment to think more seriously about secondary schooling or higher education, officials gathered in Brazzaville generally clung to the notion that African elites should be trained within a primary-level school system composed of several different tiers. The conference concluded that "it is necessary to open, in all the territories of the Empire, professional schools, higher primary schools, and specialized schools, necessary for the training of natives who will be called upon to hold a larger and larger number of jobs in commerce, industry and the administration."[26] But although little was said of secondary education in Brazzaville, French officials soon found this subject increasingly difficult to avoid.

Since its founding, at the beginning of the twentieth century, the colonial school system had never included secondary education. As was often the case, situations proved more complicated in Senegal's largest towns, where growing populations of Europeans and originaires had created pressures for secondary schooling early on. Although these pressures eventually led to the opening of a secondary school in Saint-Louis, and another in Dakar, these remained the only schools of their kind in French West Africa prior to World War II. Before examining the broadening contests over secondary education that erupted during the mid-1940s, we need to cast our eyes briefly backward to see how Senegal came to possess two very exceptional lycées.

The history of secondary education in Senegal had begun in earnest in 1884, when colonial authorities commissioned the Ploërmel Brothers to open and operate a secondary school in Saint-Louis.[27] This school opened soon after the Four Communes were formally constituted as exceptional spaces of direct administration, within a rapidly expanding West African empire that was coming to be ruled more expediently. In the end this school operated for only two decades before being shut down in 1903, as the administration rolled out its plans for a federal school system that would be confined to the primary level. Many prominent originaires were quick to denounce the closing of the secondary school in Saint-Louis, which they saw as a direct assault on their educational rights and opportunities. Throughout the first decade of the twentieth century originaire politicians and notables called for the school to be reopened. Faced with this steady pressure, the colonial administration eventually agreed, in 1909, to establish an embryonic secondary school, called the Cours secondaire de Saint-Louis. By the eve of World War I this school had come to include a number of grades. Conspicuously lacking, however, were the three final years of secondary schooling: *la seconde*, *la première*, and *la terminale*.[28] Among other things, this meant that students could not finish their secondary studies or prepare for the *baccalauréat* without traveling to France. At the time, even relatively affluent originaires found such trips increasingly out of reach, as a result of sharp reductions in the number of scholarships.

World War I eventually produced new openings. Wielding the considerable influence that he had accrued during the war, Blaise Diagne secured a commitment from authorities in Paris to establish a full lycée in Saint-Louis. Metropolitan officials sought to present this lycée as a form of compensation for the vast contributions that West Africans had made to the war effort. In June 1919 Minister of Colonies Henry Simon explained that "after the heroic sacrifices made by the populations of West Africa for the defense of France, the moment has come to respond to the wish of these populations, expressed particularly forcefully in recent years, to be equal to our most favored colonies when it comes to public education. It is appropriate to begin this work by founding a lycée." Simon went on to note that the Colony of Senegal, as a result of its unique history, was especially well prepared to receive such an institution: "Having been French for almost as long as our old colonies in the Americas, Senegal in particular can assert both its unquestionable attachment to the mother country, and the excellent results that a complete French education produces in the natives of that land, provided that they are carefully chosen and brought progressively toward our culture. There, we will not encounter, either in the intellectual traditions or in the political aspirations, any obstacle to complete assimilation."[29] For a moment it seemed as if Diagne and the originaires had won a clear victory.

By the end of 1920 colonial officials were making plans to inaugurate the new secondary school as the Lycée Faidherbe. The new minister of colonies, Albert Sarraut, wrote the French president to explain the symbolic importance of this institution. Sarraut stressed that "amid the festivities which will commemorate the armistice, this inauguration of a new institution of intellectual progress must appear as a symbol and a form of gratitude that France shows the sons of her colonies for their participation in the victory." Sarraut went on to explain that the school was being named after Louis Faidherbe, one of the chief artisans of France's colonial expansion in West Africa.[30] Inaugurated in this way, the lycée was meant to symbolize not only the repayment of wartime debts but also the continuity of France's colonial mission in West Africa.

Many colonial officials remained skeptical about this new institution, whose founding had been decided in Paris and not in Dakar. After taking up his post in the fall of 1919 Governor General Merlin did his best to ignore the recently announced plans. The Ministry of Colonies eventually contacted Merlin in late 1920, as the lycée was being officially inaugurated, to ask when the upper grades would be added so that students could begin working toward the baccalauréat.[31] Merlin proceeded to wait over a year before replying, and even then, the governor general made it clear that he was in no hurry. Following a circular reasoning, Merlin informed the ministry that planning for the baccalauréat could only be completed "in the fairly distant future," since teachers were lacking, and since the final three grades had still not been added.[32] Although a *classe de seconde* was eventually created in time for the 1922–23 school year, colonial authorities continued to drag their feet when it came to the last two grades. By this time even the Ministry of Colonies was beginning to recommend a more cautious approach to the new lycée. In November 1922 Sarraut wrote to Merlin to say that, for the time being, the development of the lycée did not require the addition of the two uppermost grades.[33] Stalling tactics of this sort prompted pointed questions from elected officials in the Four Communes as well as from Diagne in Paris. This publicity eventually made it difficult for colonial authorities to continue to defer the opening of the final two grades.[34]

Before making plans to complete the Lycée Faidherbe, colonial officials sought to learn more about the students who were already attending this institution. An inquiry in 1922 revealed that the school's student body consisted of 79 "Black originaires," 24 "Métis originaires," 33 "Europeans from France," 19 "Natives," and 9 "Syrians."[35]

The categories used in this report are themselves quite revealing. Although the originaires had been recognized as French citizens in 1916, authorities in Dakar and Saint-Louis were clearly not ready to lump originaire students together with students of metropolitan origin. Moreover, after distinguishing the originaires from "Europeans from France," colonial officials then went on to subdivide the originaire students into two distinct racial categories. As we will see, racializing visions of the lycée's "student body" remained quite commonplace throughout the interwar period and had hardly been abandoned by the end of World War II.

At first glance the 1922–23 enrollment report seems to suggest that the new lycée served the originaires ahead of all other groups. Upon closer inspection, however, one can see how students of color—regardless of their legal status—quickly became targets of racial discrimination. During the early 1920s the school's principal, Antoine Morel, clearly hoped to add the final two grades so that he could finally preside over a bona fide lycée. However, Morel also understood that most colonial officials chafed at the prospect of seeing even small handfuls of Africans work toward the baccalauréat—a degree that, even in metropolitan France, served as a marker of privilege. Keenly aware of the prestige and social function of the baccalauréat, Morel sought to explain to the lieutenant governor of Senegal that most of the Senegalese students at the Lycée Faidherbe would never study for the baccalauréat. In a 1923 note the school director opined: "As to the natives [at the Lycée Faidherbe], I feel that I can declare, after 20 years of experience in Senegal, that very few will make it to the baccalauréat. Most of those who attend the lycée only remain in the first cycle for between 2 and 4 years. At the end of this time, they go to work for businesses or the administration." In yet another revealing choice of words, Morel described all of the school's black students as "natives," even though most were actually originaires, and thus French citizens. After making dismissive comments about the academic prospects of black students, Morel went on to speak very differently about the school's *métis* and white students. The principal noted matter-of-factly that "the lycée in Saint-Louis includes a fairly large number of white and métis students for whom the end goal is the baccalauréat."[36]

Through Morel's remarks, we can see how racial considerations immediately informed and constrained plans to expand secondary education in Senegal. Jules Carde, who replaced Merlin as governor general in 1923, apparently approved of Morel's vision of how the Lycée Faidherbe should develop and function. At the beginning of 1924 Carde addressed a note to the Ministry of Colonies in which he repeated Morel's deprecating assessment of black students almost verbatim. Carde went on to conclude, in his own words, that "as a result, serious reservations must be formulated when it comes to the black element. But since the lycée includes a fairly large number of white and métis students whose studies lead to baccalauréat, it is necessary for the curricula of the Lycée de Saint-Louis to correspond to those of lycées in France."[37] It was with these racialist and indeed racist assumptions in mind that colonial officials finally allowed a full lycée to take shape in Saint-Louis. In addition to adding the last two grades, colonial authorities also helped to prepare a 1924 reform, which allowed for the baccalauréat to be administered and awarded in French West Africa. However, in what was an important distinction, the baccalauréat in AOF would bear the name of *brevet de capacité colonial*.[38] A similar diploma had already been created in Madagascar and Indochina, respectively, in 1912 and 1914. This newly established brevet could be converted rather easily into a metropolitan baccalauréat once a student completed the necessary formalities at a French university. However, this arrangement also meant that African students who were unable to travel to France would be left with a local diploma, which the colonial administration could refuse to recognize as a true baccalauréat.[39]

The founding of a full lycée in Saint-Louis ultimately amounted to a very partial victory for Senegal's originaires. Across the interwar period relatively few originaires advanced into the school's uppermost grades, where preparing for the baccalauréat became the consuming priority.[40] Education officials defended the necessity and wisdom of these restrictive, racially informed policies. In a report presented in

1937 the school's director, E. Braillon, was at pains to show just how rigorous the selection process remained for African students. Braillon explained that "on average, the Lycée Faidherbe turns out about five or six native *bacheliers* a year, blacks and mulattos. Unlike other types of education in AOF, which are adapted, our secondary education ... is assimilationist. To avoid the dangers that could result from this assimilation if it were hasty and indiscriminate, it is reserved for those who have shown themselves to be worthy of it, those who can prove that they deserve it, and that they can raise themselves up to it."[41] Whereas school officials had sometimes sought to provide métis students with easier pathways toward the baccalauréat, Braillon's comments suggest that both blacks and métis faced formidable obstacles. As we will now see, non-European students at Senegal's other secondary school had to contend with many of these same hurdles.

During World War I Senegal's European community began setting up a private secondary school in Dakar to accommodate children who could not return to France as a result of the war. With the growth of Senegal's European community during the 1920s, the Cours secondaire de Dakar soon took on a more permanent function.[42] This became especially clear after the colonial administration assumed responsibility for the school in 1925. The school's enrollment grew swiftly, from just sixty students in 1921, to three hundred in 1931, and then to five hundred by 1936.[43] The student body continued to grow thereafter, prompting colonial authorities to undertake the construction of a large, modern school building on a new site. As it moved to its new premises in 1939, the school was renamed the Lycée Van Vollenhoven.[44]

Throughout these transformations the secondary school in Dakar continued to admit only small handfuls of African students, most of whom were originaires. Léopold Senghor was one of the rare Africans to progress through the upper grades and then obtain the baccalauréat. After transferring to the Cours secondaire de Dakar in 1926, Senghor became the only black student in the *classe de première*. During his second and final year at this school, Senghor was one of two blacks in his class.[45] Although many African students would have liked to follow in Senghor's footsteps, very few succeeded. The problem was not just that school officials used racial criteria when deciding whom to admit; racial considerations also helped to determine which students would be promoted from one grade to the next. Moreover, even when African students "survived" all the way to the uppermost grades, they still had to contend with education officials who often frowned on their efforts to pass the baccalauréat.

Historical evidence suggests that baccalauréat juries, which were composed entirely of French men, routinely graded African candidates more stringently than their European peers. The results of the June 1935 baccalauréat session in Senegal illustrate broader patterns. Of the twenty-three candidates who sat for the first part of the baccalauréat, seven passed, one African and six Europeans. Of the sixteen candidates who took the second part, six succeeded, one African and five Europeans.[46] Lamine Guèye, the prominent originaire politician who had recently founded the Senegalese Socialist Party, published and vigorously denounced these results in his newspaper, *L'AOF*.[47] In a follow-up article also published in *L'AOF*, an unnamed contributor went further, declaring that "it seems that it is a crime for blacks to study for the baccalauréat. They are told that this degree is pointless. The Minister of Education and Agriculture in AOF [a facetious reference to Albert Charton, the inspector general of education] advises them all to give up studying for the baccalauréat in order to grow cabbage, lettuce and peanuts."[48] Sardonic humor aside, the author of this article pointed up an important reality: colonial officials often worked to discourage African students from setting their sights on the baccalauréat.

Despite all the obstacles and dissuasion, small numbers of Senegalese elites remained quite focused on the baccalauréat. When official routes to this diploma were blocked, young elites sometimes opted for more unconventional pathways. Without ever attending one of Senegal's two secondary schools, a string of Senegalese schoolteachers studied independently for the baccalauréat examinations, as French regulations allowed. Mamadou Dia, whom we encountered at length in chapter 6, was one of these determined schoolteachers. Although he had a full-time job at a primary school in Saint-Louis, Dia spent much of his free time preparing for baccalauréat examinations. After passing the first part of the baccalauréat during the early 1930s, Dia went on to fail the second part—or perhaps, more accurately, school officials made sure to fail him—any number of times. While carrying out an inspection of Dia's classroom during the first half of 1935, Charton came across philosophy and history notebooks, which the schoolteacher was using as he prepared, yet again, for the second part of the baccalauréat. In his report, the inspector general of education noted disapprovingly that Dia's teaching was suffering as a result of these extraneous scholarly pursuits.[49] In Dia's case, however, perseverance ultimately paid off; he finally passed the second part of the baccalauréat in 1937, perhaps not coincidentally during the more liberal Popular Front period.[50] A handful of other Senegalese schoolteachers displayed similar persistence. In 1935 Alioune Sarr signed up to take the first part of the baccalauréat, for the eighth time! That same year, Fara Sow registered to take the second part of the baccalauréat for the third time. Sow had finally passed the first part of the exam in 1933, on his fifth try, only to fail the second part twice in 1934.[51]

The first years of World War II partially reshaped Senegal's two secondary schools. As a result of restrictions on travel between Senegal and France, the Lycée Van Vollenhoven accepted record numbers of European students. No fewer than 727 Europeans were enrolled at the school at the beginning of 1942. Like many lycées in France, the Lycée Van Vollenhoven offered not only the secondary school grades but also *classes primaires*, where younger students could complete their primary education. Of the European students attending the Lycée Van Vollenhoven in early 1942, 314 were studying in the primary grades. As one might expect, the lycée's wartime expansion did not benefit Senegalese students to the same degree. The school had come to include 100 Senegalese students, 58 of whom were enrolled in the primary grades. As had become customary, the administration's statistics continued to refer to African students as *indigènes*, eliding the fact that most were originaires, and thus French citizens. No longer referencing métis students as a separate group, wartime statistics now folded them into the category of "natives."[52]

Colonial officials had never been overly worried by the growth of the lycée in Dakar, since this school had always served European children ahead of other groups. Attitudes remained rather different when it came to the Lycée Faidherbe, which had been founded—at least on paper—as a lycée for the Senegalese. As late as 1938 the total enrollment of the Lycée Faidherbe still stood at only 220. With the onset of the war, however, the school's student body quickly doubled, reaching 450 by 1943.[53] Some of this growth stemmed from wartime uncertainties and travel disruptions, which led larger numbers of European children to complete their secondary studies in Saint-Louis. However, the expanded enrollments of the Lycée Faidherbe were also the result of conscious choices made by the school's new director, V. Delarue, who had decided to admit larger numbers of urban Senegalese.

By late 1942, however, Delarue's admissions policies had begun to alarm high officials in Dakar. When he learned how many Africans were studying at the Lycée Faidherbe, High Commissioner Boisson immediately wrote to the governor of Senegal to denounce Delarue's conception of a "lycée noir." The high commissioner noted: "I don't approve of his [Delarue's] views regarding the dissemination of secondary education in native milieus. These views directly contradict the educational policy that I have resolved to follow." Unlike Delarue, Boisson worried about the fate of African students who were weeded out of the Lycée Faidherbe after just a few years of schooling. Drawing on well-worn colonial stereotypes regarding African minds, Boisson underscored "the ephemeral character of everything we try stamp onto a docile material, whose very malleability makes it difficult to have a lasting impact." Of African students who did not make it all the way to the baccalauréat, Boisson wrote: "These demi-évolués are actually misfits, satellites of our customs, which they have briefly encountered but not mastered." Boisson insisted that the school henceforth accept only small numbers of Africans. In something of a new departure, the high commissioner now argued that these reduced cohorts should be pushed all the way to the baccalauréat.[54] Issued in late 1942, these directives had scarcely been carried out by the time Boisson was forced to resign, in the summer of 1943. As Gaullist officials took over the

Government General in Dakar and Senegal's administration in Saint-Louis, they inherited lycées that had been deeply marked by the war.

SECONDARY EDUCATION AND THE
UNCERTAINTIES OF "DEMOCRATIZATION"

In metropolitan France, the war shook the foundations of the reigning educational order. French society had long been shaped by two parallel school systems, each of which had its own teachers, students, curricula, diplomas, and cultural codes. Most French children completed their entire education within the primary school system, which included a number of different tiers: primary schools, higher primary schools, *cours complémentaires*, and normal schools. Far smaller numbers of children, drawn overwhelmingly from bourgeois families, attended more prestigious collèges and lycées.[55] Enrollment figures from 1928–29 can help us to appreciate just how bifurcated schooling remained in Third Republic France. During that school year some 4,712,000 French children were enrolled in the various levels of the metropolitan primary school system (public and private schools combined). During the same year, the number of students attending secondary schools (public and private combined) stood at only 291,000.[56]

Although many factors helped to maintain a deep divide between the primary and secondary school systems, school fees played a particularly important role. Whereas public primary schooling had long been free, public secondary schools continued to charge substantial fees until the early 1930s. The existence of a limited number of state scholarships helped to assuage the sensibilities of Third Republic elites, by preserving the possibility that outsiders could find their way into secondary schools by virtue of their academic merit. In practice, however, these scholarships remained too few in number to significantly attenuate the elitist nature of secondary education. Although secondary schools drew some of their students from middle socioeconomic strata, the sons and daughters of peasants and workers remained rarities.[57] All this led one contemporary critic to refer to the baccalauréat as a *brevet de bourgeoisie*.[58]

During World War II, social and educational segregation of this sort became the object of new critiques. Resistance networks, many of which brought bourgeois and working-class constituencies together in novel ways, issued appeals for unity across class lines. First formed during the spring of 1943, the common leadership structure known as the National Council of the Resistance (CNR) went on the following March to publish a comprehensive program, which included both urgent measures aimed at countering Nazi occupation and other reforms to be implemented after the Liberation. When it came to postwar education reforms, the program called for "the real possibility for all children to benefit from education and attain the highest culture regardless of the financial situation of their parents, so that the highest positions will be truly accessible to all those who have the capacities necessary to hold them and so that a true elite, not of birth but of merit, will be promoted and constantly renewed through working-class contributions."[59] In making these recommendations, the CNR sought to make it clear that the narrowly recruited elite of the interwar period had let the nation down and that the colossal task of rebuilding and renewing France would require dynamic, forward-looking leaders, who could represent the broader interests of the French nation.[60]

Promoting interclass solidarities and a more meritocratic school system subsequently became key priorities of the Langevin-Wallon Commission, which was created in November 1944 and charged with framing broad education reforms for the postwar period. More than anything else, this commission sought to chart a course toward a more unified school system. The commission's report recommended that all students complete a common curriculum before being oriented toward courses of study in keeping with their personal abilities and talents. Echoing some of the language of the CNR program, the Langevin-Wallon Commission stressed that "all children, regardless of their family, social, and ethnic backgrounds, have an equal right to develop their particular abilities to the fullest. They must not encounter limitations other than that of their own aptitudes."[61] We now need to examine the ways in which solidarities born of the Resistance, and calls for a more democratic school system, filtered into

French West Africa. To be sure, situations were not equivalent in the empire, where class differences among Europeans tended to be more fluid, especially when compared to the ethno-racial divide that had been erected between colonizers and the colonized.[62] Nonetheless, discourses regarding the democratization of education soon began to make their way overseas.

As we will see, the arrival of a new cadre of Gaullist officials in French West Africa did not initially lead to more liberal and inclusive policies in the area of secondary education. On the contrary, during the lead-up to the Brazzaville Conference prominent officials worked to defend traditional understandings of Senegal's two lycées. Edmond Cabrière, the director of the Lycée Van Vollenhoven in Dakar, was clearly worried that his school might be asked to open its doors to larger numbers of Africans. In addition to being the principal of this lycée, Cabrière also served as head of secondary schooling within the Government General's education department. In a report to Yves Aubineau, the newly appointed director general of education in AOF, Cabrière insisted that Senegal's two lycées needed to do everything they could to accommodate all European children, who deserved to find in Senegal the same educational opportunities that they would have had in metropolitan France.[63] However, when it came to African students, the lycée director immediately struck a very different note.

In his correspondence with Aubineau, Cabrière did not hesitate to describe African students as generally unfit for secondary schooling. In his efforts to explain the putative incompatibilities between African minds and *la culture secondaire*, Cabrière drew on ethnic and racial tropes that had flourished throughout the interwar period before reaching a climax under the Vichy regime. After noting that the specificity of secondary education lay in the classical culture that it bestowed, Cabrière went on to ask: "Who can doubt that young Europeans, conscious or unconscious heirs to Mediterranean civilization, are more fit than natives to receive this culture?" Cabrière added that "although well represented in the lower grades, natives form a small minority in the last two grades. Several of them pass the baccalauréat thanks to their efforts and their memories, but very few give the impression of having assimilated la culture secondaire and of being able to go on." In an effort to substantiate his claims, Cabrière provided a breakdown of the baccalauréats awarded in Senegal between 1939 and 1943. These figures revealed that a total of 131 Europeans had obtained the baccalauréat during these years, against only 27 Africans. After citing this "evidence," Cabrière felt comfortable affirming: "In conclusion, secondary education in the colonies remains an education for Europeans, and, if it is only humane to open the door for a few carefully chosen natives, it seems pointless and inopportune to broaden indigenous recruitment." In yet another example of the ways in which racial distinctions often trumped other types of classification, Cabrière continued to refer to all black students as "natives" even though most were originaires, and consequently French citizens.[64]

Despite his commitment to using racial criteria in admissions decisions, Cabrière showed a certain awareness of changing contexts. By the end of the war explicit racial preferences were clearly becoming more problematic. Leading Gaullist officials were struggling to move beyond the taint of the Vichy period, when any number of new segregationist policies had been enacted and when racist slurs had reached a notorious peak. However, rather than viewing school integration as the way of the future, Gaullist officials began a rather frantic search for new ways to limit the number of Africans at Senegal's lycées without openly invoking race. Governor General Cournarie and Director General of Education Yves Aubineau both suggested that school fees could be used more aggressively to reserve spaces for Europeans in AOF's secondary schools.[65] However, even as they proposed this solution, these officials wondered how long school fees would remain an available option.

Fees for public secondary schooling had recently been eliminated in metropolitan France. An important step was taken in 1930, when a finance law dropped fees for the first year of secondary education (la sixième) at all public collèges and lycées. Fees were subsequently dropped for la cinquième in 1931 and la quatrième in 1932, before a 1933 finance law went considerably further, by discontinuing fees for all secondary grades.[66] As the French historian Antoine Prost has pointed out, the move away from school fees stemmed from several factors and not only from a desire to make secondary schools more "democratic." In the context of the early 1930s, policymakers were especially focused on the need to maintain secondary school enrollments at a time when adolescents were fewer in number.[67] Whatever the precise mix of motivations was, the abandonment of school fees began to bring growing numbers of students from middle socioeconomic strata into collèges and lycées. In the end, the Government General in Dakar chose not to adopt these metropolitan reforms. Although I have not been able to adequately determine how fees were used at the Lycée Van Vollenhoven during the 1930s, it is clear that the Lycée Faidherbe continued to charge fees throughout this decade.[68]

Even in metropolitan France the issue of school fees had not been fully laid to rest. If public collèges and lycées could no longer charge fees for secondary grades, the same was not true for their classes primaires. Although not technically part of the secondary school system, these elite primary classes remained heavily marked by their location within the walls of collèges and lycées. Among other things, these classes served to funnel bourgeois children directly into collèges and lycées as of their very first years of schooling. This arrangement was abruptly called into question at the end of the war. In March 1945 France's provisional government—which had moved from Algiers to Paris—published an ordinance calling for the progressive elimination of the primary grades housed in collèges and lycées. The authors of this ordinance sought to lay the foundations for a fully unified primary school system, so that children of all backgrounds would be placed on a more even footing. Among other things this ordinance declared that "public primary schools are open to children of every social category, and it is among the most talented, and not among a minority of affluent children, that secondary school students will be selected."[69] As it turned out, this ordinance did not prevent collèges and lycées from continuing to house classes primaires.[70] What the ordinance did do, however, was to reduce distinctions between these classes and those located in ordinary primary schools, by finally banning the use of fees.

The decision to eliminate all remaining fees at France's public secondary schools quickly placed new pressures on officials in French West Africa. As of the summer of 1945 the Ministry of Colonies requested that local authorities make plans to implement the ordinance that had recently been issued in the metropole.[71] Clearly caught off guard, officials at the Government General scrambled to defend school fees, and the gate-keeping role that they played. Officials focused not only on the Lycée Faidherbe and the Lycée Van Vollenhoven but also on the newly founded Cours secondaire d'Abidjan, which had sprung up during the war to accommodate European families unable to send their children to France. In a letter to the governor of Ivory Coast, Governor General Cournarie recognized that the phasing out of school fees would conform to "the democratic ideal that inspired this reform in France." However, after referencing this ideal, Cournarie went on to dismiss such a course of action, noting that without school fees, "these classes, soon loaded down with native elements,... [would] no longer be able to accommodate the young Europeans for whom they were created." Cournarie emphasized that for European families, fees for the primary grades offered at the Lycée Van Vollenhoven, the Lycée Faidherbe, and the Cours secondaire d'Abidjan represented "a very modest burden, compared to the advantages of their colonial situation."[72]

Cabrière, the director of the Lycée Van Vollenhoven, became quite distraught when he learned that authorities in Paris were pushing for an end to all remaining school fees at public secondary schools. Since being named as school principal at the end of 1943, Cabrière had cast himself as a staunch advocate of Senegal's European population, which was having to adjust to a changing educational landscape. The "European classes" that certain public primary schools had maintained were being wound down. In Senegal these classes had already lost some of their importance during the interwar period, as growing numbers of European families began to enroll their younger children in the primary grades offered at Dakar's secondary school. In a 1935 report, Inspector General of Education Albert Charton observed, quite candidly, that this school's lower grades "essentially serve as a primary school for children of European education. The breakdown of the students in these classes bears this out: 249 European students; 22 natives. Obviously, this education is not free: school fees [are] 450 francs per year."[73] By the end of World War II the lower grades of the Lycée Van Vollenhoven had expanded to take in even more of the European children in Senegal.

During the summer of 1945 Cabrière worked to defend this arrangement. In a note to Aubineau, the school director explained that the primary grades at the Lycée Van Vollenhoven were now "the only institution providing public primary education for young Europeans." In worried tones, Cabrière went on to note that "in light of this reality, I have systematically given priority, over the last two years, to European applicants. . . . If the PL [*petit lycée*] becomes a school like all the others, it will likely be overrun with students of all backgrounds; even the personnel might cease to be completely European; many parents will pull out their children and put them in private schools."[74] Cabrière did not hesitate to conjure up the "white flight" that would occur if Europeans ceased to enjoy majority status in the various grades of his school. To protect the European character of the Lycée Van Vollenhoven, he even expressed interest in raising the fees charged for the primary grades, which he considered so low as to be "ridiculous." However, given the position recently taken by France's provisional government and the Ministry of Colonies, Cabrière reluctantly conceded that fee increases could probably not be envisioned at the present time.

Although Cabrière remained unbending in his defense of European privilege and the need for race-based admissions policies, other prominent officials in AOF displayed greater openness to change. Even Governor General Cournarie, who often adhered to rather conservative positions, was beginning to recognize that AOF's secondary schools would have to begin admitting more Africans. In a July 1945 note to the governor of Ivory Coast, Cournarie suggested that the secondary school in Abidjan would need to open its doors to qualified Africans. The governor general explained: "Created initially for European and assimilated children, the secondary school cannot forever exclude native students, especially since I intend to allow those with clear aptitudes to pursue solid classical studies, to make it to the baccalauréat and then to higher education. It is necessary to plan, as of right now, for the secondary training of native students." But after this rather bold opening, Cournarie spent the rest of his letter backpedaling, especially when it came to the use of school fees, as a way to ensure that European students would remain solidly in the majority.[75]

Colonial officials such as Cournarie, Aubineau, and Cabrière ultimately failed to contain the mounting pressures surrounding secondary education. These pressures emanated from several different sources. As we will see in detail in chapter 8, the new cohorts of African politicians who emerged as of the second half of 1945 made education reform one of their core priorities. So too did African students, and especially more advanced students, who chafed at the many restrictions that had long confined them to primary-level studies. However, in important ways, the new impetus to develop secondary education in the African colonies also sprang from governmental circles in Paris.

Colonial Minister Paul Giacobbi was determined to reach out to African students and school graduates, in an effort to win their support. In a March 1945 circular to the governors general of AOF, AEF and Madagascar, Giacobbi stressed the need to show African populations that "we are not restricting the possibilities open to the évolués and that we do not consider that they, on principle, only have a right to subaltern positions." Giacobbi added: "They will doubtless begin in such positions but we must not conclude that they will remain there." The Gaullist minister went on to explain that in order to secure the future of the colonies, "France must promote a sentimental attachment, a plebiscite of the hearts. We will only succeed if indigenous elites, unfettered by our policies of goodwill and confidence, come back toward us in a common movement."[76] However, even as he made these rather forward-looking remarks, Giacobbi was forced to acknowledge the uncomfortable fact that only tiny numbers of Africans had been allowed to enroll in secondary schools. At the beginning of the 1945–46 school year, a mere 174 Africans were pursuing secondary education in the entire Federation of French West Africa.[77]

Authorities in Paris eventually became impatient with the

foot-dragging of officials in Dakar. Disturbed by Cabrière's open defense of race-based admissions policies, the Ministry of Colonies finally called for the latter's resignation.[78] But as Cabrière prepared to leave, in September 1945, senior officials in Dakar stood by their colleague. Inspector General of Education Aubineau openly lamented to Cournarie that "the departure of M. Cabrière will be a big loss for colonial secondary education. He has been an ideal colleague from every point of view and I had complete confidence in him."[79] Aubineau had been so fond of his colleague that he had helped to make Cabrière head of secondary education for AOF and second in command at the education department in Dakar. Even as Cabrière was pushed out of his position in Dakar, his career as a colonial education official was hardly over. Receiving a promotion of sorts, Cabrière would eventually be appointed as director of education in Madagascar.[80] Clearly, within the overseas administrations, attitudes toward Africans and their education were changing rather slowly.

Looking back at the Gaullist period, we can observe efforts to partially rethink education and the colonial order in French West Africa. As we have seen throughout this chapter, these efforts emanated largely from the Gaullist leadership based in Algiers, and subsequently in Paris. Adopting a much more conservative posture, officials in AOF often worked to defend existing conceptions of colonial schooling and colonial society. As a result of these and other tensions, the broad discussions of Gaullist period led only to rather incremental changes on the ground. The founding of the Fourth Republic would soon produce much fuller transformations. Colonial schools had long been tasked with educating "subject" populations. This state of affairs changed quite abruptly in May 1946, when all of the inhabitants of the African "territories" were declared to be citizens. As we will see in the final chapter of this study, African citizenship and the Fourth Republic soon spawned intense new controversies over schooling and the future of AOF.

8

The Education of African "Citizens"

STRUGGLES OVER INTEGRATION

As the Fourth Republic was being founded in 1946, many struggled to understand the shifting parameters of French citizenship. Among the metropolitan French there was a widely shared expectation that republican citizenship would be not only reestablished after the Vichy interlude but also refashioned to reflect solidarities and aspirations that had grown up in and around the Resistance. Two years earlier French women had finally won the right to vote and to be elected to political offices. Rather quickly, deliberations about postwar citizenship also led to far-reaching questions about the status and rights of overseas populations. To a growing number of French politicians, the existence of millions of colonial "subjects" seemed increasingly out of step with the postwar world. But if there was a new willingness to imagine some form of citizenship for these populations, the contours and content of such citizenship remained very much in question as the Constituent National Assembly began its work in late 1945.

This was the complex and uncertain context that the freshly elected African deputies encountered as they took up their positions within France's first postwar assembly. Senghor had been elected to represent Senegal's subject populations, whereas his political mentor and ally,

Lamine Guèye, went to Paris as the delegate of Senegal's citizens. The other African territories had also elected small numbers of deputies to the Constituent Assembly.[1] Despite their numerical weakness, the overseas deputies converged on Paris with a keen awareness of new possibilities. The war had disrupted many old assumptions and expectations, and the October 1945 elections had produced the most left-leaning legislative body that France had ever known. The French Communist Party had taken the most seats (161), followed closely by the Socialist Party and the Christian Democrats (the newly founded Mouvement républicain populaire), each of which had claimed 150 seats. The primary goal of this assembly was to draft a constitution that would provide a new institutional framework, both for war-ravaged France and for the deeply unsettled empire. However, while devoting itself to this formidable task, this assembly also used its legislative powers to pass several laws that dramatically shifted the contours of republican citizenship.[2]

Senghor assumed a prominent role in the Constituent Assembly, serving on the commission charged with drafting the new constitution and on the Commission on Overseas Territories, which had been created to reflect on colonial reform and recommend provisions for "Overseas France" within the emerging constitution.[3] During the first months of 1946 Senghor carefully followed the unfolding plans of his close friend Aimé Césaire, who had been elected to one of Martinique's two seats in the Constituent Assembly. Césaire quickly emerged as the leading sponsor of a bill proposing to transform the old colonies of Martinique, Guadeloupe, French Guiana, and Réunion into overseas departments (*départements d'outre-mer*, or DOM).[4] Eventually passed on 19 March 1946, this "departmentalization" law stipulated that standing metropolitan legislation and decrees would be extended to the overseas departments by the beginning of 1947 and that most new metropolitan laws would also be implemented in the DOM.[5]

Although the inhabitants of the old colonies had been French citizens since 1848, most still did not enjoy the full complement of citizens' rights, benefits, and opportunities. This was especially the case for darker-skinned populations, who frequently remained trapped in underclasses and condemned to work on plantations run in very "colonial" fashion. Throughout the Third Republic the old colonies had continued to be ruled through indeterminate regimes that looked toward metropolitan practices and norms even as they remained mired in colonial expedients and exceptions. The historian Gary Wilder has fittingly described the governance of the old colonies as "a hybrid form of colonial rule over quasi-citizens inhabiting demidepartments."[6] The French philosopher and political scientist Silyane Larcher has captured many of the same tensions in the concise expression "colonies of citizens."[7] At the end of World War II many political elites in the old colonies imagined that tighter integration with the metropole would enable local populations to practice their citizenship more fully.[8] Although departmentalization would soon come to be seen more problematically, this course of reform enjoyed strong local support immediately after the war.[9]

The day after the passage of the departmentalization law, the Constituent Assembly launched into broad discussions of the rest of France's overseas possessions. These discussions spilled over five days and covered many issues, including shortages of goods, economic planning and development, labor regimes, the newly founded United Nations, the French Union, and salary and benefit disparities between the European and African civil servants.[10] With so many issues on the table, Senghor worried that deputies might lose sight of the urgency of education reform. Taking the floor of the Constituent Assembly on 21 March, the Senegalese deputy devoted his maiden speech almost entirely to the critical state of education in French West Africa. While scholars have often noted the important role that Senghor played in the political life of the nascent Fourth Republic, his deep engagement with the intricacies of education reform has drawn far less attention. The present chapter explores the complex ways in which Senghor and a number of other actors imagined and pursued education reform during the second half of the 1940s. Throughout this period, struggles over schooling were directly connected to broader contests over the future of French West Africa.[11]

In his first speech to the Constituent Assembly Senghor delivered a stinging critique of the colonial administration's handling of education. Tapping into the developing rhetoric about the obsolescence of subjecthood and the new reach of citizenship, he contended that the colonial administration continued to believe in the "training [*dressage*] of subjects" and not in the education of "free citizens."[12] Senghor had no trouble pointing up the deficiencies of existing schools. He remarked that spending on education still accounted for only 5 percent of total public expenditures in French West Africa and that, as a result of prolonged neglect, only one school-age child in twenty-four actually attended a French-run school.[13] While denouncing the colonial administration's failure to extend primary education, Senghor also drew attention to the paltry state of secondary education. After noting that the three secondary schools in AOF enrolled a combined total of only 174 Africans, Senghor went on to assert: "The truth is that they [colonial authorities] oppose the training of native elites by every possible means."[14] He explained that the federation's secondary schools routinely admitted European students ahead of Africans, and that even those African students who found spaces were often unfairly weeded out before they could prepare for the *baccalauréat*. In a bold flourish, Senghor called not only for the rapid expansion of primary and secondary education but also for the founding of a university in Dakar. He observed that higher education was still unavailable in AOF, even though the British were already making plans for a second university college in West Africa.

In making his case Senghor did not hesitate to remind the assembled deputies that the international community was watching France: "You are not unaware," he declared, "that certain nations have proposed placing all the colonies under international trusteeship." Underscoring the allegiance but also the high expectations of African populations, Senghor added: "We want to belong to the French Union, but only on the condition that democracy does not fear getting its feet wet by crossing the Mediterranean. And we want first of all for it to be established in public education."[15] Toward the end of his speech Senghor expressed his confidence in Marius Moutet, the Popular Front's minister of colonies, who had recently been named as the first minister of "Overseas France."[16] However, while willing to believe that Moutet would support an overhaul of education in AOF, Senghor remained convinced that most of the colonial bureaucracy would work to block broad reforms. Addressing Moutet, who sat listening in the hemicycle of the Palais Bourbon, the Senegalese deputy concluded: "I know, monsieur le ministre, that your bureaus are in agreement with me in the area of education. . . . But I am sure that local authorities are putting up and will continue to put up fierce resistance that will have to be crushed."[17]

THE HORIZONS OF CITIZENSHIP

By the spring of 1946 most of those sitting in the Constituent Assembly were prepared to extend some form of citizenship to the inhabitants of the African territories. However, when it came to precisely defining this status, consensus remained elusive. Would African populations become French citizens, like the inhabitants of the old colonies, or would they be granted a form of "overseas citizenship," whose content might be defined somewhat differently? These were not theoretical questions: the new class of African politicians that emerged at the end of the war tended to view citizenship as a powerful lever that might be used to secure practical gains in a variety of sectors.

Not too long ago, scholars working on late French colonialism in Africa tended to focus largely on struggles and reforms that could be inserted into decolonization narratives, which moved, haltingly but predictably, toward decentralization, territorial autonomy, and eventually national independence. More recently a spate of new scholarship has begun to give more weight to the various possibilities and contingencies of the immediate postwar period. In a series of publications Frederick Cooper has pointed out the liabilities of linear narratives that naturalize certain processes of decolonization, while downplaying or eliding alternate pathways of reform that remained both available and credible to postwar actors. Among other things, Cooper has shown just how powerful the concept and rhetoric of citizenship could be, once it was extended to all of the inhabitants of the African territories.[18] After French voters narrowly rejected the first constitutional draft, in a national referendum held on 5 May 1946, the First Constituent Assembly came together, in one of its final acts, to pass a far-reaching law declaring that "all the inhabitants of the overseas territories have the quality of citizens in the same way as French nationals from the metropole."[19]

Although the legal category of "French subjects" suddenly ceased to exist, the citizenship that had been extended to overseas populations remained something of an abstraction, whose practical implications had yet to be determined. Cooper has highlighted both the uncertainties and the new possibilities that were bundled into the new citizenship legislation. Many of the uncertainties emanated from the law's final clause, which stipulated that "particular laws will establish the conditions under which they [the inhabitants of the overseas territories] will exercise their citizens' rights."[20] While declaring African populations to be equal citizens, the Constituent Assembly had allowed that citizenship might need to be practiced differently in the African territories. This provision created the all too real possibility of a second-tier citizenship that would fail to provide all the rights, benefits, and opportunities granted to "metropolitan" citizens. But even as they took stock of this slipperiness, African leaders were already imagining the ways in which they might use the egalitarian rhetoric surrounding republican citizenship to demand a range of concessions from the French state.

Battles over citizenship during the Fourth Republic reverberated with earlier contests stretching back across the first half of the twentieth century and beyond. Lamine Guèye, the chief sponsor of the May 1946 citizenship law, was all too mindful of these connections. As a young man Guèye had been deeply influenced by the battles of Blaise Diagne, and particularly by the latter's campaign to have the originaires recognized as full French citizens during World War I.[21] After the second Diagne law was passed, in 1916, Guèye observed first-hand the many obstacles that the originaires encountered as they attempted to practice their new citizenship. As a prominent lawyer and politician during the interwar period, Guèye worked to secure and defend the rights of the originaires, which colonial authorities often sought to curtail. Sharply limited access to metropolitan schooling and metropolitan diplomas remained one—but hardly the only—barrier to more complete citizenship. Mindful of this longer history, Guèye saw the May 1946 law as more than just a bid to extend citizenship beyond originaire communities, to all the inhabitants of the African territories. He was also trying to accomplish something that the Diagne law of 1916 had failed to do—namely, to provide African citizens with all the rights, benefits, and opportunities available to their metropolitan counterparts. This dimension of the 1946 law has been overlooked by scholars, who tend to treat originaire citizenship between the wars as a rather straightforward fact, rather than as an ongoing struggle or as a partially unfulfilled promise.[22]

Even as he tried to avoid the pitfalls that had undermined the Diagne law of 1916, Guèye must have felt a sense of déjà vu as he observed the controversies that began to swirl around the new citizenship law. As the Second Constituent Assembly carried out its deliberations during the summer and fall of 1946, colonial interest groups and a surprising number of French politicians campaigned to repeal—or at least narrow—the citizenship that had been extended to African populations. Many of the detractors of the May 1946 law insisted that Africans were at best ready for a form of junior citizenship. After much doubt and discussion, the African deputies ultimately helped to preserve the existing citizenship provisions, which became article 80 of the new constitution of the Fourth Republic.[23] However, these politicians knew better than to expect that these provisions would automatically filter down to the realm of practice. Having publicly advocated for the rights of the originaires between the wars, Guèye understood better than others that the rights associated with citizenship would need to be instituted and enforced on the ground, in the face of considerable colonial opposition.

Taken as a whole the constitution that was promulgated on 27 October provided a rather ambiguous framework for the overseas territories, with many important details still needing to be worked out. The creation of a number of new political bodies was meant to suggest a more democratic, consensual relationship between France and its overseas possessions, which together now formed the "French Union." The new constitution provided for the creation of a consultative Assembly of the French Union, which would deliberate in Paris.[24] The constitution also called for an elected assembly to be set up in each of the overseas territories and for broader assemblies to be formed within the various federal groupings. In AOF the territorial assemblies were called general councils (*conseils généraux*), after the assemblies by the same name that existed in the departments of metropolitan France. The federal assembly was dubbed the Grand Council of AOF.[25] Although they possessed only narrowly defined prerogatives, these bodies were not insignificant. In addition to their fairly powerful symbolism, they served as important training grounds for a new class of African politicians. They also functioned as prominent conveyor belts, carrying the language and practice of a new style of politics out into African societies. Nonetheless, African and French politicians clearly understood that responsibility for overseas reform lay primarily with the National Assembly and the coalition governments that it produced. Although their numbers remained very limited, the African deputies who sat in the newly constituted National Assembly were determined to make the most of their positions.[26]

As noted in the introduction to this chapter, Senghor began to draw powerful connections between citizenship and educational rights in early 1946, before all the inhabitants of the African territories had actually become citizens. Once the citizenship law was passed on 7 May, and later enshrined in the October constitution, these connections became even more potent. If Senghor and other African deputies stressed linkages between citizenship and educational rights, so too did French officials of a more progressive stripe, such as the Socialists Marius Moutet and René Barthes. After serving as overseas minister in the provisional governments of 1946, Moutet went on to keep his ministerial portfolio for almost all of the following year. He had an important hand in the nomination of René Barthes as governor general of French West Africa in early 1946 and in the decision keep Barthes in Dakar throughout 1947. These two men had already worked closely together under the Popular Front, when Moutet had first held the position of minister of colonies. At that time Barthes had served as director of Moutet's cabinet. Having doubtless learned lessons from their rather hapless attempts to reform colonialism under the Popular Front, both men now sought to chart a more resolute course. Like many fellow Socialists, Moutet and Barthes considered that putting an end to old-style colonialism and creating a durable French Union could be best accomplished by integrating the African territories more fully into the institutions of the newly founded Fourth Republic.[27]

Moutet and Barthes both saw education as a central driver of this process of integration. In early December 1946, barely one week after the promulgation of the new constitution, Barthes instructed the governors of the West African territories to begin preparing for a raft of education reforms. Announcing the direction that these reforms would take, the governor general explained: "To put an end to the confusion that has prevailed up to this point, it seems indispensable to organize education in AOF on the same basis as in the metropole.... Henceforth, we will rigorously conform to the rules and regulations of the Education Ministry, adopting them entirely, or with a few modifications if necessary. Please inform the directors of your education departments of my intentions and please ask that they scrupulously implement all the rulings that you will soon be receiving on this subject."[28] While allowing that "a few modifications" could be made "if necessary," Barthes nonetheless made it clear that bundled reforms would begin to bring AOF's school system toward a metropolitan framework. The immediate postwar context provided enough of an opening and impetus for officials like Moutet and Barthes to move ahead with integrationist reforms that were far from intuitive for many members of France's colonial establishment.

Even before receiving the new directives announced by Barthes, some education officials in AOF had begun to adjust to the changing times. After spearheading the defense of rural schools at the time of the Brazzaville Conference, Yves Aubineau, the director general of education in AOF, now seemed to accept that education reform would entail a progressive alignment with metropolitan norms and practices. By August 1946 Aubineau could concede to Barthes that

FIG. 3. Postcard depicting an outdoor classroom in the Casamance region of Senegal during the early 1950s. From the author's personal collection.

"for reasons of a political nature and so as to honestly keep promises that we have a duty to honor, we must no longer distinguish between metropolitan and African education. The levels have to be exactly the same. It is certainly not necessary for [school] subjects to be absolutely identical. However, without fearing a refusal from [the Ministère de] l'Éducation nationale, we must be able to prepare students for the diplomas awarded in the Metropole, and no longer for 'African' diplomas, which are considered, by those who obtain them, as a veritable swindle."[29] In the space of just two and a half years Aubineau had done the equivalent of an about-face.

Although Moutet, Barthes, and Aubineau were all pushing for a progressive alignment with metropolitan educational norms, situations on the ground—at schools across French West Africa—often changed more slowly. Rural schools, and the conceptions of "native education" that had underpinned them, had been officially disavowed. But in many interior regions it would be years before more solidly built schoolhouses were constructed to replace the rustic and often leaky structures that had served as rural schools. In many cases, there

FIG. 4. Promotional photograph of a modern classroom in Bamako during the Fourth Republic. Produced by the Ministère de la France d'outre-mer. From the author's personal collection.

were still no schoolhouses at all. To take but one example, students in a particular corner of the Casamance region of Senegal continued to have class outside as late as the early 1950s, as they waited for a schoolhouse to be built (see fig. 3). The immediate postwar period did, however, produce a broadened commitment to building schools, many of which were financed through the new development fund known as the Fonds d'investissement pour le développement économique et social (FIDES).[30] And whereas the schools of the interwar period were usually designed and constructed so as to have a distinctly rustic quality, those of the post–World War II period frequently aspired to be more modern. Officials hoped that these new constructions could be used to showcase the concrete results of French development plans. To this end the Ministry of Overseas France produced and distributed photographs depicting solidly built, well-equipped classrooms and the new educational ambitions of the Fourth Republic (see fig. 4).

As they developed their plans to overhaul the school system in AOF, Moutet and Barthes forged closer relationships with officials at the French Education Ministry. For the most part, the latter ministry welcomed new opportunities to extend its activities overseas. These opportunities contrasted sharply with the situation that had prevailed between the wars, when most of the empire had lain beyond the reach of this metropolitan ministry. Prior to World War II, responsibility for overseas education fell largely to the Ministry of Colonies, the Ministry of Foreign Affairs, and the local administrations that these ministries fielded in the various parts of the French empire. Unlike the situation in metropolitan France, where the purviews of ministries corresponded to areas of professional or technical competence, ministerial responsibilities overseas tended to be defined geographically. Following this logic, the Ministry of Colonies held blanket authority over all sectors within the African colonies.[31] Although the Ministry of Colonies had long maintained regular exchanges with the Education Ministry, much of this contact was limited to personnel issues: the overseas school systems required infusions of French teachers and the Education Ministry was regularly called upon to provide the needed personnel. This situation began to change at the end of the war, as a series of reforms started to erode established administrative compartmentalizations.[32]

The Ministère de l'Éducation nationale was partially restructured so that it would be more prepared for its expanding purview. In August 1945 this ministry (hereafter also referred to as l'Éducation nationale) added a new Coordination Bureau for Education in Overseas France.[33] The following spring the First Constituent Assembly voted to give l'Éducation nationale a more official mandate overseas. A law passed on 18 May 1946 finalized the composition and expansive role of a new supervisory council within the Education Ministry, known as the Superior Council of National Education. Among other things, this law stipulated that this council "must be consulted, and must give its opinion, on all educational questions that are of general importance, regardless of which ministry they concern."[34]

Whereas the school systems of the empire had formerly resembled a decentralized patchwork, the tide was now running clearly in the other direction. A brochure published by l'Éducation nationale in 1946 described the shifts that were under way:

> Until recently ... it was accepted that this ministry did not need to be informed of the development of education in territories placed under the authority of the Ministry of Foreign Affairs or the Ministry of Colonies. Its role was simply to lend, "détacher," personnel to the various local administrations upon receiving requests. ... At the Liberation ... such nonintervention was rightly seen as excessive and dangerous. It appeared possible and desirable—without undermining the authority that belongs to the governors and residents general, without infringing on the prerogatives granted to the competent ministries—to coordinate this immense effort to develop education of all levels in all the territories open to our cultural initiatives.[35]

The authors of this brochure were at pains to avoid confrontational language that might pique the Ministry of Foreign Affairs, the Ministry of Overseas France, or the overseas administrations. But despite the conciliatory tone, l'Éducation nationale was clearly moving into new territories.

The expanding mandate of l'Éducation nationale can also be seen at the level of personnel. The decision to appoint Jean Capelle as the new director general of education in AOF signaled a clear departure from established precedents. Capelle was a pure product of l'Éducation nationale, who had little in common with the "colonials" who had preceded him in this position.[36] Arriving in Dakar in January 1947, Capelle took over a school system that had already entered into a period of structural change. But while integrationist reforms were clearly gaining ground, a gaping divide still separated the educational system in French West Africa from that found in metropolitan France. Convinced that more robust forms of integration were required, Capelle began to lay the foundations for a new *académie*.

Since Napoleonic times metropolitan France has been divided up into large school districts known as académies. After some early fluctuations, especially during the regime changes of the mid-nineteenth century, these administrative units eventually came to enjoy a remarkable stability. From the early Second Empire until the first years of the Fourth Republic, metropolitan France was divided into sixteen académies.[37] Central authorities in Paris appointed a chief administrator, or *recteur*, to oversee each of these large school districts. In practice recteurs tended to be primarily concerned with secondary schools and institutions of higher learning, leaving much of the management of primary education to officials operating at the level of individual departments.[38] However, recteurs did maintain an important official representative, or *inspecteur d'académie*, in each of the departments that they oversaw.[39] Developed by both Bonapartist and republican regimes, this administrative architecture reflected longstanding efforts to give unity and cohesion to France's national school system.

Upon arriving in Dakar, Capelle already imagined that these metropolitan structures could and should be introduced overseas and that French West Africa should become France's newest académie. This was no small ambition: in metropolitan France, académies had grown up over a period of almost 150 years; and while there was a precedent for an overseas académie, the Académie d'Alger had been founded in the very different historical context of the Second Republic. Moreover, unlike the northern portions of Algeria, which had been administratively organized as departments of France, French West Africa remained a colonial federation, made up of "overseas territories." None of these territorial units had metropolitan equivalents. Questions of scale only added to these complications. Although the académies of metropolitan France already amounted to large school districts, they would clearly be dwarfed by the proposed Académie de l'Afrique occidentale française, a school district that would cover an area eight and a half times the size of metropolitan France.

Convinced that the structures and practices of l'Éducation nationale had demonstrated their effectiveness, Capelle was not deterred by the large challenges that awaited him in Dakar. One of his first moves was to hire inspecteurs d'académie, certified by the Education Ministry, to head up the education departments (*services de l'enseignement*) in the various West African territories. Up until this time local education departments had been headed by *chefs de service*, officials who had risen through the colonial education bureaucracy and usually lacked the qualifications of their metropolitan counterparts.[40] In addition to hiring metropolitan inspecteurs d'académie, Capelle also sought to ensure that even ordinary education inspectors would henceforth be certified by l'Éducation nationale. The local *concours* that had formerly been used to select colonial education inspectors was held for the last time in November 1946. Although many colonial education officials were incorporated into the new corps of inspectors, most were forced to accept diminished roles and new superiors.[41] With these reforms, the education administration in French West Africa came to resemble more closely that found in a metropolitan académie.[42] For Capelle, the logical next step was to bring the schools and school administration of AOF formally into the metropolitan educational framework. In proposing such a program of reform, Capelle knew he could count on the support of the Education Ministry.[43]

From the moment he arrived in Dakar, Capelle worked to link his reformist agenda with the integrationist spirit of the early Fourth Republic. In a "lettre-programme" to Overseas Minister Moutet, the new director general of education sought to explain the logic and coherence of the reforms he planned to carry out. Capelle began by noting that "if we accept the idea that we must not colonize AOF, but rather, make it an extension of France, according to the wishes of the vast majority of Africans, it follows that education in AOF must be controlled, on a professional level, by the Ministère de l'Éducation nationale."[44] It is unclear how Capelle imagined that he could speak for the "wishes of the vast majority of Africans." And Capelle was far from the mark in asserting that Africans wished to make their territories into "an extension of France." Most African politicians were working to put an end to the colonial system of the Third Republic by pushing for the full complement of citizens' rights, benefits, and opportunities. But when it came to institutional relationships linking metropolitan France and the African territories, African political figures tended to remain both circumspect and strategic, as they worked to understand the shifting possibilities of the postwar period.[45]

However, beyond these misrepresentations, Capelle's program of reform did capture core demands of many African elites. So as to underscore these shared objectives, a group of African politicians—which included both Senghor and Guèye—insisted on signing their names to Capelle's lettre-programme.[46] However, even as they expressed their confidence in Capelle, African politicians were not content to leave the matter of education reform in the hands of an appointed official in Dakar, who reported to the Ministry of Overseas France. As we will see in the next section, Senghor and other African deputies were determined to turn education reform into a potent political issue.

CHANGING COURSE: LÉOPOLD SENGHOR
AND POSTWAR EDUCATION REFORM

It is not an overstatement to say that Senghor used the terrain of education reform both to imagine and to contest the future of French West Africa. The end of the war marked a fundamental turning point in Senghor's thinking. As we saw in chapter 5, he had spent a considerable portion of the Popular Front period campaigning for improvements to the colonial school system, while refusing to support a move toward a metropolitan educational framework, which he argued could only lead to cultural alienation. At the time Senghor saw no reason to make an exception for Senegal's Four Communes, even though many originaires insisted that they should enjoy the same educational rights and opportunities as other French citizens. As late as the first part of 1945 Senghor remained broadly supportive of the orientations of the colonial school system, even as he continued to propose certain adjustments.[47]

It was not until the second half of 1945 that Senghor's understanding of school reform began to veer in a new direction. This shift corresponded with his decision to enter politics by running for one of Senegal's two seats in the Constituent Assembly. As he campaigned around Senegal in preparation for the October 1945 elections, the professor turned politician must have heard a litany of complaints about existing schools. In previous chapters we have had many occasions to observe African discontent with colonial schools, which had escalated to new levels during the 1930s and World War

II. In the more liberal context of the immediate postwar period this discontent burst into full view. Politicians seeking election could ill afford to ignore mounting pressures for broad education reform, all the more so since the sharply limited political franchise in AOF was skewed toward graduates of colonial schools.[48] At the close of the war Senghor's political mentor and ally Lamine Guèye rode to political victories by harnessing demands for equality, in education and other areas.[49] Although such demands ran especially deep in the Four Communes, they could be heard across Senegal. As he took stock of public opinion, Senghor became more aware of the politics of education and the bankruptcy of colonial schools. As we observed at the opening of this chapter, by the time he delivered his maiden speech to the First Constituent Assembly, in March 1946, the newly elected deputy had developed a sweeping critique of the colonial administration's handling of education.

During the months that followed, Senghor moved from denunciations to concrete proposals. Having concluded that the colonial administration could not be trusted when it came to educational matters, he now contended that a metropolitan educational framework would provide needed guarantees. By mid-1947 African deputies affiliated with the French Socialist Party had begun work on a bill "aiming to place education in the overseas territories under the control of the Ministry of National Education." Senghor emerged as the leading sponsor of this legislation, while the Guinean deputy, Yacine Diallo, served as the bill's rapporteur.

As they charted their way forward in the National Assembly, these two politicians saw Capelle as an ally, whom they could ask for practical advice. Writing to Capelle in July 1947 to announce the bill that he was helping to prepare, Diallo noted: "We have begun the battle that will liberate education in AOF. You are aware of the opponents and obstacles. The Commission on Overseas Territories has appointed me to present the bill to the National Assembly. I would like to *be convincing*; for that I will need *technical* and *legal* arguments. You are well positioned to provide them to me."[50] For Diallo, Senghor, Guèye, and other African deputies operating in the context of 1947,

FIG. 5. Léopold Sédar Senghor, 1949. Photo by Felix Man/Picture Post/Hulton Archive. © Getty Images.

"liberating education" increasingly meant putting an end to the constrictive control of the colonial administration and forging new ties with l'Éducation nationale. From today's perspective, these tactics can seem surprising. After all, we know that "liberation" would come to be defined quite differently by the mid to late 1950s, as the West African territories began to move more definitively toward decentralization, internal autonomy, and then independence. Diallo's use of the word "liberation" reminds us that during the second half of the 1940s, prominent actors considered that there were multiple ways to combat the colonial system of the Third Republic and the Vichy regime.

While continuing his efforts in Paris, Senghor also worked to explain his bill to constituencies in French West Africa. Although a highly skilled pubic speaker, writer, and rhetorician, Senghor clearly had some explaining to do, given how much his own positions on education reform had shifted. At the beginning of 1948 the Senegalese deputy took up the subject of school reform in his newly founded newspaper, *Condition Humaine*. On the front page of the paper's inaugural issue, Senghor sought to highlight the logic and urgency of the bill he was sponsoring. In a lengthy article titled "The Condition of Our Development: Education Reform," he insisted that "this concrete reform would correspond to legitimate aspirations and to the Constitution, which has made overseas populations into citizens of the French Republic." As he had done on the floor of the First Constituent Assembly, Senghor proceeded to offer a scathing assessment of the state of education in AOF. As far as he was concerned, the causes of this neglect were not hard to discern. Senghor explained that "the pitiful state of education in the overseas territories is due to the fact that it has been under the control of the Ministry of Colonies. This ministry, under the Third Republic and the regime of the indigénat, saw education only as a political and economic tool."[51]

After contrasting the colonialism of the Third Republic with the new regime outlined in the 1946 constitution, Senghor went on to question whether the colonial administration had really accepted "this revolution." Among other things, he noted that Albert Charton still headed up the education department at the Overseas Ministry. After reminding his readers that Charton had been one of the chief architects of the rural school movement during the 1930s, Senghor declared that the real purpose of these schools "was to fight against ... the development of critical thinking and the formation of authentic elites, who would demand their place under the African sun." The Senegalese deputy then mockingly recalled what had been a mantra of colonial officials under the Third Republic: "We mustn't train intellectuals!" Confessing that he had been naïve to support rural schools during the Popular Front period, Senghor now insisted that Africans would be better served by l'Éducation nationale, which was well positioned to bring liberal, high-quality schooling to French West Africa.[52]

Although support for integrationist solutions ran deepest among Socialists such as Senghor, Diallo, and Guèye, these politicians had no trouble finding allies in other parties. Members of the Rassemblement démocratique africain (RDA)—the biggest political formation in French West Africa—had proposed a similar program of education reform at the group's inaugural conference in October 1946. The resolution adopted at that time called for a massive expansion of primary schooling, and for a turn toward metropolitan curricula and diplomas, especially at higher primary schools and normal schools. The RDA's resolution also demanded that each territory be equipped with a lycée and that a university be opened in Dakar no later than November 1947. Although RDA leaders had not sought to determine which ministry should have authority over education in AOF, their overall vision of education reform was quite compatible with that of Senghor, Diallo, and Guèye.[53]

Senghor also found considerable support within the Grand Council of AOF, the newly created federal assembly, which met for the first time in December 1947. Although its prerogatives were quite limited, this body discussed a broad array of issues and frequently made official recommendations. Following a well-established French tradition known as *le cumul des mandats*—which allowed and even encouraged politicians to hold two or more elective offices simultaneously—Senghor had been elected not only to the National Assembly but also to Senegal's General Council and to the Grand Council of AOF.[54]

In January 1948 Senghor asked the Grand Council to adopt a resolution in support of integrationist reforms, which would bring the educational system in AOF under the authority of l'Éducation nationale. The text that Senghor presented began by declaring that "the extremely pitiful state of education in French West Africa, where only one school-age child in twenty attends school," was "a consequence of the Code de l'indigénat, now abolished, which was a system that alienated men from their true selves." Moving from the past to the present, this resolution stressed that "the Constitution of the Fourth Republic has made all of the inhabitants of the overseas territories into French citizens," and that the school system in AOF had a duty "to make these new citizens into men worthy of this name, by preparing them to exercise their rights and responsibilities." Although Africans across the federation had been de jure citizens since 1946, Senghor contended that citizenship would remain stunted without broad accompanying reforms in key areas such as education. Apparently convinced by these arguments, the members of the Grand Council promptly voted to approve Senghor's resolution.[55]

The Grand Council returned to this issue during the summer of 1949. So as to help frame the discussion Senghor prepared and distributed a report, which explained once again why French West Africa needed to be constituted as an académie, placed under the jurisdiction of l'Éducation nationale.[56] During the ensuing debate at least one councilor did raise a dissenting voice. Boubou Hama, who represented the territory of Niger, bluntly asked his colleagues "how one can reconcile a concern for the preservation of African originality with the founding of an académie tied to the Ministry of National Education, which entails assimilation."[57] Hama's question was not unreasonable, given that the reforms being considered would invite a powerful metropolitan administration, whose centralization was legendary, to assume a broad role in AOF. Senghor was himself keenly aware of the centralization of France's school system and the standardization of French school curricula—features he had singled out for criticism during the Popular Front period. Although he had not abandoned these criticisms completely, Senghor had come to view the structures and traditions of l'Éducation nationale more favorably. On a practical level, he now saw the introduction of a metropolitan educational framework in AOF as a way to guarantee academic standards and secure educational rights, while also curtailing the meddling of colonial authorities.

As he worked with others to bring the school system in French West Africa under the purview of l'Éducation nationale, Senghor also hoped that he might be able to help reshape the mission of this ministry. Repeatedly invoking the preamble of the new constitution, which proclaimed that "the French Union is composed of nations and peoples who have joined their efforts to promote their respective civilizations," Senghor insisted that the French school system needed to open itself up to the peoples and cultures of Overseas France. In several articles published in *Condition Humaine*, the Senegalese deputy pointedly contrasted the broad and inclusive "spirit of the French Union" with the rather inward-looking orientations of the French educational system. Having himself attended metropolitan schools, Senghor was all too aware of the negligible place that Africa occupied in French curricula and schoolbooks. The founding of the French Union had scarcely altered this state of affairs. When they evoked the overseas territories at all, French schools tended to recycle demeaning stereotypes about primitive and colorful lands that France was generously bringing into the march of progress.[58]

Writing in *Condition Humaine*, Senghor outlined some of the ways in which France's "national" school system needed to be reworked, in order to reflect the spirit and vocation of the French Union. In an article published in the spring of 1949, Senghor declared that "the first measure that needs to be taken is rather general. More space must be given to overseas history, overseas geography, and overseas civilizations in school curricula of every level. More space, to be sure, but I would also say a privileged space. For it is not enough to teach about other civilizations; we must also restore their dignity, that is to say, their humanistic values. We must banish contempt [for other civilizations], that absurd form of ignorance, from French schools."[59] However, even as he faulted the French school system for not living up to the inclusive, multicultural principles that had been enshrined in the 1946 constitution, Senghor projected a future-oriented optimism. He went so far as to imagine that the French school system might become a transcontinental space for enriching cultural exchanges and *métissages*.[60]

If Senghor was now able to view the French educational system in this way, it was partly because his own thinking about cultures and cultural interactions had evolved since the late 1930s. The war itself had served as an important catalyst. As Nazi forces continued their rapid advances across France in mid-June 1940, Senghor found himself in a military unit operating in Burgundy, near the town of La-Charité-sur-Loire. After unsuccessful attempts to halt German advances in the region, Senghor and other members of his unit were eventually taken prisoner on 20 June. Senghor spent the following eighteen months in several different POW camps, where he came face to face with Nazi racism. At one point, he and a group of African soldiers were forced in front of a firing squad because of the color of their skin, only to be spared at the last moment after a French officer spoke out in their defense.[61]

In a series of articles and interviews Senghor subsequently explained how his prolonged captivity had altered his thinking, causing him to become more attuned to the dangers of cultural and racial essentialisms and to the importance of solidarities that could bring peoples together across differences. Amid the hatreds and destruction of World War II, he began to think more deeply about beneficent exchanges among peoples and cultures, which in other times had produced great flowerings of civilization. Summing up these shifts in perspective, Senghor later contended that by the time he was finally released in February 1942, he had been "cured of ghetto Negritude" and had come to embrace a more positive view of cultural métissage, as one of the central drivers of human progress.[62]

While recommending broad reforms to France's educational system, Senghor also suggested that some special provisions needed to be granted to the schools of French West Africa. When it came to proposing these provisions, Senghor proceeded cautiously. As we have seen, the notion of distinct forms of "adapted education" had been badly compromised by the colonial administration. Highly mindful of this legacy, Senghor now contended that the process of adapting French education to AOF should be guided, not by colonial authorities but by academic and research institutions, such as the Centre national de la recherche scientifique (CNRS), the Institut d'ethnologie de Paris, the Institut français d'Afrique noire, and the Sorbonne. As far as Senghor was concerned, these bodies were much more capable than the colonial administration of understanding the African territories and their educational needs.[63] The Senegalese deputy went one step further, by calling for the creation of "autonomous" overseas académies, which would possess needed flexibility and expanded prerogatives, while still remaining under the jurisdiction of l'Éducation nationale. Senghor imagined that a partially decentralized arrangement of this sort would "temper the universalist tendency of the French school system, which might [otherwise] lead to standardization."[64]

As the preceding comments suggest, Senghor was not proposing that a preexisting metropolitan educational framework simply be transferred to French West Africa. As the historian Gary Wilder has argued, Senghor chose to imagine that African citizenship and the creation of the French Union might constitute revolutionary events, capable not only of transforming the overseas territories but also of remaking France itself, into a federal, multicultural republic.[65] Senghor hoped that the French educational system might provide a fertile space for this process of renegotiation and reinvention. However improbable such prospects might seem from the perspective of today, these possibilities had not been foreclosed during the late 1940s. But even as Senghor imagined broad, "revolutionary" transformations, he knew that many in France's colonial establishment clung to much narrower visions of the future.

REFORM AND REACTION IN THE
COLONIAL ADMINISTRATION

Many colonial officials found reasons to lament the trend toward integration that developed after World War II. This trend could be observed in a variety of sectors, as postwar approaches to planning and modernization began to challenge established separations between metropolitan France and the overseas territories. The historians Véronique Dimier and William B. Cohen have both documented the anxieties and disappointments of colonial officials, who struggled to adjust to a rapidly changing landscape that required them to share authority with a proliferation of outside entities and experts.[66] Although many colonial functionaries viewed these developments suspiciously, they were initially rather unsuccessful in opposing them, all the more so since Marius Moutet, the first minister of Overseas France, often supported integrationist reforms that led metropolitan entities to become more involved in the African territories.

However, when Moutet was replaced, in October 1947, dynamics started to shift. Moutet was succeeded by Paul Coste-Floret, a leading figure in the center-right Christian Democratic party, the Mouvement républicain populaire or MRP. When it came to the postwar development of the African territories, the MRP tended to favor decentralized arrangements that would preserve—albeit in updated forms—longstanding separations between the metropole and Overseas France.[67] Coste-Floret presided over the Overseas Ministry for two years before being replaced by Jean Letourneau, who was also a member of the MRP. Encouraged by this change in leadership and ideological orientation, colonial officials in Paris and Dakar soon began to organize more concerted opposition to integrationist reforms.

Officials at the Overseas Ministry were keenly aware of their diminished influence over educational policy in AOF and in other parts of Overseas France. One official in the ministry's education department observed: "It seems that, during the last several years, the ministry has not had a clearly defined educational policy, or has not managed to advocate effectively for its policy." This official lamented the weakened position of his own department, which had been downgraded from a *direction* to a *service* in the spring of 1946. In the world of French administration, this change amounted to a considerable loss of prestige and authority. This official went on to recommend that the education department within the Overseas Ministry be restored to its former status so that it could more forcefully resist the growing "intrusions" of l'Éducation nationale.[68]

Officials at the Overseas Ministry became alarmed in the spring of 1949, when they learned that Capelle was drafting a decree proposal that called for the creation of an Académie de l'AOF. Upon receiving a copy of Capelle's proposal, the head of the ministry's education department (G. Gaston) immediately contacted his colleagues to request advice on how to proceed.[69] In his reply the ministry's director of personnel insisted that Capelle's plan "blatantly contradicts fundamental principles which have, until now, always given the overseas minister exclusive control over all aspects of administration in the overseas territories."[70] In another note this same official argued that, on account of l'Éducation nationale's increasing intrusiveness, it was necessary "to defend vigorously the prerogatives of the overseas minister."[71] The director of political affairs—none other than Robert Delavignette—concurred with his colleagues, stressing that "the overseas minister, who is solely responsible for the territories placed under the authority of his ministry, must remain the sole judge of all problems in these territories, especially when, as in the case of education, they might have political consequences."[72]

After listening to the opinions of these key officials, Overseas Minister Coste-Floret wrote to Capelle in July 1949 to explain why he could not support the latter's decree proposal. Coste-Floret noted: "I subscribe to your view that colonial education must be replaced by education which meets metropolitan standards, and which is sanctioned, *whenever possible*, by metropolitan diplomas. This does not mean, however, that a metropolitan education administration should be transplanted overseas." So as to underscore this last point, the minister added that "the administrative structures of l'Éducation nationale do not apply overseas."[73] Coste-Floret's letter was forwarded to Education Minister Yvon Delbos, perhaps by Capelle, who was careful to enlist the support of his colleagues in the metropole. In his response to Coste-Floret, Delbos reiterated that l'Éducation nationale could not be bypassed when it came to setting education policies in the overseas territories. The education minister explained that the only "rational" and "efficient" solution was to equip the overseas territories with education administrations like that in France.[74] Clearly upset by this reply, Gaston, the head of the Overseas Ministry's education department, opined to a colleague: "I am very displeased with these results, [and] and even more displeased to see that the minister of National Education is not abandoning his policy of centralization and assimilation (even though he denies this second charge). For him, the French nation encompasses the overseas territories, and the troubles we have overseas are the making of colonial ministers and their functionaries."[75]

While encountering new levels of obstruction at the Overseas Ministry, Capelle also found his efforts increasingly undermined by officials in Dakar. Whereas Governor General Barthes had been a powerful ally, his successor, Paul Béchard, ultimately proved less dependable. A Socialist like Barthes, Béchard had initially supported plans to develop a metropolitan educational framework in AOF.[76] This stance had put Béchard at odds with officials at the Overseas Ministry.[77] Capelle soon learned, however, that pledges of support from Béchard did not guarantee the backing of other colonial functionaries, many of whom chafed at the growing involvement of l'Éducation nationale in the African territories.[78] After concluding that he could no longer carry out his mission, Capelle asked, in March 1949, to be relieved of his duties so that he could return to France and take up a position he had recently been offered, as recteur of the Académie de Nancy.[79]

When they heard about these plans, Senghor and other African politicians quickly intervened, urging Capelle to reconsider.[80] In a private meeting with Capelle, Béchard made a similar appeal. Believing that he had secured new pledges of support from the governor general, Capelle agreed to stay on in Dakar to continue the program of reform that he had begun.[81] However, when he discovered that colonial officials in Dakar and Paris were continuing to block his efforts to create an Académie de l'AOF, Capelle offered his resignation a second time. No longer prepared to stand with Capelle, Béchard now acquiesced. In July 1949 Capelle returned to France to become the new recteur of the Académie de Nancy.[82] Although he left Dakar without having accomplished his primary goal, Capelle had helped to set into motion a powerful process of integrationist reform. As we will see, plans to formally institute a metropolitan educational framework in AOF would soon gain new traction. Moreover, within a few years Capelle would himself return to Dakar to preside once again over AOF's school system.[83]

While viewing Capelle's departure as a temporary setback, Senghor, Diallo, and other African deputies pressed on with their reform efforts. In August 1949 Senghor wrote to Capelle, both to praise his work in AOF and to enlist his continued support. The Senegalese deputy confided: "I think that if we remain vigilant we will be able to continue, not without difficulties it is true, the magnificent undertaking you have begun. I am counting on your support when it comes to metropolitan education officials. For my part, I think it is necessary to strike at the top, that is to say, to bring my bill . . . to a successful conclusion. That is the only way to put an end to the obstruction of local authorities and the education department at the Overseas Ministry."[84] Despite the disappointments of the first half of 1949, the alliances that had been forged among African politicians, Capelle, and the Ministry of National Education remained intact. As political dynamics in Paris and French West Africa began to shift, the prospects of major education reforms soon brightened.

By 1950 France found itself mired in a series of deepening conflicts overseas. French forces were tied down in escalating battles in Indochina, just as nationalist movements in Morocco and Tunisia were entering a bold new phase. Although the nationalist insurrection and bloody repression in Madagascar had subsided, a pro-independence party was becoming increasingly active in Cameroon.[85] Compared to these hot spots, French West Africa could still appear relatively calm. But even in AOF, conflicts had been escalating. For several years colonial authorities had locked themselves into a policy of confrontation with the Rassemblement démocratique africain (RDA) and its local affiliates in the various West African territories. Authorities had shown outward hostility toward the RDA ever since this umbrella party decided to align itself nominally with the French Communist Party (PCF) in 1946. By 1950 conflicts had grown particularly acute in the Ivory Coast, where the political party of Félix Houphouët-Boigny, the Parti démocratique de la Côte d'Ivoire (PDCI), served as a powerful RDA affiliate.[86] Given the many conflicts that they were managing overseas, authorities in Paris soon found new reasons to explore other policy options in French West Africa.

An important turning point came in July 1950, with the formation of a new government led by René Pleven and his party, the Union démocratique et socialiste de la Résistance (UDSR). Behind the leadership of the freshly appointed overseas minister, François Mitterrand, French authorities began to pull back from direct confrontation with the PDCI in the hope of establishing a new dynamic in Ivory Coast and other West African territories. By this time African politicians such as Houphouët-Boigny had few remaining illusions about the influence of the PCF, which had been frozen out of French governments ever since May 1947. In response to French overtures and his own shifting political calculus, Houphouët-Boigny eventually helped to orchestrate a severing (*désapparentement*) of the RDA from the French Communist Party. Consummated in September 1950, this move eventually produced a palpable détente, not only in Ivory Coast but also in other territories where the RDA was firmly implanted.[87]

Although de-escalation with the RDA did not begin until the second half of 1950, overseas reforms had begun to acquire new momentum as of the beginning of the year. Passed in January, the "second Lamine Guèye law" established that African civil servants would no longer be distinguished from their European counterparts when it came to salaries and benefits.[88] Even the perennially stalled deliberations over an overseas labor code seemed to gain new momentum. Modeled after France's Code du travail, this code was intended to provide a comprehensive framework for such things as worker protections, worker rights, and industrial relations. Efforts to craft and introduce a labor code for the African territories were not unrelated to concurrent struggles to found a new Académie de l'AOF. In both cases reformers hoped that metropolitan frameworks might provide a reliable way forward. As Frederick Cooper has shown in the case of the labor code, African and French reformers pursued only partially overlapping goals. More than anything else, French authorities were seeking to find frameworks that could stabilize the overseas territories by channeling

African demands toward development objectives that were compatible with continued French rule. African reformers, on the other hand, sought first and foremost to wrest tangible gains from the reformist colonial state, while remaining open-minded about future political arrangements. Despite such tensions, there was ultimately enough common ground for integrationist reforms to advance.[89]

Unlike his immediate predecessors at the Overseas Ministry, Mitterrand saw no reason to continue blocking plans to bring AOF's school system under the purview of the Ministry of National Education. In a 1950 letter to Education Minister Pierre-Olivier Lapie, Mitterrand took stock of the deep changes that had already reshaped the education administration in French West Africa. The overseas minister observed that "in all the territories the education departments have been placed under the authority of an inspecteur d'académie. The structure of the education administration in AOF is now that of an académie and it appears that we have an interest, so as to show the will of the French government to equip our territories with a solid school system, in acknowledging this evolution by creating an Académie d'A.O.F."[90] It had been three and a half years since Capelle and the African deputies had first proposed such a reform. On 27 November 1950, Pleven, Mitterrand, Lapie, and Secretary of State for Overseas France Louis-Paul Aujoulat finally signed an interministerial decree creating the new académie.[91]

Although Senghor's bill had served as an important stimulus, it was never passed into law. Given the volatility of the National Assembly during the Fourth Republic, and the instability of French governments, reforming by decree frequently proved more expedient than reforming through legislative means.[92] The November 1950 decree brought a final, belated blow to the colonial school system of the Third Republic, which had in many ways already ceased to exist. African politicians and officials at the Ministry of National Education could savor a hard-won victory. The education minister's chief of staff summed up by noting that the creation of the new académie was "the result of long negotiations, during which we never stopped offering our support. We fully embraced the SENGHOR plan."[93]

As we have seen throughout this chapter, the growing trend toward educational integration did not result from a natural French penchant for assimilationist solutions, even though such a view has been repeated often in scholarly studies of late colonialism. Much of the French colonial establishment did not support forms of educational integration that would bring a rival ministry more and more deeply into the African territories. If the school system in AOF came to be increasingly recast along metropolitan lines, it was partly because colonial authorities had little remaining credibility in educational matters, and partly because a cross-cutting coalition of French reformers and African politicians came together to advocate for such a course of reform. Motivations differed. Governmental authorities in France saw the establishment of a metropolitan educational architecture in AOF as a means of firming up ties with the African territories, at a time when European empires faced mounting challenges. Officials in France's Education Ministry were motivated partially by corporatist objectives as they moved to extend the activities, structures, and personnel of l'Éducation nationale to broad new spheres overseas. African leaders, on the other hand, were generally seeking to chart a reliable course away from the colonial system of the Third Republic and the Vichy period and the restrictive, inferior schools that had been set up to train "colonial subjects." During the early Fourth Republic, integrationist reforms could appear as a clear step toward equality and new opportunities associated with citizenship and not subjecthood. The fact that most African politicians put at least some stock in these reforms does not mean that they saw the future solely in terms of increased integration. In the complex and quickly changing context of the Fourth Republic, many African politicians proceeded strategically and flexibly as they tried to understand and exploit new possibilities.[94]

Although 1950 marks the formal endpoint of this study, the epilogue to this book looks briefly toward the last decade of colonial rule and the first decade of African independence. The integrationist educational reforms that were carried out during the early Fourth Republic would have important legacies during the 1950s and 1960s, inflecting the process of decolonization and the construction of postcolonial relationships.

Epilogue

Across the first half of the twentieth century schools remained closely tied up with broader battles over French West Africa and its development. By 1950 the separate forms of schooling that had been crafted for colonial subjects had given way to a process of educational integration, as various groups of African and French actors struggled to define the new parameters and possibilities of citizenship. Although AOF's school system had clearly entered into a period of structural reform, it would be rather easy to overstate the changes that had occurred. In many ways the legacies of a half century of colonial education remained all too apparent. Statistics for the 1949–50 school year revealed that there were still fewer than 139,000 students—or a mere 4.2 percent of the school-age population—in the recognized schools of French West Africa.[1]

And whereas formal primary education still reached fewer than one child in twenty, the development of secondary schools remained even more stunted. By the late 1940s secondary schooling was no longer confined to Dakar and Saint-Louis, as it had been throughout the interwar period. But even as a scattering of collèges and lycées sprang up in the other West African territories, the growth of secondary education remained quite modest. Perpetuating an old colonial trope, many French officials continued to view the extension of primary education as the overriding priority, which should not be compromised by a premature focus on secondary schooling. Capelle noted with apparent satisfaction that 250 students from AOF obtained the *baccalauréat* in 1956—a fifteen-fold increase from 1948.[2] However, these same figures could just as easily be used to underscore a very different point: as late as the mid-1950s, the vast Federation of French West Africa, with a population approaching 20 million, was still producing a mere 250 *bacheliers* per year. The contrast with the state of affairs in France could scarcely have been more striking. Secondary schooling in the metropole entered into a period of rapid expansion in the wake of World War II. With slightly more than forty-two thousand students passing the baccalauréat in France in 1956, the annual production of bacheliers had already doubled since 1938, and even steeper increases were just around the corner.[3] By comparison, the "democratization" of secondary education in AOF had scarcely begun. This could be seen not only in the numbers of African secondary school students and bacheliers but also in the attitudes of many Europeans, who were reluctant to see the federation's lycées lose their white majorities.

It is of course problematic to hold up metropolitan French norms as goals toward which Africans should aspire. This sort of norming would itself become a powerful legacy of the late colonial period, especially when it came to schooling.[4] In the end metropolitan norms had only been partially transferred to AOF by the time the sweeping loi-cadre was passed, in June 1956. Spearheaded by Overseas Minister Gaston Defferre and approved by the National Assembly, this omnibus legislation soon loosened normative frameworks, paving the way for a cascade of decentralizing reforms that would transfer many aspects of administration—and an expanding list of governmental functions—to the level of individual territories.[5]

It quickly became apparent that these bundled reforms would leave little room for large territorial groupings such as the Federation of French West Africa. The loi-cadre, and the application decrees that flowed from it, called for most of the federal services in Dakar to be broken up and partitioned out to the administrations and proto-governments of individual territories. Certain key functions were returned to central authorities in Paris. In the wake of the loi-cadre, much of the federal educational bureaucracy in Dakar was hollowed out, as education departments in the different territories took on new functions and personnel. Although the Dakar-based administration of the Académie de l'AOF continued to exist, its role quickly shrank to that of a coordinating body, charged with overseeing curricula, diplomas, and the training of teachers.[6] As it turned out, many of the most zealous decentralizers hailed from the Ministry of Overseas France. Long uncomfortable with the integrationist thrust of many postwar reforms, officials at the Ministry of Overseas France could briefly imagine that the loi-cadre might allow them to regain some of their former primacy.

Times were rapidly changing, however. Whereas many African politicians had remained suspicious of decentralizing measures in the immediate aftermath of World War II, such a course of reform drew considerable support during the mid to late 1950s. If growing numbers of African politicians embraced decentralization in the form of "territorialization," it was partly because these reforms were finally coupled with a decisive move toward fuller democratic participation. The loi-cadre introduced universal suffrage, while also establishing a single electoral college in each of the eight territories of AOF. In 1957 voters proceeded to elect "territorial assemblies" with broad new mandates.[7] These assemblies in turn helped to select councils of government, which possessed considerable responsibility over internal matters, including primary, secondary, and technical education. Senghor emerged as perhaps the most outspoken opponent of the territorializing ambitions of the loi-cadre. Convinced that larger groupings afforded needed guarantees in the twentieth century, the Senegalese deputy ominously described the dismantling of French West Africa as a process of "balkanization" that would create a string of awkwardly divided, weak states.[8] Such warnings ultimately had little impact on historical events, as African independence soon confirmed territorial divisions. By the time the new West African nations declared their independence, in 1960, the Federation of French West Africa had already expired.[9] After being undermined by the provisions of the loi-cadre, AOF was officially abolished two years later by the Constitution of the Fifth Republic, even if it took some additional months to finish unwinding the federation.

As the new West African nations worked to consolidate their control over various state functions, one could reasonably wonder what "decolonization" and "independence" would mean in the field of education. If Africans had contested colonial schooling in a variety of ways during the first half of the twentieth century, many of these contests had been structured by demands for educational equality and an expanded set of educational and professional opportunities. Although eminently meaningful in the context of French West Africa, these contests did little to prepare Africans to think about schooling in new "postcolonial" or "national" terms. This helps to explain why, at independence, African governments quickly negotiated bilateral cooperation agreements with France, which preserved an array of linkages with the former colonial power. Although these agreements concerned many sectors, provisions in the field of education proved particularly extensive, especially when it came to secondary and higher education.[10]

The cooperation accords tended to cast France as a supplier of teachers, educational expertise, and standards and the new African nations as rather willing clients. Unbalanced bilateral relationships were not the whole story, however. Shared standards made it possible for African secondary school and university students to migrate around francophone West Africa and especially to France, in pursuit of educational opportunities. The francophone African states also began to meet collectively to discuss educational policies and challenges, with a view to sharing approaches and preserving broad consistencies across the region. The French Ministry of National Education served as a key participant in these regional meetings, as did the newly created French Ministry of Cooperation.

Over time, the new educational systems were slowly "Africanized" and "nationalized," even if many found this process to be slow and rather inconclusive. By the late 1960s growing numbers of African politicians, students, teachers, and intellectuals had begun to criticize more publicly the continuing dependency on French educational models and, in many cases, French teachers and professors. Denunciations of this sort became explosive around the time of May 1968, particularly in Senegal, where the French presence had remained rather striking. Shifting views of schooling would soon complicate the standing of Senghor and other governing African elites. Senghor's long postwar battle for educational equality increasingly faded from view, as younger generations came to see him as a leading defender of France's cultural and educational presence in the region. Such views did not do justice to Senghor's complexities. As we have seen, during the Popular Front period, Senghor emerged as a daring spokesman for African cultures and languages and for new forms of Franco-African education. Even as he came to promote educational integration during the Fourth Republic, Senghor remained a highly visible champion of Negritude. His understanding of Negritude had shifted in important ways since the late 1930s, becoming more open to cultural *métissage* and the need for worldwide cultural exchanges. However, despite these adjustments, Senghor continued to serve as a powerful spokesman for African cultures, literatures, and arts during his long presidency. During these two decades (1960–80) Senghor helped to turn his new nation into a key gathering place for black intellectuals and artists. When it came to schools, however, Senghor ultimately favored a cautious course of Africanization—or "Senegalization"—that would preserve strong linkages to France.

In Senegal as in the other nations that emerged from French West Africa—Benin, Burkina Faso, Guinea, Ivory Coast, Mali, Mauritania, and Niger—ties to the French educational system ultimately weakened. However, in many ways, the fashioning of truly "national" school systems has remained a strikingly unfinished project. As the colonial period recedes deeper into history, the region's school systems have increasingly faced a range of other obstacles, such as fragile economies, governance problems, and a world order that has eroded the resources, structures, and legitimacy of African states. If the task of consolidating and improving national school systems across the region remains daunting in the early twenty-first century, it has never been more important. Although the struggles examined in this book were shaped by different historical contexts, my hope is that they will provide insights and encouragement to present-day actors seeking to craft the schools—and possibilities—of tomorrow.

NOTES

Introduction

1. On the mapping of colonized spaces, see Edney, *Mapping an Empire*; Barrow, *Making History, Drawing Territory*; and Blais et al., *Territoires impériaux*. On mapping in colonial Africa, see Surun, "French Military Officers and the Mapping of West Africa"; and Surun, "Une souveraineté à l'encre sympathique." See also Bassett, "Cartography and Empire Building."

2. On these infrastructure projects, see Conklin, *A Mission to Civilize*, chap. 2.

3. For two older but still useful sources on railway construction in AOF, see Mangolte, "Le chemin de fer de Conakry au Niger"; and Faur, "La mise en valeur ferroviaire de l'A.O.F."

4. Fall, *Le travail forcé*, chap. 3.

5. On French educational efforts in nineteenth-century Senegal, see Bouche, *L'enseignement*, vol. 1; Duke Bryant, *Education as Politics*; and Foster, *Faith in Empire*, chaps. 1–2.

6. Ponty, "Discours du Gouverneur Général," 24. Unless otherwise indicated, all translations are my own.

7. Eugen Weber colorfully captured these realities in his landmark study, *Peasants into Frenchmen*, esp. part 1. Certain scholars have suggested that Weber overstated the isolation of rural communities by focusing on particularly remote regions. Even if one accepts this point, it remains true that sizeable portions of rural France remained heavily marked by local particularisms at the dawn of the Third Republic. For a related study, see Lehning, *Peasant and French*.

8. On the founding and impact of republican schools, see Ozouf, *L'école, l'Église et la République*, chaps. 1–5; Ozouf and Ozouf, with Aubert and Steindecker, *La République des instituteurs*; Mayeur, *Histoire générale de l'enseignement et de l'éducation en France*, 3:581–635; Prost, *Histoire de l'enseignement*, chaps. 9, 12, 14, 16; and Déloye, *École et citoyenneté*.

9. For two contrasting accounts of the influence of primary schools on the process of national integration, see Weber, *Peasants into Frenchmen*, esp. chaps. 18 and 29; and Chanet, *L'école républicaine*.

10. I discuss the originaires in depth in chapters 1 and 2.

11. As we will see, primary schools in metropolitan France and in the colonies were organized into several different tiers.

1. Conflicting Visions

1. Johnson, *The Emergence*.

2. See esp. Johnson, "The Rivalry between Diagne and Merlin"; Johnson, "The Senegalese Urban Elite"; and Johnson, "The Impact of the Senegalese Elite."

3. Mamadou Diouf, Elizabeth Foster, Hilary Jones, and David Robinson have helped to renew the study of the originaires during the nineteenth century. See Diouf, "The French Colonial Policy of Assimilation"; Diouf, "Assimilation coloniale et identités religieuses"; Foster, *Faith in Empire*, chaps. 1 and 3; Jones, *The Métis of Senegal*; and Robinson, *Paths of Accommodation*, chaps. 5–6. For a detailed recent study that situates the originaires squarely within the first two decades of the twentieth century, see Thiam, *La révolution*.

4. A 1921 census conducted in Senegal determined that there were 18,458 originaires. "Colonie du Sénégal, Recensement 1921," ANS, FAOF, Sous-série 17G: Affaires politiques (hereafter 17G), 239/108.

5. On the long history of these towns, and particularly Saint-Louis, see Sinou, *Comptoirs et villes coloniales*, part 1; Biondi, *Saint-Louis du Sénégal*; Bonnardel, *Saint-Louis du Sénégal*; and Dozon, *Saint-Louis du Sénégal*.

6. On the slave trade and its impact on West Africa, see esp. Klein, *Slavery and Colonial Rule in French West Africa*; Barry, *Senegambia*; and Manning, *Slavery and African Life*.

7. Slavery had been officially abolished once before, in 1794, by the revolutionary government known as the National Convention. In the event this measure was applied unevenly in the old colonies before Napoleon's government reinstituted slavery in 1802. See Dubois, *A Colony of Citizens*; Dubois, *Avengers of the New World*; and Benot, *La Révolution française et la fin des colonies*.

8. On Faidherbe's rule in Senegal, see Barry, *Senegambia*, esp. chaps. 12–18; Saint-Martin, *Le Sénégal sous le Second Empire*; and Amselle, *Affirmative Exclusion*, chap. 3 ("Faidherbe: A Republican Raciologist").

9. First created during the French Revolution, communes have remained important territorial units ever since. For a history of French communes, see Fougère, Machelon, and Monnier, *Les communes et le pouvoir*.

10. On the new political institutions established in the Four Communes during the early Third Republic, see Johnson, *The Emergence*, chap. 2; Légier, "Les institutions municipales"; Idowu, "Assimilation in 19th Century Senegal"; and Idowu, "The Establishment of Elective Institutions."

11. Initially the colony's governor selected the town mayors from among the members of the municipal councils. After 1882 the municipal councils began to elect the mayors from among their members. See Légier, "Les institutions municipales," 424, 453.

12. Senegal's General Council was initially made up of sixteen members, ten from Saint-Louis, four from Gorée-Dakar, and two from Rufisque. Councilors were elected for six-year terms. In addition to a regular session once each year, the General Council was also routinely convened for extraordinary sessions.

13. The inhabitants of Saint-Louis and Gorée elected a deputy for the first time in 1848, with the advent of the Second Republic. This political position was quickly lost, with the fall of the republic and the founding of the Second Empire. After being reinstituted in 1871, this deputyship was again taken away in 1875, before being reestablished for good in 1879. See Binoche, "Les élus d'outre-mer au Parlement," esp. 82–88. See also Johnson, *The Emergence*, 49–52; and Idowu, "The Establishment of Elective Institutions," 269.

14. During the first decades of the Third Republic, colonial authorities in Senegal often did their best to oppose the introduction of elective bodies modeled after those in the metropole. In the end the creation of such institutions was decided primarily in Paris, against the recommendations of Senegal's governors. Idowu, "The Establishment of Elective Institutions," 265–69; Foster, *Faith in Empire*, 25.

15. On disannexation, see esp. Searing, "Accommodation and Resistance," 70–75; and Foster, *Faith in Empire*, 47, 64–67. For a contemporary French overview of disannexation, see "La désannexation des territoires indigènes," *Bulletin du Comité de l'Afrique Française*, no. 6 (June 1895): 184–85.

16. See Jones, *The Métis of Senegal*, chap. 2; Robinson, *Paths of Accommodation*, 108–39. See also Searing, "Accommodation and Resistance," 274–84, 324–43.

17. Originaire populations were composed of a majority of blacks and a minority of *métis*. I describe the composition of originaire communities in more detail later in this chapter and again in chapter 2. In both chapters, I use the French term *métis* to designate mixed-race populations, rather than choosing an English-language equivalent or the rival French term *mulâtres* (mulattoes), which tended to have more negative connotations.

18. The General Council met in Saint-Louis. On the expanding influence of *métis* politicians, see Thiam, *La révolution*, 13–22; Johnson, *The Emergence*, chap. 6; Zuccarelli, *La vie politique sénégalaise*, 80–90; Jones, *The Métis of Senegal*, chaps. 6–7; and Manchuelle, "Métis et colons."

19. During the same space of time a different trend could be observed on the island of Gorée, where the local population experienced a protracted decline, falling to 1,306. These figures are taken from a table provided in Johnson, *The Emergence*, 35. For a fuller account of the changes that reshaped these towns, see Sinou, *Comptoirs et villes coloniales*.

20. The early Third Republic played an important role in crystallizing the citizen-subject binary, which had remained more fluid during much of the nineteenth century. See esp. Saada, *Les enfants de la colonie*, chap. 4.

21. Daughton, *An Empire Divided*. See also White and Daughton, *In God's Empire*.

22. Foster, *Faith in Empire*.

23. In the event the 1904 law was not fully applied and many recognized

congregations were able to maintain their schools. For detailed accounts of challenges to congregations and their schools, see Boyer, "La législation anti-congréganiste 1901–1904"; Delpal, "L'application des lois anticongréganistes"; and Sorrel, *La République contre les congrégations*.

24. On these metropolitan conflicts, see Baubérot, *Histoire de la laïcité en France*, esp. chaps. 4–5; Ozouf, *L'école, l'Église et la République*, chap. 7; and Weil, *Politiques de la laïcité au XXe siècle*.

25. On the partial translation of church-state conflicts to imperial settings, see Foster, *Faith in Empire*, chap. 3; Achi, "Laïcité d'empire"; and Duteil, "Laïcisation dans les colonies françaises."

26. J. P. Daughton contends that by World War I overseas missions had generally begun to situate their evangelizing efforts more directly within the framework of Third Republic colonialism. Daughton, *An Empire Divided*, esp. chap. 8. Elizabeth Foster finds that relations between missionaries and the colonial administration in Senegal did improve during World War I. However, Foster goes on to show how relationships again became quite strained during the interwar period as a result of conflicting priorities. Foster, *Faith in Empire*, chaps. 4–6. In his work on schooling and language policies in French Cameroon, Kenneth J. Orosz also finds ample evidence of enduring conflicts between missionaries and the colonial administration. Orosz, *Religious Conflict and the Evolution of Language*, chaps. 4–5.

27. On the schools run by these missionary orders, see Bouche, *L'enseignement*, 1: chaps. 3 and 10; Foster, *Faith in Empire*, 26–29; and Jones, *The Métis of Senegal*, 98–105.

28. Bouche, *L'enseignement*, 1:165–69.

29. On education in late nineteenth-century Senegal, see Bouche, *L'enseignement*, vol. 1; and Duke Bryant, *Education as Politics*. Whereas Bouche studies the development of schools from the perspective of colonial authorities, Duke Bryant is primarily interested in local responses to colonial schooling.

30. On efforts to develop schooling in French Soudan during the late nineteenth century, see Bouche, "Les écoles françaises au Soudan." After officially becoming a colony in 1892, French Soudan was subsequently integrated into the new territorial unit of Haut-Sénégal-Niger in 1904. On early educational efforts in Dahomey, see Garcia, "L'organisation de l'instruction publique au Dahomey"; and Bouche, *L'enseignement*, 2:683–91.

31. "Rapport de M. le Gouverneur Camille Guy sur la situation de l'enseignement au Sénégal en 1903," ANS, FAOF, Série J: Enseignement jusqu'en 1920 (hereafter Série J), 19. On the mounting pressure to curb the *écoles congréganistes* in the Four Communes, see also Foster, *Faith in Empire*, 74–83.

32. In the end the Government General did not follow the gradual approach that Guy had endorsed. Within a few years almost all the *écoles congréganistes* of the Four Communes had been converted into "official" schools, run directly by the colonial administration. See Bouche, *L'enseignement*, 2:476–96, 579–84; and Foster, *Faith in Empire*, 74–83. Bouche portrays the *laïcisation* of schools as a draconian event, whereas Foster describes a more complicated process. Foster notes, for example, how some French nuns found ways to continue teaching in the Four Communes.

33. "Rapport de M. le Gouverneur Camille Guy sur la situation de l'enseignement au Sénégal en 1903," ANS, FAOF, Série J.

34. "Rapport de M. le Gouverneur Camille Guy sur la situation de l'enseignement au Sénégal en 1903."

35. "Rapport de M. le Gouverneur Camille Guy sur la situation de l'enseignement au Sénégal en 1903."

36. Guy's introductory report to Roume, dated 15 October 1903, and the three *projets d'arrêté* were published in Conseil de gouvernement de l'Afrique occidentale française, *Organisation du service de l'enseignement*, 1–21.

37. "Arrêté organisant le service de l'enseignement dans les colonies et territoires de l'Afrique occidentale française," 24 November 1903, *Bulletin Administratif du Gouvernement Général de l'Afrique Occidentale Française*, no. 11 (November 1903): 825–34. For other accounts of the school system established by the 1903 *arrêtés*, see Bouche, *L'enseignement*, 2: chap. 14; and Conklin, *A Mission to Civilize*, 75–86.

38. On regional schools, see "Arrêté organisant le service de l'enseignement," 826–27.

39. The 1903 *arrêté* provided for an *école supérieure professionnelle* (l'École Pinet-Laprade), an *école primaire supérieure et commerciale* (l'École Faidherbe), and an *école normale*. The first was founded in Dakar, while the other two were located in Saint-Louis. "Arrêté organisant le service de l'enseignement," 827–33.

40. "Arrêté organisant le service de l'enseignement," 827.

41. Guy's introductory report to Roume, 15 October 1903, in Conseil de gouvernement de l'Afrique occidentale française, *Organisation du service de l'enseignement*, 5.

42. During the 1904–5 school year the eleven urban schools enrolled 2,157 students, against 203 students at Senegal's two regional schools, and 830 students at the colony's twenty rural schools. See Lemé, *L'enseignement*, 45–46. Despite the progress of *laïcisation*, Catholic orders still operated thirteen schools in Senegal; however these schools no longer enjoyed any official authorization and were required to make do without subsidies from the colonial administration. In 1904–5, there were six *écoles congréganistes* for boys and seven for girls, with respective combined enrollments of 93 and 182. There was also one school run

by Protestants reporting 34 boy students. Lemé, *L'enseignement*, 46. In AOF as a whole, there were still fifty-three *écoles congréganistes*, with a combined total of 2,745 students. Lemé, *L'enseignement*, 74.

43. In his 1906 book on schooling in French West Africa, René Lemé notes the existence of an urban school in Conakry (Guinea) but makes no mention of an urban school in Haut-Sénégal-Niger, Ivory Coast, or Dahomey. Lemé, *L'enseignement*, part 2, chaps. 4–7.

44. On the secondary school in Saint-Louis, see Bouche, *L'enseignement*, 1: chap. 4, esp. 203–14. Diagne graduated from this school in 1890, at the head of his class. Johnson, *The Emergence*, 155; Thiam, *La révolution*, 157; and Dieng, *Blaise Diagne*, 54–55.

45. "Rapport de M. le Gouverneur Camille Guy sur la situation de l'enseignement au Sénégal en 1903," ANS, FAOF, Série J. See also Guy's introductory report to Roume, 15 October 1903, in Conseil de gouvernement de l'Afrique occidentale française, *Organisation du service de l'enseignement*, 2–4.

46. On the École Faidherbe, see Bouche, *L'enseignement*, 2:503–8.

47. Ponty, "Discours du Gouverneur Général," 24. The Conseil de gouvernement, or Council of the Government General, met at least once a year to discuss the broad orientations of colonial policy. It was made up of the governor general, the lieutenant governors, the heads of the different departments at the Government General, and a scattering of other officials.

48. Ponty, "Discours du Gouverneur Général."

49. Ponty to lieutenant governor of Senegal, 13 September 1909, ANS, FAOF, Série J, 19.

50. Ponty to lieutenant governor of Senegal, 13 September 1909, ANS, FAOF, Série J, 19.

51. On originaire populations during the early years of the twentieth century, see Thiam, *La révolution*; Johnson, *The Emergence*, chaps. 6–8; Jones, *The Métis of Senegal*, chap. 7; Robinson, *Paths of Accommodation*, chaps. 5–6; Duke Bryant, *Education as Politics*, chap. 5; and Searing, "Accommdation and Resistance," 324–43.

52. Gaudart to Ponty, 10 April 1909, ANS, FAOF, Série J, 19.

53. "Arrêté fixant la répartition des écoles élémentaires du Sénégal dans les diverses catégories établies par l'arrêté du 24 novembre 1903," 8 Octobre 1909, *JOS*, 1909, 581–82. On this reform, see also Bouche, *L'enseignement*, 2:602–3.

54. "Arrêté fixant la répartition des écoles élémentaires du Sénégal," 582. Another *arrêté*, passed the same day, also concerned urban schools: "Arrêté relatif à l'organisation du service dans les écoles urbaines," *JOS*, 1909, 576–77.

55. The Colony of Senegal continued to maintain its own diplomas. See "Arrêté

instituant au Sénégal un certificat d'études primaires élémentaires," 8 October 1909, *JOS*, 1909, 581; and "Arrêté instituant au Sénégal un certificat d'études élémentaires professionnelles," 8 October 1909, *JOS*, 1909, 582.

56. On attitudes toward segregation in AOF and British West Africa, see Goerg, "From Hill Station (Freetown) to Downtown Conakry (First Ward)"; Goerg, *Pouvoir colonial, municipalités et espaces urbains*; and Bigon, *A History of Urban Planning in Two West African Colonial Capitals*.

57. Here my interpretation is rather different from that of Alice Conklin, who finds that republican ideology remained a defining feature of Ponty's administration. Conklin, *A Mission to Civilize*, chap. 4.

58. Peuvergne had already served as lieutenant governor of Senegal once before, in 1908.

59. See d'Anfreville de la Salle, *Conférences sur l'hygiène coloniale*.

60. D'Anfreville de la Salle, *Notre vieux Sénégal*, 116–19, quote at 117–18.

61. D'Anfreville de la Salle, *Notre vieux Sénégal*, 118.

62. Saada, *Les enfants de la colonie*, esp. chap. 3. I discuss the *métis* communities of the Four Communes in greater detail in chapter 2.

63. Peuvergne to Ponty, marked "confidential," 16 April 1910, ANS, FAOF, Série J, 19. On the mobilization of public health justifications in support of segregation, see Echenberg, *Black Death, White Medicine*; Ngalamulume, "Keeping the City Totally Clean"; and Betts, "The Establishment of the Medina in Dakar." For broader accounts, see Osborne, *The Emergence of Tropical Medicine in France*; and Chakrabarti, *Medicine and Empire*.

64. Peuvergne to Ponty, marked "confidential," 16 April 1910, ANS, FAOF, Série J, 19.

65. Peuvergne to Ponty, 16 April 1910 and 10 May 1919, ANS, FAOF, Série J, 19.

66. Masson, "Ville de Dakar: Rapport sur le service de l'instruction primaire de la commune de Dakar pour l'année 1909," 15 February 1909, ANS, FAOF, Série J, 19.

67. The composition and prerogatives of the General Council were laid out in "Décret instituant le Conseil général au Sénégal et dépendances," 4 February 1879, *Moniteur du Sénégal et Dépendances*, no. 1208 (1 April 1879): 64–68. On this body, see also Johnson, *The Emergence*, 55–62; Jones, *The Métis of Senegal*, 127–30; and Searing, "Accommodation and Resistance," 369–81. When it was founded, the General Council initially controlled non-mandatory expenditures in the entire Colony of Senegal. However, colonial authorities soon sought to curb the powers of this elective body. In 1892 Senegal's governor (Henri Félix de Lamothe) introduced a reform that deprived the General Council of any budgetary authority over the protectorate regions of Senegal.

68. Devès belonged to a prominent *métis* family that controlled considerable

business interests in Senegal. Over the years, several members of the Devès family had become well-known figures in local politics. On the influence of this family, see Jones, *The Métis of Senegal*, *passim*; Robinson, *Paths of Accommodation*, 108–16; Manchuelle, "Métis et colons"; Foster, *Faith in Empire*, 30–34, 41–42; and Idowu, "Café au Lait."

69. On the rise of Justin Devès as a political powerbroker in the Four Communes, see Thiam, *La révolution*, 43–49; and Johnson, *The Emergence*, 113–22.

70. Colonie du Sénégal, *Conseil général: Session ordinaire de décembre 1909* (Saint-Louis: Imprimerie du Gouvernement, 1912), 204–7. This discussion continues through p. 217. Most issues of the official periodical *Colonie du Sénégal: Conseil général* are now available through Gallica, the digital library of the Bibliothèque nationale de France.

71. First elected to the General Council in 1888, Hyacinthe Devès remained a fixture in this body until his death in 1910. For a portrait of this powerful spokesman, see Idowu, "Café au lait," 281.

72. Colonie du Sénégal, *Conseil général: Session ordinaire de décembre 1909*, 211.

73. Colonie du Sénégal, *Conseil général: Session ordinaire de décembre 1909*, 212–13.

74. On Galandou Diouf, see Thiam, *La révolution*, 35–43; and Johnson, *The Emergence*, 87, 118–19, 144–47. At the time Diouf's first name was often spelled N'Galandou. I have chosen to use the spelling that would become customary in subsequent years: Galandou.

75. Colonie du Sénégal, *Conseil général: Session ordinaire de décembre 1909*, 215.

76. Colonie du Sénégal, *Conseil général: Session ordinaire de décembre 1909*, 223–34.

77. For examples of this treatment, see Bouche, *L'enseignement*, 2:604–12, 866–76.

78. On the closing of the European teaching *cadre* to Senegalese schoolteachers, and on Senegalese efforts to find new routes into these ranks, see Jézéquel, "Grammaire de la distinction coloniale"; and Ly, *Les instituteurs au Sénégal*, chap. 23. See also my discussion in chapter 4.

79. Decree signed by President Félix Faure on 18 Decembre 1896. This decree and an accompanying report by Minister of Colonies André Lebon were published in *JORF*, 23 December 1896, 7016.

80. In France the law of 19 July 1889 had made primary school teachers *fonctionnaires de l'État*, who were paid with state funds according to standard pay scales. See the "Loi sur les dépenses ordinaires de l'instruction primaire publique et les traitements du personnel de ce service," *JORF*, 20 July 1889, 3557–61.

81. See, for example, "Voeu au sujet de l'enseignement public," in Colonie du Sénégal, *Conseil général: Session ordinaire de mai 1910* (Saint-Louis: Imprimerie du Gouvernement, 1912), 305–12. A similar situation prevailed in the old colonies

of Martinique, Guadeloupe, French Guiana, and Réunion. During the first decades of the Third Republic many elected officials in these old colonies hoped that local teachers would come to be governed by metropolitan legislation. However, in the end the 1889 legislation was not extended to the old colonies, meaning that teacher salaries continued to weigh heavily on local communes. It was only in 1946—when the old colonies were transformed into *départements d'outre-mer*—that local schoolteachers became *fonctionnaires de l'État*. See Farraudière, *L'école aux Antilles françaises*, 45–79. See also Lucas, *Bourbon à l'école*.

82. Peuvergne to Ponty, 4 March 1910, ANS, FAOF, Série J, 19.

83. For figures on the numbers of *métis*, blacks, and Europeans attending this school, see Duke Bryant, *Education as Politics*, 133.

84. Peuvergne to Ponty, 24 February 1910 and 16 April 1910, ANS, FAOF, Série J, 19. For another account of these confrontations in Saint-Louis, see Duke Bryant, *Education as Politics*, chap. 5.

85. Peuvergne to Ponty, 4 March 1910, ANS, FAOF, Série J, 19. See also Peuvergne to Ponty, 16 April 1910, ANS, FAOF, Série J, 19.

86. See the discussion "Au sujet d'une distinction d'origine entre ses élèves faite par le Directeur de l'école de garçons de Dakar," in Colonie du Sénégal, *Conseil général: Session ordinaire de juin 1911* (Saint-Louis: Imprimerie du Gouvernement, 1911), 156–57.

87. For other examples, see Duke Bryant, *Education as Politics*, 124–28.

88. All told, the public schools of the Four Communes were to include a total of sixteen classes that would follow the urban school curricula, sixteen classes that would adhere the regional school curricula, and fifteen classes that were to use the rural school curricula. Arrêté n. 1907, 3 November 1912, "fixant la répartition des écoles primaires du Sénégal dans les diverses catégories établies par les arrêtés du 24 novembre 1903 et du 28 octobre 1911 de M. le Gouverneur Général," *JOS*, 1912, 862–63. See also Bouche, *L'enseignement*, 2:610–12.

89. After being named as the new inspector of education in AOF in 1912, Georges Hardy sent a caustic report to Ponty, describing the general confusion and aggravation that the 1912 reform had caused. Hardy's "Rapport sur l'enseignement au Sénégal en 1912–1913," 31 December 1913, ANS, FAOF, Série J, 20.

90. The *agrégation* was, and still is, a highly comptetitive national examination that serves, among other things, to select elite lycée professors in various fields.

91. Hardy remained a prominent figure into World War II but thereafter lost credibility as a result of his active support of the Vichy Regime. On Hardy's broad influence within the French colonial establishment, see esp. Singaravélou, *Professer l'Empire*.

92. See Bouche, *L'enseignement*, 2:778, 794–876.

93. See, for example, Segalla, *The Moroccan Soul*. General accounts of Hardy's tenure in Dakar can also be found in Conklin, *A Mission to Civilize*, 133–39; and Eizlini, "Le Bulletin de l'Enseignement."

94. Bouche, *L'enseignement*, 2:790–94.

95. On this reform, see Hardy, *Une conquête morale*, 25–26; and Bouche, *L'enseignement*, 2:795–96.

96. See Hardy, *Une conquête morale*, 28–29.

97. On continuing tensions between education officials in Dakar and Saint-Louis, see Bouche, *L'enseignement*, 2:778–89.

98. "Arrêté rattachant au Gouvernement général de l'Afrique occidentale française l'École normale d'instituteurs de Saint-Louis, l'École supérieure professionnelle Pinet-Laprade et l'École des pupilles mécaniciens de la Marine," 25 October 1912, *JOS*, 7 Novembre 1912, 853–54. The normal school had been administratively attached to the Government General between 1903 and 1907, before being transferred to the Colony of Senegal. See Bouche, *L'enseignement*, 2:520.

99. The move took place in 1913; the name change followed Ponty's death in 1915. On the reorganization of the normal school, see Bouche, *L'enseignement*, 2:508–25, 801–4; and Hardy, *Une conquête morale*, 131–40. I examine the École William Ponty in detail in chapter 4.

100. "Circulaire relative aux programmes scolaires" and "Annexe," 1 May 1914, *JOAOF*, 1914, 462–82. On these curricula, see also Bouche, *L'enseignement*, 2:806–12; and Conklin, *A Mission to Civilize*, 133–39.

101. Hardy, *Une conquête morale*, 22.

102. For a history of this publication, see Eizlini, "Le Bulletin de l'Enseignement."

103. Cited in Hardy, *Une conquête morale*, 30.

104. "Circulaire relative aux programmes scolaires," 1 May 1914, *JOAOF*, 23 May 1914, 476.

105. "Circulaire relative aux programmes scolaires," 1 May 1914, 477.

2. *The Lessons of War*

1. Ponty was hardly the first governor general to challenge the originaires. His immediate predecessor, Ernest Roume, had also worked to rein in the originaires and particularly the General Council. See Searing, "Accommodation and Resistance," 373–82.

2. "Colonie du Sénégal, Recensement 1921," ANS, FAOF, 17G, 239/108. One could go further in breaking down the populations of the Four Communes. For example, the colonial state employed a number of black and *métis* West Indians hailing from France's old colonies. In the 1921 census these men were almost

certainly lumped into the category of "French Europeans." On Antilleans in the African colonies, see Hélénon, *French Caribbeans in Africa*. The census also did not directly identify the small but growing numbers of Lebanese in Senegal. See Arsan, *Interlopers of Empire*.

3. On the struggle to determine who was an originaire around the time of World War I, see esp. the doctoral thesis of Guèye, "De la situation politique des Sénégalais originaires," 43–47.

4. On the development and use of the *état civil* in France, see Noiriel, "L'identification des citoyens."

5. "Relevé statistique des jugements supplétifs d'actes de naissance rendus par les tribunaux de Saint-Louis et de Dakar de 1913 à 1921," ANS, FAOF, 17G, 239/108. See also Buell, *The Native Problem*, 1:952–53; and Searing, "Accommodation and Resistance," 424–25.

6. On the system of native tribunals that was established in 1903, see Roberts, *Litigants and Households*, chaps. 2–3, quote at 82. See also Manière, "Deux conceptions de l'action judiciaire." For a comparative study of the ways in which British and French colonial administrations developed and used customary law, see Mamdani, *Citizen and Subject*, chap. 4.

7. For an overview of the *indigénat* in AOF, see Mann, "What Was the *Indigénat*?" For more general accounts, see Le Cour Grandmaison, *Anatomie d'un "monstre" juridique*; and Merle, "Retour sur le régime de l'indigénat." As Mann points out, the *indigénat* often bore little resemblance to a "code." Its ill-defined, changing nature meant that it often created a space of almost unregulated violence. Mann, "What Was the *Indigénat*?," esp. 331–33, 337–38.

8. In practice there was considerable confusion about the relative roles of these two systems of native justice. Colonial administrators could frequently choose, whether capriciously or strategically, which system they wanted to use to punish a particular infraction. On this point, see Manière, "Deux conceptions de l'action judiciaire."

9. For a summary of this situation, see Sarr and Roberts, "The Jurisdiction of Muslim Tribunals." See also Christelow, "The Muslim Judge and Municipal Politics." On the Kayes tribunal, see Shereikis, "From Law to Custom."

10. Diouf, "The French Colonial Policy of Assimilation," esp. 675, 685–93.

11. For a discussion of this decree and its implications, see Conklin, *A Mission to Civilize*, 119–30.

12. On the decree of 16 August 1912 and the controversy that it sparked, see Guèye, *Itinéraire africain*, 23–26; and Guèye, "De la situation politique des Sénégalais originaires," 28–31. See also Moleur, "L'indigène aux urnes," 91–92.

13. In at least two cases colonial officials did use the provisions of the *indigénat* to

arrest—on dubious charges—originaires who had ventured outside the Four Communes. Searing, "Accommodation and Resistance," 340–42.

14. "Colonie du Sénégal, Recensement 1921," ANS, FAOF, 17G, 239/108.

15. These approximations are based on a table provided in Buell, *The Native Problem*, 1:947. Buell's figures refer to the number of African citizens found in the various colonies in 1921. The exact figures he provides are 22,771 in Senegal, 1,164 in Soudan, 491 in Guinea, 308 in Ivory Coast, 121 in Dahomey, 116 in Mauritania, 17 in Upper Volta, and 9 in Niger. It should be noted that not all these citizens were originaires. A May 1912 naturalization decree had opened up the possibility of naturalization to Africans residing anywhere in AOF. In the end, however, the conditions and procedures that were laid out proved so stringent that only 94 African requests for citizenship were accepted between 1914 and 1922. An additional 14 Africans took advantage of special naturalization provisions briefly extended to decorated veterans at the end of World War I. Buell, *The Native Problem*, 1:946–47.

16. Thiam, *La révolution*, 61, 89–94. Colonial authorities eventually realized that the controversy over access to French courts had become a windfall for originaire politicians skilled at harnessing public discontent. Backing down, authorities issued a follow-up decree on 9 March 1914, which guaranteed that the originaires would continue to have access to French courts wherever these existed in French West Africa. The decree of 9 March 1914 and the accompanying "rapport de présentation" are reprinted in Guèye, *Itinéraire africain*, 26–29.

17. Carpot's speech on 19 December 1919, *JORF*, *Débats Parlementaires*, 20 December 1912, 3282–87, quote at 3283.

18. On the decisions of the Cour de cassation, see Moleur, "L'indigène aux urnes," 88–90; Guèye, *Itinéraire africain*, 26–27; and Guèye, "De la situation politique des Sénégalais originaires," 19–21.

19. Carpot's speech of 19 December 1912, *JORF*, *Débats Parlementaires*, 20 December 1912, 3283–85.

20. Ponty, introductory letter and report to minister of colonies, 6 August 1913, ANS, FAOF, 17G, 47/17.

21. A law passed on 24 April 1833 had stipulated: "Any person born free or having legally acquired freedom enjoys in the French colonies: 1) civil rights; 2) political rights according to the conditions set forth by the laws." Law cited in Guèye, "De la situation politique des Sénégalais originaires," 12. This law was promulgated in the Colony of Senegal in the same year.

22. Ponty appended a naturalization decree proposal to his introductory letter and report to the minister of colonies, 6 August 1913, ANS, FAOF, 17G, 47/17.

23. Ponty, introductory letter and report to minister of colonies, 6 August 1913, ANS, FAOF, 17G, 47/17.

24. As a freemason Ponty often shied away from publically supporting Catholics and Catholicism. However, as Elizabeth Foster has shown, Ponty was often willing to provide more discreet assistance. See Foster, *Faith in Empire*, 122–23, 149–53.

25. See Saada, *Les enfants de la colonie*; and Stoler, *Carnal Knowledge and Imperial Power*.

26. On approaches to the *métis* in AOF, see White, *Children of the French Empire*; and Badji, "Le statut juridique des enfants métis."

27. On these shifts, see Johnson, *The Emergence*, chaps. 7–8; and Thiam, *La révolution*, 35–43.

28. Johnson, *The Emergence*, 154. Iba Der Thiam points out that Diagne's candidacy had been announced in a local newspaper as early as the spring of 1913. Thiam, *La révolution*, 136.

29. I discuss Diagne's education in more detail in chapter 4.

30. On Diagne's career leading up to his election as deputy, see esp. Thiam, *La révolution*, 157–79. See also Johnson, *The Emergence*, 154–59; and Dieng, *Blaise Diagne*, 51–61.

31. According to Iba Der Thiam, Diagne had returned home one other time, at the end of the 1890s. See Thiam, *La révolution*, 168–69.

32. "Rapport de M. Leredu sur l'élection de M. Daigne en 1914," 7 July 1914, ANS, FAOF, 17G, 234/108. Leredu was the rapporteur for the *commission de recensement des votes* that supervised the election in Senegal. For a highly detailed account of Diagne's campaign and the responses it generated in Senegal, see Thiam, *La révolution*, 138–379. See also Johnson, *The Emergence*, 161–72; and Searing, "Accommodation and Resistance," 387–400.

33. Contingents of West Africans had been recruited into military service across the nineteenth century. Military service became more formalized in 1857, when Louis Faidherbe created new colonial units known as the *tirailleurs sénégalais*. During the nineteenth century, recruiting methods varied widely and often involved some degree of coercion. Former slaves, purchased by colonial authorities, were sometimes incorporated into *tirailleur* units, where they served alongside men who had freely enlisted. The 1912 decree laid groundwork for a dramatic increase in the number of *tirailleurs*. By the beginning of 1914 *tirailleur* units already included almost eighteen thousand men. See Echenberg, *Colonial Conscripts*, 7–30.

34. For an overview of this standoff, see Johnson, *The Emergence*, 181–83.

35. These soldiers were discharged after the Conseil d'État ruled that originaires

could not be conscripted into French military units since they were not citizens. See Thiam, *La révolution*, 366. See also Guèye, "De la situation politique des Sénégalais originaires," 33–34; and Moleur, "L'indigène aux urnes," 94. A discussion of these events took place in Senegal's General Council. See *Conseil général: Session ordinaire de juin 1911*, 33–35.

36. See esp. Dumont, *L'amère patrie*, chap. 1. For a broader account of the often truncated citizenship of ex-slave populations in the old colonies, see Larcher, *L'autre citoyen*.

37. For a table comparing the advantages of service in the regular French army to the much more unfavorable terms of service in *tirailleur* units, see Johnson, *The Emergence*, 190. See also "Comparaison entre la situation militaire des originaires et celle des indigènes," n.d. (early 1920s), ANS, FAOF, 17G, 233/108.

38. Article published on 29 December 1915 and cited in Johnson, *The Emergence*, 188–89. On the paper *La Démocratie du Sénégal*, see Johnson, *The Emergence*, 104; and Thiam, *La révolution*, 77, 194.

39. On the two "Diagne Laws," see Guèye, *Itinéraire africain*, 23–39; Guèye, "De la situation politique des Sénégalais originaires," 33–50; and Johnson, *The Emergence*, 183–91.

40. During World War I French reformers proposed a similar arrangement for certain groups of Muslims in Algeria. In the end, however, the settler lobby succeeded in blocking these initiatives. The "loi du 4 février 1919 sur l'accession des indigènes d'Algérie aux droits civiques" required that Muslim Algerians renounce their personal status in order to be considered for French citizenship. As a result of this requirement and other stringent conditions, very few Algerian Muslims chose to apply for French citizenship. See Weil, *Qu'est-ce qu'un Français*, 337–68, esp. 359–63.

41. See the "report to the president of the French Repubic," dated 14 January 1918 and signed by Clemenceau, Colonial Minister Henry Simon, and Finance Minister Louis-Lucien Klotz. See also the accompanying presidential decree appointing Diagne as "commissaire de la République dans l'Ouest africain." *JORF*, 17 January 1918, 678. On Diagne's prominent role in the 1918 recruiting campaigns, see Johnson, *The Emergence*, 192–95; Michel, *Les Africains et la Grande Guerre*, 68–78; and Searing, "Accommodation and Resistance," 426–34.

42. Fogarty, *Race and War*, 51. For a table containing the numbers of soldiers recruited from the various parts of the empire during the years 1914–18, see Fogarty, *Race and War*, 27.

43. This certainly does not mean that Diagne's recruiting drives avoided coercion. After the war, a range of African elites would seek to discredit Diagne by denouncing his tolerance for forced recruitment. See Conklin, "Who Speaks

for Africa?" It is reasonable to conclude, however, that Diagne's 1918 recruiting efforts were less coercive than previous campaigns.

44. These decrees and their accompanying reports were published in *JORF*, 17 January 1918, 677–81. Following G. Wesley Johnson, historians have often incorrectly stated that the French government promised—at the same time—to open a secondary school in Saint-Louis. In reality this promise was made the following year. I examine the development of secondary education in AOF in chapter 7.

45. See, for example, the article by the deputy from Guadeloupe, Gratien Candace, "La mission Diagne: Les premiers résultats," *Le Petit Parisien*, 12 June 1918.

46. Draft of Angoulvant's circular to the lieutenant governors and to the commissioners in the civilian territory of Mauritania and the military territory of Niger, n.d., ANS, FAOF, Série J, 16. Extensive excerpts of the final version of this circular, dated 1 November 1918, can be found in Ly, *Les instituteurs au Sénégal*, 203–4.

47. Through the end of World War I, higher primary schools were usually called *groupes centraux*. Located in the various administrative capitals (Bingerville, Bamako, Conakry, Porto-Novo, and Saint-Louis), these schools included *cours normaux*, which trained *moniteurs* (low-level teachers) as well as candidates for the federal normal school, the École William Ponty. *Groupes centraux* also included other sections that trained students for subaltern positions in different branches of the colonial administration. During the interwar period, these schools would come to be called *écoles primaires supérieures*, or higher primary schools. Hardy, *Une conquête morale*, 40, 83–88.

48. Draft of circular from the governor general to the lieutenant governors and to the commissioners in the civilian territory of Mauritania and the military territory of Niger, n.d., ANS, FAOF, Série J, 16.

49. "Rapport sur l'École Normale William Ponty," prepared by Georges Gallin, who had been recently appointed as the school's interim director, November 1919, ANS, FAOF, Série J, 58.

50. Antonetti added: "I fear that Hardy, in wanting to go to fast, might compromise our entire mission." All quotations are taken from "Extrait d'une lettre personnelle de M. le Gouverneur Antonetti. a/s intituteurs indigenes," 3 juin 1918 (date when this excerpt was forwarded to Hardy by the cabinet of the governor general), ANS, FAOF, Série J, 16. In a letter to Angoulvant, Hardy responded to Antonetti's tirades. Hardy to Angoulvant, 18 June 1918, ANS, FAOF, Série J, 16. The governor general subsequently sent a rebuke to Antonetti. Governor general to lieutenant governor of Ivory Coast, 20 June 1918, ANS, FAOF, Série O: Enseignement, sciences et arts (hereafter Série O), 21/31.

51. Although Antonetti and other officials focused their criticism on the École William Ponty, the other professional schools also drew increased scrutiny. These schools included the École Faidherbe, which had recently been founded on Gorée to train African clerks for various branches of the colonial administration. This school replaced the school by the same name that had formerly existed in Saint-Louis, between 1903 and 1907. Gorée was also home to the École Pinet-Laprade, which trained skilled tradesmen for employment around the federation. On the professional schools that the Government General operated during World War I, see Bouche, *L'enseignement*, 2:839–48.

52. "Lieutenant Governor of Côte d'Ivoire to Martial-Henry Merlin," in Hill, *Marcus Garvey*, 9:253.

53. "Lieutenant Governor of Côte d'Ivoire to Martial-Henry Merlin." Antonetti misleadingly suggests that all these students had been dismissed for indiscipline. A report on the 1918–19 school year indicates that of the eighteen expulsions that occurred at the École William Ponty that year, seven were attributable to indiscipline, one to illness, and ten to "other reasons." "Écoles du Gouvernement général: année scolaire 1918–1919: Répartition des élèves exclus durant cette année," n.d., ANS, FAOF, Série J, 58.

54. On all these elections, see Johnson, *The Emergence*, 197–205.

55. Telegram addressed to Diagne, dated 1 December 1919, ANS, FAOF, 17G, 234/108.

56. On Merlin's background, see esp. Johnson, "The Rivalry between Diagne and Merlin," 303–5.

57. On colonial reactions to Diagne and his supporters, see Johnson, *The Emergence*, 197–210; Johnson, "The Rivalry between Diagne and Merlin"; Conklin, *A Mission to Civilize*, 155–59; Searing, "Accommodation and Resistance," 456–516; and Genova, *Colonial Ambivalence*, chaps. 1 and 3.

58. "Politique de M. Diagne au Sénégal—Le Diagnisme," n.d. (1922), ANS, FAOF, 17G, 233/108.

59. For more on the political vision and objectives of Diagne, see Johnson, *The Emergence*, 209–10, 217–18; Searing, "Accommodation and Resistance," 466–76; and Michel, "René Maran et Blaise Diagne," esp. 161–62.

60. On this entity, see Wilder, *The French Imperial Nation-State*, chaps. 1–2.

61. "Note de l'inspecteur de police Vallet sur l'état d'esprit des populations indigènes, en particulier au Sénégal, 1922," ANS, FAOF, 17G, 239/108.

62. A report produced by the Government General echoed the grave warnings that had been coming in from local administrations. See "Note pour Monsieur le Gouverneur Général," 5 August 1921. Found in folder labeled "Note du Gouverneur Général sur l'esprit frondeur d'indigènes sortant des écoles européennes (1921)," ANS, FAOF, 17G, 239/108.

63. Merlin's "Note pour Monsieur le Directeur de l'Enseignement," 13 August 1921. Found in folder labeled "Note du Gouverneur Général sur l'esprit frondeur d'indigènes sortant des écoles européennes (1921)," ANS, FAOF, 17G, 239/108.

64. Merlin contended that African societies were bereft of moralizing influences and that moral education had to be provided almost entirely by schools: "Here [in AOF, one finds] no philosophical ideas or religious education, no family or social discipline that has a truly moralizing effect." Merlin, "Note pour Monsieur le Directeur de l'Enseignement," 13 August 1921, ANS, FAOF, 17G, 239/108.

65. Figures are taken from a report by the interim inspector of education in AOF, J. L. Monod, "Situation d'ensemble pour la période triennale 1920–1923," 25 October 1923, ANS, FAOF, Sous-série 2G: Rapports périodiques des gouverneurs, administrateurs, et chefs de services depuis 1895 (hereafter 2G), 23/84. The changes that reshaped the École William Ponty during the interwar period are closely examined in chapter 4.

66. On this paper, see Johnson, *The Emergence*, 104. On Hardy's confrontations with the originaires, see also Segalla, *The Moroccan Soul*, 79–86.

67. An official in Saint-Louis compiled excerpts from articles on schooling that had appeared in Diagne's papers during the first half of 1919. See "Extraits d'articles parus dans la Démocratie du Sénégal du 12 janvier au 30 mars 1919 et dans l'Ouest-Africain Français du 5 avril au 17 mai 1919," ANS, FAOF, Série J, 16.

68. Article from *La Démocratie du Sénégal*, cited in "Extraits d'articles."

69. This figure of 7,200 is taken from Fogarty, *Race and War*, 241.

70. On the demobilization of African soldiers and the anxieties that this event produced in the colonial administration, see esp. Mann, *Native Sons*, chap. 2.

71. On the identity of Amadou l'Artilleur, see Thiam, *La révolution*, 191.

72. Originally published in *La Démocratie du Sénégal* on 9 February 1919, this article was excerpted in "Extraits d'articles."

73. "Arrêté portant application des programmes métropolitaines dans les écoles communales de St.-Louis, Dakar, Rufisque, Gorée," 22 Novembre 1921, ANS, Fonds Sénégal colonial, Sous-série 1G: Enseignement (hereafter 1G), 12. See also Merlin to minister of colonies, "a/s organisation actuelle de l'enseignement," 9 September 1921, ANS, FAOF, Série O, 28/31; letter from the Inspection de l'enseignement, Colonie du Sénégal, to Merlin, 19 October 1921; and Merlin's response, 14 November 1921, ANS, FAOF, Série O, 714/31.

74. See the report of the Conseil supérieur de l'enseignement, session of 18 juin 1923, *BEAOF*, no. 54 (April–June 1923): 25.

75. Jules Carde, "Circulaire sur la réorganisation de l'enseignement," 1 May 1924,

and "Arrêté fixant l'organisation générale de l'enseignement en Afrique occidentale française," 1 May 1924, *JOAOF*, 10 May 1924, 309–47.

76. This represented a further restriction compared to the 1914 guidelines, which had included adapted curricula designed specifically for urban schools. See chapter 1.

77. Carde, "Circulaire sur la réorganisation de l'enseignement," 312; and "Arrêté fixant l'organisation générale de l'enseignement en Afrique occidentale française," 317.

78. Larcher, *L'autre citoyen*, 328.

3. Toward the Interior

1. Crouzet's opening remarks were reprinted in the conference's published proceedings, Exposition coloniale internationale de 1931, *L'adaptation de l'enseignement*, 289.

2. Crouzet's opening remarks, in Exposition Coloniale, *L'adaptation de l'enseignement*, 289. Crouzet's official title was inspecteur-conseil de l'instruction publique au Ministère des Colonies. This position was created at the end of World War I. Having been seconded by the Ministry of Public Instruction, Crouzet also had the title of inspecteur de l'Académie de Paris.

3. Exposition coloniale, *L'adaptation de l'enseignement*, 291. Gautier was "chef de cabinet" for Mario Roustan, the minister of public instruction and fine arts.

4. For an overview of the rival ideologies of assimilation and association, see Betts, *Assimilation and Association in French Colonial Theory*, esp. chaps. 5–8. See also Ageron, *France coloniale ou parti colonial?*, chap. 6.

5. On Lyautey's career in Morocco and his conception of the protectorate, see especially Rivet, *Lyautey et l'institution*; and Hoisington, *Lyautey and the French Conquest of Morocco*.

6. On approaches to urban planning in French Morocco, see Wright, *The Politics of Design in French Colonial Urbanism*, chap. 3; Rabinow, *French Modern*, chap. 9; and Abu-Lughod, *Rabat, Urban Apartheid in Morocco*.

7. On Lyautey's influence on the Colonial Exposition, see Morton, *Hybrid Modernities*.

8. "Allocution de M. le Maréchal Lyautey," in Exposition coloniale, *L'adaptation de l'enseignement*, 302–3. The italics do not appear in the original.

9. Taboulet, "Rapport sur l'Indochine," in Exposition coloniale, *L'adaptation de l'enseignement*, 173.

10. Taboulet, "Rapport sur l'Indochine," 174.

11. Taboulet, "Rapport sur l'Indochine," 174–82. On these reforms, see also Kelly, "Franco-Vietnamese Schools, 1918–1933"; and Kelly and Kelly, *French Colonial*

Education. Additional studies include Bezançon, *Une colonisation éducatrice*; and Van Thao, *L'école française en Indochine*.

12. In 1930 Indochina's franco-indigène school system included a total of 383,518 students. A full 338,379 students were enrolled in the elementary cycle, while 40,367 were studying in the subsequent primary cycle. The federation's higher primary schools had a combined enrollment of 4,615 students, while franco-indigène secondary schools claimed a mere 157 students. Direction générale de l'instruction publique, *Le Service de l'instruction publique en Indochine en 1930* (Hanoi: Imprimerie d'Extrême-Orient, 1930), 31. Report cited in Ha, "From 'Nos Ancêtres les Gaulois' to 'Leur Culture Ancestrale,'" 115n15.

13. See Devaux, "Rapport sur Madagascar," in Exposition coloniale, *L'adaptation de l'enseignement*, 130. Devaux was the assistant to the director of education in Madagascar.

14. Devaux, "Rapport sur Madagascar," 135–50, quote at 136.

15. Devaux indicated that of the 110,000 students enrolled in the administration's schools, only 3,000 were studying beyond the first primary cycle. Devaux, "Rapport sur Madagascar," 164. On education in interwar Madagascar, see Koerner, *Histoire de l'enseignement privé et officiel à Madagascar*, 197–233; and Deleigne, "Entre la plume et l'angady (*la bêche*)." See also Duteil, "Enseignants coloniaux."

16. Brunot, "Rapport sur le Maroc," in Exposition coloniale, *L'adaptation de l'enseignement*, 34.

17. Brunot, "Rapport sur le Maroc," 35. For general accounts of education in the Moroccan Protectorate, see Segalla, *The Moroccan Soul*, chaps. 4–6; Vermeren, *La formation des élites marocaines et tunisiennes*; and Rivet, *Lyautey et l'institution*, 2:241–52.

18. Brunot explained that the sons of Moroccan elites who studied at *collèges musulmans* did receive some training in classical Arabic. Brunot, "Rapport sur le Maroc," 36–38.

19. Access to more advanced education remained considerably more limited in the old colonies than in the metropole. Primary education also lagged behind that in the metropole, partly because the salaries of schoolteachers continued to be paid out of local budgets, rather than by the French state. See chap. 1, n. 81.

20. Magdeleine, "Rapport sur la Martinique," in Exposition coloniale, *L'adaptation de l'enseignement*, 63. In the same volume, see also Girard, "Rapport sur la Guadeloupe"; Boris, "Rapport sur la Guyane française"; and Gautier, "Rapport sur la Réunion."

21. See Jules Carde, "Circulaire sur la réorganisation de l'enseignement," 1 May 1924, and "Arrêté fixant l'organisation générale de l'enseignement en Afrique occidentale française," 1 May 1924, *JOAOF*, 10 May 1924, 309–47.

22. Davesne, "Rapport sur l'Afrique occidentale française," in Exposition coloniale, *L'adaptation de l'enseignement*, 88. Davesne was inspector of primary education at the Government General in Dakar. He was also the author of a new series of schoolbooks written specifically for African students. Launched in 1929, Davesne's "Mamadou and Bineta" series soon became a staple at schools across French West Africa.

23. Davesne, "Rapport sur l'Afrique occidentale française," 86.

24. Brévié, *Discours prononcé par M. J. Brévié*, 1930, 39.

25. Brévié and his administration referred to these schools variously as *écoles rurales*, *écoles populaires*, and *écoles rurales populaires*. Here they are simply called rural schools.

26. Brévié, *Discours prononcé par M. J. Brévié*, 1930, 40.

27. "Arrêté fixant l'organisation générale de l'enseignement en Afrique occidentale française," *JOAOF*, 10 May 1924, 319. The exclusivity of instruction in French had already been reaffirmed just two years earlier, in a decree relating to private schools in AOF. This decree established that "education must be given exclusively in French, [since] the use of native idioms is forbidden." "Décret du 14 février 1922, réglementant l'enseignement privé et l'exercise de la propagande confessionnelle en Afrique occidentale française," *JOAOF*, 1 April 1922, 190–91.

28. This was evident in the report on education in AOF that André Davesne delivered to the Intercolonial Conference on Education in the Colonies and Overseas Territories. A strong proponent of education in French, Davesne felt the need to defend the administration's traditional position against growing pressures for education in local languages. See Davesne's appendix, "L'enseignement en langue indigène dans l'Afrique noire," in Exposition coloniale, *L'adaptation de l'enseignement*, 100–106.

29. Brévié, *Discours prononcé par M. J. Brévié*, 1931, 58–59.

30. I return to the subject of language policy in chapters 5 and 6.

31. Report titled "L'enseignement massif et l'école indigène," 21 Octobre 1930, ANS, FAOF, Série O, 22/31.

32. This colony was created after World War I, when the super-colony of Upper Senegal and Niger was broken up to form French Soudan and Upper Volta. Niger had been split off somewhat earlier, in 1912.

33. During the 1920s the Government General's educational bulletin published a series of circulars that Assomption had addressed to education officials in French Soudan. By 1923 this bulletin was already describing Assomption as "Soudan's education inspector, a preeminent schoolteacher, who is among the most experienced and authoritative." From the preface to the column titled "Pédagogie pratique: Conseils aux maîtres," *BEAOF*, no. 54 (April–June 1923): 31.

34. Assomption's circular to "personnel enseignant du Soudan français," n.d. (early 1930s), ANS, FAOF, Série O, 226/31.

35. Ponty, "Circulaire relative aux programmes scolaires," 1 May 1914, *JOAOF*, 23 May 1914, 467.

36. Angoulvant issued instructions stipulating that all village and regional schools should be in compliance with the 1914 school programs—requiring school gardens and agricultural education—by the beginning of the 1916–17 school year. Schoolteachers were to attend training sessions on agricultural education and students studying to be schoolteachers were to demonstrate a certain level of competency in the area of agricultural education. Finally, Angoulvant announced the creation of prizes for both teachers and students, to reward excellence in agricultural education. Angoulvant, "Instructions relatives à l'enseignement et à la vulgarisation agricoles," 5 August 1916, *JOAOF*, 12 August 1916, 493–96.

37. On AOF's role in the *ravitaillement* of metropolitan France, see Michel, *Les Africains et la Grande Guerre*, chaps. 8–9.

38. "Arrêté fixant l'organisation générale de l'enseignement en Afrique occidentale française," 1 May 1924, *JOAOF*, 10 May 1924, 313.

39. "Arrêté fixant l'organisation générale de l'enseignement en Afrique occidentale française," 1 May 1924, 320. On agricultural education in AOF, see also Bouche, *L'enseignement*, 2:628–31, 831–35; and Bouche, "L'école rurale en Afrique occidentale française," 272–76.

40. Carde's circular to the lieutenant governors, 17 April 1930, ANS, FAOF, Série O, 131/31.

41. On the Depression years in France, see Berstein, *La France des années 30*, chap. 2; and Weber, *The Hollow Years*, chaps. 2–3.

42. The classic account of this Depression-era economic strategy is found in Marseille, *Empire colonial et capitalisme français*, chaps. 6–8.

43. Brévié, *Discours prononcé par M. J. Brévié*, 1930, 63.

44. Assomption, "Circulaire au sujet de l'enseignement pratique agricole," 41–42.

45. "L'école rurale au Soudan," *BIR*, no. 121 (24 November 1936).

46. See, for example, "Rapport statistique d'ensemble pour l'année scolaire 1934–1935," *L'Éducation Africaine*, no. 93 (January–March 1936): 63–67.

47. Ponty's circular on *mutuelles scolaires*, 22 July 1913. Cited in Bouche, *L'enseignement*, 2:835.

48. Governor General Angoulvant, "Instructions relatives à l'enseignement et à la vulgarisation agricoles," 5 August 1916, *JOAOF*, 12 August 1916, 493–96. Hardy enthusiastically endorsed *mutuelles scolaires* in his 1917 book on colonial education. See Hardy, *Une conquête morale*, 166–69. On the early history of *mutuelles scolaires*, see also Bouche, *L'enseignement*, 2:835–39.

49. Carde, "Circulaire sur la réorganisation de l'enseignement," 1 May 1924, *JOAOF*, 10 May 1924, 313.

50. "Les mutuelles scolaires," *BIR*, no. 96 (7 April 1936): 13. The rationale of *mutuelles scolaires* overlapped somewhat with that of *sociétés indigènes de prévoyance*, which were also promoted by the colonial administration. African farmers paid dues to these savings associations, which then provided seed grain and credit for the planting season as well as financing for small-scale rural development projects. These associations soon came to be riddled with abuses. See Searing, "Accommodation and Resistance," 294–99, 554–55; and Mann and Guyer, "Imposing a Guide on the *Indigène*."

51. For examples of these stereotypes, see Hardy, *Une conquête morale*, 155–58, 166–67.

52. "L'école rurale au Soudan," *BIR*, no. 121 (24 November 1936).

53. If the percentage of total expenditures (local and federal budgets combined) devoted to education rose from 2.9 to 3.54 between 1927 and 1932, this did not mean that increased sums of money were being channeled toward schools. Rather, budgets for education were trimmed with more restraint than were other budgets. "L'emprunt de l'AOF et l'enseignement," ANS, FAOF, Série O, 146/31. As this report indicates, when French West Africa secured a large loan from the metropole in 1932, only one half of one percent of the borrowed sum went toward education.

54. "Rapport statistique d'ensemble pour l'année scolaire 1934–1935." See also Brévié's letter to the governor of Dahomey, 3 March 1936, ANS, FAOF, Série O, 507/31.

55. Quotation from "L'école rurale en Côte d'Ivoire," *BIR*, no. 77 (27 September 1935): 14–15. See also "L'enseignement en Côte d'Ivoire," *BIR*, no. 207 (5 December 1938); "La réforme scolaire de 1935 en Côte d'Ivoire," *BIR*, no. 223 (17 July 1939): 366–67.

56. Other differences also distinguished these two types of schools. When Governor General Joost Van Vollenhoven visited a certain number of village schools in 1917, he was shocked by what he saw. Most were tumbledown, unhygienic structures that lacked everything in the way of educational materials. Most of the teachers at village schools were poorly trained *moniteurs*, who were often only semi-literate in French. These discoveries led Van Vollenhoven to argue for a generalization of the regional school model. His recommendation was not heeded. Van Vollenhoven, "Circulaire au sujet d'un plan d'action scolaire," 5 October 1917, *JOAOF*, 6 October 1917, 531–34.

57. On the positions that school graduates went on to hold, see Lawrance, Osborn, and Roberts, *Intermediaries, Interpreters, and Clerks*. I discuss African schoolteachers at length in chapter 4.

58. In 1934–35 the eight higher primary schools collectively enrolled 816 students. "Rapport statistique d'ensemble pour l'année scolaire 1934–1935," *L'Éducation Africaine*, no. 93 (January–March 1936): 67.

59. Brévié's circular to the governors of AOF, 30 March 1932, ANS, FAOF, Série O, 22/31.

60. On the Depression's effects on rural Africa, see esp. Coquery-Vidrovitch, "L'Afrique coloniale française et la crise de 1930"; and Coquery-Vidrovitch, "La colonisation française, 1931–1939," 227–43.

61. Gouvernement général de l'Afrique occidentale française, *Circonscription de Dakar et dépendances*, 1–2, 24–25. As part of these reforms, authority over greater Dakar shifted from the administration of the Colony of Senegal to the Government General.

62. Seck, *Dakar*, 211.

63. In 1934 the populations of Saint-Louis, Porto-Novo, and Bamako were respectively 29,827, 25,724, and 20,929. These figures are from a chart published in *BIR*, no. 32 (18 October 1934): 16–17. On the early history of urbanization in sub-Saharan Africa, see Coquery-Vidrovitch, *The History of Cities South of the Sahara*. For studies that extend into the twentieth century, see Coquery-Vidrovitch, "The Process of Urbanization in Africa"; and Freund, *The African City*.

64. On Delavignette, see especially Mouralis and Piriou, *Robert Delavignette*. For additional biographical information, see "Introduction: The Career of Robert Delavignette," in Cohen, *Robert Delavignette on the French Empire*, 1–18.

65. Moulin, *Peasantry and Society*, 136–37.

66. As late as 1872, 69 percent of France's total population still lived in rural communes. By 1911 the share of the French population residing in rural communes had fallen to 56 percent. Moulin, *Peasantry and Society*, esp. 66–68, 101–3.

67. See Weber, *Peasants into Frenchmen*; and Lehning, *Peasant and French*, esp. chap. 2.

68. On changing literary treatment of peasants, see Moulin, *Peasantry and Society*, 122–23; and Thiesse, *Écrire la France*. On representations of peasants in the visual arts, see Golan, *Modernity and Nostalgia*, esp. 40–55. Pierre Bourdieu insightfully suggested that peasants generally function as a *classe objet*, defined by and for others. See Bourdieu, "Une classe objet."

69. According to Jean Pitié, it was in 1903 that a French-language book first included the expression *l'exode rural* in its title. Pitié, *L'exode rural*, 3. The book to which Pitié alludes was perhaps Vandervelde's *L'exode rural et le retour aux champs*. A prominent member of the Belgian Labor Party, Vandervelde wrote about the rural exodus in his country.

70. A 1931 census revealed that—for the first time in the nation's history—more than half of the French population lived in urban communes. However, as has

often been noted, official censuses overstated the extent of rural out-migration since they classified as urban any commune whose *chef-lieu* was home to two thousand or more inhabitants. Such a low threshold meant that many "urban" Frenchmen actually belonged to worlds that were still predominantly rural. On this point, see Berstein, *La France des années 30*, 7–8.

71. Delavignette, *Les paysans noirs*. On the broad influence of this book, see Cohen, *Rulers of Empire*, 100–101.

72. See Michel, *Les Africains et la Grande Guerre*, chap. 9; and Fall, *Le travail forcé*, 130–40.

73. On the forced recruitment of laborers for these private ventures and the problems that it raised, see Cooper, *Decolonization and African Society*, 31–43; Fall, *Le travail forcé*, chap. 7; Roberts, *Two Worlds of Cotton*, chap. 7; and Conklin, *A Mission to Civilize*, 235–45.

74. These figures come from Delavignette, *Service africain*, 183. See also Mande, "Labor Market Constraints and Competition in Colonial Africa." Upper Volta was created in 1919, when the large colony known as Upper Senegal and Niger was carved up. Largely to facilitate the flow of laborers, most of Upper Volta was later incorporated into Ivory Coast, in 1933. The Colony of Upper Volta was not reconstituted until 1947.

75. On the forced labor that was used to develop these irrigation projects, see Fall, *Le travail forcé*, 161–99. For more general accounts of irrigation schemes and the Office du Niger, see Roberts, *Two World of Cotton*, chaps. 6 and 10; Schreyger, *L'Office du Niger au Mali*; and van Beusekom, *Negotiating Development*.

76. On this escalating criticism, see Cooper, *Decolonization and African Society*, 89–91; Coquery-Vidrovitch, "The Popular Front and the Colonial Question," 158–62; and Roberts, *Two Worlds of Cotton*, 238–42. For a contemporary critique, see Pierre Herbart, *Le chancre du Niger*, with a preface by André Gide.

77. On the ILO convention and French reactions to it, see Cooper, *Decolonization and African Society*, 28–31, 37–39, quotes at 29. See also Cooper, "Conditions Analogous to Slavery"; Conklin, *A Mission to Civilize*, 228–35; and Fall, *Le travail forcé*, chap. 8.

78. The Ministry of Colonies drafted a decree in 1930 that sought to clarify and restrict the situations in which forced labor could be used. This decree was not officially promulgated in AOF until 1933. Conklin, *A Mission to Civilize*, 234–35, 242–43.

79. Delavignette, "Notes sur l'Afrique du juste-milieu en A.O.F.," 110–11.

80. Delavignette, "Notes sur l'Afrique du juste-milieu en A.O.F.," 103. On Delavignette's reformist visions, see also Piriou, "Les enjeux d'une 'Afrique du juste-milieu'"; and Dimier, "For a Republic," 53–58.

81. Delavignette, "Pour les paysans noirs, pour l'esprit africain," 387. See also Delavignette, *Service africain*, 217–18.
82. Cited in Piriou, "Les enjeux d'une 'Afrique du juste-milieu,'" 185.
83. Hardy, "Rapport général," in *Congrès international et intercolonial de la société indigène*, 609.
84. Hardy, "Rapport général," 609.
85. Delavignette, *Les vrais chefs de l'empire*, 88–90.

4. Reorienting African Schoolteachers

1. For studies that focus on the trajectories of Ponty students and graduates, see Jézéquel, "'Les mangeurs de craies'"; Jézéquel, "Les enseignants comme élite politique en AOF"; and Jézéquel, "Histoire de bancs, parcours d'élèves." For an institutional history, see Sabatier, "Educating a Colonial Elite." For a detailed six-volume study of Senegalese schoolteachers, including their training, see Ly, *Les instituteurs*. On the training of women schoolteachers, see Barthélémy, *Africaines et diplômées*. On normal schools in another colonial location, see esp. Colonna, *Instituteurs algériens*.
2. On this new section, see Ly, *Les instituteurs*, 3:203–9.
3. The administrative section was eventually reopened in 1933, once the revamping of the École William Ponty had begun. On the administrative section after 1933, see Sabatier, "Educating a Colonial Elite," chap. 8.
4. On the École de médecine, see Sabatier, "Educating a Colonial Elite," chap. 7; and Barthélémy, *Africaines et diplômées*, chap. 1.
5. During the early 1920s a total of 81 students graduated from the administrative section, before it was abruptly closed. The medical section turned out a total of 139 graduates during the 1920s, compared to 306 for the teaching section. See Sabatier, "Educating a Colonial Elite," 78–79.
6. For other accounts of this scholarship program, see Ly, *Les instituteurs*, 5:257–69; and Sabatier, "Educating a Colonial Elite," 68–69, 88–91, 446–47.
7. Sabatier, "Educating a Colonial Elite," 89; Ly, *Les instituteurs*, 5:257.
8. By the turn of the century such scholarships had become increasingly rare, as a result of financial pressures in the Four Communes, the founding of the federal school system in AOF, and the administration's growing determination to curtail study trips to France. On these scholarships and their decline, see Bouche, *L'enseignement*, 1: chap. 6; and Duke Bryant, "The Politics of Education in Senegal," chap. 4. The number of scholarships continued to be cut back during the first decades of the twentieth century. See Bouche, *L'enseignement*, 2:559–63, 858–59.
9. On Diagne's time in Aix-en-Provence, see Duke Bryant, "'In My Senegalese Quality and as a Compatriot.'"

10. Candidates for admission to metropolitan normal schools were required to possess the *brevet élémentaire* already.

11. This diploma was not officially required of public schoolteachers in France until 1932. In practice, however, many schoolteachers possessed the *brevet supérieur* prior to this date. See Prost, *Histoire de l'enseignement*, 377.

12. Gleyze, directeur de l'École normale d'Aix, "Rapport sur les élèves de l'A.O.F. (promotion 1920–23)," 30 September 1923, ANS, FAOF, Série O, 211/31.

13. The archives mention, without further explanation, that these four students did not pass this examination as a result of "une tentative de fraude"—presumably some form of cheating. "École normale primaire d'instituteurs d'Aix, a/s proposition d'exclusion de deux élèves noirs boursiers du Sénégal: Extrait du registre des délibérations du Conseil des professeurs, séance du 19 novembre 1923," ANS, FAOF, Série O, 211/31.

14. "École normale primaire d'instituteurs d'Aix, a/s proposition d'exclusion de deux élèves noirs," ANS, FAOF, Série O, 211/31.

15. Gleyze to the inspecteur général de l'enseignement in AOF, 27 November 1923, ANS, FAOF, Série O, 211/31.

16. Gleyze, "Rapport sur les élèves de l'A.O.F. (promotion 1920–23)," 30 September 1923, ANS, FAOF, Série O, 211/31.

17. Letter dated 5 September 1925, cited in Ly, *Les instituteurs*, 5:265–67.

18. Arrêté dated 12 Septembre 1923, ANS, FAOF, Série O, 211/31. On these changes, see also Ly, *Les instituteurs*, 5:264–65.

19. Dewitte, *Les mouvements nègres*, 35. Dewitte mistakenly asserts that the first African *boursiers* arrived at the normal school in Aix in 1923 and that two students were expelled in 1923 for poor grades (p. 34). As we have seen, the first African students arrived in 1920; N'Diaye and Coulibaly were expelled in 1923 for disciplinary reasons.

20. On Kouyaté and his activism, see Dewitte, *Les mouvements nègres*, esp. chaps. 4–5 and 10; Edwards, *The Practice of Diaspora*, chap. 5; and Derrick, *Africa's "Agitators."* I briefly discuss the development of African communities in France in chapter 5.

21. Cited in Suret-Canale, *Afrique noire, occidentale et centrale*, 486.

22. Sabatier, "Educating a Colonial Elite," 68. Sabatier explains that the number of twenty-three students is a close approximation. See the table listing the names of Ponty graduates who went on to study in Aix in Sabatier, "Educating a Colonial Elite," 446.

23. At the time there was confusion as to whether this diploma was equavalent to the metropolitan diploma by the same name. See Jézéquel, "Grammaire de la distinction coloniale," 9.

24. The new diplomas were known as the *certificat d'aptitude à l'enseignement* and the *diplôme supérieur d'études primaires*. See Ly, *Les instituteurs*, 5:232; and Jézéquel, "Grammaire de la distinction coloniale," 10.

25. During the first two decades of the twentieth century the names of the two teacher *cadres* shifted, becoming less overtly racially marked: the *cadre européen* was renamed the *cadre général* in 1908, while the *cadre indigène* became the *cadre local* in 1916. However, as Jean-Hervé Jézéquel has shown, these name changes did nothing to restrain the discriminatory function of these professional categories, which actually increased over time, as the colonial state became more and more determined to firm up boundaries between colonizers and the colonized. However, despite this clamping down, the *cadre européen* (or *cadre général*) never became entirely hermetic. A handful of Senegalese schoolteachers continued to piece together pathways into the *cadre général*. See Jézéquel, "Grammaire de la distinction coloniale." On the diplomas and *cadres* that structured the status of African schoolteachers, see also Ly, *Les instituteurs*, 5: chap. 23.

26. Ly, *Les instituteurs*, 5:264, 268–69.

27. Dupont served as the school's director between 1927 and 1931. On the reforms that he oversaw, see Sabatier, "Educating a Colonial Elite," 70, 119–24; and Ly, *Les instituteurs*, 5:269–78.

28. Dupont, "Rapport sur le fonctionnement de l'École W. Ponty pendant l'année scolaire 1927–1928," cited in Ly, *Les instituteurs*, 5:271–72.

29. Arrêté dated 8 August 1928. See Ly, *Les instituteurs*, 5:273–78.

30. During oral interviews conducted in the late twentieth century, historian Boubacar Ly found that a surprising number of retired—and quite elderly—Senegalese schoolteachers still remembered Dupont and the powerful impression he had made during his tenure at Ponty. Ly, *Les instituteurs*, 5:269–70, 272n2. Positive memories of Dupont can be found in other places, such as in Ousmane Socé's *Mirages de Paris*. While traveling to France on a steamer in 1931, the Senegalese protagonist of this novel encounters a school director named Dupont. The narrator presents Dupont as someone whose liberal ideas confronted the color prejudice increasingly in evidence in colonial circles (21–23). Having graduated from Ponty in 1928 and having subsequently worked at the school for a year, Socé knew Dupont personally. Chapter 6 includes a detailed discussion of Socé. For other recollections of Dupont, see Dia, *Vicissitudes*, 21–23.

31. On Prat's support for the *section du brevet* at Ponty, see Ly, *Les instituteurs*, 5:272–73. For a portrait of Prat, see Vaillant, *Black, French, and African*, 61–63.

32. On Charton's opinions of the recent reforms at Ponty, see Ly, *Les instituteurs*, 5:285–93. Charton was the first official to have the title of inspecteur

général de l'enseignement. His predecessors held the position of inspecteur de l'enseignment.

33. Ly, *Les instituteurs*, 5:278–93.

34. Charton's report to Brévié, 11 June 1931, ANS, FAOF, Série O, 22/31.

35. The normal school moved from Saint-Louis to Gorée in 1913 and was named the École William Ponty in 1915. On this move, see Bouche, *L'enseignement*, 2:801–4; and Hardy, *Une conquête morale*, 116–40.

36. Carde's circular on educational policy to the various lieutenant governors, 31 December 1923, ANS, Fonds Sénégal colonial, 1G, 12. In France and in the colonies, *leçons de choses* implied the use of concrete objects to illustrate subjects covered in the school curricula.

37. Davesne, "Rapport sur l'Afrique occidentale française," 93. Emphasis in the original.

38. At this point the Circonscription de Dakar et dépendances became coterminous with the commune of Dakar. Gouvernement général de l'Afrique occidentale française, *Circonscription de Dakar et dépendances*, 30. I continue to use the expression "Four Communes" to refer to Senegal's old coastal towns. By 1929 this expression had become so customary that almost no one seemed ready to speak of the "Three Communes."

39. Davesne, "Rapport sur l'Afrique occidentale française," 94.

40. Davesne, "Rapport sur l'Afrique occidentale française," 99.

41. Student reports were archived by school officials. All in all, students produced some eight hundred of these *cahiers*. They can be consulted today at the library of the Institut fondamental d'Afrique noire (IFAN) in Dakar. For an overview of these reports, see Sabatier, "Educating a Colonial Elite," 137–42; Warner, "Para-Literary Ethnography and Colonial Self-Writing," 1–20.

42. Charton, "Les études indigènes à l'École William-Ponty," *BEAOF* 84 (July–December 1933): 199.

43. Charton, "Les études indigènes à l'École William-Ponty," 199.

44. Brévié, "Arrêté créant un prix annuel destiné à récompenser les travaux d'ordre scientifique et documentaire dus à des indigènes originaires de l'Afrique occidentale française," 30 January 1931, ANS, FAOF, Série O, 605/31.

45. Charton added that "it is not forbidden to think that these modest projects have a certain documentary, or even scientific, value." Charton, "Les études indigènes à l'École William-Ponty," 199.

46. Anderson argues that the "territorial" identities of Guinea, Ivory Coast, Soudan, etc. did not really take root until after World War II, when elites began to follow more circumscribed trajectories that usually culminated in local capitals such as Conakry, Abidjan, and Bamako. Select students continued to

embark on study trips outside their home colonies. But as Anderson points out, these trips increasingly led to France, rather than to the federal capital of Dakar. Anderson, *Imagined Communities*, 123–24.

47. Chanet, *L'école républicaine*; Thiesse, "Les deux identités de la France"; and Thiesse, *Ils apprenaient la France*. For a study that explores layered identities in both the metropole and the empire, see Lebovics, *True France*.

48. Maupoil, "Le théâtre dahoméen," 301–6.

49. On the development of theater at Ponty, see Maupoil, "Le théâtre dahoméen," 301–18; Traoré, *Le théâtre négro-africain*, 45–114. See also Mouralis, "William Ponty Drama," 130–40; Sabatier, "Educating a Colonial Elite," 176–82; Cornevin, *Le théâtre en Afrique noire et à Madagascar*, 51–74; and Jézéquel, "Le 'théâtre des instituteurs.'"

50. For an overview of Béart's career, see Sabatier, "Educating a Colonial Elite," 166.

51. Béart, "Le théâtre indigène," 13–14.

52. Béart, "Le théâtre indigène," 12.

53. Béart quipped: "Our goal is to develop the full potential of native art, not to cultivate a form of exoticism." Béart, "Le théâtre indigène," 12.

54. The play was published in "Le théâtre indigène et la culture franco-africaine," a special issue of *L'Éducation Africaine* (1937), 82–93.

55. *BIR*, no. 51 (28 February 1935): 8. Charles Béart offered an almost identical interpretation of this skit in *L'Éducation Africaine*, noting that the members of the chorus "make fun of one of their own kind [who has] returned from the city most grotesquely decked out in European fashion, and aping in the most ridiculous way possible those Whites whom he admired so." Béart, "Compte-rendu de la fête de l'École William-Ponty," 179.

56. The programs for the performances in 1936 and 1937 were reproduced in "Le théâtre indigène et la culture franco-africaine," a special issue of *L'Éducation Africaine* (1937), 17–19, 65–67. This issue also includes the full texts of the plays that were presented.

57. Traoré, *Le théâtre négro-africain*, 50–51; final report on AOF's section at the World's Fair, n.d., ANOM, Fonds ministériel 628, dossier 1077. On Josephine Baker's début and subsequent performance of race in Paris, see Boittin, *Colonial Metropolis*, chap. 1.

58. "Trente élèves de l'École William-Ponty sont partis pour l'Exposition," *BIR*, no. 154 (26 July 1937): 2.

59. "Trente élèves de l'École William-Ponty," 2.

60. Bernard Mouralis concludes, erroneously in my view, that "all our records concerning the actual conditions in which these activities were carried out reveals [*sic*] an open and liberal pedagogical climate." Mouralis, "William

Ponty Drama," 136. Cornevin arrives at much the same conclusion. Cornevin, *Le théâtre en Afrique noire et à Madagascar*, 74.

61. Sabatier concludes that there was real freedom but within limits: "There were clear if unspoken limits to the freedom to write and produce plays at the school. . . . However limits on the theater were largely self-imposed and internalized. Most graduates stressed that there was no such thing as overt censorship, and it would be an exaggeration to contend that the school administration controlled the theater in an active sense." Sabatier, "Educating a Colonial Elite," 176.

62. Traoré speaks of a "théâtre dirigé" and notes that "students did not initiate this theater: it was proposed to them." Traoré, *Le théâtre négro-africain*, 102, 109. Traoré himself studied at Ponty after World War II, by which time the school had already taken new directions.

63. Jean-Hervé Jézéquel comes closest to the mark, when he stresses the ways in which colonial authorities sought to exploit these productions, as part of their broader efforts to reposition young African elites. Jézéquel, "Le 'théâtre des instituteurs,'" 195–98.

64. Chapter 6 further develops this point by showing how young African elites redirected celebrations of African culture and folklore during World War II.

65. Brévié, *Discours prononcé par M. J. Brévié*, 1932, 48.

66. Charton, "Le problème de l'éducation en Afrique noire," paper given in 1932 at the Congrès international de Nice, ANS, FAOF, Série O, 184/31.

67. Charton, "Rôle social de l'enseignement en Afrique occidentale française," 191.

68. Although there was considerable slippage between these two words, "civilization" tended to imply something broader and more venerable. On the histories of these words, see Bénéton, *Histoire de mots*.

69. Quotations are taken from a paper that Dirand presented at a conference held during the Paris World's Fair. Dirand, "La formation intellectuelle et la culture franco-africaine à l'École William-Ponty," 38–39.

70. "Conseil supérieur de l'enseignement (session du 23 décembre 1935), extraits de l'exposé de M. l'inspecteur général de l'enseignement," *L'Éducation Africaine*, no. 93 (January–March 1936): 90–91.

71. Students at Ponty studied a common curriculum during their first year before being assigned to one of the school's sections for two additional years of study. As previously mentioned, the school's administrative section was not reopened until 1933. Sabatier, "Educating a Colonial Elite," 86–88, 155–58; Ly, *Les instituteurs*, 3:207–12, 216–25.

72. Davesne, "Rapport sur l'Afrique occidentale française," 94.

73. Sabatier notes: "One of the most frequently given reasons for the move to

Sébikotane was the necessity of keeping students in contact with the land. Alienation from the rural milieu, in fact, had been one of the recurring criticisms of the Gorée-trained teachers. Ironically, however, students' main contact with the soil at 'Sébi' was in cutting flowers around their dormitories, planting trees and laying out trails, and building an outdoor theater. Hired laborers did all the heavy work in the fields, garden, and with the livestock, undoubtedly reinforcing Ponty students' very rational sense of their superior position in African society. In theory, at least one student a day on a rotating basis was responsible for keeping track of these workmen and thus familiarizing himself with agricultural techniques and activities, but many graduates interviewed could not remember having done this." Sabatier, "Educating a Colonial Elite," 146–47.

74. For an overview of this reformist movement, see Ohayon, Ottavi, and Savoye, *L'éducation nouvelle*; Gutierrez, Besse, and Prost, *Réformer l'école*; Médici, *L'éducation nouvelle*.

75. On education reform under the Popular Front, see Ory, *La belle illusion*, 613–711; Antoine Prost, "Les instructions de 1938," in Prost, *Jean Zay et la gauche du radicalisme*, chap. 12; and Prost, *Du changement dans l'école*, chap. 2. On education reform under the Vichy regime, see Barreau, *Vichy contre l'école de la République*; and Déloye, *École et citoyenneté*, chap. 7.

76. Charton, "La réforme de l'enseignement en AOF: Le centre de Sébikotane," *BIR*, no. 110 (18 August 1936): 7–8.

77. On metropolitan normal schools and the reform movements that reshaped them, see Chanet, *L'école républicaine*.

78. Brévié's circular to the governors, 25 July 1935, ANOM, GGAOF (microfilm), Sous-série 17G: Affaires politiques (hereafter 17G), 256.

79. Brévié, *Discours prononcé par M. J. Brévié*, 1934, 65.

80. Plans for such schools had first developed in metropolitan France. In 1927 Education Minister Édouard Herriot issued instructions calling for the creation of rural normal schools to train schoolteachers for service in heavily rural areas. The plan was to convert normal schools in twenty-six departments to this new model. In the end, however, rural normal schools never got off the ground in metropolitan France. Chanet, *L'école républicaine*, 170–72.

81. "Discours prononcé par M. Charton, à l'inauguration de l'École normale rurale de Katibougou (30 janvier 1935)," *L'Éducation Africaine*, no. 89 (January–March 1935): 105.

82. Assomption, "Une nouvelle conception de l'enseignement en Afrique occidentale française."

83. Assomption's 1933 description of Katibougou's mission, cited in You, "Assomption pédagogique," 36.

84. "Discours prononcé par M. Charton, à l'inauguration de l'École normale rurale de Katibougou," 104. See also Rémondet, "La création des écoles normales rurales en A.O.F."

5. Léopold Sédar Senghor

1. Senghor, "Le problème culturel en A.O.F.," 53. Senghor's talk was later published in Senghor, *Liberté 1: Négritude et humanisme.* However, this later version was edited in numerous ways, making it a less reliable transcript of the speech that Senghor actually gave on 4 September 1937. For this reason I refer only to the version published in 1945. For his talk, Senghor translated the words of McKay's character (Ray) into French. I have provided the original English. See McKay, *Banjo,* 172.

2. For general accounts of the Popular Front's engagement with empire and imperial reform, see Chafer and Sackur, *French Colonial Empire and the Popular Front;* Cohen, "The Colonial Policy of the Popular Front"; Thomas, *The French Empire between the Wars,* chap. 9; and Bernard-Duquenet, *Le Sénégal et le Front populaire.*

3. Edwards, *The Practice of Diaspora,* esp. 7–15.

4. For a general history of the Popular Front, see Jackson, *The Popular Front in France.* For cultural histories of the Popular Front period, see Ungar and Andrew, *Popular Front Paris;* and Ory, *La belle illusion.* On social and labor questions, see Prost, *Autour du Front populaire.*

5. On Moutet's attempts at colonial reform during the Popular Front period, see Gratien, *Marius Moutet,* esp. 145–96. On the Ligue des droits de l'Homme, see Irvine, *Between Justice and Politics;* and Claveau, *Une sélection universaliste.*

6. On the evolving colonial views of the Socialist Party, see Koulaksiss, *Le Parti socialiste et l'Afrique du Nord;* Candar, "La gauche coloniale en France"; Semidei, "Les socialistes français et le problème colonial"; Sibeud, "La gauche et l'empire colonial avant 1945"; Liauzu, *Aux origines des tiers-mondismes,* chap. 7; Cohen, "The Colonial Policy of the Popular Front," 371–74, 389–90; and Girardet, *L'idée coloniale,* 156–67, 211–20.

7. The PCF had refused to accept any ministerial positions in the new government. On the PCF's attitude toward the colonies, see Liauzu, *Aux origines des tiers-mondismes,* chap. 1; Cohen, "The Colonial Policy of the Popular Front," 374–76, 391–92; and Girardet, *L'idée coloniale,* 202–11, 220–24.

8. During the interwar period Albert Sarraut served as one of the Radical Party's leading spokesmen on colonial questions. See Thomas, "Albert Sarraut." For a summary of the Radical Party's involvement with empire, see also Cohen, "The Colonial Policy of the Popular Front," 368–71.

9. Lagana, "L'échec de la commission," 82–83.

10. Procès-verbal de la séance inaugurale de la Commission d'enquête dans les territoires de la France d'outre-mer, ANOM, GGAOF, 17G, 252.

11. On the Senate's efforts to hamstring this commission, see Lagana, "L'échec de la commission," 94–96.

12. A copy of the commission's letter of resignation, dated 7 July 1938, can be found in ANOM, Commission Guernut, 9.

13. See, for example, Lagana, "L'échec de la commission"; Cohen, "The Colonial Policy of the Popular Front," 387–88; and Coquery-Vidrovitch, "The Popular Front and the Colonial Question," 157–58.

14. This goal had been spelled out in the first article of the 20 January 1937 law creating the parliamentary commission. See "Procès-verbal de la séance inaugurale de la Commission d'enquête dans les territoires de la France d'outre-mer," ANOM, GGAOF, 17G, 252.

15. Circular from the parliamentary commission to overseas bodies (trade unions, professional organizations, associations, etc.), n.d. (summer 1937), ANOM, Commission Guernut, 15.

16. Although some of these groups had primarily European memberships, others were largely or exclusively Senegalese. Letter from the administrator of the Circonscription de Dakar et dépendances to Governor General de Coppet, 16 September 1937, ANOM, GGAOF, 17G, 252.

17. For a biographical portrait of de Coppet, see Couturier, *Le gouverneur et son miroir*.

18. Cooper, *Decolonization and African Society*, 92–98.

19. De Coppet, *Discours prononcé par M. M. de Coppet*, 1937, 9.

20. Cooper, *Decolonization and African Society*, 98.

21. See Cooper, *Decolonization and African Society*, 73–109; Omar Guèye, *Sénégal*, chap. 2; and Bernard-Duquenet, *Le Sénégal et le Front populaire*.

22. De Coppet, *Discours prononcé par M. M. de Coppet*, 1937, 9.

23. "Organisation agricole et artisanale de l'École de Médina à Dakar," *L'Éducation Africaine*, no. 94 (April–June 1936): 209–13; and "Une nouvelle réalisation sociale: L'École de Médina," *BIR*, no. 82 (21 November 1935): 7–8.

24. Senghor later reported on the outcry that this rural school had provoked. See Senghor, "La résistance de la bourgeoisie sénégalaise à l'école rurale populaire," 44.

25. Letter from the Association des notables de Saint-Louis à Dakar to Marius Moutet, 25 September 1936, ANS, FAOF, Série O, 45/31.

26. In an effort to assert more control over Senegal's General Council, colonial authorities moved at the end of World War I to dilute originaire representation by adding a number of non-elective seats, which were distributed to chiefs and

notables ostensibly representing the various regions of Senegal. In practice, appointed councilors usually became rather compliant allies of the colonial administration. As they reformed this body, colonial authorities also imposed the new name of Colonial Council. See esp. Searing, "Accommodation and Resistance," 489–517.

27. "Motion concernant la nomination du chef du service de l'enseignement du Sénégal," in Colonie du Sénégal, *Conseil colonial: Session ordinaire de juin 1935* (Saint-Louis: Imprimerie du Gouvernement, 1935), 212. Most such published reports and issues of the official periodical *Colonie du Sénégal: Conseil Colonial* are now available through Gallica, the digital library of the Bibliothèque nationale de France.

28. See, for example, Colonie du Sénégal, *Conseil colonial: Session extraordinaire de novembre 1936* (Saint-Louis: Imprimerie du Gouvernement, 1937), 136–45.

29. "Profession de foi de M. Lamine Guèye, candidat du P.S.S," *L'AOF* (newspaper), 25 April 1936. Although Guèye lost this election, he remained a powerful voice for reform throughout the Popular Front period. On Guèye's political career during the 1930s, see Dieng, *Lamine Guèye*, esp. chap. 2; and Zuccarelli, *La vie politique sénégalaise*, chap. 10.

30. Louis Martin, "Pour nos enfants," *Le Périscope Africain*, 18 June 1936. See also Martin, "L'enseignement en AOF," *Le Périscope Africain*, 20 April 1935.

31. Pierre André, "Les détracteurs de l'enseignement aux colonies," *Le Périscope Africain*, 27 June 1936.

32. See, for example, the following three articles in *La Voix du Dahomey*: "En marge de l'enseignement," 1 September 1936; "En marge de l'enseignement (suite)," 1 December 1936; and "En marge de l'enseignement (suite)," 1 June 1937. On *La Voix du Dahomey* and its repeated confrontations with the colonial administration, see Lokossou, "La presse au Dahomey"; and Codo, "La presse dahoméenne face aux aspirations des 'évolués.'"

33. On Senghor's scholarly and literary interests at this time, see Vaillant, *Black, French, and African*, chap. 5.

34. Senghor insinuates that Lalouse pushed him toward the Cours secondaire de Dakar after finding him inadequately suited for the priesthood. Senghor, *La poésie de l'action*, 49–55. After analyzing correspondence between Lalouse and his superior, Janet Vaillant concludes that the priest deeply admired Senghor's academic abilities and sought to help the latter to pursue more advanced studies. Vaillant, *Black, French, and African*, 58–59.

35. I discuss secondary education in detail in chapter 7.

36. On Senghor's formal education in Senegal, see Vaillant, *Black, French, and African*, 19–24, 29–33, 58–63; and Senghor, *La poésie de l'action*, 47–55.

37. Vaillant, *Black, French, and African*, 61–62.

38. On the founding of this residential community after World War I, see Blanc, "La constitution du domaine de la Cité internationale universitaire de Paris."

39. On Senghor's educational experiences in France, see Vaillant, *Black, French, and African*, chaps. 3–5; Senghor, *La poésie de l'action*, 56–61; and Sirinelli, "Deux étudiants 'coloniaux.'"

40. Senghor passed the *agrégation de grammaire* in the fall of 1935, on his third try. Vaillant, *Black, French, and African*, 88–89, 104–7.

41. This was the case for Ousmane Socé, another ascendant Senegalese intellectual, who came to know Senghor in Paris. I discuss Socé at length in chapter 6.

42. In Paris Césaire enrolled in the *classes préparatoires* of the prestigious Lycée Louis-le-Grand; from there he won admission to the École normale supérieure. Damas followed a more unsettled pathway that led him to the École nationale des langues orientales vivantes and then to the Sorbonne, where he studied law and literature. On Césaire's educational trajectory, see Toumson and Henry-Valmore, *Aimé Césaire*, 31–48; and Fonkoua, *Aimé Césaire*, chaps. 1–2. On Damas's education, see Racine, *Léon-Gontran Damas*, 25–30. For other book-length studies of Damas, see Rano, *Créolitude*; Miller, *Rethinking Négritude*; and Ojo-Ade, *Léon-Gontran Damas*.

43. On the early Negritude movement, see esp. Wilder, *The French Imperial Nation-State*, chaps. 6–8; Kesteloot, *Black Writers in French*, chaps. 1–8; Taoua, *Forms of Protest*, chap. 2; Vaillant, *Black, French, and African*, chaps. 4–5; and Irele, *The Negritude Moment*.

44. See esp. Sharpley-Whiting, *Negritude Women*; Edwards, *The Practice of Diaspora*, chap. 3; and Boittin, *Colonial Metropolis*, chap. 5.

45. From page titled "Our Aim," *La Revue du Monde Noir*, no. 1 (1931): 4. Reprinted in *La Revue du Monde Noir/The Review of the Black World, 1931–1932*, 2. On *La Revue du Monde Noir*, see Sharpley-Whiting, *Negritude Women*, chaps. 2–4; Edwards, *The Practice of Diaspora*, chap. 3; Malela, *Les écrivains afro-antillais*, esp. 110–32; Wilder, *The French Imperial Nation-State*, 171–75; and Dewitte, *Les mouvements nègres*, 256–67.

46. As Edwards compellingly notes, contributions to this journal remained rather disparate in their focus, hardly suggesting a unified "movement." Moreover, despite the publication's title, which was clearly meant to evoke affinities among African and Antillean students, Senghor was the only African contributor. See Edwards, *The Practice of Diaspora*, 178–81.

47. Césaire, "Nègreries: Jeunesse noire et assimilation."

48. Senghor, "L'humanisme et nous."

49. Césaire is reported to have invented the term around the middle of the decade, but even during the second half of the 1930s the term was used only sparingly.

Césaire dramatically evoked his Negritude in his monumental poem *Cahier d'un retour au pays natal*, which was first published in 1939. The first poem by Senghor to contain the term "Negritude" was apparently "Le portrait," from 1936. In this poem, Senghor writes of "the demands of my imperious Negritude." See *Vaillant, Black, French, and African*, 120.

50. Senghor, "Réflexions sur l'éducation africaine: De l'assimilation," *Paris-Dakar*, 6 January 1937.

51. See Senghor, "Réflexions sur l'éducation africaine: L'école rurale populaire," *Paris-Dakar*, 9 January 1937.

52. Letter from de Coppet to the Governor of Senegal, n.d., ANOM, GGAOF, 17G, 470.

53. For a general account of Seghor's trip to Senegal, see Vaillant, *Black, French, and African*, 147–55.

54. On Senghor's trip home in 1932, see Vaillant, *Black, French, and African*, 103, 149–50.

55. "Avec M. Léopold Senghor," *Paris-Dakar*, 3 September 1937.

56. "Le problème culturel en AOF: Tel est le sujet que traitera ce soir M. Léopold Sédar Senghor," *Paris-Dakar*, 4 September 1937.

57. Senghor's speech was published in four installments in *Paris-Dakar*, in the issues of 7, 8, 10, and 11 September. *Le Périscope Africain* reproduced the speech in its issues of 18 September and 2 October.

58. Senghor was not the first Senegalese intellectual to be offered such a speaking engagement. Ousmane Socé had given a talk titled "Impressions of Europe" on 31 July 1937. On Socé, see chapter 6.

59. Letter from de Coppet's cabinet to Senghor, 2 September 1937, ANOM, GGAOF, 17G, 470.

60. Vaillant, *Black, French, and African*, 151.

61. Senghor, "Le problème culturel en A.O.F.," 44–45. For other accounts of Senghor's speech, see Vaillant, *Black, French, and African*, 151–55; and Wilder, *The French Imperial Nation-State*, 234–38.

62. Senghor, "Le problème culturel en A.O.F.," 45.

63. Senghor proceeded to explain that "civilizations" were the more tangible manifestations of cultures, or "the totality of concepts and technologies of a given people at a particular moment in its history." Senghor, "Le problème culturel en A.O.F.," 45.

64. Senghor had encountered Frobenius's work in the mid-1930s. In 1936 Césaire offered Senghor a volume that had just been translated into French, *Histoire de la civilisation africaine*. See Senghor, "Les leçons de Leo Frobenius," 398. On the impact that Frobenius had on Senghor, see also Vaillant, *Black, French, and African*, 123–25; and Riesz and Bjornson, "Senghor and the Germans."

65. Senghor, "Le problème culturel en A.O.F.," 45.

66. Senghor, "Le problème culturel en A.O.F.," 47. Senghor changed the word *bipolarité* to *bicéphalisme* in the version of his speech that was subsequently published as part of his collected writings. See "Le problème culturel en A.O.F.," in Senghor, *Liberté 1*, 14.

67. Senghor, "Le problème culturel en A.O.F.," 51. Senghor had recently begun work on a doctoral dissertation devoted to several languages spoken in Senegal. Senghor, *La poésie de l'action*, 17, 18, 60; and Vaillant, *Black, French, and African*, 116, 121.

68. Senghor, "Le problème culturel en A.O.F.," 51.

69. Describing how his propositions were received in 1937, Senghor later noted: "In 1937, in a talk titled *The Cultural Problem in A.O.F.* ... my calls for a return to our roots, and hence to Negro-African languages, caused an uproar among Negro-African elites." Senghor, "Le problème des langues vernaculaires," 228.

70. De Coppet even published an article on the subject, titled "L'enseignement vernaculaire aux colonies," which his cabinet forwarded to Senghor. Letter from Edmond Louveau (director of de Coppet's cabinet) to Senghor, 28 October 1937, ANOM, GGAOF, 17G, 470.

71. Decree dated 29 September 1938, *JORF*, 7 October 1938, 11721. See also the note from minister of colonies, Georges Mandel, to the president of the French Republic, Albert Lebrun, 29 September 1938, CADN, Fonds Dakar 339; and Mandel's letter to the governor general of AOF, 10 October 1938, ANS, FAOF, Série O, 93/31.

72. Senghor, "Le problème culturel en A.O.F.," 46.

73. For an overview of this section of the fair, see Hodeir, "La France d'Outre-Mer."

74. On Rivet, see esp. Laurière, *Paul Rivet, le savant et le politique*; Conklin, *In the Museum of Man*, esp. chap. 5; and de L'Estoile, *Le goût des autres*, chap. 3.

75. On these ethnographic missions, see Conklin, *In the Museum of Man*, 199–211; and de L'Estoile, *Le goût des autres*, 138–51.

76. A list of participants was later published in *Congrès international de l'évolution culturelle*, 21–24.

77. Blanche, "Préface," 16.

78. In 1937 Hazoumé published *Le pacte de sang au Dahomey*; the following year he published *Doguicimi*. For an analysis of Hazoumé's writings, see Riesz, "From Ethnography to the African Novel"; and Coundouriotis, *Claiming History*, chaps. 3–4.

79. Senghor, "La résistance de la bourgeoisie," 40–44.

80. Sissoko, "Les noirs et la culture." I have concluded that Sissoko did not attend the conference since, unlike Hazoumé, he does not appear on the *liste des congressistes*, and unlike Senghor, he is not mentioned in the conference's

program. Sissoko continued to develop his essentialist thinking about the development of cultures and races during the late 1930s. During World War II he circulated a longer statement of his views, which eventually became the basis for a book, published in 1950, under the title *Les noirs et la culture: Introduction au problème de l'évolution culturelle des peuples africains.*

81. For another account of Senghor's conference paper, see Vaillant, *Black, French, and African*, 155–62.

82. Senghor, "La résistance," 42. Throughout his paper Senghor chooses to refer to urban Senegalese elites as the local "bourgeoisie." Senghor may well have imagined that this term would undermine the legitimacy of these elites, since in France, Popular Front officials were attuned in new ways to popular culture and the working class.

83. Senghor, "La résistance," 44.

84. See Blanche, "Préface," 18.

85. Blanche, "Préface," 18.

86. Blanche, "Préface," 18.

87. Blanche, "Préface," 18–19.

88. Blanche, "Préface," 18–19.

89. Blanche, "Préface," 15.

90. Blanche, "Préface," 15.

91. On *la culture légitime*, see esp. Bourdieu and Passeron, *La reproduction*.

92. On Senghor's studies in ethnology and African liguistics, see Vaillant, *Black, French, and African*, 104, 121–26.

93. On the struggle to speak for "Africans," see de L'Estoile, "Au nom des 'vrais Africains.'"

94. Labouret headed the second subcommission, which was charged with investigating the sub-Saharan colonies, including Madagascar and Réunion, along with the remaining French colonies in the Americas.

95. Senghor to Labouret, 26 October 1937, ANOM, Commission Guernut, 107, dossier 20.

96. Labouret to Senghor, 28 October 1937, ANOM, Commission Guernut, 107, dossier 20.

97. De Coppet, *Discours prononcé par M. M. de Coppet*, 1937, 18–19. See also p. 42.

98. In two interviews conducted with Jacques Hymans in 1960, Senghor claimed that he declined de Coppet's offer because he was not ready to enter the world of politics. At the time, he still considered his cause to be primarily cultural in nature. Senghor also feared that his conception of educational reform would fail to generate adequate support among Senegalese elites. See Hymans, *Léopold Sédar Senghor*, 95–96. In an interview conducted in 1976 Senghor explained

to Janet Vaillant that he had turned down this position because he doubted that he could sufficiently influence the views of the colonial administration. See Vaillant, *Black, French, and African*, 154–55. On these points, see also Wilder, *The French Imperial Nation-State*, 234, 354n83.

99. De Coppet to Senghor, 23 November 1937; de Coppet to Senghor, 8 December 1937, ANOM, GGAOF, 17G, 470.

100. Senghor's report to de Coppet, titled "L'enseignement en AOF," ANS, FAOF, Série O, 614/31.

101. In 1934 there were thirteen urban schools in AOF, with a combined total of 929 students. "L'année scolaire 1933–1934 en A.O.F.: Rapport statistique d'ensemble," *BIR*, no. 30 (4 October 1934): 7.

102. De Coppet to Laborde, April 1938, ANS, FAOF, Série O, 45/31. See also the reports that the head of de Coppet's cabinet wrote as he and de Coppet inspected schools in French Soudan. ANOM, GGAOF, 17G, 378.

103. During his time in France, de Coppet planned to tend to the protracted respiratory illness from which he had been suffering. Letter from de Coppet to the director of finance and accounting at the Government General, 13 July 1938, ANOM, GGAOF, 17G, 379.

104. On these strikes, see Cooper, *Decolonization and African Society*, 104–7; and Bernard-Duquenet, *Le Sénégal et le Front populaire*, 182–211.

105. Correspondence announcing de Coppet's arrivals and departures can be found in ANOM, GGAOF, 17G, 379.

106. Mandel to governors general of AOF, AEF, Madagascar, and Indochina, the commissioners of Togo and Cameroon, and the governor of New Caledonia, 18 November 1938, CADN, Fonds Dakar 340.

107. Mandel to Boisson, 9 March 1939; Boisson to Mandel, 20 March 1939, ANS, FAOF, Série O, 230/31.

108. Miller, *Nationalists and Nomads*, 40. See also Midiohouan, *L'idéologie dans la littérature négro-africaine*, 107–12.

109. In Wilder's words: "Interwar Negritude was a politically moderate project to reform French colonialism. Its writers never called explicitly for the political independence of colonized peoples. They deliberately collaborated with colonial humanism, sometimes challenged it, and unwittingly reproduced many of its problematic positions." Wilder, *The French Imperial Nation-State*, 253.

6. The National Revolution

1. See, for example, Jennings, *Vichy in the Tropics*; Cantier, *L'Algérie sous le régime de Vichy*; Cantier and Jennings, *L'Empire colonial sous Vichy*; and Ginio, *French Colonialism Unmasked*.

2. The Colony of Gabon remained a holdout until November 1940, when troops loyal to the Free French finally took control. On wartime events in French Africa, see Jennings, *Free French Africa in World War II*; Thomas, *The French Empire at War*, esp. part 2; and Akpo-Vaché, *L'AOF et la Seconde Guerre mondiale*.

3. The present chapter builds on my previous article "The National Revolution in French West Africa."

4. "Décret du 25 juin 1940 portant création d'un Haut-Commissariat de l'Afrique française," ANS, FAOF, Série O, 170/31.

5. On Boisson's colonial career prior to the summer of 1940, see Ramognino, *L'Affaire Boisson*, chaps. 1–4. Ramognino's account of Boisson is overly sympathetic. Among other things, Ramognigno mistakenly concludes that Boisson was known for his left-leaning tendencies during the Popular Front period. In reality Boisson's appointment as commissioner of Cameroon in 1936 hardly proves that he identified with the Popular Front governments and their priorities. The same could be said of Jules Brévié, who was promoted to the position of governor general of Indochina by the first Popular Front government. Subsequently both men quickly assumed positions of responsibility within the Vichy Regime.

6. Circular dated 31 August 1940, ANOM, Fonds ministériels, Affaires politiques, 883/20. On this important shift, see also Jennings, *Vichy in the Tropics*, 200–201.

7. Lémery to Boisson, 16 August 1940, CADN, Fonds Dakar 113.

8. Boisson to "toutes colonies Afrique française et circonscription Dakar et dépendances," 18 November 1940, CADN, Fonds Dakar 113. On Boisson's leadership in Dakar, see Ramognino, *L'Affaire Boisson*, part 2; and Ramognino, "L'Afrique de l'Ouest sous le proconsulat de Pierre Boisson."

9. One measure of this increased despotism was the surge in the number of punishments handed out under the provisions of the *indigénat*. In 1942 Senegal's administration issued 2,150 prison sentences and 231 fines. This represented a marked change from the Popular Front period: in 1937 the colony's administration had handed out 830 prison sentences and 54 fines. "Colonie du Sénégal: Rapport politique, année 1942," CADN, Fonds Dakar 178. The corresponding political report for 1937 can be found in CADN, Fonds Dakar 176. On the use of the *indigénat* during the war, see also Ginio, *French Colonialism Unmasked*, 28–30.

10. Boisson's circular "Trois directives de colonisation africaine," 21 August 1941, ANOM, GGAOF, 17G, 119.

11. See Boisson to Lémery, 18 November 1940, ANS, FAOF, Série O, 31/31; and especially Boisson's circular to the governors of AOF, 18 November 1940, CADN, Fonds Dakar 113. On interwar travel restrictions, see also Mann, *From Empires to NGOs in the West African Sahel*, 124–27.

12. Circulaire from Boisson to the governors, 26 April 1939, ANOM, GGAOF, 17G, 119.

13. Circulaire from Boisson to the governors, 26 April 1939.

14. On the move toward ethnic and racial definitions of Frenchness in other parts of the French empire, see esp. Saada, *Les enfants de la colonie*. On similar trends in metropolitan France, see Camiscioli, *Reproducing the French Race*.

15. Circulaire from Boisson to the governors, 26 April 1939, ANOM, GGAOF, 17G, 119. See also the follow-up circular, outlining these same priorities, that Senegal's governor (Georges Parisot) sent to local commandants, 26 August 1939, CADN, Fonds Dakar 155.

16. A growing number of historical studies have investigated the role of sports in the French empire. In many cases the Vichy period proved to be a watershed moment. See Deville-Danthu, *Le sport en noir et blanc*; Combeau-Mari, *Le sport colonial à Madagascar*; Combeau-Mari, *Sports et loisirs dans les colonies*; Singaravélou and Sorez, *L'Empire des sports*; and Dubois, *Soccer Empire*.

17. Boisson's circular "Trois directives de colonisation africaine," 21 August 1941, ANOM, GGAOF, 17G, 119.

18. Akpo-Vaché, *L'AOF et la Seconde Guerre mondiale*, 127–28; and Atlan, "Élections et pratiques électorales au Sénégal," chap. 3.

19. For an assessemnt of the Legion in AOF, see Akpo-Vaché, *L'AOF et la Seconde Guerre mondiale*, 73–79. Membership figures are provided on p. 76. The figure for Senegal (10,535 on 30 April 1942) also includes members in Mauritania, who must have been relatively few in number. On the Legion in AOF, see also Ginio, *French Colonialism Unmasked*, 50–53; and Ramognino, *L'Affaire Boisson*, 116–20.

20. Rey, "telegramme-lettre" to "administrateurs, tous cercles," 13 March 1942, CADN, Fonds Dakar 113. See also Rey's "confidential" letter to Boisson, 7 March 1942, CADN, Fonds Dakar 155.

21. Boisson to Rey, 24 October 1942, ANS, FAOF, Série O, 524/31. On mounting tensions between Boisson's administration and the Legion, see Akpo-Vaché, *L'AOF et la Seconde Guerre mondiale*, 77–79.

22. On wartime racism and segregation, see Guèye, *Itinéraire africain*, 110–11; and Ginio, *French Colonialism Unmasked*, 109–11. Although less virulent than antisemitism, antiblack racism also surged in metropolitan France during the war years. See Ndiaye, *La condition noire*, 177–83; and Jennings, "Vichy fut-il aussi antinoir?"

23. Boisson's circular to the governors of AOF, 28 June 1941, ANOM, GGAOF, 17G, 119.

24. Racial epithets seem to have remained quite commonplace. In late September 1943 the governor of Senegal, Hubert Deschamps, found it necessary to issue a strongly worded circular urging more restraint and respect. Circular cited in Guèye, *Itinéraire africain*, 111–12.

25. By early 1943 only two dailies were still being published in Dakar: *Paris-Dakar*

and a bulletin put out by the Chamber of Commerce. *Dakar-Jeunes* was the only weekly. Note from N. Valroff, "Directeur des Services d'Information de Presse et de Radiodiffusion," to the "Inspecteur des Colonies, Chef de la Délégation de l'AOF en Afrique du Nord," 17 February 1943, ANOM, GGAOF, 17G, 412. On the history of *Paris-Dakar*, see Koumé, "L'évolution de la presse quotidienne au Sénégal, Paris-Dakar." For a broader account of the press in Senegal, see Barry, *Histoire des médias au Sénégal*.

26. "Note au sujet de l'organisation de l'information et de la propagande au Haut-Commissariat de l'Afrique française," April 1942, ANOM, GGAOF, 17G, 412.

27. "Paysans du Berry: Un chant dans les labours," *Dakar-Jeunes*, 12 March 1942.

28. G. Etcheverry, "Pays Basque: Une terre—sa race—ses traditions," *Dakar-Jeunes*, 11 June 1942.

29. Ousmane Socé, "Un témoignage: L'évolution culturelle de l'AOF," *Dakar-Jeunes*, 29 January 1942.

30. During the 1930s and the war years he tended to write under the name of Ousmane Socé, even though his full name was Ousmane Socé Diop.

31. On Socé's trajectory, see Sabatier, "Educating a Colonial Elite," 100; and Ly, *Les instituteurs*, 5:300–301.

32. See Wilder, *The French Imperial Nation-State*, 185–86; and Vaillant, *Black, French, and African*, 99.

33. For more critical commentary on Socé's novels, see Miller, *Nationalists and Nomads*, chap. 2; Malela, *Les écrivains afro-antillais*, 141–55; and Hill, "Imagining Métissage."

34. Socé's talk was less ambitious than Senghor's and is not discussed here. See Socé, "Impressions d'Europe," *Paris-Dakar*, 4 August 1937 and 7 August 1937.

35. In September 1937 a reporter for *Paris-Dakar* could already observe that Senghor and Socé "are not always of the same mind." "Le problème culturel en AOF: Tel est le sujet que traitera ce soir M. Léopold Sédar Senghor," *Paris-Dakar*, 4 September 1937.

36. Scholars sometimes assume that Senghor was always a proponent of cultural *métissage*. But in fact this term does not appear in Senghor's writings from the 1930s. Senghor did employ other terms such as "Afro-French" and "Franco-African," which might seem to have similar connotations. In reality, however, Senghor's avoidance of the expression *métissage culturel* was a reflection of his more essentialist understanding of cultures and races. Senghor's experiences during World War II eventually led him to revise his views of cultures and cultural *métissage*. On these postwar evolutions, see my discussion in chapter 8.

37. For examples of his reprising of African legends, see Socé, "La légende de Ghana," *Paris-Dakar*, 11 March 1938; Socé "La légende de Silamakan," *Paris-Dakar*,

21 and 22 December 1938; and Socé, "Takhara ou la légende d'El Adji Omar," *Paris-Dakar*, 23 and 24 December 1938.

38. These biographical details are taken from Dia, *Vicissitudes*, 35.

39. Fara Sow, "La jeunesse se confie à Dakar-Jeunes," *Dakar-Jeunes*, 5 March 1942.

40. Sow, "La jeunesse se confie à Dakar-Jeunes."

41. Massata N'Diaye, "Fidelité spirituelle," *Dakar-Jeunes*, 4 June 1942.

42. N'Diaye, "Fidelité spirituelle."

43. Socé, "Le danger," *Paris-Dakar*, 29 September 1937.

44. Biographical information about Diawara and some other participants in the *Dakar-Jeunes* debates can be found in Jézéquel, "Les enseignants comme élite politique"; and Jézéquel, "Les 'mangeurs de craies.'"

45. Daouda Diawara, "Une opinion soudanaise," *Dakar-Jeunes*, 23 April 1942.

46. After the war Dia would emerge as an important political figure and a close ally of Senghor. Dia was elected to represent Senegal in the French Senate (Conseil de la République) in 1948. He gave up his Senate seat in 1956, when he was elected to the French National Assembly. Dia later went on to become Senegal's first prime minister at independence. For these and other biographical details, see Dia, *Vicissitudes*, chaps. 1–2.

47. Dia, *Vicissitudes*, 34.

48. Dia, "Une culture africaine," *Dakar-Jeunes*, 12 March 1942.

49. Dia, *Vicissitudes*, 35–36. Dia notes that other leaders of this group included Abdoulaye Sadji, Joseph M'Baye, and Fara Sow. Dia's recollection of Sow's position in the wartime cultural debates stands in tension with Sow's article in *Dakar-Jeunes*, discussed earlier. Sow found Dia's views excessively idealistic. In a letter to Dia that was intercepted by French authorities, he wrote: "You are a passionate soul and like all the enamoured people of your type, you have not managed to distinguish dreams from reality, wishes from what is possible." Letter dated 10 March 1942, CADN, Fonds Dakar 155.

50. Dia, *Vicissitudes*, 36.

51. Dia remembers: "I was thus, in those days, a type of protester who did not like politics. I considered that politics were something dirty and that everyone who got involved in politics ran the risk of becoming sullied." Dia, *Vicissitudes*, 46.

52. Dia, *Vicissitudes*, 36.

53. Sumus, "Pour un épanouissement essentiel du génie africain," *Dakar-Jeunes*, 11 June 1942.

54. Joseph M'Baye, "Le métissage culturel ne doit pas être un but mais un moyen," *Dakar-Jeunes*, 26 March 1942. At the time, M'Baye was vice-president of the Amicale des instituteurs du Sénégal, an association with which Dia was also deeply involved. See Dia, *Vicissitudes*, 35.

55. M'Baye, "Le métissage culturel ne doit pas être un but mais un moyen."

56. Letter intercepted and reproduced by the Commission de contrôle postal in Saint-Louis, CADN, Fonds Dakar 155.

57. Letter from Ibrahima M'Baye to Joseph M'Baye, 18 May 1942, CADN, Fonds Dakar 155.

58. *Sénégal: Bulletin d'Information et de Liaison*, no. 2 (21 March 1942): 32. This new association resulted from the fusion of two existing associations, the Association des anciens élèves du Lycée Faidherbe and the Saint-Louisienne.

59. Letter from Merlo (who worked at Senegal's administrative headquarters in Saint-Louis) to Rey, 25 September 1941, CADN, Fonds Dakar 113.

60. Rey, "telegramme-lettre" to "administrateurs, tous cercles," 13 March 1942, CADN, Fonds Dakar 113. Rey described many of these same directives in a confidential note to Boisson, 7 March 1942, CADN, Fonds Dakar 155.

61. Jennings, "Conservative Confluences." Describing the tactics of Decoux's administration, Jennings writes: "Convinced that they could play the cards of diversity, ethnicity, and difference to their advantage, as had countless French officials before them, Vichyite administrators embarked on a calculated strategy of bolstering local allegiances, stoking patriotic sentiment, fostering rediscovery, and strengthening particularism" (621).

62. Rey's "confidential" letter to Boisson, 29 April 1942, ANS, FAOF, Série O, 31/31.

63. Note from the directeur des affaires politiques et administratives to the directeur des services de l'information, 13 May 1942, ANS, FAOF, Série O, 31/31.

64. Émile Zinsou, "Une opinion de Cotonou," *Dakar-Jeunes*, 14 May 1942.

65. Charles Béart, "A propos d'une littérature indigène d'expression française," *Dakar-Jeunes*, 18 June 1942.

66. Béart, "A propos d'une littérature indigène d'expression française."

67. Report from Mady Diallo (who worked as an "agent de sûreté" for the police department in Saint-Louis) to the chief of police in Saint-Louis, 24 June 1942, CADN, Fonds Dakar 155.

68. I disagree with Ruth Ginio when she argues that "the enthusiastic response of educated Africans to the colonial idea of launching a cultural debate in *Dakar-Jeunes* may also point to a certain support for the regime. After all, a relatively safe way to express discontent would simply have been to ignore this literary discussion." Ginio, *French Colonialism Unmasked*, 109.

69. This is how one colonial official in Saint-Louis summed up the task facing African *évolués*. Merlo to Governor Rey, 2 July 1942, CADN, Fonds Dakar 155.

70. On AOF's rupture with Vichy France, see Akpo-Vaché, *L'AOF et la Seconde Guerre mondiale*, chaps. 7–8; Thomas, *The French Empire at War*, 159–77; and Ramognino, *L'Affaire Boisson*, chaps. 13–14.

71. On the accusations and trials that Boisson faced after leaving Dakar, see Hitchcock, "Pierre Boisson, French West Africa, and the Postwar *Epuration*"; and Ramognino, *L'Affaire Boisson*, chaps. 15–19.

7. Gaullist Hesitations

1. See Cooper, *Decolonization and African Society*, 176–202, esp. 177–83; and Cooper, *Citizenship between Empire and Nation*, chap. 1.

2. For a fuller account of this evolution, see Thomas, *The French Empire at War*, chap. 6; and Cantier, *L'Algérie sous le régime de Vichy*, chap. 8.

3. On this external focus, see Levy, "Les origines de la Conférence de Brazzaville"; and Ageron, "La préparation de la Conférence de Brazzaville."

4. On American skepticism about European imperialism, see Nwaubani, "The United States and the Liquidation of European Colonial Rule," 506–18; Hubbard, *The United States and the End of British Colonial Rule*; and Louis and Robinson, "The United States and the Liquidation of British Empire."

5. On these efforts, see Cooper, *Decolonization and African Society*, 110–41.

6. For accounts of the Brazzaville Conference, see esp. L'Institut Charles-de-Gaulle, *Brazzaville*; Cooper, *Decolonization and African Society*, esp. 177–83; Shipway, *The Road to War*, 21–40; and Chafer, *The End of Empire*, 56–61.

7. At the time Laurentie was director of political affairs at the CFLN's Commissariat aux colonies. On the various participants, see the conference's published report and recommendations, *La Conférence africaine française*, 11–16.

8. African opinions were represented only by a collection of reports that local elites had forwarded to Félix Éboué, the governor general of AEF. Éboué read from these reports at the Brazzaville Conference. Exerpts were subsequently published in *La Conférence africaine française*, 87–105.

9. "Programme général de la Conférence de Brazzaville," n.d. (November 1943), CADN, Fonds Dakar 160. This document was written primarily by Herni Laurentie, who also developed his views on the problem of colonial education in an internal report written around the same time. See Laurentie, "Note sur l'enseignement des indigènes et les oeuvres de jeunesse indigène dans les colonies françaises," 21 December 1943, ANOM, Fonds ministériels, Affaires politiques, 874/3.

10. Reports and minutes from the "Conférence des chefs de service de l'enseignement," Bamako, 14–18 January 1944, ANS, FAOF, Série O, 492/31.

11. You, "Colonie du Soudan: Conférence de Brazzaville: Enseignement," n.d., ANS, FAOF, Série O, 171/31.

12. E. Cabrière, the principal of the Lycée Van Vollenhoven in Dakar, who also worked at the Direction générale de l'enseignement, asserted: "We are again

being criticized for having maladapted education. Rural education has just started to pay dividends and already people have to attack it, before it has even had time to develop? ... Who has studied natives sufficiently to be able to assert that rural schools have not succeeded in native society, that they do not have a record of excellent results? ... It would be a mistake to reexamine our policies, for this would ruin a fifteen-year undertaking whose benefits have just started to be felt." Cabrière's report to Governor General Cournarie, 10 January 1944, ANS, FAOF, Série O, 171/31.

13. For another account of the conference's engagement with educational questions, see Chafer, "Decolonizaton and the Politics of Education," 40–43.

14. "Plan d'enseignement: Conférence africaine de Brazzaville," n.d., ANS, FAOF, Série O, 171/31. On this plan and the committee that produced it, see also Gardinier, "Les recommandations de la Conférence de Brazzaville."

15. "Plan d'enseignement: Conférence africaine de Brazzaville," n.d., ANS, FAOF, Série O, 171/31.

16. Similar conceptions of girls' education had structured the thinking of colonial officials during the interwar period, and particularly during the 1930s. See Barthélémy, *Africaines et diplômées*, esp. chap. 2.

17. "Conseil de gouvernement, 1943: Enseignement primaire officiel," n.d., ANS, FAOF, Série O, 171/31.

18. These figures are from Le Goff, "Écoles de filles et enseignement ménager en A.O.F.," 55–56.

19. Haut-Commissariat de l'AOF, *Annuaire statistique de l'AOF*, 2:79. I would like to thank Pascale Barthélémy for sharing this reference and for helping me to gauge more precisely the evolution of girls' schooling in AOF.

20. The conference's official recommendations were published in *La Conférence africaine française*. Recommondations regarding schooling are found on pp. 43–44. See also Gardinier, "Les recommandations de la Conférence de Brazzaville."

21. *La Conférence africaine française*, 44. Capitalization in the original. In making this declaration, officials were returning to a position that had already been clearly established by the 1924 school directives and the 1922 regulations regarding private schools. See chapter 3.

22. Cournarie to the governors, 10 March 1944, ANS, FAOF, Série O, 688/31.

23. "Extrait des discours prononcés au Conseil de gouvernement de 1944 et 1945 par Monsieur le Gouverneur Général de l'A.O.F.," *L'Éducation Africaine*, nos. 109–10 (1944–45): 35.

24. "Arrêté réorganisant l'enseignement primaire en Afrique occidentale française," 22 August 1945, reprinted in *L'Éducation Africaine*, nos. 109–10 (1944–45). The pagination is irregular.

25. See Bouche, "L'école rurale," 285–86.
26. *La Conférence africaine française*, 43–44. Raphaël Saller, the governor of the Côte des Somalis, who originally hailed from Martinique, was one of the lone officials to speak out in favor of secondary education. See Gardinier, "Les recommandations de la Conférence de Brazzaville," 175.
27. On secondary schooling in nineteenth-century Senegal, see Bouche, *L'enseignement*, 1: chap. 4.
28. The administration's plans for this new secondary school were presented to Senegal's General Council in late 1909, prompting spirited debates. Colonie du Sénégal, *Conseil général: Session ordinaire de décembre 1909*, 186–217, 221–34, 378–404. On the reopening of a secondary school in Saint-Louis, see also Bouche, *L'enseignement*, 2:549–59, 854–56, 871–73.
29. Simon, "Rapport au président de la République," 20 June 1919. See also the accompanying presidential decree calling for the establishment of a lycée in Saint-Louis. *JORF*, 26 June 1919, 6579–80.
30. Sarraut's letter to French president Alexandre Millerand and the accompanying presidential decree, dated 10 November 1920, ANS, FAOF, Série O, 246/31.
31. Note from Paul Crouzet, who was responsible for educational questions at the Ministry of Colonies, to Merlin, 25 November 1920, ANS, FAOF, Série O, 246/31.
32. Merlin's reply to Crouzet, 31 Janvier 1922, ANS, FAOF, Série O, 246/31.
33. Sarraut's telegram to Merlin, 11 November 1922, ANS, FAOF, Série O, 246/31.
34. This is clear from Merlin's note to officials in Saint-Louis, 17 March 1923, ANS, FAOF, Série O, 246/31.
35. "Lycée de Saint-Louis: État indiquant le nombre d'élèves au cours du premier trimestre 1922 répartis selon leur origine," ANS, FAOF, 17G, 239/108.
36. Morel's note "A/S la réforme de l'enseignement secondaire" to the lieutenant-governor of Senegal, 7 January 1923, ANS, FAOF, Série O, 246/31.
37. Carde to Inspection-conseil de l'instruction publique at the Ministry of Colonies, 24 January 1924, ANS, FAOF, Série O, 246/31.
38. The *brevet de capacité colonial* was created by a presidential decree published on 28 March 1924. See *JORF*, 30 March 1924, 3041. See also the "arrêté promulguant en A.O.F. le décret du 28 Mars 1924 portant création en A.O.F. d'un brevet de capacité correspondant au baccalauréat," 17 Avril 1924, ANS, FAOF, Série O, 246/31.
39. For a summary of this situation, as seen by a prominent originaire, see Louis Martin, "Pour nos enfants," *Le Périscope Africain*, 13 June 1936.
40. For the sake of simplicity, I use the term *baccalauréat*. In their correspondence,

even colonial authorities often opted for this term, as opposed to the rather clunky label of *brevet de capacité colonial*.

41. Braillon, "L'enseignement secondaire," 29–30.

42. On the European community in Senegal, see Cruise O'Brien, *White Society in Black Africa*, esp. chap. 2. Population figures are provided on p. 275.

43. Braillon, "L'enseignement secondaire," 27. On the early history of this school, see also Bouche, *L'enseignement*, 2:857–58.

44. Between 1936 and 1939 this school briefly bore the name of Lycée de Dakar. Today this historic school is known as the Lycée Lamine Guèye.

45. On Senghor's time at this school, see Senghor, *La poésie de l'action*, 55–56; and Vaillant, *Black, French, and African*, 58–63.

46. Between 1874 and 1965 students had to pass the first part of the *baccalauréat*, taken at the end of *la première*, before they were cleared to take the second part at the end of the following year. These respective parts underwent several changes over the years. For more details, see "La longue histoire du baccalauréat I: Quand le baccalauréat signait l'appartenance à l'élite"; and "La longue histoire du baccalauréat II: Quand le baccalauréat remplace le certificat d'études primaires," in Prost, *Regards historiques*, 239–46.

47. Lamine Guèye, "Le baccalauréat au Sénégal," *L'AOF* (newspaper), 16 November 1935.

48. Nédos Lignorant (pseud.), "Lettre ouverte à MM. les ministres de l'Éducation nationale et des Colonies," *L'AOF*, 23 November 1935.

49. Charton's "confidential" report to Brévié, 31 May 1935, ANS, FAOF, Série O, 183/31.

50. Dia, *Vicissitudes*, 34.

51. Charton's "confidential" report to Brévié, 31 May 1935, ANS, FAOF, Série O, 183/31.

52. "Lycée Van Vollenhoven: Effectif au 5 janvier 1942," ANS, FAOF, Série O, 190/31. The administration's statistics also indicated that 175 "Lebanese" attended this lycée. These students were confined almost entirely to the *classes primaires*. On Lebanese populations in AOF, see Arsan, *Interlopers of Empire*. Arsan estimates that there were some six thousand Lebanese in AOF by the late 1930s (pp. 5–6).

53. "Discours prononcé par M. Hubert Deschamps, Gouverneur du Sénégal, à la session ordinaire du Conseil colonial, 23 août 1943," in Colonie du Sénégal, *Conseil colonial: Procès-verbal de la séance du 23 août 1943* (Saint-Louis: Imprimerie du Gouvernement, 1943), 4.

54. Boisson to Governor Rey, 24 October 1942, ANS, FAOF, Série O, 524/31.

55. Today collèges are roughly equivalent to U.S. middle schools, while lycées correspond, broadly speaking, to U.S. high schools. The situation was quite

different during the Third Republic. At that time collèges and lycées frequently offered many of the same grades. Although smaller and less prestigious than lycées, collèges sometimes provided a full course of secondary education. In other cases collèges lacked certain grades, most typically *la terminale*. See the entry "Grands lycées et petits collèges" in Prost, *Regards historiques*, 109–12.

56. These figures are taken from Prost, *Histoire générale de l'enseignement et de l'éducation en France*, 4:232–33.

57. On scholarships for secondary schools, see Sirinelli, "Des boursiers conquérants?"; and Hugot, *La gratuité de l'enseignement secondaire*, chap. 8.

58. See Goblot, *La barrière et le niveau*. See also Lallement, *Logique de classe*, esp. 214–16.

59. Hessel, *Le programme du Conseil national de la Résistance*, 87–88. On the National Council of the Resistance, see Wieviorka, *Histoire de la Résistance*, 280–91.

60. The historian Marc Bloch was hardly the only one to conclude that the elites of the late Third Republic had hastened France's defeat. See Bloch, *Strange Defeat*. Bloch discusses the failings of the French educational system on pp. 151–62. For an overview of the educational reformism that grew out of the war, see Shennan, *Rethinking France*, chap. 7.

61. Cited in Compagnon and Thévenin, *L'école et la société française*, 101. For overviews of the Langevin-Wallon Commission, see also Chapoulie, *L'école d'État conquiert la France*, 364–81; and Prost, *Histoire générale*, 263–67. For additional details, see Sorel, *Une ambition pour l'école*.

62. On the softer nature of class boundaries in the colonies, and on more salient distinctions between colonizers and the colonized, see Memmi, *The Colonizer and the Colonized*, esp. 3–18.

63. Cabrière's report to Aubineau on "l'enseignement secondaire et la question indigène (Conférence de Brazzaville)," n.d., ANS, FAOF, Série O, 171/31.

64. Cabrière's report to Aubineau on "l'enseignement secondaire et la question indigène."

65. Aubineau discusses this strategy in a note to the Direction de l'enseignement et de la jeunesse at the Ministry of Colonies, n.d. (from the summer of 1945), ANS, FAOF, Série O, 45/31. See also Cournarie's note to the governor of Ivory Coast, 24 July 1945, ANS, FAOF, Série O, 184/31.

66. On the phasing out of school fees, see Prost, *Histoire générale*, 241–51, 714n28; and Hugot, *La gratuité de l'enseignement secondaire*, chap. 13.

67. The dip in birth rate that France experienced during World War I was acutely felt in the early 1930s, as particularly thin age cohorts moved into their adolescent years. On this point, see Prost, *Histoire générale*, 241–48.

68. In 1938 students boarding at the Lycée Faidherbe had to pay a yearly fee of 2,400 francs. Reductions were granted for families who enrolled more than

one child. Students who were not boarders also had to pay fees, ranging from 120 to 160 francs for the *classes primaires*, from 160 to 200 francs for the first cycle of secondary studies, and from 200 to 240 francs for the second cycle. "Lycée Faidherbe: Année scolaire 1938–1939," *JOAOF*, 8 October 1938, 1185–86. This document also describes a range of other restrictive policies. Maximum age limits were set for each class year, and before each year of study students had to pass a qualifying examination.

69. Ordonnance nº 45–318 du 3 mars 1945 relative à la suppression des classes primaires et élémentaires des lycées et collèges, *JORF*, 4 March 1945, 1132.

70. As Antoine Prost notes, many collèges and lycées continued this practice into the 1960s. It was during that decade that this longstanding traditon was finally abandoned. Prost, *Histoire générale*, 170–71.

71. Note from Lucien Paye, directeur de l'enseignement et de la jeunesse at the Ministry of Colonies, to Aubineau, 9 July 1945. This note is clearly referenced in Cabrière's note to Aubineau, dated 20 July 1945, ANS, FAOF, Série O, 45/31.

72. Cournarie to the governor of Ivory Coast, 24 July 1945, ANS, FAOF, Série O, 184/31.

73. Charton, "Rapport à Monsieur le Gouverneur Général de l'Afrique occidentale française," 22 February 1935, ANS, FAOF, Série O, 183/31.

74. Cabrière to Aubineau, 20 July 1945, ANS, FAOF, Série O, 45/31.

75. Lettre from Cournarie (signed by Yves Digo, the secretary-general) to the governor of Ivory Coast, 24 July 1945, ANS, FAOF, Série O, 184/31.

76. Giacobbi's "secret" circular to the governors general of AOF, AEF, and Madagascar, 23 March 1945, CADN, Fonds Dakar 160.

77. "Enseignement du second degré: tableau récapitulatif au 1er octobre 1945," in Ministère de l'Éducation nationale (Service de coordination de l'enseignement dans la France d'outre-mer), *L'enseignement dans les territoires français d'outre-mer*, 45.

78. At a meeting of teachers and education officials in mid-1946 two professors at the Lycée Van Vollenhoven continued to express bitterness over the way in which Cabrière had been forced out. "Compte rendu de la conférence tenue le lundi 3 juin 1946 a/s enseignement primaire supérieur et formation des instituteurs africains," ANS, FAOF, Série O, 688/31.

79. Aubineau to Cournarie, 11 September 1945, ANS, FAOF, Série O, 247/31.

80. Cabrière served as chef du service de l'enseignement in Madagascar from 1950 to 1954, and then from 1955 to 1957. Duteil, "Enseignants coloniaux," 2:521.

8. The Education of African "Citizens"

1. All told, six Africans and four Frenchmen were elected to represent French West Africa (and Togo). French Equatorial Africa elected two black Africans, one

métis, and three Frenchmen. A two-college system was used so as to guarantee the election of candidates representing the metropolitan French. For a fuller list of the parliamentary seats granted to the empire, see Cooper, *Citizenship*, 61–64; and Archives de la Chambre des députés, *Tableau des élections du 21 octobre 1945 à l'Assemblée nationale constituante*, esp. 20.

2. On the deliberations of the First Constituent Assembly, see Cooper, *Citizenship*, 67–91; and Guèye, *Itinéraire africain*, 133–46. For a contemporary account, see Devèze, *La France d'outre-mer*, chap. 5.

3. Senghor was named to the Commission des territoires d'outre-mer on 29 November 1945. He officially joined the Commission de la Constitution on 19 February 1946. See *JORF, Débats de l'ANC*, 30 November 1945, 139; 20 February 1946, 365.

4. See the preparatory report on departmentalization that Césaire presented in February 1946, published in the official periodical *Documents de l'Assemblée Nationale Constituante*, annexe no. 520 (séance du 26 février 1946).

5. This law was debated several times in the First Constituent Assembly. See especially the debate that took place during the first session of 12 March 1946. *JORF, Débats de l'ANC*, 13 March 1946, 659–66. See also the debate held during the first session on 14 March 1946. *JORF, Débats de l'ANC*, 15 March 1946, 751–62. The departmentalization law that was finally passed pulled back somewhat from earlier drafts, which had specified that *all* new metropolitan laws would apply to the overseas departments. The ultimate wording established that new metropolitan legislation would apply to the DOM provided that this intent was spelled out in the laws themselves. On this point, see Wilder, *Freedom Time*, 111–12.

6. Wilder, *Freedom Time*, 117. On the truncated citizenship of many inhabitants of the old colonies, see Larcher, *L'autre citoyen*, chaps. 4–6; and Dumont, *L'amère patrie*, chaps. 1–3.

7. Larcher, *L'autre citoyen*, 235.

8. On the broad support for departmentalization that existed among the political parties in Martinique, see Nicholas, *L'histoire de la Martinique*, 3: chap. 2; and Dumont, *L'amère patrie*, 68–74, 86–87, 155–58.

9. Departmentalization reduced but did not put an end to differential treatment, leading to disappointment and new demands. See Wilder, *Freedom Time*, 122–32, chap. 7; Dumont, "La quête de l'égalité aux Antilles"; Dumont, *L'amère patrie*, chap. 5; Finch-Boyer, "'The Idea of the Nation Was Superior to Race'"; Childers, "Departmentalization, Migration, and the Politics of the Family." For an array of perspectives on departmentalization and its consequences, see Constant and Daniel, *1946–1996*; and the special issue (on departmentalization) of the *International Journal of Francophone Studies* 11, nos. 1–2 (June 2008).

10. See *JORF*, *Débats de l'ANC*, 21 March 1946, 899–913; 22 March 1946, 931–49; 23 March 1946, 994–1003; 24 March 1946, 1028–45; 27 March 1946, 1051–58.

11. This chapter partially builds on my earlier article "La crise de l'enseignement en Afrique occidentale française."

12. Senghor's speech was subsequently published under the title "L'enseignement, base de l'évolution des peuples," quotes at 9–10.

13. Senghor noted that there was a grand total of 108,911 students in French West Africa; this figure included students in public and private primary schools as well as students in secondary schools. He calculated the total school-age population to be 2.7 million. Senghor, "L'enseignement, base de l'évolution des peuples," 11.

14. Senghor, "L'enseignement, base de l'évolution des peuples," 11.

15. Senghor, "L'enseignement, base de l'évolution des peuples," 13.

16. In January 1946 the Ministry of Colonies officially became the Ministry of Overseas France. In related semantic shifts the colonies were rebranded as "territories," while the empire was increasingly referred to as the French Union. If the terms "empire" and "French Union" had different resonances, they also embraced somewhat different geographies. Unlike the empire, the French Union included both the metropole and Overseas France. In the end some of France's overseas possessions (principally Morocco, Tunisia, and the "protected states" of French Indochina) were never fully integrated into the French Union. See Isoart, "Le septennat de Vincent Auriol."

17. Senghor, "L'enseignement, base de l'évolution des peuples," 18.

18. See Cooper, *Decolonization and African Society*, part 2; and Cooper, *Citizenship*, chaps. 2–4. Other important works that challenge conventional narratives about decolonization by taking integrationist reforms seriously include Shepard, *The Invention of Decolonization*; Wilder, *Freedom Time*; and Lawrence, *Imperial Rule and the Politics of Nationalism*.

19. "Loi no. 46–940 du 7 mai 1946 tendant à proclamer citoyens tous les ressortissants des territoires d'outre-mer," *JORF*, 8 May 1946, 3888. This law is sometimes referred to as the "Lamine Guèye law," after its leading sponsor.

20. "Loi no. 46–940 du 7 mai 1946 tendant à proclamer citoyens."

21. In his doctoral dissertation, defended in 1921, Guèye provided a legal and historical analysis of the originaires' quest for French citizenship. See Guèye, "De la situation politique des Sénégalais originaires." Diagne provided early support to Guèye, as the latter sought to acquire metropolitan academic credentials and use them to his advantage in Senegal. Among other things, Diagne helped Guèye win incorporation into the European *cadre* of schoolteachers, against the wishes of colonial authorities. Guèye soon gave up his career as a

schoolteacher to devote himself to law and politics. During the 1920s his relations with Diagne grew progressively more complicated. On these intersections,
see Dieng, *Lamine Guèye*, 57–61; and Ly, *Les instituteurs*, 2:250–51, 5:254–57.

22. Much work still needs to be done on the "practice" of originaire citizenship
between the wars. Although the uniqueness of originaire citizenship declined
markedly after World War II, important legal distinctions continued to separate originaire citizens from the millions of new citizens created by the law
of 7 May 1946. Most notably, the originaires enjoyed universal voting rights,
whereas other African citizens had to meet certain requirements to be eligible to vote. This changed with the loi-cadre of 1956–57, when voting rights
became universal everwhere in AOF. For a brief analysis of these technicalities,
see Coquery-Vidrovitch, "Nationalité et citoyenneté en Afrique occidentale
française," 296–304.

23. On struggles to defend the Lamine Guèye law, see Cooper, *Citizenship*, 91–123.
Articles 81 and 82 of the new constitution also bore directly on questions of
citizenship. The former declared that French nationals and the inhabitants
of the French Union were all citizens the French Union, who enjoyed the
rights and liberties defined in the constitution's preamble. The latter article
stipulated that citizens who did not possess French civil status would retain
their personal status unless they decided to renounce it. This article went on
to state that rights and liberties pertaining to citizens could not be limited or
denied to those citizens who did not have French civil status. For the full text of
the constitution of 27 octobre 1946, see http://www.conseil-constitutionnel.fr
/conseil-constitutionnel/francais/la-constitution/les-constitutions-de-la-france
/constitution-de-1946-ive-republique.5109.html.

24. The Assembly of the French Union drew half of its members from the metropole
and the other half from France's overseas possessions. This assembly was
not convened for its first meeting until December 1947. Thereafter it quickly
became clear that this body would serve a largely symbolic function. See
Michel, "L'empire colonial dans les débats parlementaires," 210–15.

25. For more details on these political bodies, see Benoist, *L'Afrique occidentale
française*, 81–82, 93–101.

26. On the activities of African deputies in the legislatures of the Fourth Republic,
see Cooper, *Citizenship*, chaps. 3–5; Benot, *Les parlementaires africains à Paris*,
chaps. 4–7; Morgenthau, *Political Parties in French-Speaking West Africa*, esp.
chap. 3; Guillemin, "Les élus d'Afrique noire à l'Assemblée nationale"; and
Michel, "L'empire colonial dans les débats parlementaires."

27. On the Socialist Party's approach to colonial reform after World War II, see

Ageron, "De l'Empire à la dislocation de l'Union française (1939–1956)," 429–33. See also Gratien, *Marius Moutet*, 219–28, 283–301.

28. Circular dated 6 December 1946, cited in Capelle, *L'éducation en Afrique noire*, 40.

29. Letter from Aubineau to Governor General Barthes, 3 August 1946, ANS, FAOF, Série O, 1/31.

30. The first step toward creating this fund was taken on 30 April 1946, with the passage of a law "tendant à l'établissement, au financement et à l'exécution de plans d'équipement et de développement des territoires relevant du ministère de la France d'outre-mer," *JORF*, 1 May 1946, 3655–56. This fund was consolidated during the months that followed.

31. Whereas the Ministry of Colonies held administrative responsibility for the largest portion of the empire, including AOF, AEF, Madagascar, Indochina, and the old colonies, the Ministry of Foreign Affairs oversaw the administration of the French protectorates in Morocco and Tunisia, and the French mandate for Syria and Lebanon. Things were somewhat more complicated in Algeria, which included three French *départements*. The Interior Ministry possessed the broadest purview in Algeria, even though other metropolitan ministries had also acquired prerogatives there. For an overview of these administrative divisions, see Thobie, "Le Bilan colonial en 1914," 7–13.

32. For an overview of this trend, see Chafer, *The End of Empire*, 87–90.

33. On the creation of this entity, see Ministère de l'Éducation nationale, "Introduction," 3–6.

34. The Constituent Assembly initially created the Conseil supérieur de l'éducation nationale in early April. See *JORF, Débats de l'ANC*, 5 April 1946, 1433. The precise composition and functions of this body were debated and approved two weeks later. See *JORF, Débats de l'ANC*, 21 April 1946, 2084–89. A final law establishing this council was passed on 18 May 1946. See *JORF*, 19 May 1946, 4323–29. This new council replaced the Conseil supérieur de l'instruction publique, which had functioned between 1850 and 1945, and the Conseil supérieur de l'enseignement public that had been established on 26 April 1945.

35. Ministère de l'Éducation nationale (Service de coordination de l'enseignement dans la France d'outre-mer), *L'enseignement dans les territoires français d'outre-mer*, 3.

36. Capelle had studied at both the École des mines and the École normale supérieure—two of France's most prestigious grandes écoles. After completing his doctorate at the Sorbonne in 1938, with a specialization in mechanics and engineering, he eventually went on to hold a professorship at the University of

Nancy, before being tapped to head up education in AOF. See the biographical sketch provided in Prost, *Regards historiques*, 81–84.

37. This does not include the Académie d'Alger, which was founded in 1848. On the evolution of France's *académies* since the First Empire, see Condette, *Les recteurs d'académie*, 1:125–44.

38. Each *académie* encompassed a number of departments, ranging anywhere from three to eight. See Condette, *Les recteurs d'académie*, 1:137.

39. On the evolving responsibilities of *recteurs* and their subordinates, see Condette, *Les recteurs d'académie*, 1: chap. 1.

40. Capelle, *L'éducation en Afrique noire*, 38, 40–41, 50.

41. Capelle's letter to the director of personnel at the Government General, 11 September 1947, ANS, FAOF, Série O, 511/31.

42. Report by P. and M. Drouin (inspecteurs généraux at the Education Ministry), "L'enseignement du premier degré en AOF: Année 1948–1949," Archives nationales de France, Pierrefitte-sur-Seine, AN 19770508/54; Capelle, *L'éducation en Afrique noire*, 50.

43. Before sending Capelle to Dakar, the Education Ministry had first awarded him with the metropolitan rank of *recteur*. By sending a *recteur* to Dakar, officials in Paris sought to suggest that educational structures in AOF should come to resemble those of a metropolitan *académie*. They also wanted to make sure that Capelle went to Dakar with enough authority to carry out reforms in the face of colonial opposition. Capelle, *L'éducation en Afrique noire*, 58.

44. Capelle's "lettre-programme" to the overseas minister, 3 April 1947, cited in Capelle, *L'éducation en Afrique noire*, 40–41.

45. Frederick Cooper and Gary Wilder have both emphasized this point. See Cooper, *Citizenship*; and Wilder, *Freedom Time*, esp. chaps. 6 and 8.

46. Signatories included not only Senghor and Guèye but also Yacine Diallo (deputy from Guinea), Jean Silvandre (deputy from Soudan), Jean-Hilaire Aubame (deputy from Gabon), and Ousmane Socé Diop (senator from Senegal). Capelle, *L'éducation en Afrique noire*, 42.

47. See Senghor's essay "Vues sur l'Afrique noire ou assimiler, non être assimilés." Originally published in Lemaignen, Youtévong, and Senghor, *La communauté impériale française*, this text was later reprinted in Senghor, *Liberté 1*, 39–69. Senghor discusses educational matters on pp. 62–68.

48. Several months before the elections to the First Constituant Assembly, an ordinance dated 22 August 1945 specified the categories of Africans who would be allowed to vote in the electoral colleges reserved for "subjects." These categories included "notables évolués," members and former members of local assemblies, representatives of cooperatives and unions, recipients of a variety of honorary

medals and distinctions, retired and active civil servants, holders of diplomas equivalent or superior to the local primary school certificate, members of native tribunals, former officers and petty officers, military veterans having served outside their home territory during either of the world wars, former soldiers receiving a retirement or disability pension, licensed merchants, and chiefs or representatives of "collectivités indigènes." Ordinance reprinted in Guèye, *Itinéraire africain*, 133–34.

49. After being elected as mayor of Dakar in July 1945, Guèye went on to be elected as deputy by citizens in Senegal in October 1945. For more details, see Atlan, "Élections et pratiques électorales," chap. 7.

50. Diallo's note to Capelle, 21 July 1947, cited in Capelle, *L'éducation en Afrique noire*, 42. Italics in original.

51. Senghor, "La condition de notre évolution: Réforme de l'enseignement," *Condition Humaine*, 11 February 1948.

52. Senghor, "La condition de notre évolution."

53. Chafer, "Decolonization and the Politics of Education," 74–75. See in particular the RDA's October 1946 resolution on education, which is reproduced on pp. 429–31.

54. Eligible voters in the African territories directly elected the members of the various *conseils généraux*. All the colonies except Senegal used a double college system, which ensured that European populations would retain strong representation. Each *conseil général* then elected, from among its own members, representatives to serve on the Grand conseil de l'AOF.

55. See "Voeu tendant à la création d'une Académie de l'Afrique noire," 30 January 1948, in *Bulletin du Grand Conseil de l'A.O.F. Procès-verbaux et Délibérations*, no. 2 (April 1948), available in Bibliothèque nationale de France.

56. During its discussion the previous year, the Grand Council of AOF had focused largely on Senghor's bill. In June 1949 the Grand Council took up a decree proposal, prepared by Capelle, which sought to accomplish much the same thing. However, whereas Senghor's bill proposed to create an Académie de l'Afrique noire, Capelle's decree proposal called for the founding of an Académie de l'AOF. See Senghor's report "sur le projet de décret portant création d'une Académie de l'AOF et sur le projet de décret portant création d'un Institut universitaire à Dakar," 3 June 1949, Archives nationales de France, Pierrefitte-sur-Seine, AN 19770641/8.

57. "Procès-verbal de la séance du vendredi 3 juin 1949," in *Bulletin du Grand Conseil de l'A.O.F. Procès-verbaux des Délibérations* (1949).

58. See Semidei, "De l'Empire à la décolonisation," esp. 71–86. Semidei argues that the first deep changes to the ways in which Overseas France was represented came only in the late 1950s.

59. Senghor, "La formation des professeurs pour la France d'outre-mer (allocution prononcée à la Radiodiffusion nationale, sous le patronage de la Commission nationale de l'UNESCO)," *Condition Humaine*, 15 March 1949; see also Senghor's article "Culture et organisation de l'enseignement (2e résolution votée à l'issue des journées d'études des I.O.M.)," *Condition Humaine*, 7 November 1950.

60. In the inaugural issue of *Condition Humaine*, Senghor declared that "it is the French educational system that will create the French Union, that symbiosis of cultures which will lead to the blossoming of a new civilization, made for the twentieth century, made to the measure of the universe and mankind." Senghor, "La condition de notre évolution."

61. On Senghor's experiences as a soldier and as a prisoner, see Scheck, "Léopold Sédar Senghor, prisonnier de guerre allemand"; and Vaillant, *Black, French, and African*, 166–77.

62. On these shifts, see Senghor, *La poésie de l'action*, quote at 184; Senghor, "Le Message de Goethe"; Senghor, "La Négritude, comme culture des peuples noirs," esp. 107; and Senghor, "Négritude et germanité I," esp. 15. For accounts written by others, see Vaillant, *Black, French, and African*, 175–77; and Wilder, *Freedom Time*, 52–59.

63. Senghor, "La condition de notre évolution."

64. Senghor, "La formation des professeurs pour la France d'outre-mer."

65. See Wilder, *Freedom Time*, chap. 6.

66. See Dimier, *Le gouvernement des colonies*, chaps. 5 and esp. 6; and Cohen, *Rulers of Empire*, 172–83.

67. On the MRP's views and positions on colonial affairs, see esp. Thomas, "The Colonial Policies of the Mouvement Républicain Populaire"; and Lewis, "The MRP and the Genesis of the French Union."

68. "Note sur la transformation du service de l'Enseignement en direction de l'Enseignement," prepared for the minister of Overseas France by the Inspection générale de l'enseignement et de la jeunesse. Signed Fasson, n.d., MAMEN, F17bis 3275. As of 1947 the education department at the Ministry of Overseas France came to be called the Inspection générale de l'enseignement et de la jeunesse. Although this implied a step up from a "service," it still did not match the former denomination of "direction."

69. Note from Gaston (the inspecteur général de l'enseignement et de la jeunesse) to the director of political affairs at the Overseas Ministry (Robert Delavignette), 17 May 1949; note from Gaston to the overseas minister's "directeur du cabinet," 24 May 1949; note from Gaston to the director of personnel at the Overseas Ministry, 15 June 1949; note from Gaston to the director of personnel and the director of political affairs, 21 June 1949, MAMEN, F17bis 3273.

70. Note from the director of personnel to Gaston, 15 June 1949, MAMEN, F17bis 3273.

71. Note from the director of personnel to the Inspection générale de l'enseignement et de la jeunesse, 19 December 1949, MAMEN, F17bis 3273.

72. Note from Delavignette to Gaston, 31 May 1949, MAMEN, F17bis 3273.

73. Coste-Floret's letter to Capelle, 4 July 1949, cited in Capelle, *L'éducation en Afrique noire*, 70–71, italics in the original.

74. Delbos to Coste-Floret, 1 August 1949, cited in Capelle, *L'éducation en Afrique noire*, 72.

75. Gaston's letter to G. H. Camerlynck (who succeeded Capelle as director general of education in AOF), n.d. (Fall 1949), MAMEN, F17bis 3273.

76. Béchard's letter to the president of the Grand Council of AOF, n.d. (Spring 1949), MAMEN, F17bis 3273.

77. These tensions can be seen in Béchard's letter to Overseas Minister Coste-Floret, 9 April 1949, cited in Capelle, *L'éducation en Afrique noire*, 68–70.

78. The second in command at the Government General, Secretary-General Paul Chauvet, was particularly hostile to Capelle's reforms. Capelle, *L'éducation en Afrique noire*, 61–63.

79. Capelle to Béchard, 19 March 1949, ANS, FAOF, Série O, 711/31.

80. Capelle to directeur général de l'enseignement supérieur (Pierre Donzelot), Ministère de l'Éducation nationale, 30 March 1949, ANS, FAOF, Série O, 711/31. See also the letter that ten African politicians addressed to the overseas minister on 7 May 1947. Reprinted in Capelle, *L'éducation en Afrique noire*, 74–75.

81. Capelle to Béchard, 29 March 1949; Capelle to the directeur général de l'enseignement supérieur (Pierre Donzelot), Ministère de l'Éducation nationale, 30 March 1949. ANS, FAOF, Série O, 711/31.

82. Letter from Capelle to Béchard, 13 April 1949, ANS, FAOF, Série O, 711/31. See also Capelle, *L'éducation en Afrique noire*, 61–63.

83. On Capelle's second stint in Dakar, between 1954 and 1957, see Capelle, *L'éducation en Afrique noire*, chaps. 10–20. During the early 1960s Capelle would emerge as one of the leading architects of important educational reforms in metropolitan France. For a brief overview, see Prost, *Regards historiques*, 83–84, 145–48.

84. Letter dated 4 August 1949; see also Senghor's letter of 27 September 1949. Both are cited in Capelle, *L'éducation en Afrique noire*, 92.

85. For an overview of these challenges, see Thomas, Moore, and Butler, *Crises of Empire*, esp. chaps. 7, 8, and 10.

86. On the RDA and its clashes with the colonial administration, see Schmidt, *Cold War and Decolonization in Guinea*, esp. chaps. 1–2; Cooper, *Citizenship*, 165–78; Keese, "A Culture of Panic"; and Morgenthau, *Political Parties*, 176–205.

87. Mitterrand described his efforts to promote this détente in his book *Présence française et abandon*, 171–200.

88. On this law, see Guèye, *Itinéraire africain*, 97–101; and Cooper, *Decolonization and African Society*, 282–83.

89. First proposed at the end of the war, this code remained stalled for several years before the National Assembly began to consider it again in November 1950. Final passage was not secured until November 1952. On these debates and struggles, see Cooper, *Decolonization and African Society*, esp. chap. 7.

90. Mitterrand to education minister, n.d. (fall 1950), MAMEN, F17bis 3273.

91. "Décret no. 50–1467 portant création d'une Académie d'Afrique occidentale française," 27 November 1950, *L'Éducation Africaine*, nos. 8–9 (1950): 5.

92. Capelle and Senghor discussed these realities. See Senghor to Capelle, 9 October 1950; Capelle to Senghor, 14 October 1950, letters cited in Capelle, *L'éducation en Afrique noire*, 93.

93. Note from the "chef de service, cabinet du ministre de l'Éducation nationale," n.d. (1950), Archives nationales de France, Pierrefitte-sur-Seine, AN 19770641/8.

94. Here my conclusions align broadly with those of Frederick Cooper. However, Cooper does not emphasize the corporatism of particular ministries and administrations in the way that I do. See Cooper, *Decolonization and African Society*, esp. chap. 7; and Cooper, *Citizenship*.

Epilogue

1. From table provided in Capelle, *L'éducation en Afrique noire*, 56. The figures provided include students enrolled at both public schools (105,276) and private schools (32,709). These statistics do not include less formal types of education or education at Koranic schools.

2. Capelle, *L'éducation en Afrique noire*, 191. Capelle indicates that 194 of these *baccalauréats* were awarded in AOF. The others were presumably obtained in France. Capelle returned to AOF, where he once again headed up the federation's school system, between 1954 and 1957. During his second stint in Dakar Capelle held the title of *recteur*.

3. Jean-Claude Chesnais calculates that 42,286 *baccalauréats* were awarded in 1956, against 20,542 in 1938. This figure included *baccalauréats* granted in Algeria but not those conferred in the overseas territories and departments. Chesnais, "La population des bacheliers en France," 533–35.

4. For two critiques along these lines, see Chakrabarty, *Provincializing Europe*; and Chatterjee, *Nationalist Thought and the Colonial World*.

5. Loi no. 56–619 du 23 juin 1956 autorisant le Gouvernement à mettre en oeuvre les réformes et à prendre les mesures propres à assurer l'évolution des territoires

relevant du ministère de la France d'outre-mer, *JORF*, 24 juin 1956, 5782. For analyses of the loi-cadre and its consequences, see Cooper, *Decolonization and African Society*, chap. 11; Cooper, *Citizenship*, chap. 5; Chafer, *The End of Empire*, chap. 6; and Benoist, *La balkanisation*, part 3.

6. An *inspecteur d'académie* was assigned to each territorial educational department. However, these officials were now placed under the authority of education ministers, who belonged to the councils of government in the various territories. On these changing institutional arrangements, see Capelle, *L'éducation en Afrique noire*, 261–67.

7. Prior to this time the assemblies in the various African territories had been called *conseils généraux*, after the local assemblies that existed in the departments of metropolitan France.

8. Senghor published many articles on this subject. See for example Senghor, "Balkanisation ou fédération"; Senghor, "Union française et fédéralisme"; and Senghor, "Les décrets d'application de la loi-cadre ou 'donner et retirer ne vaut.'" For broader accounts of Senghor's evolving positions during the mid to late 1950s, see Wilder, *Freedom Time*, 152–66, 206–40; and Cooper, *Citizenship*, 226–78.

9. The territory of Guinea attained independence two years earlier, in October 1958, after an overwhelming majority of voters there rejected the constitutional draft being proposed by the interim government of Charles de Gaulle.

10. For an excellent overview of what the cooperation accords specified in the area of education, see Manière, "La politique française pour l'adaptation de l'enseignement." Although bilateral in nature, the provisions of the various cooperation agreements were so similar across francophone Africa that Manière rightly speaks of an institutionalized "system."

BIBLIOGRAPHY

Archival Sources

Archives nationales d'outre-mer (Aix-en-Provence)
  Fonds ministériels, Ministère des Colonies
    Affaires politiques
    Agence de la France d'outre-mer
    Commission d'enquête dans les territoires d'outre-mer
      (Commission Guernut)
  Gouvernement général de l'AOF (microfilm)
    Sous-série 17G: Affaires politiques
Archives nationales de France (Pierrefitte-sur-Seine)
  Fonds du Ministère de l'Éducation nationale
Archives nationales de la République du Sénégal (Dakar)
  Fonds de l'AOF, 1895–1959
    Sous-série 4E: Conseil général ou colonial, assemblée territoriale
      du Sénégal
    Sous-série 1G: Études générales, monographies, thèses
    Sous-série 2G: Rapports périodiques des gouverneurs,
      administrateurs, et chefs de services depuis 1895
    Sous-série 3G3: Commune de Saint-Louis
    Sous-série 17G: Affaires politiques
    Série J: Enseignement jusqu'en 1920
    Série O: Enseignement, sciences et arts

Fonds Sénégal colonial
Sous-série 1G: Enseignement
Centre des Archives diplomatiques de Nantes
Archives des colonies et territoires d'outre-mer
Fonds du Gouvernement général de l'A.O.F., puis du Haut-
Commissariat ("Fonds Dakar")
Mission des archives, Ministère de l'Éducation nationale (Paris)
F17bis 3273
F17bis 3275

In 1998–99 these two bundles of documents were being housed rather informally in offices belonging to the Mission des archives of the French Education Ministry. These bundles included important correspondance of the Inspection générale de l'enseignement et de la jeunesse of the Ministère de la France d'outre-mer, from the late 1940s to the early 1950s. It appears that these documents were subsequently incorporated into the *fonds* named Service universitaire des relations avec l'étranger et l'outre-mer (SUREOM) at the main Pierefitte-sur-Seine location of the French National Archives. However, to date, archivists in Paris have not been able to identify the new *cotes* of the bundles I consulted.

Official Periodicals

These official sources are housed in various archives, and many are now available through Gallica, the digital library of the Bibliothèque nationale de France.

Bulletin Administratif du Gouvernement Général de l'Afrique Occidentale Française
Bulletin de l'Enseignement de l'A.O.F. (L'Éducation Africaine)
Bulletin d'Information et de Renseignements du Gouvernement Général de l'A.O.F.
Bulletin du Comité de l'Afrique Française
Documents de l'Assemblée Nationale Constituante
Journal Officiel de l'A.O.F.
Journal Officiel de la République Française, Débats de l'Assemblée Nationale Constituante
Journal Officiel de la République Française, Débats Parlementaires
Journal Officiel de la République Française, Lois et Décrets
Journal Officiel du Sénégal
Moniteur du Sénégal et Dépendances

Published Sources

Abu-Lughod, Janet L. *Rabat, Urban Apartheid in Morocco*. Princeton: Princeton University Press, 1980.

Achi, Raberh. "Laïcité d'empire: Les débats sur l'application du régime de séparation à l'islam impérial." In *Politiques de la laïcité au XXe siècle*, edited by Patrick Weil, 237–63. Paris: Presses Universitaires de France, 2007.

Ageron, Charles-Robert. "De l'Empire à la dislocation de l'Union française (1939–1956)." In *Histoire de la France coloniale*, vol. 2, *1914–1990*, by Jacques Thobie, Gilbert Meynier, Catherine Coquery-Vidrovitch, and Charles-Robert Ageron, 311–570. Paris: A. Colin, 1990.

———. *France coloniale ou parti colonial?* Paris: Presses Universitaires de France, 1978.

———. "La préparation de la Conférence de Brazzaville et ses enseignements." In *Brazzaville, janvier-février 1944: Aux sources de la décolonisation*, edited by l'Institut Charles-de-Gaulle, 29–41. Paris: Plon, 1988.

Akpo-Vaché, Catherine. *L'AOF et la Seconde Guerre mondiale (septembre 1939–octobre 1945)*. Paris: Karthala, 1996.

Amselle, Jean-Loup. *Affirmative Exclusion: Cultural Pluralism and the Rule of Custom in France*. Translated by Jane Marie Todd. Ithaca NY: Cornell University Presss, 2003.

Anderson, Benedict. *Imagined Communities: Reflections on the Origin and Spread of Nationalism*. Rev. ed. London: Verso, 1991.

Archives de la Chambre des députés. *Tableau des élections du 21 octobre 1945 à l'Assemblée nationale constituante*. Paris: Imprimerie de l'A.N.C., 1946.

Arsan, Andrew. *Interlopers of Empire: The Lebanese Diaspora in Colonial French West Africa*. New York: Oxford University Press, 2014.

Assomption, Frédéric. "Circulaire au sujet de l'enseignement pratique agricole." *Bulletin de l'Enseignement de l'A.O.F.*, no. 55 (July–September 1923): 41–42.

———. "Une nouvelle conception de l'enseignement en Afrique occidentale française: L'École normale rurale de Katibougou." *Bulletin d'Information et de Resneignements du Gouvernement Général de l'A.O.F.*, no. 202 (26 September 1938): 376–77.

Atlan, Catherine. "Élections et pratiques électorales au Sénégal (1940–1958): Histoire sociale et culturelle de la décolonisation." Thèse de doctorat, École des hautes études en sciences sociales, 2001.

Badji, Mamadou. "Le statut juridique des enfants métis nés en Afrique Occidentale Française de parents inconnus: Entre idéalisme républicain et turpitudes coloniales." *Droit et Cultures* 61 (2011): 257–83.

Barreau, Jean-Michel. *Vichy contre l'école de la République*. Paris: Flammarion, 2000.

Barrow, Ian J. *Making History, Drawing Territory: British Mapping in India, c. 1756–1905*. New Delhi: Oxford University Press, 2003.

Barry, Boubacar. *Senegambia and the Atlantic Slave Trade*. Translated by Ayi Kwei Armah. Cambridge: Cambridge University Press, 1998.

Barry, Moustapha. *Histoire des médias au Sénégal: De la colonisation à nos jours*. Paris: L'Harmattan, 2013.

Barthélémy, Pascale. *Africaines et diplômées à l'époque coloniale (1918–1957)*. Rennes: Presses Universitaires de Rennes, 2010.

Bassett, Thomas J. "Cartography and Empire Building in Nineteenth-Century West Africa." *Geographical Review* 84, no. 3 (July 1994): 316–35.

Baubérot, Jean. *Histoire de la laïcité en France*. Paris: Presses Universitaires de France, 2000.

Béart, Charles. "Compte-rendu de la fête de l'École William-Ponty." *L'Éducation Africaine*, nos. 90–91 (April–September 1935): 179–80.

———. "Le théâtre indigène et la culture franco-africaine." *L'Éducation Africaine*, special issue titled "Le théâtre indigène et la culture franco-africaine" (1937): 3–14.

Becker, Charles, Saliou Mbaye, and Ibrahima Thioub, eds. *AOF: Réalités et héritages: Sociétés ouest-africaines et ordre colonial, 1895–1960*. 2 vols. Dakar: Direction des Archives du Sénégal, 1997.

Bénéton, Philippe. *Histoire de mots: Culture et civilisation*. Paris: Presses de la Fondation Nationale des Sciences Politiques, 1975.

Benoist, Joseph-Roger de. *La balkanisation de l'Afrique occidentale française*. Dakar: Nouvelles Éditions Africaines, 1979.

———. *L'Afrique occidentale française: De la conférence de Brazzaville (1944) à l'indépendance (1960)*. Dakar: Nouvelles Éditions Africaines, 1982.

Benot, Yves. *La Révolution française et la fin des colonies: Essai*. Paris: La Découverte, 1987.

———. *Les parlementaires africains à Paris: 1914–1958*. Paris: Éditions Chaka, 1989.

Bernard-Duquenet, Nicole. *Le Sénégal et le Front populaire*. Paris: L'Harmattan, 1985.

Berstein, Serge. *La France des années 30*. 2nd ed. Paris: Armand Colin, 1993.

Betts, Raymond F. *Assimilation and Association in French Colonial Theory, 1890–1914*. 1960. Reprint, Lincoln: University of Nebraska Press, 2004.

———. "The Establishment of the Medina in Dakar, Senegal, 1914." *Africa: Journal of the International African Institute* 41, no. 2 (April 1971): 143–52.

Bezançon, Pascale. *Une colonisation éducatrice: L'expérience indochinoise, 1860–1945*. Paris: L'Harmattan, 2002.

Bigon, Liora. *A History of Urban Planning in Two West African Colonial Capitals: Residential Segregation in British Lagos and French Dakar (1850–1930)*. Lewiston NY: Edwin Mellen Press, 2009.

Binoche, Jacques. "Les élus d'outre-mer au Parlement de 1871 à 1914." *Revue Française d'Histoire d'Outre-Mer* 58, no. 210 (1971): 82–115.

Biondi, Jean-Pierre. *Saint-Louis du Sénégal: Mémoires d'un métissage*. Paris: Denoël, 1987.

Blais, Hélène, Florence Deprest, and Pierre Singaravélou, eds. *Territoires impériaux: Une histoire spatiale du fait colonial*. Paris: Publications de la Sorbonne, 2011.

Blanc, Brigitte. "La constitution du domaine de la Cité internationale universitaire de Paris." *In Situ: Revue des Patrimoines* 17 (2001), doi: 10.4000/insitu.855.

Blanchard, Pascal. "Discours, politique et propagande: L'AOF et les Africains au temps de la Révolution nationale (1940–1944)." In *AOF, réalités et héritages: Sociétés ouest-africaines et ordre colonial, 1895–1960*, vol. 1, edited by Charles Becker, Saliou Mbaye, and Ibrahima Thioub, 315–37. Dakar: Direction des Archives du Sénégal, 1997.

Blanche, Denis. "Préface." In *Congrès international de l'évolution culturelle des peuples coloniaux, 26, 27, 28 septembre 1937: Rapports et compte rendu*, 13–20. Paris: Exposition Internationale de Paris, 1938.

Bloch, Marc. *Strange Defeat: A Statement of Evidence Written in 1940*. Translated by Gerard Hopkins. New York: W. W. Norton and Company, 1968.

Boittin, Jennifer Anne. *Colonial Metropolis: The Urban Grounds of Anti-Imperialism and Feminism in Interwar Paris*. Lincoln: University of Nebraska Press, 2010.

Bonnardel, Régine. *Saint-Louis du Sénégal: Mort ou naissance?* Paris: L'Harmattan 1992.

Bouche, Denise. "Autrefois, notre pays s'appelait la Gaulle … Remarques sur l'adaptation de l'enseignement au Sénégal de 1817 à 1960." *Cahiers d'Études Africaines* 8, no. 29 (1968): 110–22.

———. "L'école rurale en Afrique occidentale française de 1903 à 1956." In *Études africaines offertes à Henri Brunschwig*, 271–296. Paris: Éditions de l'École des Hautes Études en Sciences Sociales, 1982.

———. *L'enseignement dans les territoires français de l'Afrique occidentale de 1817–1920: Mission civilisatrice ou formation d'une élite?* 2 vols. Lille: Atelier Reproduction des Thèses, 1975.

———. "Les écoles françaises au Soudan à l'époque de la conquête, 1884–1900." *Cahiers d'Études Africaines* 6, no. 22 (1966): 228–67.

Bourdieu, Pierre. "Une classe objet." *Actes de la Recherche en Sciences Sociales* 17–18 (1977): 2–5.

Bourdieu, Pierre, and Jean-Claude Passeron. *La reproduction: Éléments pour une théorie du système d'enseignement*. Paris: Éditions de Minuit, 1970.

Boyer, Alain. "La législation anticongréganiste 1901–1904." In *Le grand exil des congrégations religieuses françaises, 1901–1914*, edited by Patrick Cabanel and Jean-Dominique Durand, 21–58. Paris: Éditions du Cerf, 2005.

Braillon, E. "L'enseignement secondaire et le développement de la culture indigène et Afrique occidentale française." In *Congrès international de l'évolution culturelle des peuples coloniaux, 26, 27, 28 septembre 1937: Rapports et compte rendu*, 27–33. Paris: Exposition Internationale de Paris, 1938.

Brévié, Jules. *Discours prononcé par M. J. Brévié, Gouverneur Général de l'Afrique occidentale française, à l'ouverture de la session du Conseil de gouvernement, décembre 1930*. Gorée: Imprimerie du Gouvernement Général, 1930.

———. *Discours prononcé par M. J. Brévié, Gouverneur Général de l'Afrique occidentale française, à l'ouverture de la session du Conseil de gouvernement, décembre 1931*. Gorée: Imprimerie du Gouvernement Général, 1931.

———. *Discours prononcé par M. J. Brévié, Gouverneur Général de l'Afrique occidentale française, à l'ouverture de la session du Conseil de gouvernement, novembre 1932*. Gorée: Imprimerie du Gouvernement Général, 1932.

———. *Discours prononcé par M. J. Brévié, Gouverneur Général de l'Afrique occidentale française, à l'ouverture de la session du Conseil de gouvernement, décembre 1934*. Gorée: Imprimerie du Gouvernement Général, 1934.

Buell, Raymond Leslie. *The Native Problem in Africa*. Vol. 1. New York: Macmillan, 1928.

Camiscioli, Elisa. *Reproducing the French Race: Immigration, Intimacy, and Embodiment in the Early Twentieth Century*. Durham NC: Duke University Press, 2009.

Candar, Gilles. "La gauche coloniale en France: Socialistes et radicaux (1885–1905)." *Mil Neuf Cent* 27 (2009): 27–56.

Cantier, Jacques. *L'Algérie sous le régime de Vichy*. Paris: Odile Jacob, 2002.

Cantier, Jacques, and Eric T. Jennings, eds. *L'Empire colonial sous Vichy*. Paris: Odile Jacob, 2004.

Capelle, Jean. *L'éducation en Afrique noire à la veille des indépendances (1946–1958)*. Paris: Karthala and Agence de Coopération Culturelle et Technique, 1990.

Césaire, Aimé. *Cahier d'un retour au pays natal*. 1939. Reprint, Paris: Présence Africaine, 1983.

———. "Nègreries: Jeunesse noire et assimilation." *L'Étudiant Noir*, no. 1 (March 1935): 3.

Chafer, Tony. "Decolonizaton and the Politics of Education in French West Africa, 1944–1958." PhD diss., University of London, 1993.

———. *The End of Empire in French West Africa: France's Successful Decolonization?* Oxford: Berg, 2002.

Chafer, Tony, and Amanda Sackur, eds. *French Colonial Empire and the Popular Front: Hope and Disillusion*. New York: St. Martin's Press, 1999.

Chakrabarty, Dipesh. *Provincializing Europe: Postcolonial Thought and Historical Difference*. Princeton NJ: Princeton University Press, 2008.

Chakrabarti, Pratik. *Medicine and Empire: 1600–1960*. Basingstoke, Hampshire, UK: Palgrave Macmillan, 2014.

Chanet, Jean-François. *L'école républicaine et les petites patries*. Paris: Aubier, 1996.

Chapoulie, Jean-Michel. *L'école d'État conquiert la France: Deux siècles de politique scolaire*. Rennes: Presses Universitaires de Rennes, 2010.

Charton, Albert. "Conseil supérieur de l'enseignement (session du 23 décembre 1935), extraits de l'exposé de M. l'inspecteur général de l'enseignement." *L'Éducation Africaine*, no. 93 (January–March 1936): 90–91.

———. "Discours prononcé par M. Charton, à l'inauguration de l'École normale rurale de Katibougou (30 janvier 1935)." *L'Éducation Africaine*, no. 89 (January–March 1935): 104–5.

———. "Rôle social de l'enseignement en Afrique occidentale française." *Outre-Mer: Revue Générale de Colonisation* 6, no. 2 (June 1934): 188–202.

Chatterjee, Partha. *Nationalist Thought and the Colonial World: A Derivative Discourse*. Minneapolis: University of Minnesota Press, 1993.

Chesnais, Jean-Claude. "La population des bacheliers en France: Estimation et projection jusqu'en 1995." *Population* 30, no. 3 (1975): 527–50.

Childers, Kristen Stromberg. "Departmentalization, Migration, and the Politics of the Family in the Post-War French Caribbean." *History of the Family* 14 (2009): 177–90.

Christelow, Allan. "The Muslim Judge and Municipal Politics in Colonial Algeria and Senegal." *Comparative Studies in Society and History* 24, no. 1 (January 1982): 3–24.

Claveau, Cylvie. *Une sélection universaliste de l'altérité dans l'entre-deux-guerres: L'autre à la Ligue des droits de l'Homme et du citoyen en France, 1920–1940*. Saarbrücken, Germany: Éditions Universitaires Européennes, 2010.

Codo, Bellarmin Coffi. "La presse dahoméenne face aux aspirations des 'évolués': La 'Voix du Dahomey' (1927–1957)." Thèse de doctorat, Université Paris VII, 1978.

Cohen, William B. "The Colonial Policy of the Popular Front." *French Historical Studies* 7, no. 3 (Spring 1972): 368–93.

———, ed. *Robert Delavignette on the French Empire: Selected Writings*. Chicago: University of Chicago Press, 1977.

———. *Rulers of Empire: The French Colonial Service in Africa, 1880–1960*. Stanford: Hoover Institution Press, 1971.

Colonna, Fanny. *Instituteurs algériens: 1883–1939*. Paris: Presses de la Fondation Nationale des Sciences Politiques, 1975.

Combeau-Mari, Évylyne. *Le sport colonial à Madagascar, 1896–1960*. Paris: Publications de la Société Française d'Histoire d'Outre-mer, 2009.

———, ed. *Sports et loisirs dans les colonies, XIXè–XXè siècles*. Paris: Le Publieur, 2004.

Compagnon, Béatrice, and Anne Thévenin. *L'école at la société française*. Brussels: Éditions Complexe, 1995.

Condette, Jean-François. *Les recteurs d'académie en France de 1808 à 1940*. Vol. 1, *La formation d'une élite administrative au service de l'instruction publique*. Lyon: Institut National de Recherche Pédagogique, 2006.

Congrès international de l'évolution culturelle des peuples coloniaux, 26, 27, 28 septembre 1937: Rapports et compte rendu. Paris: Exposition Internationale de Paris, 1938.

Congrès international et intercolonial de la société indigène (5–10 octobre 1931). Paris: Exposition Coloniale Internationale, 1931.

Conklin, Alice L. *In the Museum of Man: Race, Anthropology, and Empire in France, 1850–1950*. Ithaca NY: Cornell University Press, 2013.

———. *A Mission to Civilize: The Republican Idea of Empire in France and West Africa, 1895–1930*. Stanford: Stanford University Press, 1997.

———. "Who Speaks for Africa? The René Maran–Blaise Diagne Trial in 1920s Paris." In *The Color of Liberty: Histories of Race in France*, edited by Sue Peabody and Tyler Stovall, 302–37. Durham NC: Duke University Press, 2003.

Conseil de gouvernement de l'Afrique occidentale française. *Organisation du service de l'enseignement*. Saint-Louis: Imprimerie du Gouvernement, 1903.

Constant, Fred, and Justin Daniel, eds. *1946–1996: Cinquante ans de départmentalisation outre-mer*. Paris: L'Harmattan, 1997.

Cooper, Frederick. *Citizenship between Empire and Nation: Remaking France and French Africa, 1945–1960*. Princeton: Princton University Press, 2014.

———. "Conditions Analogous to Slavery: Imperialism and Free Labor Ideology in Africa." In *Beyond Slavery: Explorations of Race, Labor, and Citizenship in Postemancipation Societies*, by Frederick Cooper, Thomas C. Holt, and Rebecca J. Scott, 107–49. Chapel Hill: University of North Carolina Press, 2000.

———. *Decolonization and African Society: The Labor Question in French and British Africa*. Cambridge: Cambridge University Press, 1996.

Coquery-Vidrovitch, Catherine. "La colonisation française, 1931–1939." In *Histoire de la France coloniale*, vol. 2, *1914–1990*, by Jacques Thobie, Gilbert Meynier, Catherine Coquery-Vidrovitch, and Charles-Robert Ageron, 213–308. Paris: A. Colin, 1990.

———. "L'Afrique coloniale française et la crise de 1930: Crise structurelle et genèse du sous-développement." *Revue Française d'Histoire d'Outre-Mer* 63, no. 232 (1976): 386–424.

———. *The History of Cities South of the Sahara: From the Origins to Colonization*. Translated by Mary Baker. Princeton NJ: Markus Wiener Publishers, 2005.

———. "Nationalité et citoyenneté en Afrique occidentale française: Originaires et citoyens dans le Sénégal colonial." *Journal of African History* 42, no. 2 (2001): 285–305.

———. "The Popular Front and the Colonial Question. French West Africa: An Example of Reformist Colonialism." In *French Colonial Empire and the Popular Front: Hope and Disillusion*, edited by Tony Chafer and Amanda Sackur, 155–69. New York: St. Martin's Press, 1999.

———. "The Process of Urbanization in Africa (from the Origins to the Beginning of Independence)." *African Studies Review* 34, no. 1 (1991): 1–98.

Cornevin, Robert. *Le théâtre en Afrique noire et à Madagascar.* Paris: Le Livre Africain, 1970.

Coundouriotis, Eleni. *Claiming History: Colonialism, Ethnography, and the Novel.* New York: Columbia University Press, 1999.

Couturier, Alain. *Le gouverneur et son miroir: Marcel de Coppet (1881–1968).* Paris: L'Harmattan, 2006.

Cruise O'Brien, Rita. *White Society in Black Africa: The French of Senegal.* Evanston IL: Northwestern University Press, 1972.

D'Anfreville de la Salle, Léon. *Conférences sur l'hygiène coloniale faites aux instituteurs et institutrices de Saint-Louis pour les élèves indigènes des colonies de l'Afrique occidentale.* Paris: A. Picard, 1908.

———. *Notre vieux Sénégal: Son histoire. Son état actuel. Ce qu'il peut devenir.* Paris: Augustin Challamel, 1909.

Daughton, J. P. *An Empire Divided: Religion, Republicanism, and the Making of French Colonialism, 1880–1914.* New York: Oxford University Press, 2006.

De Coppet, Marcel. *Discours prononcé par M. M. de Coppet, Gouverneur Général de l'Afrique occidentale française, à l'ouverture de la session du Conseil de gouvernement, novembre 1937.* Gorée: Imprimerie du Gouvernement Général, 1937.

Delavignette, Robert. *Les paysans noirs: Récit soudanais en douze mois.* Paris: Stock, 1931.

———. *Les vrais chefs de l'empire.* Paris: Gallimard, 1939.

———. "Notes sur l'Afrique du juste-milieu en A.O.F." *Outre-Mer: Revue Générale de Colonisation* 3, no. 2 (1931): 103–19.

———. "Pour les paysans noirs, pour l'esprit africain." *Esprit* 4, no. 39 (December 1935): 367–90.

———. *Service africain.* Paris: Gallimard, 1946.

Deleigne, Marie-Christine. "Entre la plume et l'angady (*la bêche*): Les jardins scolaires des écoles du premier degré à Madagascar (1916–1951)." *Histoire de l'Éducation* 128 (October–December 2010): 103–27.

Déloye, Yves. *École et citoyenneté: L'individualisme républicain de Jules Ferry à Vichy: Controverses.* Paris: Presses de la Fondation Nationale des Sciences Politiques, 1994.

Delpal, Bernard. "L'application des lois anticongréganistes: Éléments pour un bilan, 1901–1904." In *Le grand exil des congrégations religieuses françaises, 1901–1914,* edited by Patrick Cabanel and Jean-Dominique Durand, 59–87. Paris: Éditions du Cerf, 2005.

Derrick, Jonathan. *Africa's "Agitators": Militant Anti-Colonialism in Africa and the West, 1918–1939.* London: Hurst, 2008.

Devèze, Michel. *La France d'outre-mer: De l'empire colonial à l'Union française, 1938–1947.* Paris: Hachette, 1948.

Deville-Danthu, Bernadette. *Le sport en noir et blanc: Du sport colonial au sport africain dans les anciens territoires français d'Afrique occidentale (1920–1965).* Paris: L'Harmattan, 2000.

Dewitte, Philippe. *Les mouvements nègres en France, 1919–1939*. Paris: L'Harmattan, 1985.

Dia, Mamadou. *Vicissitudes de la vie d'un militant du Tiers-Monde: Si mémoire ne ment...* Paris: Publisud, 1985.

Dieng, Amady Aly. *Blaise Diagne: Député noir de l'Afrique*. Paris: Éditions Chaka, 1990.

———. *Lamine Guèye: Une des grandes figures politiques africaines (1891–1968)*. Dakar: L'Harmattan Sénégal, 2013.

Dimier, Véronique. "For a Republic 'Diverse and Indivisible?' France's Experience from the Colonial Past." *Contemporary European History* 13, no. 1 (2004): 45–66.

———. *Le gouvernement des colonies, regards croisés franco-britanniques*. Brussels: Éditions de l'Université de Bruxelles, 2004.

Diouf, Mamadou. "Assimilation coloniale et identités religieuses de la civilité des originaires des Quatre Communes (Sénégal)." *Canadian Journal of African Studies* 34, no. 3 (2000): 565–87.

———. "The French Colonial Policy of Assimilation and the Civility of the Originaires of the Four Communes (Senegal): A Nineteenth Century Globalization Project." *Development and Change* 29, no. 4 (October 1998): 671–96.

Dirand, Alfred. "La formation intellectuelle et la culture franco-africaine à l'École William-Ponty." In *Congrès international de l'évolution culturelle des peuples coloniaux, 26, 27, 28 septembre 1937: Rapports et compte rendu*, 35–39. Paris: Exposition Internationale de Paris, 1938.

Dozon, Jean-Pierre. *Saint-Louis du Sénégal: Palimpseste d'une ville*. Paris: Karthala, 2012.

Dubois, Laurent. *Avengers of the New World: The Story of the Haitain Revolution*. Cambridge MA: Belknap Press of Harvard University Press, 2004.

———. *A Colony of Citizens: Revolution & Slave Emancipation in the French Caribbean, 1789–1804*. Chapel Hill: University of North Carolina Press, 2004.

———. *Soccer Empire: The World Cup and the Future of France*. Berkeley: Univerisity of California Press, 2011.

Duke Bryant, Kelly M. *Education as Politics: Colonial Schooling and Political Debate in Senegal, 1850s-1914*. Madison: University of Wisconsin Press, 2015.

———. "'In My Senegalese Quality and as a Compatriot': Senegalese Students in the Metropolis and the Language of Affinity, 1880–1890." *African and Black Diaspora: An International Journal* 2, no. 1 (2009): 55–65.

———. "The Politics of Education in Senegal, 1885–1914." PhD diss., Johns Hopkins University, 2009.

Dumont, Jacques. *L'amère patrie: Histoire des Antilles françaises aux XXe siècle*. Paris: Fayard, 2010.

———. "La quête de l'égalité aux Antilles: La départementalisation et les manifestations des années 1950." *Le Mouvement Social* 230, no. 1 (January–March 2010): 79–98.

Duteil, Simon. "Enseignants coloniaux: Madagascar, 1896–1960." 2 vols. Thèse de doctorat, Université du Havre, 2009.

———. "Laïcisation dans les colonies françaises: Le cas de Madagascar (1904–1913)." In *Politiques de la laïcité au XXe siècle*, edited by Patrick Weil, 265–284. Paris: Presses Universitaires de France, 2007.

Echenberg, Myron. *Black Death, White Medicine: Bubonic Plague and the Politics of Public Health in Colonial Senegal, 1914–1945*. Portsmouth NH: Heinemann, 2002.

———. *Colonial Conscripts: The Tirailleurs Sénégalais in French West Africa, 1857–1960*. Portsmouth NH: Heinemann, 1991.

Edney, Matthew H. *Mapping an Empire: The Geographical Construction of British India, 1765–1843*. Chicago: University of Chicago Press, 1997.

Edwards, Brent Hayes. *The Practice of Diaspora: Literature, Translation, and the Rise of Black Internationalism*. Cambridge MA: Harvard University Press, 2003.

Eizlini, Carine. "Le Bulletin de l'Enseignement de l'AOF, une fenêtre sur le personnel d'enseignement public, expatrié en Afrique Occidentale française (1913–1930)." Thèse de doctorat, Université Paris Descartes, 2012.

Exposition coloniale internationale de 1931. *L'adaptation de l'enseignement dans les colonies: Rapports et compte-rendu du Congrès intercolonial de l'enseignement dans les colonies et les pays d'outre-mer, 25–27 septembre 1931*. Paris: Henri Didier, 1932.

Fall, Babacar. *Le travail forcé en Afrique-occidentale française, 1900–1946*. Paris: Karthala, 1993.

Farraudière, Sylvère. *L'école aux Antilles françaises: Le rendez-vous manqué de la démocratie*. Paris: L'Harmattan, 2007.

Faur, Jean-Claude. "La mise en valeur ferroviaire de l'A.O.F. (1880–1939)." Thèse de doctorat, Faculté de Lettres de Paris, 1969.

Finch-Boyer, Héloïse. "'The Idea of the Nation Was Superior to Race': Transforming Racial Contours and Social Attitudes and Decolonizing the French Empire from La Réunion, 1946–1973." *French Historical Studies* 36, no. 1 (Winter 2013): 109–40.

Fogarty, Richard S. *Race and War in France: Colonial Subjects in the French Army, 1914–1918*. Baltimore: Johns Hopkins University Press, 2008.

Fonkoua, Romuald. *Aimé Césaire (1913–2008)*. Paris: Perrin, 2010.

Foster, Elizabeth A. *Faith in Empire: Religion, Politics, and Colonial Rule in French Senegal, 1880–1940*. Stanford: Stanford University Press, 2013.

Fougère, Louis, Jean-Pierre Machelon, and François Monnier. *Les communes et le pouvoir: Histoire politique des communes françaises de 1789 à nos jours*. Paris: Presses Universitaires de France, 2002.

Freund, Bill. *The African City: A History*. New York: Cambridge University Press, 2007.

Frobenius, Leo. *Histoire de la civilisation africaine*. Translated by H. Back and D. Ermont. Paris: Gallimard, 1936.

Gamble, Harry. "La crise de l'enseignement en Afrique occidentale française (1944–1950)." *Histoire de l'Éducation* 128 (2010): 129–62.

———. "The National Revolution in French West Africa: *Dakar-Jeunes* and the Shaping of African Opinion." *International Journal of Francophone Studies* 10, nos. 1–2 (2007): 85–103.

———. "Peasants of the Empire: Rural Schools and the Colonial Imaginary in 1930s French West Africa." *Cahiers d'Études Africaines* 195, no. 3 (2009): 775–804.

Garcia, Luc. "L'organisation de l'instruction publique au Dahomey, 1894–1920." *Cahiers d'Études Africaines* 11, no. 41 (1971): 59–100.

Gardinier, David E. "Les recommandations de la Conférence de Brazzaville sur les problèmes d'éducation." In *Brazzaville, janvier–février 1944: Aux sources de la décolonisation*, edited by l'Institut Charles-de-Gaulle, 170–80. Paris: Plon, 1988.

Genova, James E. *Colonial Ambivalence, Cultural Authenticity, and the Limitations of Mimicry in French-Ruled West Africa, 1914–1956*. New York: Peter Lang, 2004.

Ginio, Ruth. *French Colonialism Unmasked: The Vichy Years in French West Africa*. Lincoln: University of Nebraska Press, 2006.

———. "La Propagande impériale de Vichy." In *L'Empire colonial sous Vichy*, edited by Jacques Cantier and Eric T. Jennings, 117–33. Paris: Odile Jacob, 2004.

Girardet, Raoul. *L'idée coloniale en France: De 1871 à 1962*. Paris: La Table Ronde, 1972.

Goblot, Edmond. *La barrière et le niveau: Étude sociologique sur la bourgeoisie française moderne*. 1925. Reprint, Paris: Presses Universitaires de France, 2010.

Goerg, Odile. "From Hill Station (Freetown) to Downtown Conakry (First Ward): Comparing French and British Approaches to Segregation in Colonial Cities at the Beginning of the Twentieth Century." *Canadian Journal of African Studies* 32, no. 1 (1998): 1–31.

———. *Pouvoir colonial, municipalités et espaces urbains: Conakry-Freetown des années 1880 à 1914*. 2 vols. Paris: L'Harmattan, 1997.

Goheneix-Minisini, Alice. "Le français colonial: Politiques et pratiques de la langue nationale dans l'Empire (1880–1962)." Thèse de doctorat, Institut d'études politiques de Paris, 2011.

Golan, Romy. *Modernity and Nostalgia: Art and Politics in France between the Wars*. New Haven: Yale University Press, 1995.

Gouvernement général de l'Afrique occidentale française. *Circonscription de Dakar et dépendances*. Paris: Société d'Éditions Géographiques, Maritimes et Coloniales, 1931.

Gratien, Jean-Pierre. *Marius Moutet: Un socialiste à l'outre-mer*. Paris: L'Harmattan, 2006.

Guèye, Lamine. *De la situation politique des Sénégalais originaires des communes de plein exercice, telle qu'elle résulte des lois des 19 octobre 1915, 29 septembre 1916 et de la jurisprudence antérieure: Conséquences au point de vue du conflit des lois françaises et musulmanes en matière civile.* Published PhD diss. Paris: Éditions "de la vie universitaire," 1921.

———. *Itinéraire africain.* Paris: Présence Africaine, 1966.

Guèye, Omar. *Sénégal: Histoire du mouvement syndical: La marche vers le Code du travail.* Paris: L'Harmattan, 2011.

Guillemin, Phillipe. "Les élus d'Afrique noire à l'Assemblée nationale sous la Quatrième République." *Revue Française de Science Politique,* no. 4 (1958): 861–77.

Gutierrez, Laurent, Laurent Besse, and Antoine Prost, eds. *Réformer l'école: L'apport de l'éducation nouvelle (1930–1970).* Grenoble: Presses Universaires de Grenoble, 2012.

Ha, Marie-Paule. "From 'Nos Ancêtres les Gaulois' to 'Leur Culture Ancestrale': Symbolic Violence and the Politics of Colonial Schooling in Indochina." *French Colonial History* 3 (2003): 101–17.

Hardy, Georges. *Une conquête morale: L'enseignement en A.O.F.* 1917. Reprint, Paris: L'Harmattan, 2005.

Haut-Commisariat de l'AOF. *Annuaire statistique de l'AOF.* Vol. 2. Paris: Imprimerie Nationale, 1951.

Hazoumé, Paul. *Doguicimi.* Paris: Maisonneuve et Larose, 1938.

———. *Le pacte de sang au Dahomey.* Paris: Institut d'Ethnologie, 1937.

Hélénon, Véronique. *French Caribbeans in Africa: Diasporic Connections and Colonial Administration, 1880–1939.* New York: Palgrave Macmilllan, 2011.

Herbart, Pierre. *Le chancre du Niger.* With a preface by André Gide. Paris: Gallimard, 1939.

Hessel, Stéphane, ed. *Le programme du Conseil national de la Résistance: 15 mars 1944.* Le Bouscat, France: L'Esprit du Temps, 2012.

Hill, Edwin. "Imagining *Métissage*: The Politics and Practice of *Métissage* in the French Colonial Exposition and Ousmane Socé's *Mirages de Paris*." *Social Identities* 8, no. 4 (2002): 619–45.

Hill, Robert A., ed. *The Marcus Garvey and Universal Negro Improvement Association Papers.* Vol. 9, *Africa for the Africans, 1921–1922.* Berkeley: University of California Press, 1995.

Hitchcock, William I. "Pierre Boisson, French West Africa, and the Postwar *Epuration*: A Case from the Aix Files." *French Historical Studies* 24, no. 2 (Spring 2001): 305–41.

Hodeir, Catherine. "La France d'Outre-Mer." In *Cinquantenaire de l'Exposition internationale des arts et des techniques dans la vie moderne,* 284–91. Paris: Institut Français d'Architecture–Paris-Musées, 1987.

Hoisington, William A., Jr. *Lyautey and the French Conquest of Morocco.* New York: St. Martin's Press, 1995.

Hubbard, James P. *The United States and the End of British Colonial Rule in Africa, 1941–1968.* Jefferson NC: McFarland and Company, 2011.

Hugot, Philippe. *La gratuité de l'enseignement secondaire: L'application des premières mesures démocratiques dans l'enseignement secondaire, 1918–1939.* Paris: L'Harmattan, 2005.

Hymans, Jacques Louis. *Léopold Sédar Senghor: An Intellectual Biography.* Edinburgh: Edinburgh University Press, 1971.

Idowu, H. Oludare. "Assimilation in 19th Century Senegal." *Cahiers d'Études Africaines* 9, no. 34 (1969): 194–218.

——. "Café au Lait: Senegal's Mulatto Community in the Nineteenth Century." *Journal of the Historical Society of Nigeria* 6, no. 3 (December 1972): 271–88.

——. "The Establishment of Elective Institutions in Senegal, 1869–1880." *Journal of African History* 9, no. 2 (1968): 261–77.

L'Institut Charles-de-Gaulle, ed. *Brazzaville, janvier-février 1944: Aux sources de la décolonisation.* Paris: Plon, 1988.

Irele, F. Abiola. *The Negritude Moment: Explorations in Francophone African and Caribbean Literature and Thought.* Trenton NJ: Africa World Press, 2010.

Irvine, William D. *Between Justice and Politics: The Ligue Des Droits de l'Homme, 1898–1945.* Stanford: Stanford University Press, 2007.

Isoart, Paul. "Le septennat de Vincent Auriol (1947–1954) ou l'échec de l'État associé." In *L'ère des décolonisatons: Actes du colloque d'Aix-en-Provence*, edited by Charles-Robert Ageron and Marc Michel, 96–112. Paris: Karthala, 1995.

Jackson, Julian. *The Popular Front in France: Defending Democracy, 1934–1938.* Cambridge: Cambridge University Press, 1988.

Jennings, Eric T. "Conservative Confluences, 'Nativist' Synergy: Reinscribing Vichy's National Revolution in Indochina, 1940–1945." *French Historical Studies* 27, no. 3 (Summer 2004): 601–35.

——. *Free French Africa in World War II: The African Resistance.* New York: Cambridge University Press, 2015.

——. "Vichy fut-il aussi antinoir?" In *L'Empire colonial sous Vichy*, edited by Jacques Cantier and Eric T. Jennings, 213–31. Paris: Odile Jacob, 2004.

——. *Vichy in the Tropics: Pétain's National Revolution in Madagascar, Guadeloupe, and Indochina, 1940–1944.* Stanford: Stanford University Press, 2001.

Jézéquel, Jean-Hervé. "Grammaire de la distinction coloniale: L'organisation des cadres de l'enseignement en Afrique occidentale française (1903–fin des années 1930)." *Genèses* 69 (December 2007): 4–25.

——. "Histoire de bancs, parcours d'élèves: Pour une lecture 'configurationnelle' de la scolarisation à l'époque coloniale." *Cahiers d'Études Africaines* 169–70 (2003): 409–33.

——. "Les enseignants comme élite politique en AOF (1930–1945): Des 'meneurs de galopins' dans l'arène politique." *Cahiers d'Études Africaines* 178 (2005): 519–43.

——. "'Les mangeurs de craies': Socio-histoire d'une catégorie lettrée à l'époque coloniale: Les instituteurs diplômés de l'École normale William Ponty." Thèse de doctorat, École des hautes études en sciences sociales, 2002.

———. "Le 'théâtre des instituteurs' en Afrique occidentale française (1930–1950): Pratique socio-culturelle et vecteur de cristallisation de nouvelles identités urbaines." In *Fêtes urbaines en Afrique: Espaces, identités et pouvoirs*, edited by Odile Goerg, 181–200. Paris: Karthala, 1999.

Jobs, Richard Ivan. *Riding the New Wave: Youth and the Rejuvenation of France after the Second World War*. Stanford: Stanford University Press, 2007.

Johnson, G. Wesley. *The Emergence of Black Politics in Senegal: The Struggle for Power in the Four Communes, 1900–1920*. Stanford: Stanford University Press, 1971.

———. "The Impact of the Senegalese Elite Upon the French, 1900–1940." In *Double Impact: France and Africa in the Age of Imperialism*, edited by G. Wesley Johnson, 155–78. Westport CT: Greenwood Press, 1985.

———. "The Rivalry between Diagne and Merlin for Political Mastery of French West Africa." In *AOF, réalités et héritages: Sociétés ouest-africaines et ordre colonial, 1895–1960*, vol. 1, edited by Charles Becker, Saliou Mbaye and Ibrahima Thioub, 303–14. Dakar: Direction des Archives du Sénégal, 1997.

———. "The Senegalese Urban Elite, 1900–1945." In *Africa and the West: Intellectual Responses to European Culture*, edited by Philip D. Curtin, 139–87. Madison: University of Wisconsin Press, 1972.

Jones, Hilary. *The Métis of Senegal: Urban Life and Politics in French West Africa*. Bloomington: Indiana University Press, 2013.

Keese, Alexander. "A Culture of Panic: 'Communist' Scapegoats and Decolonization in French West Africa and French Polynesia (1945–1957)." *French Colonial History* 9 (2008): 131–45.

Kelly, Gail Paradise. "Franco-Vietnamese Schools, 1918–1933." PhD diss., University of Wisconsin, 1975.

Kelly, Gail Paradise, and David H. Kelly. *French Colonial Education: Essays on Vietnam and West Africa*. New York: AMS Press, 2000.

Kesteloot, Lilyan. *Black Writers in French: A Literary History of Negritude*. Translated by Ellen Conroy Kennedy. Philadephia: Temple University Press, 1974.

Klein, Martin A. *Slavery and Colonial Rule in French West Africa*. Cambridge: Cambridge University Press, 1998.

Koerner, Francis. *Histoire de l'enseignement privé et officiel à Madagascar (1820–1995)*. Paris: L'Harmattan, 1999.

Koulaksiss, Ahmed. *Le Parti socialiste et l'Afrique du Nord de Jaurès à Blum*. Paris: Armand Colin, 1991.

Koumé, Mamadou. "L'évolution de la presse quotidienne au Sénégal, Paris-Dakar (1937–1961), Dakar-Matin (1961–1970)." Thèse de doctorat, Université Paris 2, 1991.

La Conférence africaine française: Brazzaville (30 janvier–8 février 1944). Algiers: Commissariat aux Colonies, 1944.

Lagana, Marc. "L'échec de la commission d'enquête coloniale du Front populaire." *Historical Reflections/Réflexions Historiques* 16, no. 1 (Spring 1989): 79–97.

Lallement, Michel. *Logique de classe: Edmond Goblot, la bourgeoisie et la distinction sociale*. Paris: Belles Lettres, 2015.

Larcher, Silyane. *L'autre citoyen: L'idéal républicain et les Antilles après l'esclavage*. Paris: Armand Colin, 2014.

La Revue du Monde Noir/The Review of the Black World, 1931–1932: Collection complète, nos. 1 à 6. Paris: Jean Michel Place, 1992.

Laurière, Christine. *Paul Rivet, le savant et le politique*. Paris: Publications Scientifiques du Muséum National d'Histoire Naturelle, 2008.

Lawrance, Benjamin N., Emily Lynn Osborne, and Richard L. Roberts, eds. *Intermediaries, Interpreters, and Clerks: African Employees in the Making of Colonial Africa*. Madison: University of Wisconsin Press, 2006.

Lawrence, Adria K. *Imperial Rule and the Politics of Nationalism: Anti-Colonial Protest in the French Empire*. New York: Cambridge University Press, 2013.

Lebovics, Herman. *True France: The Wars over Cultural Identity, 1900–1945*. Ithaca NY: Cornell University Press, 1992.

Le Cour Grandmaison, Olivier. *Anatomie d'un "monstre" juridique: Le droit colonial en Algérie et dans l'Empire français*. Paris: Éditions La Découverte, 2010.

Légier, Henri Jacques. "Les institutions municipales et politique coloniale: Les communes du Sénégal." *Revue Française d'Histoire d'Outre-mer* 55, no. 201 (1968): 414–64.

Le Goff, Germaine. "Écoles de filles et enseignement ménager en A.O.F." In *Congrès international de l'évolution culturelle des peuples coloniaux, 26, 27, 28 septembre 1937: Rapports et compte rendu*, 55–68. Paris: Exposition Internationale de Paris, 1938.

Lehmil, Linda S. "À l'école du français: Politiques coloniales de la langue 1830–1944." PhD diss., Tulane University, 2007.

Lehning, James R. *Peasant and French: Cultural Contact in Rural France during the Nineteenth Century*. Cambridge: Cambridge University Press, 1995.

Lemaignen, Robert, Prince Sisowath Youtévong, and Léopold Sédar Senghor. *La communauté impériale française*. Paris: Éditions Alsatia, 1945.

Lemé, René. *L'enseignement en Afrique occidentale française*. Paris: Émile Larose, 1906.

L'Estoile, Benoît de. "Au nom des 'vrais Africains': L'hostilité à l'anthropologie des élites africaines scolarisées (1930–1950)." *Terrain* 28 (March 1997): 87–102.

———. *Le goût des autres: De l'Exposition coloniale aux arts premiers*. Paris: Flammarion, 2007.

Levine, Alison J. Murray. *Framing the Nation: Documentary Film in Interwar France*. New York: Continuum, 2010.

Levy, Claude. "Les origines de la Conférence de Brazzaville, le contexte et la décision." In *Brazzaville, janvier-février 1944: Aux sources de la décolonisation*, edited by l'Institut Charles-de-Gaulle, 21–29. Paris: Plon, 1988.

Lewis, James I. "The MRP and the Genesis of the French Union, 1944–1948." *French History* 12, no. 3 (September 1998): 276–314.

Lewis, Mary Dewhurst. *The Boundaries of the Republic: Migrant Rights and the Limits of Universalism in France, 1918–1940*. Standford: Stanford University Press, 2007.

———. *Divided Rule: Sovereignty and Empire in French Tunisia, 1881–1938*. Berkeley: University of California Press, 2014.

Liauzu, Claude. *Aux origines des tiers-mondismes: Colonisés et anticolonialistes en France (1919–1939)*. Paris: L'Harmattan, 1982.

Lokossou, Clément Koudessa. "La presse au Dahomey, 1894–1960: Évolution et création face à l'administration coloniale." Thèse de doctorat, École des hautes études en sciences sociales, 1976.

Louis, William Roger, and Ronald Robinson. "The United States and the Liquidation of British Empire in Tropical Africa, 1941–1951." In *The Transfer of Power in Africa: Decolonization 1940–1960*, edited by Prosser Gifford and William Roger Louis, 31–55. New Haven: Yale University Press, 1982.

Lucas, Raoul. *Bourbon à l'école: 1815–1946*. 2nd ed. Saint-André, La Réunion: Océan Éditions, 2006.

Ly, Boubacar. *Les instituteurs au Sénégal de 1903 à 1945*. 6 vols. Paris: L'Harmattan, 2009.

Malela, Buata B. *Les écrivains afro-antillais à Paris (1920–1960): Stratégies et postures indentitaires*. Paris: Karthala, 2008.

Mamdani, Mahmood. *Citizen and Subject: Contemporary Africa and the Legacy of Late Colonialism*. Princeton: Princeton University Press, 1996.

Manchuelle, François. "Métis et colons: La famille Devès et l'émergence politique des Africains au Sénégal, 1881–1897." *Cahiers d'Études Africaines* 24, no. 96 (1984): 477–504.

Mande, Issiaka. "Labor Market Constraints and Competition in Colonial Africa: Migrant Workers, Population, and Agricultural Production in Upper Volta, 1920–1932." In *Movements, Borders, and Identities in Africa*, edited by Toyin Falola and Aribidesi Usman, 285–303. Rochester NY: University of Rochester Press, 2009.

Mangolte, Jacques. "Le chemin de fer de Conakry au Niger." *Revue Française d'Histoire d'Outre-mer* 55, no. 198 (1968): 37–105.

Manière, Laurent. "Deux conceptions de l'action judiciaire aux colonies: Magistrats et administrateurs en Afrique occidentale française (1887–1912)." *Clio@Thémis:*

Revue Électronique d'Histoire du Droit, no. 4 (2001), http://www.cliothemis.com /Deux-conceptions-de-l-action.

————. "La politique française pour l'adaptation de l'enseignement en Afrique après les indépendances (1958–1964)." *Histoire de l'Éducation* 128 (2010): 163–90.

Mann, Gregory. *From Empires to NGOs in the West African Sahel: The Road to Non-governmentality.* New York: Cambridge University Press, 2015.

————. *Native Sons: West African Veterans and France in the Twentieth Century.* Durham NC: Duke University Press, 2006.

————. "What Was the *Indigénat*? The 'Empire of Law' in French West Africa." *Journal of African History* 50, no. 3 (2009): 331–53.

Mann, Gregory, and Jane I. Guyer. "Imposing a Guide on the *Indigène*: The Fifty Year Experience of the *Sociétés de Prévoyance* in French West and Equatorial Africa." In *Credit, Currencies and Culture: African Financial Institutions in Historical Perspective*, edited by Endre Stiansen and Jane I. Guyer, 118–45. Uppsala, Sweden: Nordiska Afrikainstitutet, 1999.

Manning, Patrick. *Slavery and African Life: Occidental, Oriental, and African Slave Trades.* Cambridge: Cambridge University Press, 1990.

Marseille, Jacques. *Empire colonial et capitalisme français: Histoire d'un divorce.* Paris: Albin Michel, 1984.

Maupoil, Bernard. "Le théâtre dahoméen: Les auteurs-acteurs de l'École William-Ponty, Gorée-Dakar 1934–1937." *Outre-Mer: Revue Générale de Colonisation* 9, no. 4 (September 1937): 301–21.

Mayeur, Françoise. *Histoire générale de l'enseignement et de l'éducation en France.* Vol. 3, *De la Révolution à l'école républicaine (1789–1930)*. Paris: Éditions Perrin, 2004.

McKay, Claude. *Banjo.* 1929. Reprint, London: X Press, 2000.

Médici, Angéla. *L'éducation nouvelle: Ses méthodes—ses progrès.* 3rd ed. Paris: Presses Universitaires de France, 1948.

Memmi, Albert. *The Colonizer and the Colonized.* Translated by Howard Greenfeld. Boston: Beacon Press, 1991.

Merle, Isabelle. "Retour sur le régime de l'indigénat: Genèse et contradictions des principes répressifs de l'empire français." *French Politics, Culture and Society* 20, no. 2 (2002): 77–97.

Meynier, Gilbert. "La France coloniale de 1914 à 1931." In *Histoire de la France coloniale*, vol. 2, *1914–1990*, by Jacques Thobie, Gilbert Meynier, Catherine Coquery-Vidrovitch, and Charles-Robert Ageron, 71–179. Paris: Armand Colin, 1990.

Michel, Marc. "L'empire colonial dans les débats parlementaires." In *L'année 1947*, edited by Serge Berstein and Pierre Milza, 189–217. Paris: Presses de Sciences Po, 2000.

———. *Les Africains et la Grande Guerre: L'appel à l'Afrique (1914–1918)*. Paris: Karthala, 2003.

———. "René Maran et Blaise Diagne: Deux négritudes républicaines." *Présence Africaine: Revue Culturelle du Monde Noir*, nos. 187–88 (2013): 153–66.

Midiohouan, Guy Ossito. *L'idéologie dans la littérature négro-africaine d'expression française*. Paris: L'Harmattan, 1986.

Miller, Christopher L. *Nationalists and Nomads: Essays on Francophone African Literature and Culture*. Chicago: University of Chicago Press, 1998.

Miller, F. Bart. *Rethinking Négritude through Léon-Gontran Damas*. Amsterdam: Editions Rodopi B.V., 2014.

Ministère de l'Éducation nationale. "Introduction: Le Service de coordination de l'enseignement dans la France d'outre-mer." *Carnets de Documentation sur l'Enseignement dans la France d'Outre-Mer*, no. 1 (1946).

Ministère de l'Éducation nationale (Service de coordination de l'enseignement dans la France d'outre-mer). *L'enseignement dans les territoires français d'outre-mer*. Paris: Imprimerie Nationale, 1946.

Mitterrand, François. *Présence française et abandon*. Paris: Plon, 1957.

Moleur, Bernard. "L'indigène aux urnes: Le droit de suffrage et la citoyenneté dans la colonie du Sénégal." In *Les droits de l'Homme et le suffrage universel, 1848–1948–1998: Actes du colloque de Grenoble, avril 1998*, edited by Gérard Chianéa and Jean-Luc Chabot, 65–97. Paris: L'Harmattan, 2000.

Morgenthau, Ruth Schachter. *Political Parties in French-Speaking West Africa*. Oxford: Clarendon Press of Oxford University Press, 1964.

Morton, Patricia. *Hybrid Modernities: Architecture and Representation at the 1931 Colonial Exposition, Paris*. Cambridge MA: MIT Press, 2000.

Moulin, Annie. *Peasantry and Society in France since 1789*. Translated by M. C. and M. F. Cleary. Cambridge: Cambridge University Press; Paris: Éditions de la Masion des Sciences de l'Homme, 1991.

Mouralis, Bernard. "William Ponty Drama." In *European-Language Writing in Sub-Saharan Africa*, edited by Albert S. Gérard, 130–40. Budapest: Akadémiai Kiadó, 1986.

Mouralis, Bernard, and Anne Piriou, eds. *Robert Delavignette: Savant et politique (1897–1976)*. Paris: Karthala, 2003.

Ndiaye, Pap. *La condition noire: Essai sur une minorité*. Paris: Calmann-Lévy, 2008.

Ngalamulume, Kalala. "Keeping the City Totally Clean: Yellow Fever and the Politics of Prevention in Colonial Saint-Louis-du-Sénégal, 1850–1914." *Journal of African History* 45, no. 2 (2004): 183–202.

Nicholas, Armand. *L'histoire de la Martinique*. Vol. 3, *De 1939 à 1971*. Paris: L'Harmattan, 1998.

Noiriel, Gérard. "L'identification des citoyens: Naissance de l'état civil républicain." *Genèses* 13, no. 1 (1993): 3–28.

Nwaubani, Ebere. "The United States and the Liquidation of European Colonial Rule in Tropical Africa, 1941–1963." *Cahiers d'Études Africaines* 171 (2003): 505–51.

Ohayon, Annick, Dominique Ottavi, and Antoine Savoye, eds. *L'éducation nouvelle, histoire, présence et devenir.* Berne: Peter Lang, 2007.

Ojo-Ade, Femi. *Léon-Gontran Damas: Spirit of Resistance.* London: Karnak House, 1993.

Orosz, Kenneth J. *Religious Conflict and the Evolution of Language Policy in German and French Cameroon, 1885–1939.* New York: Peter Lang, 2008.

Ory, Pascal. *La belle illusion: Culture et politique sous le signe du Front populaire, 1935–1938.* Paris: Plon, 1994.

Osborne, Michael A. *The Emergence of Tropical Medicine in France.* Chicago: University of Chicago Press, 2014.

Ozouf, Jacques, and Mona Ozouf, with Véronique Aubert and Claire Steindecker. *La République des instituteurs.* 1992. Reprint, Paris: Éditions du Seuil, 2001.

Ozouf, Mona. *L'école, l'Église et la République: 1871–1914.* Paris: Éditions Cana–Jean Offredo, 1982.

Piriou, Anne. "Les enjeux d'une 'Afrique du juste-milieu.'" In *Robert Delavignette: Savant et politique (1897–1976),* edited by Bernard Mouralis and Anne Piriou, 185–204. Paris: Karthala, 2003.

Pitié, Jean. *L'exode rural.* Paris: Presses Universitaires de France, 1979.

Ponty, William. "Discours du Gouverneur Général, à l'ouverture de la session du Conseil de gouvernement." In *Situation générale de l'année 1908,* by Gouvernement général de l'Afrique occidentale française, 7–26. Gorée: Imprimerie Générale du Gouvernement Général, 1909.

Prost, Antoine. *Autour du Front populaire: Aspects du mouvement social au XXe siècle.* Paris: Éditions du Seuil, 2006.

———. *Du changement dans l'école: Les réformes de l'éducation de 1936 à nos jours.* Paris: Éditions du Seuil, 2013.

———. *Histoire de l'enseignement en France: 1860–1967.* Paris: Armand Colin, 1968.

———. *Histoire générale de l'enseignement et de l'éducation en France.* Vol. 4, *L'école et la famille dans une société en mutation (depuis 1930).* Paris: Perrin, 2004.

———, ed. *Jean Zay et la gauche du radicalisme.* Paris: Presses de Sciences Po, 2003.

———, ed. *Regards historiques sur l'éducation en France: XIXè–XXè siècles.* Paris: Belin, 2007.

Rabinow, Paul. *French Modern: Norms and Forms of the Social Environment.* Cambridge MA: MIT Press, 1989.

Racine, Daniel. *Léon-Gontran Damas: L'homme et l'oeuvre.* Paris: Présence Africaine, 1983.

Ramognino, Pierre. *L'affaire Boisson: Un proconsul de Vichy en Afrique.* Paris: Les Indes Savantes, 2006.

————. "L'Afrique de l'Ouest sous le proconsulat de Pierre Boisson (juin 1940–juin 1943)." In *L'Empire colonial sous Vichy*, edited by Jacques Cantier and Eric T. Jennings, 69–87. Paris: Odile Jacob, 2004.

Rano, Jonas. *Créolitude: Léon-Gontran Damas et la quête d'une identité primordiale.* Paris: Éditions Universitaires Européennes, 2011.

Rémondet, A. "La création des écoles normales rurales en A.O.F." *Outre-Mer: Revue Générale de Colonisation* 7, nos. 2–3 (1935): 201–3.

Riesz, János. "From Ethnography to the African Novel: The Example of Doguicimi (1938) by Paul Hazoumé (Dahomey)." *Research in African Literatures* 35, no. 4 (Winter 2004): 17–32.

Riesz, János, and Aija Bjornson. "Senghor and the Germans." *Research in African Literatures* 33, no. 4 (Winter 2002): 25–37.

Rivet, Daniel. *Lyautey et l'institution du protectorat français au Maroc, 1912–1925.* 3 vols. Paris: L'Harmattan, 1988.

Roberts, Richard L. *Litigants and Households: African Disputes and Colonial Courts in the French Soudan, 1895–1912.* Portsmouth NH: Heinemann, 2005.

————. *Two Worlds of Cotton.* Stanford: Stanford University Press, 1996.

Robinson, David. *Paths of Accommodation: Muslim Societies and French Colonial Authorities in Senegal and Mauritania, 1880–1920.* Athens: Ohio University Press; Oxford: James Currey, 2000.

Saada, Emmanuelle. *Les enfants de la colonie: Les métis de l'Empire français, entre sujétion et citoyenneté.* Paris: La Découverte, 2007.

Sabatier, Peggy. "Educating a Colonial Elite: The William Ponty School and Its Graduates." PhD diss., University of Chicago, 1977.

Saint-Martin, Yves-Jean. *Le Sénégal sous le Second Empire.* Paris: Karthala, 1989.

Salaün, Marie. *L'école indigène: Nouvelle-Calédonie 1885–1945.* Rennes: Presses Universitaires de Rennes, 2005.

Sarr, Dominique, and Richard Roberts. "The Jurisdiction of Muslim Tribunals in Colonial Senegal, 1887–1932." In *Law in Colonial Africa*, edited by Kristin Mann and Richard Roberts, 131–45. Portsmouth NH: Heinemann; London: James Currey, 1991.

Scheck, Raffael. "Léopold Sédar Senghor, prisonnier de guerre allemand: Une nouvelle approche fondée sur un texte inédit." *French Politics, Culture and Society* 32, no. 2 (Summer 2014): 76–98.

Schmidt, Elizabeth. *Cold War and Decolonization in Guinea, 1946–1958.* Athens: Ohio University Press, 2007.

Schreyger, Emil. *L'Office du Niger au Mali, 1932 à 1982: La problématique d'une grande entreprise agricole dans la zone du Sahel.* Wiesbaden: Steiner; Paris: Diffusion L'Harmattan, 1984.

Searing, James F. "Accommodation and Resistance: Chiefs, Muslim Leaders, and Politicians in Colonial Senegal 1890–1934." PhD diss., Princeton University, 1985.

Seck, Assane. *Dakar: métropole ouest-africaine*. Dakar: Institut Fondamental d'Afrique Noire, 1970.

Segalla, Spencer D. *The Moroccan Soul: French Education, Colonial Ethnology, and Muslim Resistance, 1912–1956*. Lincoln: University of Nebraska Press, 2009.

Semidei, Manuela. "De l'Empire à la décolonisation à travers les manuels scolaires français." *Revue Française de Science Politique* 16, no. 1 (1966): 56–86.

———. "Les Socialistes français et le problème colonial entre les deux guerres (1919–1939)." *Revue Française de Science Politique* 18, no. 6 (December 1968): 1115–54.

Senghor, Léopold Sédar. "Assimilation et association." In *Liberté 2: Nation et voie africaine du socialisme*, 19–28. Paris: Éditions du Seuil, 1971.

———. "Balkanisation ou fédération." In *Liberté 2: Nation et voie africaine du socialisme*, 180–83. Paris: Éditions du Seuil, 1971.

———. "La Négritude, comme culture des peuples noirs, ne saurait être dépassée." In *Liberté 5: Le dialogue des cultures*, 95–109. Paris: Éditions du Seuil, 1993.

———. *La poésie de l'action: Conversations avec Mohamed Aziza*. Paris: Stock, 1980.

———. "La résistance de la bourgeoisie sénégalaise à l'école rurale populaire." In *Congrès international de l'évolution culturelle des peuples coloniaux, 26, 27, 28 septembre 1937: Rapports et compte rendu*, 40–44. Paris: Exposition Internationale de Paris, 1938.

———. "Le Message de Goethe aux nègres-nouveaux." In *Liberté 1: Négritude et humanisme*, 83–86. Paris: Éditions du Seuil, 1964.

———. "L'enseignement, base de l'évolution des peuples." In *Liberté 2: Nation et voie africaine du socialisme*, 9–16. Paris: Éditions du Seuil, 1971.

———. "Le problème culturel en A.O.F." In *Essais et études universitaires: Édition lettres, 1–1945*, edited by Jean Dumont, 44–53. Paris: La Nouvelle Édition, 1945.

———. "Le problème culturel en A.O.F." In *Liberté 1: Négritude et humanisme*, 11–21. Paris: Éditions du Seuil, 1964.

———. "Le problème des langues vernaculaires ou le bilinguisme comme solution." In *Liberté 1: Négritude et humanisme*, 228–31. Paris: Éditions du Seuil, 1964.

———. "Les décrets d'application de la loi-cadre ou 'donner et retirer ne vaut.'" In *Liberté 2: Nation et voie africaine du socialisme*, 211–15. Paris: Éditions du Seuil, 1971.

———. "Les leçons de Leo Frobenius." In *Liberté 3: Négritude et civilisation de l'universel*, 398–404. Paris: Éditions du Seuil, 1977.

———. "L'humanisme et nous: 'René Maran.'" *L'Étudiant Noir*, no. 1 (March 1935): 4.

———. "Négritude et germanité I." In *Liberté 3: Négritude et civilisation de l'universel*, 11–17. Paris: Éditions du Seuil, 1977.

———. "Union française et fédéralisme." In *Liberté 2: Nation et voie africaine du socialisme*, 197–210. Paris: Éditions du Seuil, 1971.

———. "Vues sur l'Afrique noire ou assimiler, non être assimilés." In *Liberté 1: Négritude et humanisme*, 39–69. Paris: Éditions du Seuil, 1964.

Sharpley-Whiting, T. Denean. *Negritude Women*. Minneapolis: University of Minnisota Press, 2002.

Shennan, Andrew. *Rethinking France: Plans for Renewal 1940–1946*. Oxford: Clarendon Press, 1989.

Shepard, Todd. *The Invention of Decolonization: The Algerian War and the Remaking of France*. Ithaca NY: Cornell University Press, 2006.

Shereikis, Rebecca. "From Law to Custom: The Shifting Legal Status of Muslim Originaires in Kayes and Medine, 1903–1913." *Journal of African History* 42, no. 2 (2001): 261–83.

Shipway, Martin. *The Road to War: France and Vietnam, 1944–1947*. Providence: Berghahn Books, 1996.

Sibeud, Emmanuelle. "La gauche et l'empire colonial avant 1945." In *Histoire des gauches en France*, vol. 2, *XXè siecle: À l'épreuve de l'histoire*, edited by Jean-Jacques Becker and Gilles Candar, 341–56. Paris: La Découverte, 2004.

Singaravélou, Pierre. *Professer l'Empire: Les "sciences coloniales" en France sous la IIIè République*. Paris: Publications de la Sorbonne, 2011.

Singaravélou, Pierre, and Julien Sorez, eds. *L'Empire des sports: Une histoire de la mondialisation culturelle*. Paris: Belin, 2010.

Sinou, Alain. *Comptoirs et villes coloniales au Sénégal: Saint-Louis, Gorée, Dakar*. Paris: Karthala and ORSTOM, 1993.

Sirinelli, Jean-François. "Des boursiers conquérants? École et 'promotion républicaine' sous la IIIè République." In *Le modèle républicain*, edited by Serge Berstein and Odile Rudelle, 243–62. Paris: Presses Universitaires de France, 1992.

———. "Deux étudiants 'coloniaux' à Paris à l'aube des années trente." *Vingtième Siècle* 18 (April–June 1988): 77–88.

Sissoko, Fily-Dabo. "Les noirs et la culture." In *Congrès international de l'évolution culturelle des peuples coloniaux, 26, 27, 28 septembre 1937: Rapports et compte rendu*, 116–22. Paris: Exposition Internationale de Paris, 1938.

———. *Les noirs et la culture: Introduction au problème de l'évolution culturelle des peuples africains*. New York, 1950.

Socé, Ousmane. *Karim: Roman sénégales*. 1935. Reprint, Paris: Nouvelles Éditions Latines, 1948.

———. *Mirages de Paris: Roman*. 1937. Reprint, Paris: Nouvelles Éditions Latines, 1964.

Sorel, Etya. *Une ambition pour l'école: Le plan Langevin-Wallon (1943–1947)*. Paris: Éditions Sociales, 1997.

Sorrel, Christian. *La République contre les congrégations: Histoire d'une passion française (1899–1914)*. Paris: Éditions du Cerf, 2003.

Stoler, Ann Laura. *Carnal Knowledge and Imperial Power: Race and the Intimate in Colonial Rule*. Berkeley: University of California Press, 2002.

Suret-Canale, Jean. *Afrique noire, occidentale et centrale*. Vol. 2, *L'ère coloniale (1900–1945)*. Paris: Éditions Sociales, 1964.

Surun, Isabelle. "French Military Officers and the Mapping of West Africa: The Case of Captain Brosselard-Faidherbe." *Journal of Historical Geography* 37, no. 2 (April 2011): 167–77.

———. "Une souveraineté à l'encre sympathique? Souveraineté autochtone et appropriations territoriales dans les traités franco-africains au XIXe siècle." *Annales. Histoire, Sciences Sociales* 69, no. 2 (2014): 313–48.

Taoua, Phyllis. *Forms of Protest: Anti-colonialism and Avant-Gardes in Africa, the Caribbean, and France*. Portsmouth NH: Heinemann, 2002.

Thiam, Iba Der. *La révolution de 1914 au Sénégal, ou l'élection au Palais Bourbon du député noir Blaise Diagne (de son vrai nom Galaye Mbaye Diagne)*. Vol. 1. Dakar: L'Harmattan-Sénégal, 2014.

Thiesse, Anne-Marie. *Écrire la France: Le mouvement littéraire régionaliste de langue française entre la Belle Époque et la Libération*. Paris: Presses Universitaires de France, 1991.

———. *Ils apprenaient la France: L'exaltation des régions dans le discours patriotique*. Paris: Éditions de la Maison des Sciences de l'Homme, 1997.

———. "Les deux identités de la France." *Modern and Contemporary France* 9, no. 1 (2001): 9–18.

Thobie, Jacques. "Le bilan colonial en 1914." In *Histoire de la France coloniale*, vol. 2, *1914–1990*, by Jacques Thobie, Gilbert Meynier, Catherine Coquery-Vidrovitch, and Charles-Robert Ageron, 7–67. Paris: Armand Colin, 1990.

Thomas, Martin. "Albert Sarraut, French Colonial Development, and the Communist Threat, 1919–1930." *Journal of Modern History* 77, no. 4 (December 2005): 917–55.

———. "The Colonial Policies of the Mouvement Républicain Populaire, 1944–1954: From Reform to Reaction." *English Historical Review* 118, no. 476 (April 2003): 380–411.

———. *The French Empire at War: 1940–1945*. Manchester: Manchester University Press, 1998.

———. *The French Empire between the Wars: Imperialism, Politics, and Society*. Manchester: Manchester University Press, 2005.

Thomas, Martin, Bob Moore, and L. J. Butler. *Crises of Empire: Decolonization and Europe's Imperial States*. 2nd ed. London: Bloomsbury Academic, 2015.

Toumson, Roger, and Simonne Henry-Valmore. *Aimé Césaire: Le nègre inconsolé*. Châteauneuf-le-Rouge: Vents d'Ailleurs, 2002.

Traoré, Bakary. *Le théâtre négro-africain et ses fonctions sociales*. Paris: Présence Africaine, 1958.

Ungar, Steven, and Dudley Andrew. *Popular Front Paris and the Poetics of Culture*. Cambridge MA: Harvard University Press, 2005.

Vaillant, Janet G. *Black, French, and African: A Life of Léopold Sédar Senghor*. Cambridge MA: Harvard University Press, 1990.

Van Beusekom, Monica M. *Negotiating Development: African Farmers and Colonial Experts at the Office du Niger, 1920–1960*. Portsmouth NH: Heinemann; Oxford: James Currey; Cape Town: David Philip, 2002.

Vandervelde, Émile. *L'exode rural et le retour aux champs*. Paris: F. Alcan, 1903.

Van Thao, Trinh. *L'école française en Indochine*. Paris: Karthala, 1995.

Vermeren, Pierre. *La formation des élites marocaines et tunisiennes: Des nationalistes aux islamistes, 1920–2000*. Paris: La Découverte, 2002.

Warner, Tobias. "Para-Literary Ethnography and Colonial Self-Writing: The Student Notebooks of the the William Ponty School." *Research in African Literatures* 47, no. 1 (Spring 2016): 1–20.

Weber, Eugen. *The Hollow Years: France in the 1930s*. New York: W. W. Norton and Company, 1994.

———. *Peasants into Frenchmen: The Modernization of Rural France, 1870–1914*. Stanford: Stanford University Press, 1976.

Weil, Patrick, ed. *Politiques de la laïcité au XXe siècle*. Paris: Presses Universitaires de France, 2007.

———. *Qu'est-ce qu'un Français: Histoire de la nationalité française depuis la Révolution*. Paris: Gallimard, 2004.

Wieviorka, Olivier. *Histoire de la Résistance: 1940–1945*. Paris: Perrin, 2013.

White, Owen. *Children of the French Empire: Miscegenation and Colonial Society in French West Africa, 1895–1960*. Oxford: Clarendon Press; New York: Oxford University Press, 1999.

White, Owen, and J. P. Daughton, eds. *In God's Empire: French Missionaries and the Modern World*. New York: Oxford University Press, 2012.

Wilder, Gary. *Freedom Time: Negritude, Decolonization, and the Future of the World*. Durham NC: Duke University Press, 2015.

———. *The French Imperial Nation-State: Negritude and Colonial Humanism between the Two World Wars*. Chicago: University of Chicago Press, 2005.

Wright, Gwendolyn. *The Politics of Design in French Colonial Urbanism*. Chicago: University of Chicago Press, 1991.

You, André. "Assomption pédagogique." *L'Éducation Africaine*, no. 106 (1942): 32–36.

Zuccarelli, François. *La vie politique sénégalaise (1789–1940)*. Paris: Le Centre des Hautes Études sur l'Afrique et l'Asie Modernes, 1987.

Page numbers in italics refer to illustrations.

African elites (*continued*)
metropolitan education in Four Communes for, 132–33; migration patterns of, 61–62; National Revolution in AOF and, 181; Negritude movement and, 126; originaires and, 61–62; political rights of, 180–81, 304n48; Popular Front and, 126, 136; regional schools and, 86, 87; rural schools in urban centers and, 130–31, 133, 146, 153, 282n24; secondary education for, 28, 101–2, 255n44. See also *baccalauréat* for African elites; *évolués*; *métis* (mixed-race) elites

African languages in colonial school system, 79, 142–43, 146, 286n67, 286nn69–70

Afrique équatoriale française (AEF), 160, 161, 299n1

Afrique occidentale française (AOF): about, 1, 78, 245–46; colonies of, 3, 4, 5; future and, 8–9, 85, 124, 137, 183, 226, 241; independence of colonies in, 245–46, 247; interior regions of, 4, 9, 15, 17, 20; loi-cadre and, 244–45; population statistics for, 2–3, 52, 88–89, 244; postcolonial era and, 241, 245–48, 309n6, 309n9. See also French empire

"Afro-French" culture. See Franco-African culture

agrégation, 42, 134–35, 258n90, 284n40

agricultural exports, AOF, 81, 90, 92

agricultural irrigation schemes, AOF, 92–93, 273n78

agricultural studies and training: about, 59–60, 76–77, 155; École William Ponty and, 119–20, 121, 279n73; Four Communes and,

26–27; regional schools and, 87, 270n36; rural schools in Senegalese towns and, 81, 131, 153; rural schools of AOF and, 81, 82–84, 270n36

Algeria, French, 225, 263n40, 303n31

Allied forces, 160, 183, 185

Angoulvant, Gabriel, 59–60, 61, 81, 270n36

antiblack racism, 166–67, 204, 205, 290n22, 290n24. See also racial discrimination

Antonetti, Raphaël, 60, 61–62, 64, 100–101, 264n50, 265n51, 265n53

AOF. See Afrique occidentale française (AOF)

Assembly of the French Union (Assemblée de l'Union française), 218, 302n23

assimilation: Four Communes and, 16–17, 20, 42, 72; in French empire, 71–74, 76, 96; Léopold Sédar Senghor on, 126, 137–38, 147–49; and *métis* elites as *assimilés*, 33; and originaires as *assimilés*, 20, 54; racial segregation versus, 32–33; Senegal and, 32–33. See also integration

assimilés, 33, 54

association, 96. See also assimilation

Assomption, Frédéric, 80–81, 83, 123–24, 269n33

Aubineau, Yves, 188, 204, 205, 208, 209, 210, 220

authoritarianism, 162–63, 289n9

baccalauréat: education in France and, 194, 196, 197, 202, 244, 308n2; European students in AOF and, 195–97, 199, 205; French empire and, 197, 308n3

baccalauréat for African elites: about, 214–15; *brevet de capacité colonial* and, 197, 296n38; challenges and, 134, 169, 198, 199–200; *métis* elites and, 196–97, 198; Pierre Boisson on, 201; racial discrimination and, 196–97, 199, 207–9; secondary education in France as pathway toward, 194, 308n2; statistics for, 195–97, 199, 205, 244, 297n46, 308nn2–3

balkanization of AOF, 245

Barthes, René, 219–20, 222, 237

Béart, Charles, 112–14, 115, 181–82, 278n53, 278n55

Béchard, Paul, 237

black Muslims, 31–32, 55. *See also* Muslims

Blanche, Denis, 147–50

Blum, Léon, 127–28

Boisson, Pierre: advanced school graduates and, 163–65; antiblack racism and, 166, 167, 201; *baccalauréat* for African elites and, 201; cultural associations and, 165, 179; interracial contacts and, 164, 165; pastoral visions and, 163; political career of, 155, 161, 183, 186, 289n5; sports and, 164, 165

Bouche, Denise, 38, 42, 254n32

Braillon, E., 197–98

Brazzaville Conference (1944): about, 10–11, 185–86; African elites' education and, 192–93; attendees at, 186, 294n8; colonial order and, 186, 190; decolonization scholarship on, 185; French empire and, 186–87, 192–93; girls' education and, 189, 190, 191, 294n16; language policies in colonial school system and, 191; mass

education and, 187, 190–91; primary schools in African colonies and, 188, 191–93; rural schools and, 188–99, 294n12; secondary education and, 192–93, 201, 296n26

brevet de capacité colonial, 197, 296n38. See also *baccalauréat* for African elites

Brévié, Jules: African languages in colonial school system and, 79, 146; agricultural training in colonial schools and, 82–84; École William Ponty and, 107, 108, 118; Franco-African culture and, 117; mass education and, 77, 85; political career of, 289n5; regional schools and, 87–88; rural normal schools and, 122–23; rural schools and, 77, 79–80, 85, 146, 153, 269n25; school-run savings associations and, 84; schoolteachers in AOF and, 122; *section du brevet* and, 107

Britain. *See* Great Britain

Brunot, Louis, 75–76, 268n18

Bulletin de l'Enseignement de l'A.O.F. (L'Éducation Africaine), 44, 121

Cabrière, Edmond, 204–5, 207, 208, 209, 210, 294n12, 299n78, 299n80

cadres for schoolteachers in AOF, 26, 38, 102, 106, 276n25, 301n21

Capelle, Jean: Académie de l'AOF and, 223, 236–37, 239, 240, 305n56; African elites' relationship with, 225–26, 304n46; *baccalauréat* for African elites and, 244, 308n2; educational attainment of, 223, 303n36; education reform in France and, 307n83; *inspecteurs d'académie* and, 224–25; integration through education

72, 75–76; Third Republic and, 213, 252n20, 300n9. *See also* subjects (colonial subjects), AOF

civil rights of French citizens, 31, 53–54, 58, 211, 212

civil rights of originaires: about, 60–61; Chamber of Deputies and, 52–53, 261n16; citizen-subject binary and, 20–21, 38, 51, 70; colonial school system in AOF and, 7, 28, 70; contestations and, 20–21; *évolués* and, 60–61, 209; Four Communes and, 13, 31, 48–50, 51, 138; French courts and, 50, 51, 52, 70, 261n16; Government General and, 52; *indigénat* and, 50–51, 70, 260nn7–8, 260n13; Muslim personal status and, 51; Muslim tribunals and, 50, 51, 260n8; secondary education and, 27–28, 196, 200, 205, 209. *See also* citizenship for originaires; political rights of originaires

civil rights of subjects, 20, 28

civil servants' rights, 213, 239

class distinctions, 6–7, 202–3, 204, 298n60

Clemenceau, Georges, 58, 59

CNR (National Council of the Resistance), 203

Code de l'indigénat (*indigénat*), 50–51, 59, 70, 92, 229, 231, 260nn7–8, 260n13, 289n9

Code du travail. *See* labor code, AOF

Cohen, William B., 235

collèges in France, 202, 205, 206, 297n55

Colonial Council, Colony of Senegal (Conseil colonial, Colonie du Sénégal), 131–32, 282n26

Colonial Exposition (1931), 71, 73, 95, 267n2

colonial reform: French empire and, 127–29, 186, 282n14, 282n16; Gaullists and, 186; loi-cadre and, 244–46, 302n22; Popular Front and, 120, 128–29, 130, 132, 133, 219; urban Senegal and, 129–33, 282n16

colonial school system, Four Communes: about, 9, 26; African elites and, 28, 101–2, 255n44; Catholic missionaries and, 16, 22–23, 39; costs and, 39, 257n79; *écoles congréganistes* and, 23–25, 27, 28, 254n32; legislation and, 26, 27; *métis* elites' contestations and, 35, 36–37, 46, 257n71; metropolitan school certificates for originaires in, 131; originaires' contestations and, 8, 29, 35, 36, 37, 38, 39, 40, 44, 66–67; rural schools and, 30, 35, 38, 41, 44, 255n55, 258nn88–89; secondary education and, 28, 101–2, 255n44; segregation in, 30–35, 40, 41, 45–46, 126, 132, 256n57. *See also* metropolitan education, Four Communes; regional schools, Four Communes

colonial school system, French empire: colonial order and, 71–72; Georges Hardy and, 42, 75; higher primary schools and, 192–93; Intercolonial Conference on Education and, 71–75, 94–95, 108, 269n28; language policies and, 74, 75, 76, 79, 268n18, 295n21; metropolitan education and, 268n19; missionaries' schools and, 21, 22; primary schools and, 73, 74–75, 268n15; secondary education and, 192–93, 296n26

colonial subjects. *See* subjects (colonial subjects), AOF

communes de plein exercise (full communes), definition of, 13, 15, 251n9. *See also* Four Communes

Conseil général, Colonie du Sénégal. *See* General Council, Colony of Senegal (Conseil général, Colonie du Sénégal)

conseils généraux. See general councils (*conseils généraux*) under Fourth Republic

Conseil supérieur de l'enseignement primaire (High Council on Primary Education), 43, 303n34

Constituent National Assemblies, 14, 211–12, 213–15, 216–17, 218–19, 222, 227, 230, 240, 299n1, 301nn12–13, 303n34, 304n48

Cooper, Frederick, 216, 239, 308n94

Coste-Floret, Paul, 235, 236

costs for education: colonial school system in AOF and, 39, 84–85, 205, 206, 207, 208, 257n79, 271n53, 298n68; education in France and, 39, 202, 205–6, 257n50, 268n19, 299n70

Coulibaly, Massire, 103, 275n19

Council of the Government General (Conseil de gouvernement), 35, 117, 255n47

Cour de cassation, 53

Cournarie, Pierre, 191–92, 205, 207, 208–9

Cours secondaire d'Abidjan, 207, 208

Cours secondaire de Dakar, 134, 198, 283n34

Cours secondaire de Saint-Louis, 193–94, 196n28

courts, French, 50, 51, 52, 70, 261n16. *See*

also Chamber of Deputies (Chambre des députés); native courts

Crouzet, Paul, 71, 72, 267n2, 298n31

cultural associations, AOF: urban Senegal and, 130, 180, 292n34, 293n58; Vichy regime and, 165, 179–80, 293n58

cultural *métissage*: education in France and, 233, 306n60; Léopold Sédar Senghor and, 170, 233, 247, 291n36, 306n60; Ousmane Socé and, 168–69, 170. *See also* debates on African culture and cultural *métissage*

culture, African. *See* African culture; debates on African culture and cultural *métissage*; Franco-African culture

Dahomey: colonial school system in, 24, 254n42; École William Ponty students from, 112; geographical location of, 3, *4*, *5*; metropolitan education in, 255n43; originaires residing in, 52, 261n15; rural schools in, 85, 133; theatrical productions and, 114; urban population statistics for, 88

Dakar: colonial reform and, 129, 282n16; Four Communes and, 13, 15, 277n38; General Council members from, 16, 251n12, 272n61; Government General headquarters in, 1–2, *2*, *20*; infrastructure projects and, 3–4, *5*; Léopold Sédar Senghor's speech to Chamber of Commerce in, 125–26, 139–44, 146, 285nn57–58, 285n63, 286nn66–67; local politics in, 17, 25, 39; Lycée Lamine Guèye and, 297n44; maps of, *18*, *19*, 89; mayors of, 15–16, 251n11, 305n49;

métis elites in, 55; metropolitan education in, 31; migration patterns during Great Depression era and, 88; Muslim tribunals in, 51; *originaires des Quatre Communes* and, 7; Ousmane Socé's speech to Chamber of Commerce in, 170, 285n58, 291n34; political organization in, 15–16, 35, 251nn11–12, 272n61; population statistics for, 20, 88, 89; primary schools in, 35, 68; rural schools in, 131; segregation in colonial school system in, 35; trade/labor unions and strikes in, 129, 130, 155. *See also* secondary education, AOF

Dakar-Jeunes: about, 160–61, 167, 290n25; advanced school graduates and, 160; African culture and, 175–76; cultural *métissage* and, 168–69; National Revolution in AOF and, 180–81; regionalism in France and, 168; sports and, 167–68; Vichy regime propaganda and, 160, 167, 179

Damas, Léon-Gontran, 135, 136, 156, 284n42

D'Anfreville de la Salle, Léon, 32–34

Daughton, J. P., 21, 253n26

Davesne, André, 76–77, 108–10, 119–20, 269n22, 269n28

debates on African culture and cultural *métissage*: African elites and, 182, 293n68; in correspondence, 178–79; Daouda Diawara and, 173–74; Fara Sow and, 170–71, 174; Joseph M'Baye and, 177–78; Léopold Sédar Senghor and, 157, 291n36; Mamadou Dia and, 175–76; Massata N'Diaye and, 171–72, 174; Ousmane Socé and, 170, 173, 174;

Sumus (pen name) and, 176–77; Vichy regime in AOF and, 181–82. *See also* African culture

decolonization, 185, 216, 241, 243, 245–46. *See also* postcolonial era

de Coppet, Marcel: African culture and, 151–52; African languages in colonial school system and, 143, 286n70; health of, 288n103; Léopold Sédar Senghor and, 139, 140, 151, 170, 287n99; Ousmane Socé and, 170; political career of, 129–30, 154–55; rural schools and, 154; trade/labor unions and strikes in AOF and, 155

Decoux, Jean, 180, 293n61

Defferre, Gaston, 244

De Gaulle, Charles, 160, 185, 186, 206, 208, 289n2, 309n9

Delavignette, Robert, 89–90, 91–92, 93–94, 95–96

Delbos, Yvon, 236

democratization: education reform in AOF and, 34, 203–4, 205–6, 207, 215, 244; French empire relationship with France and, 138, 218, 243; secondary education in AOF and, 204, 206, 244. *See also* integration

departmentalization of "old colonies," 212–13, 300nn4–5, 300nn8–9

Depression. *See* Great Depression era

Deschamps, Hubert, 290n24

Devès, Hyacinthe, 37, 257n71

Devès, Justin, 36–37, 40, 256n68

Dia, Mamadou, 175–76, 199–200, 292n46, 292n49, 292n51

Diagne, Blaise: activism of, 14; as commissioner of the republic, 58–59; criticism of and challenges to, 64–65; demands for new professional

education in France: *académies* and, 223–24, 304nn37–38; *agrégation* and, 42, 134–35, 258n90, 284n40; *baccalauréat* and, 194, 196, 197, 202, 244, 308n2; Catholics and, 6, 21–22, 252n23; class distinctions in, 6–7, 202–3, 298n60; *collèges* and, 202, 205, 206, 297n55; costs for, 39, 202, 205–6, 257n50, 268n19, 299n70; cultural *métissage* and, 233, 306n60; curricula of, as multicultural, 232–33, 234, 305n58; diplomas and certificates for schoolteachers and, 102; *écoles congréganistes* and, 22; higher primary schools and, 202; *inspecteurs d'académie* and, 224; integration and, 6–7; lycées and, 202, 206, 297n55; normal schools and, 101–4, 105, 106, 121, 202, 275nn10–11, 275n13, 275n19, 275n22; postcolonial era and, 245–46, 247; primary schools and, 7, 24, 26, 27, 38, 69, 202, 205, 206, 250n11; *recteur* and, 224, 237, 304n43, 308n2; rural normal schools and, 280n80; secondary education and, 7, 194, 206, 244; Third Republic and, 6–7, 202, 250n7, 297n55
education inspectors, AOF, 42, 43, 44, 105, 132, 134
Education Ministry. *See* Ministère de l'Éducation nationale
Edwards, Brent Hayes, 127, 284n46
electoral rights of originaires. *See* political rights of originaires
elites, African. *See* African elites
European populations, AOF, 7, 32, 164, 166, 207, 305n54
European students, AOF: *baccalauréat*

for, 196–97, 205; costs for education and, 207, 208, 209; Four Communes and, 30, 31–32, 34, 40, 41, 45–46, 68; metropolitan education for, 30, 31–32, 34, 41, 45–46, 68; primary schools and, 207–8; private schools and, 198, 208; regional schools and, 40; secondary schools and, 195, 196–97, 200, 201, 204–5, 207–9; statistics for, 195–97, 205
évolués, 60–61, 150, 151, 201, 209, 227, 304n48. *See also* advanced school graduates (*jeunesse évoluée*); African elites
Exposition Coloniale (1931), 71, 73, 95, 267n2

Faidherbe, Louis, 15, 195, 262n33
Federation of French West Africa, 1. *See also* AOF (Afrique occidentale française)
Ferry, Jules, 6
Fifth Republic, 246
forced labor, AOF, 92–93, 273n78
Foster, Elizabeth A., 21, 253n26, 254n32, 262n24
Four Communes: assimilation and, 16–17, 20, 42, 72; black Muslims in, 31–32, 55; Chamber of Deputies representatives from, 14, 16, 17, 55–56, 57–58, 62, 64, 132, 252n13, 262n28, 262n32; civil rights of originaires in, 13, 31, 48–50, 138; educational rights in, 28–29, 35, 41, 131, 132; history of, 13, 15, 109, 165, 251n9, 277n38; interior regions of Senegal and, 20; Légion française des combattants in, 165–66, 290n19; local politics in, 17, 30, 31, 39, 40, 41, 55, 62, 64, 167;

231, 301n19, 301n21, 302n23; equal
benefits and salaries for African
civil servants and, 239; integration
through education reform in AOF
and, 132, 230; Jean Capelle and, 226,
304n46; political career of, 132, 211–
12, 227, 283n29, 305n49; Senegalese
Socialist Party and, 132, 199
Guinea: geographical location of, 3, 4,
5; independence of, 247; metropolitan education in, 255n43;
originaires residing in, 52, 261n15;
representatives from, 304n46;
urban population statistics for, 88
Guy, Camille, 23–26, 27–28, 30, 254n32

Hama, Boubou, 231
Hardy, Georges: *Bulletin de l'Enseignement de l'A.O.F.* and, 44, 121;
career trajectory of, 42, 68, 258n91;
consolidating federal school system
as priority of, 42–46, 61, 258n89;
École coloniale directorship and,
94; educational attainment of, 42,
258n90; historians' assessments of,
42, 259nn92–93; International and
Intercolonial Conference on Native
Society and, 95; originaires' denunciations of, 66–68; pastoral visions
and, 94, 95; Raphaël Antonetti's
criticisms of, 61, 264n50; school-run
savings associations and, 270n48;
teacher-training centers and, 43,
259n99; urban schools and, 45–46
Haut-Sénégal-Niger, 253n30, 254n42.
See also Niger
Hazoumé, Paul, 145, 286n78, 286n80
Hegel, Georg Wilhelm Friedrich, 140–41
High Council on Primary Education

(Conseil supérieur de l'enseignement primaire), 43, 303n34
higher education, AOF, 215, 224, 230, 246
higher primary schools, 60, 86, 111, 113,
122, 192–93, 202, 230, 264n47, 272n58
"higher technical education," 59–60
Houphouët-Boigny, Félix, 238–39

independence of colonies in AOF,
245–46, 247
indigénat (Code de l'indigénat), 50–
51, 59, 70, 92, 229, 231, 260nn7–8,
260n13, 289n9
Indochina, French, 74
inspecteurs d'académie, 224–25, 240, 309n6
integration: Code du travail and, 239–40,
308n89; colonial officials' opposition to, 234–37; Education Ministry
during Fourth Republic and, 215,
225, 227–32, 235, 237, 238, 240, 304n43;
Gaullists and, 205; Jean Capelle and,
225, 237, 307n78; Lamine Guèye and,
132, 230; Léopold Sédar Senghor and,
215, 227–32, 240; Marius Moutet and,
219; of metropolitan France during
early Third Republic, 6–7; Popular
Front and, 132, 133; René Barthes
and, 219–20. *See also* assimilation;
democratization
Intercolonial Conference on Education in the Colonies and Overseas
Territories, 71–76, 94–95, 108, 269n28
International and Intercolonial Conference on Native Society, 94–95
International Conference on the
Cultural Development of Colonial
Peoples, 136–37, 144–50, 286n80,
287n94
International Labor Organization, 93

Ivory Coast: boundary alteration of, 273n74; Cours secondaire d'Abidjan in, 207, 208; forced labor in, 92; geographical location of, 3, 4, 5; independence of, 247; originaires residing in, 52, 261n15; Parti démocratique de la Côte d'Ivoire in, 238–39; political leadership in, 60; rural normal schools and, 123–24; rural schools and, 85, 86; theatrical productions and, 114; urban population statistics for, 88

Jennings, Eric, 180, 293n61
jeunesse évoluée. See advanced school graduates (*jeunesse évoluée*)
Johnson, G. Wesley, 14, 264n44
Jones, Hilary, 17

Kayes, 51, 78
Kouyaté, Tiémoko Garan, 105, 156

labor code, AOF, 129, 130, 155, 165, 239, 308n89
Labouret, Henri, 145, 150, 151, 287n194
laïcisation, 21–22, 23–24, 254n32
language policies in colonial school system: African languages and, 79, 142–43, 146, 286n67, 286nn69–70; AOF and, 26, 79, 191, 269nn27–28, 295n21; French empire and, 74, 75, 76, 79, 268n18, 295n21
Lapie, Pierre-Olivier, 240
Larcher, Silyane, 69–70, 213
L'Artilleur, Amadou. *See* Ndiaye, Amadou Duguay Clédor
Laurentie, Henri, 187, 294n7, 294n9
L'Éducation Africaine (*Bulletin de l'Enseignement de l'A.O.F.*), 44, 121

Légion française des combattants, 165–66, 290n19
Lémery, Henry, 162
Letourneau, Jean, 235
loi-cadre, 244–46, 302n22
Lyautey, Louis Hubert Gonzalve, 72–73, 75
lycées, AOF. *See* secondary education, AOF
lycées, France. *See* secondary education, France

Madagascar, 74–75
Mandel, Georges, 155
manual (trades) sections, 39, 76–77, 87, 121, 131, 153, 155
Martin, Louis, 132–33
Martinique, colony of, 56–57, 69–70, 76, 212–13, 257n81. *See also* departmentalization of "old colonies"
mass education, 77, 85, 187, 190–91, 192
Masson, Émile, 35
Mauritania: geographical location of, 3, 4, 5; independence of, 247; Légion française des combattants in, 290n19; originaires residing in, 52, 261n15; urban population statistics for, 88
M'Baye, Ibrahima, 179
M'Baye, Joseph, 177–79, 292n49, 292n54
McKay, Claude, 126, 281n1
medical studies: common curriculum and sections for, at École William Ponty, 279n71; Daouda Diawara and, 173; founding of École de médecine de Dakar and, 59–60; founding of section at École William Ponty for, 101; and statistics on graduates of medical section at École William Ponty, 274n5; *travaux pratiques* for

students in medical section of École William Ponty and, 119

Merlin, Martial, 62, 64, 65–66, 68, 195, 266n64

métis (mixed-race) elites: about, 252n17; as *assimilés*, 33, 54; *baccalauréat* and, 196–97, 198; Catholicism and, 31, 54–55, 262n24; citizenship for originaires and, 54–55; colonial school system contestations by, 35, 36–37, 46, 257n71; *écoles congréganistes* and, 24–25; Four Communes and, 55; François Carpot and, 17, 52; General Council and, 17, 35, 36–37, 257n71; Government General's relations with, 30–31; local politics and, 17, 30, 31, 55, 64; lycées in AOF and, 196–97; metropolitan education in Four Communes for, 30–31, 33, 69; racial discrimination and, 33, 196, 198, 200. *See also* African elites

métissage, cultural. *See* cultural *métissage*; debates on African culture and cultural *métissage*

metropolitan diplomas, 106–8

metropolitan education: AOF and, 27, 69, 192, 255n43, 267n76; France and, 16–17; French empire and, 74, 75, 76, 268n15, 268n19

metropolitan education, Four Communes: about, 27, 255n43; African elites and, 132–33; *assimilés* and, 33, 54; certificates for, 38, 46, 131; curricula for, 27, 41, 44, 45, 258nn88–89; European students and, 30, 31–32, 34, 41, 45–46, 68; legislation and regulations on, 16–17, 27, 28, 30, 31, 32, 41, 255n54; *métis* elites and, 30–31, 33, 69; originaires and, 30–31, 38, 46, 48,

66–67, 131, 132; primary schools and, 25–26, 27–28; racial discrimination and, 32–34, 36, 41; segregation and, 30–35, 45–46, 256n57; statistics on, 28, 31, 254n42, 258n88

migration patterns, 49–50, 52, 61–62, 88, 91–92, 97, 272n69

military service for subjects: AOF and, 47–48, 56, 57–59, 262n33, 262n35, 263n43; citizenship for originaires and, 56, 57–58, 59, 262n35; Code de l'indigénat and, 59; French empire and, 56–57; *tirailleurs sénégalais* and, 56, 57, 262n33. *See also* veterans

Ministère de l'Éducation nationale, 120, 121; *académies* in French empire and, 234, 236; education reform in AOF and, 219–20, 225, 304n43; education reform in French empire and, 222–23; integration through education reform in AOF and, 215, 225, 227–32, 235, 237, 238, 240, 304n43; Jean Capelle's support from, 225, 236, 304n43

Ministry of Colonies, 215, 222, 223, 301n16, 303n31

Ministry of Foreign Affairs, 222, 223, 303n31

Ministry of Overseas France, 215, 223, 235, 236–37, 244, 245, 301n16, 306n68

missionaries: colonial administrators' relations with, 21, 22, 253n26; cost of schools and teachers for, 39; girls' education and, 22, 190; schools founded or administered in AOF by, 5, 6, 16, 21, 22–23, 39, 67, 254n42; schools founded or administered in France by, 6, 21–22, 252n23. *See also* church-state controversies

Mitterrand, François, 239, 240
Morel, Antoine, 196–97
Morocco, French Protectorate, 72–73, 75–76, 303n31
Moutet, Marius, 127–28, 215, 219, 220, 222, 225, 235
Mouvement républicain populaire (MRP), 212, 235
mulâtres (mulattoes), 252n17. See also *métis* (mixed-race) elites
Muslims: black, 31–32, 55; personal status of, 51, 53–54, 55, 58, 263n40; tribunals and, 50, 51, 260n8, 304n49
mutuelles scolaires. See school-run savings associations (*mutuelles scolaires*)

nationalist movements, 180–81, 238
National Revolution, 159, 160, 162, 166, 167, 174, 179. See also Vichy regime; Vichy regime in AOF
native courts: Code de l'indigénat and, 50–51, 59, 70, 92, 229, 231, 260nn7–8, 260n13, 289n9; French courts versus, 50, 51, 52, 261n16; tribunals and, 50, 51, 260n8, 304n49
naturalization, 54, 261n15, 261nn21–22
Ndiaye, Amadou Duguay Clédor, 67–68
N'Diaye, Guibril, 103, 104, 275n19
N'Diaye, Massata, 171–72, 174
Negritude movement: about, 135–36, 284n46, 284n49, 288n109; African elites and, 126; French empire and, 136, 284n46; Léopold Sédar Senghor and, 126, 135, 138, 156, 233, 247, 284n46, 284n49, 288n109; urban Senegal and, 126, 138–39; women and, 135

Niger: colonial school system in, 254n42; establishment of, as colony, 269n32; geographical location of, 3, 4, 5; Haut-Sénégal-Niger and, 253n30, 254n42; independence of, 247; originaires residing in, 261n15; urban population statistics for, 88
normal schools, France, 101–4, 105, 106, 121, 202, 275nn10–11, 275n13, 275n19, 275n22

old colonies. See Guadeloupe, colony of; Martinique, colony of
originaires (*originaires des Quatre Communes*): about, 7, 9, 49–50, 252n17; African elites and, 61–62; assimilation and, 20, 54; black Muslims as, 31–32; Catholic missionaries as founders of schools for, 22–23; citizen-subject binary and, 20–21; colonial order and, 13–14, 17, 41, 52; colonial school system contestations by, 8, 29, 35, 36–37, 38, 39, 40, 44, 66–67; *écoles congréganistes* and, 27, 28–29; educational rights of, 28–29, 35, 41, 44, 131; Four Communes and, 7, 13; future of, 9, 29; General Council representation by, 131–32, 282n26; Government General's relations with, 31; integration of, through education reform, 44–45; interior regions and, 17; local politics and, 17, 39, 40, 41; lycées in AOF and, 195–96, 200; metropolitan education for, 30–31, 38, 46, 48, 66–67, 126, 131, 132; metropolitan school certificates for, 38, 46, 131; migration patterns and, 49–50, 52; population statistics for, 14, 25, 49, 52, 251n4,

segregation in colonial school system: Dakar and, 35; Four Communes and, 30–35, 40, 41, 45–46, 126, 132, 256n57; *métis* elite politicians' opposition to, 34; metropolitan education in Four Communes and, 30–35, 45–46, 256n57; originaires' opposition to, 34; Popular Front and, 126, 132; Vichy regime and, 205; William Ponty and, 30–35, 256n57. *See also* racial discrimination

Semidei, Manuela, 305n58

Senegal: assimilation and, 32–33; church-state controversies in, 253n26; citizenship for originaires in, 261n21; geographical location of, 3, *4*, *5*; history of, 3, 14–15, 23, 251n7, 273n74; infrastructure projects in, 3–5, *5*, 15; Kayes, 51, 78; Louis Faidherbe as governor of, 15; missionaries in, 21; *Paris-Dakar* and, 137–39, 167, 170, 173, 290n25; and Parti socialiste du Sénégal, 132, 199; political rights of originaires in, 20; racial discrimination and, 33; regional schools in, 26–28, 44, 254n42, 258n88; rural schools in, 26, 27, 28, 44, 254n42; slavery and, 14–15, 251n7; Thiès, 28, 52, 78, 178; Ziguinchor, 28, 52, 78. *See also* Four Communes; urban Senegal

Senghor, Lamine, 156

Senghor, Léopold Sédar: Académie de l'Afrique noire and, 231, 305n56; *académies* in French empire and, 234; activism of, 126, 136, 137–38, 156–57, 176, 247; African culture and, 140–41, 147, 148–50, 154, 170, 174, 285nn63–64; African elites and, 126,

140, 146, 287n82; African languages in colonial school system and, 142–43, 286n67, 286n69; assimilation and, 126, 137–38, 147–49; *baccalauréat* and, 134, 198; Blaise Diagne and, 135; Constituent National Assemblies and, 211–12, 213–15, 300n3; constitutional drafts and, 212, 300n3; criticism of colonial school system by, 213–15, 226, 227, 229–30, 231–32, 301nn12–13; cultural *métissage* and, 170, 233, 247, 291n36, 306n60; curricula in AOF and, 233–34; curricula in France and, 232–33, 234; debates on African culture and cultural *métissage* and, 157, 291n36; democratization and, 138, 215; educational attainment of, 133–35, 150, 283n34, 284n40; educational rights and citizenship for originaires and, 214, 219, 231; Franco-African culture and, 139, 143–44, 146–47, 153–54, 156, 291n36; French Union and, 215, 232; future of AOF and, 137, 226; General Council of Senegal and, 230; Grand Council of AOF and, 230–31; integration through education reform in AOF and, 215, 227–32, 230, 238, 240; International Conference on the Cultural Development of Colonial Peoples and, 136–37, 144–50, 286n80, 287n82; Jean Capelle and, 226, 238, 304n46; l'Éducation nationale and, 215, 227–32, 238, 240; Marcel de Coppet and, 139, 140, 151, 170, 287n99; military service during World War II and, 233; National Assembly and, 227, 230, 240, 301nn12–13; Negritude movement and, 126, 135, 138, 156, 233,

247, 284n46, 284n49, 288n109; 1937
visit to Senegal and investigations
by, 136, 138–39, 152; Ousmane Socé
and, 170, 291n35; photograph of, 228;
Popular Front and, 125, 126, 133, 151,
226, 227, 231; postcolonial era and,
247; public intellectuals and, 133, 170,
247; regional schools in Four Communes and, 153–54; rural schools
in urban Senegal and, 137, 138, 146,
153–54; speech to Chamber of
Commerce in Dakar by, 125–26, 139–
44, 146, 281n1, 285nn57–58, 285n63,
286nn66–67; "territorialization" and
"balkanization" and, 245

Simon, Henry, 64, 194

Sissoko, Fily-Dabo, 146, 286n80

slavery, 14–15, 251n7

Socé, Ousmane: as author of fiction,
169–70, 291n30; cultural *métissage*
and, 168–69, 170; educational attainment of, 169, 170; Franco-African
culture and, 168–69; Jean Capelle's
education reforms and, 304n46;
Léopold Sédar Senghor and, 170,
173, 174, 291n35; Mamadou Dia's
activism and, 176; public intellectuals and, 284n41; speech to Chamber
of Commerce in Dakar by, 170,
285n58, 291n34

Socialist Party (Section française de
l'internationale ouvrière, SFIO),
127, 128, 212, 227

Sow, Fara, 170–71, 174, 200, 292n49

sports: École William Ponty and, 121;
French empire and, 290n16; Popular Front and, 130; Third Republic
and, 167–68; Vichy regime in AOF
and, 164, 165, 167–68, 290n16

statut personnel musulman (Muslim
personal status), 51, 53–54, 55, 58,
263n40. *See also* Muslims

student population statistics, 25, 195,
201n13, 214, 243, 308n1

subjects (colonial subjects), AOF: citizenship law and, 216–18, 231, 301n19,
301n21, 302n23; colonial school
system for, 7, 38, 44–45, 69; Constituent National Assemblies' debates
about, 14, 211–12, 213–15, 226–27, 230,
301nn12–13, 304n48; military service
in French empire for, 56–57; practical training for, 26–27, 29, 35, 38, 43,
254n39, 259n98; rural schools and,
26, 30, 35, 38, 41. *See also* citizen-
subject binary

suffrage, 211, 245, 302n22, 304n48

Taboulet, Georges, 74

Thiam, Iba Der, 262n28, 262n31

tirailleurs sénégalais, 56, 57, 262n33

trade (labor) unions and strikes, AOF,
129, 130, 155, 165. *See also* labor code,
AOF

tribunals, 50, 51, 260n8, 304n49

Union démocratique et socialiste de la
Résistance (UDSR), 239

universities, AOF, 215, 230

Upper Volta: establishment of, as
colony, 269n32; forced labor in, 92,
273n74; geographical location of, 3,
4, 5; originaires residing in, 261n15;
pastoral visions and, 91; population
statistics for, 89

urban Senegal: about, 3, 4, 5, 88;
activism in, 125; African elites in,
277n46; antiblack racism in, 166–67,

urban Senegal (*continued*)
290n24; colonial reform and, 129–
33, 282n16; cultural associations in,
130, 180, 292n34, 293n58; European
populations in, 7, 32, 166, 207,
305n54; Léopold Sédar Senghor's
1937 investigations in, 136, 138–39,
152; Negritude movement and, 126,
138–39; originaires in, 52; population statistics for, 20, 52, 252n19;
trade/labor unions and strikes in,
129, 130, 155, 165; Vichy regime and,
166. *See also* Four Communes

Van Vollenhoven, Joost, 270n36
veterans, 59, 130, 165, 261n15, 304n48. *See
also* military service for subjects
Vichy regime: France and, 159, 160, 161,
163, 165–66, 290n22; French empire
and, 162, 180, 290n16
Vichy regime in AOF: about, 182–83;
advanced school graduates during,
160, 163–65, 166, 169; African culture
and, 179–80, 279n64; antiblack
racism and, 204, 205; authoritarianism and, 162–63, 289n9; Code
de l'indigénat and, 289n9; cultural
associations and, 165, 179–80,
293n58; *Dakar-Jeunes* and, 160, 167,
179; debates on African culture
and cultural *métissage* during, 181–
82; education reform under, 120;
Four Communes and, 165; Légion
française des combattants and,
165–66, 290n19; National Revolution and, 160, 162, 166, 167, 174,
179; pastoral visions during, 163;
propaganda and, 160, 161–62, 167,
179; segregation in colonial school

system during, 205; sports and, 164,
165, 167–68, 290n16. *See also* World
War II era in AOF
village schools, AOF: about, 271n56;
curricula for, 26, 27, 28, 44; Four
Communes and, 30, 35, 38, 41, 44,
255n55, 258nn88–89; Senegal and,
26, 27, 28, 44, 254n42; statistics for,
28, 254n42; subjects' education
and, 26, 30, 35, 38, 41. *See also* rural
schools, AOF
voting rights, 211, 245, 302n22, 304n48

Weber, Eugen, 250n7
Wilder, Gary, 156, 213, 234, 288n109
World War I era in AOF: about, 47–48;
agricultural exports and, 81, 90,
92; citizenship for originaires laws
during, 11, 53, 57–58, 66, 69, 125, 196,
217, 301n21, 302n22; colonial order
and, 47, 64, 100; École William
Ponty during, 101, 108, 109, 112–
13; military service for subjects
and, 47–48, 56, 57–59, 233, 262n33,
262n35, 263n43; missionaries and,
22, 253n26; originaires and, 14, 46,
56–61, 64, 66–67, 261n15, 282n26;
veterans and, 59, 165, 261n15
World War II era: Allied forces and,
160, 183, 185; antiblack racism and,
166–67, 290n24; class distinctions
in France during, 202–3, 298n60;
Free French during, 160, 185, 289n2;
French empire during, 160, 180, 183,
185, 213; provisional government
during, 206, 208. *See also* Vichy
regime; Vichy regime in AOF

You, André, 188

To order or obtain more information on these or other University of Nebraska Press titles, visit nebraskapress.unl.edu.

CPSIA information can be obtained
at www.ICGtesting.com
Printed in the USA
LVHW112013150621
690290LV00010B/379/J